Challenges in Managing Sustainable Business

Susanne Arvidsson
Editor

Challenges in Managing Sustainable Business

Reporting, Taxation, Ethics and Governance

palgrave
macmillan

Editor
Susanne Arvidsson
Lund University
Lund, Sweden

ISBN 978-3-030-06625-3 ISBN 978-3-319-93266-8 (eBook)
https://doi.org/10.1007/978-3-319-93266-8

This Palgrave Macmillan imprint is published by the registered company Springer Nature Switzerland AG
The registered company address is: Gewerbestrasse 11, 6330 Cham, Switzerland

Preface: A Background to the Challenges in Managing Sustainable Business

Introduction

Today, it is more than 30 years since the Brundtland Report entitled *Our Common Future* (UNWCED, 1987) was published with the objective of drawing attention to the global need for sustainable development. Many meritorious initiatives have since resulted in a faster adaption towards sustainable development—both at national and international level. Sustainability is now a topic that is high up on the agendas in politics, business society and academia. Agenda 2030 and UNs Sustainable Development Goals (SDGs) are putting an emphasis on the vital urgency to transform our countries, companies and lives into more sustainable. As we speak, our businesses are undergoing a transformation towards more sustainable organizations. Vigorous practice development is taking place in a number of areas. This book, *Challenges in Managing Sustainable Business: Reporting, Taxation, Ethics and Governance*, explores a variety of challenges faced by businesses when becoming more sustainable organizations. These challenges are linked to economic development and have implications for e.g. reporting, assurance, finance, corruption and taxation. Showcasing an interdisciplinary approach, the chapters explore topics such as sustainability reporting and assurance, anti-corruption, business ethics, corporate responsibility, cognitive frames, sustainable finance, ethic taxation and tax governance. The book is divided into five different parts: *Sustainability Reporting*, *Sustainability Assurance*, *Sustainable Finance*, *Anti-corruption and Business Ethics* and *Ethical Taxation & Tax Transparency*. The next section provides the structure of the book, where the five parts are introduced along with a presentation of the themes at focus in the chapters.

The Structure of the Book

Part I of the book, *Sustainability Reporting* acknowledges the fierce practice developing of sustainability reporting. Here, the focus is on what challenges this means both to our companies and to the various stakeholders who try to understand and assess sustainability information and corporate performance on the sustainability arenas. The part includes five chapters that all set out to enhance our understanding of how the transformation towards more sustainable businesses has changed the landscape for corporate disclosure and communication. With this transformation, a new type of information is entered into the corporate reports, i.e. sustainability information.

In the first chapter, Arvidsson takes us on "*An Exposé of the Challenging Practice Development of Sustainability Reporting: From the First Wave to the EU Directive (2014/95/EU)*". The chapter gives a theoretical background to why companies (should) engage in sustainability reporting. Three arguments for providing sustainability reporting are at focus (i) gaining, maintaining and/or repairing legitimacy, (ii) improving stakeholder relations and (iii) decreasing information asymmetry. The chapter also acknowledges that this practice has been criticized throughout the years, not the least from the actors on the financial markets. It highlights different types of critique (PR-invention, green-, blue- or even SDG-washing activity, poor informational quality) and discusses how a new set of voluntary-sustainability standards have been developed to help companies implement, manage and report more efficiently on their sustainability activities. The chapter ends with highlighting the EU directive (2014/95/EU), which from financial year 2017 mandates the largest EU companies to provide sustainability information in their corporate reports.

In the second chapter, Torre et al. enhance our knowledge on "*Integrated Reporting and Integrating Thinking: Practical Challenges*". Integrated Reporting (<IR>) is currently a hot topic for academic research because of the practical challenges businesses encounter implementing it. The chapter focuses on the challenges of integrated thinking and examines the extant academic literature to offer contributions for future research based on <IR> practice. They authors argue that integrated thinking suffers from significant conceptual, theoretical and practical challenges, which obstruct the claimed benefits deriving from adopting <IR>. Therefore, this chapter contributes to rethinking the paradigm of integrated thinking, and it is claimed that managers need to abandon the compliance-driven logic underpinning external reporting to foster integrated thinking and unlock its potential in practice.

The third chapter is titled "*Human Capital Disclosures in Swedish State-Owned Enterprises—A Comparison of Integrated Reporting Versus Traditional Reporting*". Here, Rimmel provides us with insights on how Swedish state-owned enterprises (SOEs) make disclosures about human capital in their corporate reports. Using a GRI framework, the chapter sets out to identify patterns in disclosure and provide us with illustrating examples that compare integrated reporting with traditional corporate reporting. The findings show that SOEs applying integrated reporting tend to disclose more about employees than enterprises that follow traditional corporate reporting.

In the fourth chapter, Arvidsson and Johansson address "*Sense-Making and Sense-Giving: Reaching Through the Smokescreen of Sustainability Disclosure in the Stock Market*". Here, we learn more about how the increased focus on sustainability information in corporate reports has affected financial analysts in their important work of interpreting, assessing and communicating value-added information to their clients, i.e. the investors. Their role as information intermediaries is vital for the efficient allocation of resources on the stock market. The challenges they face relate to the ambitious nature of sustainability information and its difference from traditional financial information. How do analysts reach through this smokescreen? How do analysts make sense of sustainability information, and how do they give sense to this information when they provide investment advices to their clients? These challenges are addressed in the chapter from a cognitive-frame perspective.

Part I of the book ends with Holland's chapter on "*Changing Financial Firms Relative to ESG Issues*". This chapter investigates changes in financial firms relative to environmental, social and governance issues (ESG). An embryonic "behavioural theory of the financial firm" (BTFF) is outlined to provide a conceptual framework to analyse ESG.-change issues in financial firms. This framework is used to explore how financial firms and others can understand processes of: learning, strategic design of the firm, mobilization of resources and reporting relative to growing ESG concerns. The chapter illustrates how "top teams", advisory policy bodies, legislators and regulators can use the BTFF to inform their actions and change proposals. This can support an integrated view of the financial firm and encourage a coherent pursuit of financial *and* ESG aims throughout the financial firm.

Part II of the book, *Sustainability Assurance*, includes two chapters, which enhance our understanding of the challenges sustainability information has imposed on the assurance practices. The increased interest in developing efficient assuring of sustainability information is triggered by the critique against the poor credibility and comparability of sustainability information.

In the first chapter, Faroq and de Villiers address "*Sustainability Assurance: Who Are the Assurance Providers and What Do They Do?*". Since sustainability is a voluntary undertaking in most countries, there is no restriction on who can provide sustainability assurance services or the approach to assurance. This chapter explores the different types of sustainability assurance providers operating in the market—accounting sustainability assurance providers and non-accounting sustainability assurance providers. The similarities and differences in approach to sustainability assurance are discussed. This discussion highlights the challenges faced by assurance providers and assurance seekers (i.e. sustainability reporters) in the market for this new form of assurance.

In the next chapter, Carrington provides us with a "*A Critical Perspective on Sustainability Assurance*". What does assurance of sustainability reports mean? To answer this question, the chapter treats assurance as a word with a regulatory and etymological history, which prescribes a specific and particular interpretation of the term assurance. It is observed that sustainability assurance inherits a specific theory with a particular form of evaluating and making authoritative statements on sustainability practice from (financial) auditing. It draws on agency theory, and the form of evaluation is the indirect evaluation of statements of compliance with standards instead of a direct assessment of the company's sustainability performance. This is argued to be problematic. Even if assurance may add credibility to sustainability reporting, it does not challenge the visions and perspectives adopted by the company. This was a problem in the first place, as suggested by the Brundtland report.

In Part III of the book, *Sustainable Finance* is at focus. The part includes four chapters that highlight different challenges related to the fierce process of making finance more sustainable. Several intriguing questions are addressed in the chapters: What can we learn from the Nordic sustainable and responsible (SRI) strategy? How can accounting frameworks be improved? How can sustainability risks be recognized and integrated in credit decisions and risk-management practices? What do we mean with a sustainable infrastructure and what role does green bonds play?

In the first chapter, Hassel and Semenova focus on "*Engagement Dialogue as a Nordic Sustainable and Responsible Investment (SRI) Strategy*". This chapter conducts an in-depth analysis of engagement dialogue between Nordic institutional investors and MSCI World companies regarding environmental, social and corruption risks. The main characteristics of the Nordic model of engagement dialogue are an incident-based approach, norm-based compliance, a small number of engagement cases and long-term emphasis on risk reduction as opposed to short-term financial gains. The chapter notes that successful forms of engagement dialogue target global companies with higher levels of pre-engagement environmental, social and governance (ESG) performance, ESG transparency and operating performance than a matched sample. Their performance remains superior to the matched sample in the post-engagement period. The chapter consequently extends previous literature on SRI strategies in the Anglo-Saxon model of activism based on shareholder resolutions whereby companies are targeted owing to corporate governance risks and low financial performance.

The second chapter is titled "*Sustainable Business Practices—An Environmental Economics Perspective*". Lundgren et al. discuss corporate social responsibility (CSR) from an environmental economics perspective. The discussion is based on existing research and aims to illuminate some concepts and create an explanatory framework for understanding the corporate behaviour referred to as CSR and especially the environmental responsibility dimension. It is argued that a theory about CSR would have to include trade-offs between personal taste and values, social norms and market imperfections. The challenge with progressing academic research about CSR would be improving environmental accounting frameworks, both at the national level and at firm level. The system of double bookkeeping needs to be accompanied by environmental, social and material flows accounts in a more detailed manner than what we see today. If not, any proposed theory about CSR would run the risk of being moot as it would be impossible to put it to the test.

In the third chapter, with the controversial title "*Will the Banker Become a Climate Activist?*", Henningson argues that banks currently lack a proper understanding and incentives to manage climate-related financial risks and translate them into credit decisions. The chapter includes a discussion on how this scene gradually could change within the banking industry, mainly driven by regulators and rating agencies and potentially sudden market revaluations of climate-related risks. It is illustrated how banks, by using well-established methods further developed by rating agencies could integrate climate factors into the credit decisions and become concerned consumers of corporate climate information. The chapter ends with a discussion on the challenges the banking sector face related to the recognition and integration of climate-related risks in their risk-management practices.

The fourth and final chapter in the part Sustainable Finance is authored by Hebb and is titled "*Investing in Sustainable Infrastructure*". In this chapter, she enhances our knowledge of how sustainable business is underpinned by sustainable and resilient infrastructure. This is defined as infrastructure that integrates environmental, social and governance (ESG) aspects into a project's planning, building and operating while ensuring resilience in the face of climate change or shocks. Currently, trillions of dollars of infrastructure investment are needed to meet our needs globally. This chapter explores the shift towards greater consideration of ESG in infrastructure investment. It looks at the drivers of these phenomena and some of its implications. However, integrating ESG in infrastructure investment is not without its challenges. Given that these large institutional investors have a fiduciary duty to serve their beneficiaries in both the short and long term, incorporating sustainability in infrastructure investment raises tensions between the need for profitable financial returns and the need to contribute to a healthy and sustainable planet. These challenges are explored in greater depth at the close of the chapter.

Part IV of the book *Anti-corruption and Business Ethics* includes three chapters. The globalization has many advantages but it also gives rise to various challenges. One such challenge is to fight corruption. Today many companies invest substantial resources in the development of efficient systems for preventing, identifying and managing corruption-related incidents. In this part, the three chapters in different ways enhance our understanding not only of the complexity underlying the fighting of anti-corruption but also of its relationship with business ethics and responsibility.

The first chapter has the somewhat provocative title "*Anti-corruption: Who Cares*". Here, Sampson problematizes engagement in fighting corruption, in terms of why businesses, governments, international organizations and NGOs choose to make anti-corruption a priority and how they go about fighting corruption, including their degree of genuine engagement. Two major anti-corruptionist discourses are described: the one emphasizes the progress in fighting corruption through laws, conventions, campaigns and transparency; and the other discourse is a more pessimistic scenario emphasizing the continued persistence of corruption, as revealed by the Panama and Paradise papers and almost daily corruption scandals at the highest corporate and government levels; this second, cynical discourse highlights the failure of the anti-corruption industry to actually reduce corruption. Problematizing who cares about anti-corruption and why they care can not only help put anti-corruption in its proper sociopolitical context. It can also lead the way towards more effective anti-corruption programmes.

The second chapter is titled "*Rationalizing Deviances—Avoiding Responsibility*". In this chapter, Brytting takes his departure in the fact that only one in five instances of fraud is detected by internal and external audits and IT controls. Instances of corruption are most probably even less visible. How come, and what to do about it? This chapter treats deviances as a social and psychological problem. Rationalizations both from the fraudsters' and the bystanders' side will be discussed as important factors that obstructs the prevention of deviances. These rationalizations are interpreted as a kind of perverted modern virtues, something that might explain their persuasive power.

In the last chapter of this part, "*Organizational Anti-corruption: De-normalization Through Anxiety, Superego, Courage and Justice*", Lennerfors argues *that* major challenge for fighting corruption is our narrow conceptions about corruption and the lack of alternative, creative theorizations about both corruption and anti-corruption. The chapter responds to this challenge by discussing organizational corruption and anti-corruption in an alternative way. It reviews three different definitions of corruption and argues that corruption should be seen as the degeneration of a legitimate value. With this view of corruption, this chapter develops an anti-corruption framework by inverting Ashforth and Anand's (2003) work on the normalization of corruption in organizations. In the latter part, the chapter argues that one could relate to anti-corruption measures in any of four ways: anxiety, superego, courage and justice. It suggests that a balanced mix of these four subject positions is useful for fighting corruption.

The final part of the book is *Ethical Taxation and Tax Transparency*. This part includes two chapters, which put a focus on a new sustainability theme: tax and taxation. Triggered by the Panama and Paradise papers, the sustainability debate has started to address tax and taxation. The relationship between tax, taxation and sustainability is not an easy one. How do we define and promote responsible tax policies and ethical taxation? How can tax transparency assist in this process? These are some of the questions that are raised and discussed in this part.

In the first chapter, Gribnau and Jallai enhance our understanding about the complex relationship between "*Sustainable Tax Governance and Transparency*". The chapter will deal with the calls for increased tax transparency. Public transparency with regard to corporate tax is in many countries a rather new phenomenon. It is argued that corporate tax transparency is a key to good tax governance. Yet, it also entails various challenges. A first step is the question as to relationship between tax and sustainability; sustainable tax governance will first be dealt from a governmental perspective which requires the state to pay due attention to the quality of tax legislation. Following, it will be discussed how to relate multinational tax-planning practices to sustainability. It will be analysed whether paying taxes could be seen as a company's obligation towards society. Here, CSR is used as a proxy for sustainability. A notion of good tax governance as a response to demand of sustainable and responsible tax planning will be proposed. Furthermore, this chapter relates such good tax governance to transparency, which is considered as a necessary if challenging prerequisite for a sustainable tax planning.

The second chapter is titled "*Perspectives on Corporate Taxation from a Sustainable Business Perspective*". In this chapter, Persson Österman emphasizes the need for a legal rule-based taxation. The most important lesson social-science research provides should be that the willingness to pay taxes is a function of complicated processes and that there is no single explanation as to why an individual or a corporation chooses to pay their taxes or engage or not engage in tax planning or tax avoidance. Research also indicates that the social norm is not very clear in terms of the view on tax avoidance. The best way of securing a sustainable corporate taxation is international cooperation on the legislative level and the development of legal concepts against tax avoidance (General Anti Avoidance Rules).

Acknowledgements

I would like to express my deepest gratitude to the contributing authors not only for the time, energy and skills you have put into the making of this book but also for all the constructive, enthusiastic and positive discussions that we have had throughout the process. I hope we will get a chance to continue our discussions in future projects! I also want to thank the editors Madeleine Holder and Gabriel Everington at Palgrave Macmillan for their always so kind and prompt support. Last but not least, my daughter Charlotte and son Carl owe my special thanks for their unconditional love. Just thinking of you makes me smile! I promise that the next book will be one we can read when I put you to bed.

Lund, Sweden
May 2018

Susanne Arvidsson
Editor

Contents

Notes on Contributors

Susanne Arvidsson is Associate Professor at Lund University School of Economics and Management, Sweden. She completed her Ph.D. in 2003. For her thesis "Demand and Supply of Information on Intangibles: A focus on Knowledge-Intense Companies", she was awarded the esteemed Wallander Scholarship. Her research interests are within corporate finance and accounting and include the areas: corporate reporting and disclosure, sustainability accounting and assurance as well as corporate valuation. Her work has been published in several leading accounting and management journals, e.g. *Journal of Business Ethics and Corporate Communication: An International Journal.* Susanne is the initiator of the international SUBREA conference and head of the SUBREA network https://www.lusem.lu.se/calendar/conferences/sustainable-business-reporting-assurance. She is chairman of the Advisory Board responsible for an annual ranking of Swedish companies' sustainability performance.

Cristiana Bernardi is a Lecturer in Accounting at The Open University Business School (UK). She previously worked as a postdoctoral researcher at Roma Tre University, having been awarded her Ph.D. from that institution in May 2015. Her main research interest is in the general area of financial reporting, particularly in the information content of mandatory and voluntary disclosures concerning non-financial performance. In this regard, she has specific interests in current developments in integrated reporting and corporate social responsibility reporting and in the stock market demand for, and consequences of, the disclosure of non-financial information.

Tomas Brytting is currently Professor in Organizational Ethics at The Institute for Organizational- and Worklife ethics, Ersta Skondal Bracke University College in Stockholm, Sweden. He is Associate Professor at The Stockholm School of Economics. Apart from being a researcher, he is also active as a lecturer and consultant in related topics. He is a member of the Swedish Press Council, chairman of The Ethics Board of the Swedish Executive Search Consultants (ESK). Tomas is frequently commenting incidents concerning organizational- and worklife ethics in different public media.

Thomas Carrington is Ph.D. at Stockholm Business School at Stockholm University. His research spans a wide area from financial reporting to public sector auditing. Already in and ever since his Ph.D. thesis, where he investigated audit failure through a qualitative analysis of how different actors framed them as such, his interest in auditing has revolved around the fundamental questions of how to understand auditing and what value the phenomenon of auditing can be understood to produce. This has led him to study audits in many different contexts. Thomas is also the author of a textbook on auditing.

Lammertjan Dam is an Associate Professor at the Department of Economics, Econometrics and Finance at the University of Groningen in the Netherlands. He has a background in econometrics and focuses both on economic theory and empirical research in the fields of corporate social responsibility and financial markets.

Charl de Villiers is Professor of Accounting at the Graduate School of Management, the University of Auckland, New Zealand. His research interests include Sustainability Accounting and Integrated Reporting. He is also an adjunct professor at several South African universities and a research fellow at the Centre for Sustainability Management at

Leuphana University of Lüneburg, Germany. Charl has more than 300 research-based publications and presentations, including over 70 articles in refereed journals. He is co-editor of the Routledge book *Sustainability Accounting and Integrated Reporting*.

John Dumay is Associate Professor of Accounting at Macquarie University, Sydney, Australia. Originally a consultant, he joined academia after completing his Ph.D. in 2008. His thesis won the European Fund for Management Development and Emerald Journals Outstanding Doctoral Research Award for Knowledge Management. John researches intellectual capital, knowledge management, corporate reporting and disclosures, research methodologies and academic writing. John has written over 70 peer-reviewed articles, book chapters and edited books and is highly cited in Scopus and Google Scholar. He is the Associate Editor of the *Journal of Intellectual Capital* and *Meditari Accountancy Research* and Editor of the *eJournal of Knowledge Management*, on the Editorial Board of Advice of the highly regarded *Accounting, Auditing and Accountability Journal*, *Journal of Knowledge Management* and several other leading accounting and management journals.

Muhammad Bilal Farooq is an accounting academic at Auckland University of Technology. His research interests include sustainability accounting and the assurance of non-financial information. His research has been published in *Accounting, Auditing & Accountability Journal* and several other journals.

Hans Gribnau is professor of Tax Law at Tilburg University, the Netherlands, and professor by special appointment of Quality of tax regulation at Leiden University, the Netherlands. His research focus is taxation, tax methodology, philosophy of tax law, procedural tax law, tax law principles and tax ethics. Recent publications dealt with topics such as corporate tax governance, corporate social responsibility and voluntary compliance beyond the letter of the law, codes of conduct, public tax governance, cooperative compliance, tax transparency, reciprocity and fair play. These and other publications are available at http://ssrn.com/author=441648 and https://www.researchgate.net/profile/Hans_Gribnau/contributions?ev=prf_act.

James Guthrie is a Professor in the Department of Accounting and Corporate Governance. James has held positions at various Australian and Italian universities, in a career in accounting education that spans more than 35 years. He is editor of the highly regarded interdisciplinary accounting journal, Accounting, Auditing, and Accountability. He was Head of Academic Relations at Chartered Accountants Australia and New Zealand from 2008 to 2017, engaging with accounting academics and other stakeholders in the Australian and New Zealand higher education systems and providing thought leadership to benefit the wider accounting profession.

Lars G. Hassel holds a Dr.Sc. degree in Accounting from Åbo Akademi University in Finland. In the past, Lars worked as a Professor at Åbo Akademi University and Umeå University and additionally served as Dean for the School of Business and Economics in the latter. Lars also worked as Program Director for Sustainable Investment Research Platform for seven years at Mistra, the Foundation for Strategic Environmental Research. He is currently a Professor at the University of Gävle in Sweden. His current research interests and publications explore the economic value of ESG.

Tessa Hebb is a Senior Research Fellow and past Director of the Carleton Centre for Community Innovation, Carleton University, Canada. Her research focuses on Responsible Investment, Impact Investment and Impact Measurement. This work has been funded by the Social Sciences and Humanities Research Council, Government of Canada. Dr. Hebb is the past chair of the steering committee of the UN-backed Principles for Responsible Investment (PRI) Academic Network. She also served on the board the Heartland Network (USA). Dr. Hebb recently co-chaired the Ontario's Social Enterprise Impact Measurement Task Force. She was a board member of the Responsible Investment Association (Canada) from 2011 to 2017. Dr. Hebb is a frequent guest speaker on impact investment, responsible investment and impact measurement issues. She has published many books and articles on responsible investing and impact investing including the volumes *The Routledge Handbook of Responsible Investment*; *SRI in the 21st Century: Does it Make a Difference to Society*; *Working Capital:*

the Power of Labor's Pensions; *No Small Change: Pension Fund Corporate Engagement*; and *The Next Generation of Responsible Investing.*

Johan Henningsson is Head Sustainability and Executive Director at Swedish Export Credit Corporation. He holds a Dr. degree in Industrial Economics and Organisations from Mälardalen University and is currently associated Researcher at Örebro University School of Business. Johan has an extensive experience from various positions in the financial markets, among others as an options trader at ABB Treasury Center AB, Head of Corporate Sales at ABN Amro Bank (Sweden) and as a financial consultant. Johan's research field is within sustainable finance and sociology of finance. In his thesis, he studied how social forces affect fund managers when they make sense of information on Intellectual Capital and Sustainability.

John Holland has been an academic since 1972 and member of staff at Glasgow University in Scotland since 1979. He is an emeritus professor in the Adam Smith Business School, University of Glasgow, Scotland. He has published in journals as part of networks of academics from the UK, Scandinavia, China, Australia and Japan. He has published and researched in the areas of intangibles in financial firms (banks, fund managers, Analysts, etc.) and Financial Markets (for capital, and for information). He has published on corporate disclosure concerning the role of intangibles in company business models, their role in value creation and their valuation by financial markets and by financial firms. He has published on the role of financial firms in the governance of commercial firms. The publications have included ESG issues arising in the above areas.

See the following web page for details of publications http://eprints.gla.ac.uk/view/author/6061.html.

Ave-Geidi Jallai is a Ph.D. researcher in the Tax Law department at Tilburg University, the Netherlands. Her research focus is international corporate tax planning, corporate governance and corporate social responsibility. She has published various articles focusing on topics such as corporate tax governance, corporate social responsibility, business ethics, trust and tax transparency.

Jeaneth Johansson is full Professor at Halmstad University and at Luleå University of Technology, Sweden. She completed her Ph.D. in Accounting and Control, 2004. For her thesis "Recommendation changes in walls of glass: perceived roles and relative importance of direct contacts", she was awarded the esteemed Wallander Scholarship. Her research interests in the capital market focus on corporate communication, cognitive foundations and decision-making by different actors in the capital market, e.g. financial analysts, venture capitalists and governmental financiers. Her research on sustainability focusing on stereotypical notations and biases in allocation of finance has received much attention internationally both in research and in practice. Johansson's work is published in several leading journals, e.g. Harvard Business Review and Entrepreneurship Theory and Practice.

Jeaneth. https://www.ltu.se/staff/j/jeaneth-1.10340?l=en.

Matteo La Torre is Postdoc Research Fellow at University "G. D'Annunzio" of Chieti-Pescara (Italy). He completed his Ph.D. in Accounting and Business Administration in 2016 working on a thesis on integrated reporting, rhetoric and digital advances. Prior to his current position, he worked as a consultant for an information security consulting firm. He has been a visiting research scholar at Macquarie University (Sydney) working on a research on rhetoric and innovations. His research interests in accounting relate to intellectual capital, integrated reporting, digital corporate reporting and information security management.

Thomas Taro Lennerfors is an associate professor at the Department of Engineering Sciences at Uppsala University. His research concerns the interstices between ethics and philosophy on the one hand and business and technology on the other. In this inbetweenness, he has addressed issues such as corporate philosophy and its historical dynamics, the philosophy of maritime industries, sustainability of information and communications technology, East Asian philosophical perspectives on business ethics and ethics of technology and not the least corruption. He also teaches courses on ethics in engineering, business ethics, sustainable business, research ethics and ethics in the natural sciences.

Tommy Lundgren is an Associate Professor and Senior Researcher at the *Centre for Environmental and Resource Economics* at Umeå University. His research is mainly focused on applied policy analysis related to the environment including issues associated with corporate environmental responsibility. Currently, he is running a project assessing industrial energy demand and energy efficiency.

Roger Persson Österman is professor in Tax Law at Stockholm University (Sweden). He completed his Ph.D. in 1997. The subject was Swedish tax consequences of reorganizations of business enterprises (mergers, de-mergers, etc.). In the study, he used an economic efficiency tool in order to find the best tax policy applicable. He was postdoctoral at University of Cambridge (UK) as a visiting scholar at the Centre for European Legal Studies and Clare Hall College 1998–1999. Between 2006 and 2012, he worked as a tax practician (Wistrand Law Firm and EY International Tax Services). His current research covers the role of tax adjudication and tax rulings in terms of strengthening the taxpayer morale.

Gunnar Rimmel is full professor and holds a Chair in Accounting and is founding director of the Henley Centre for Accounting Research & Practice (HARP) at Henley Business School, University of Reading, UK. He previously worked in Sweden as a professor in Accounting at Jönköping International Business School and Gothenburg Research Institute at the University of Gothenburg. He received his Ph.D. in 2003 for the thesis "Human Resource Disclosures" from the School of Business at the School of Business, Economics and Law at Gothenburg University in Sweden. He published his articles in *International Academic Journals* like *Accounting, Auditing and Accountability Journal*, *Journal of Accounting and Public Policy* and *Accounting Forum*. Further, he has contributed with more than twenty book chapters in international books. His research and teaching interests include accounting communication, human resource accounting, international financial accounting and social and environmental reporting, specifically integrated reporting. During the past years, his research programme "Accounting for Sustainability—communication through integrated reporting" has been externally funded by the Handelsbanken research foundations. He had also received grants from the NASDAQ OMX Nordic Foundation.

Steven Sampson is Professor Emeritus of Social Anthropology at Lund University. He has researched the anti-corruption industry, NGOs and business ethics. Recent publications include "The Anti-corruption Industry: From Movement to Institution" in *Global Crime*, 2010; *Cultures of Doing Good: Anthropologists and NGOs* (co-ed., 2017), "The 'Right Way': Moral Capitalism and the Emergence of the Corporate Ethics and Compliance Officer" in the *Journal of Business Anthropology*, 2016. "All that is Normal Melts into Air: Rethinking Neoliberal Rules and Deviance" in J. Carrier (ed.) *Neoliberalism and Deviance* (Berghahn, in press) and he is currently editing a volume on the anthropology of business ethics.

Bert Scholtens is a Professor in Sustainable Banking and Finance at the Department of Economics, Econometrics and Finance at the University of Groningen in the Netherlands. Furthermore, he is a Finance Professor at the School of Management of the University of Saint Andrews, Scotland, UK. He is also affiliated with the University of Edinburgh Business School. His research is directed at international financial intermediation and environmental finance and economics.

Natalia Semenova is the corresponding author for the chapter and is currently Senior Lecturer at the School of Business and Economics, Linnaeus University, in Växjö, Sweden. Natalia received her Dr.Sc. degree in Accounting from Åbo Akademi University in Finland. Prior to her doctoral studies, she was affiliated with Ufa State Aviation Technical University in Russia. She held positions at Umeå University before joining Linnaeus University. In her research and publications, Natalia approaches ESG in companies and industries from an empirical perspective.

List of Figures

List of Tables

Part I

Sustainability Reporting

An Exposé of the Challenging Practice Development of Sustainability Reporting: From the First Wave to the EU Directive (2014/95/EU)

Susanne Arvidsson

Introduction

In 2017, it was 30 years since the Brundtland Report entitled 'Our common future' (UNWCED 1987) was published with the objective of drawing attention to the global need for sustainable development. Thus, the idea was that this wake-up call would trigger companies to speed up its transformation of becoming more sustainable organisations. As we will see later in this chapter, this transformation process has been fragmented. During these decades, many meritorious initiatives at both national and international level have seen the light and resulted in a faster adaption towards a sustainable development.

The European Commission (2013) argues that a central way of demonstrating how companies perform in the sustainability arena is to engage in sustainability reporting, i.e. disclose sustainability information

S. Arvidsson (✉)
School of Economics and Management, Lund University, Lund, Sweden
e-mail: Susanne.arvidsson@fek.lu.se

S. Arvidsson (ed.), *Challenges in Managing Sustainable Business*,
https://doi.org/10.1007/978-3-319-93266-8_1

in corporate reports (annual reports, standalone sustainability reports and/or integrated reports). Today, most companies include a more or less pronounced focus on sustainability when they communicate with their stakeholders through corporate reports (Bondy et al. 2012; KPMG 2015). There is a vigorous practice development among companies when it comes to sustainability reporting. This chapter will highlight some challenges with this reporting practice—not the least the importance to enhance the informational quality of sustainability reporting by providing value relevant, credible and comparable information on sustainability performance.

In this process, structures and guidelines can help companies to implement, manage and report sustainability activities. Until now, voluntary efforts have primarily provided this assistance. This appears to be changing. From the financial year 2017, the new EU Directive (2014/95/EU) mandating larger entities to provide sustainability reports is in force (see section 'Enhancing Sustainability Reporting Through the New EU Directive (2014/95/EU)'). There are also forthcoming national and international regulations concerning, e.g. inclusion of sustainable perspectives on investment valuations, emissions, disclosure rules, tax transparency, compliance and anti-corruption. All this imposes pressure on companies to provide structured and relevant information on these issues in their sustainability reporting.

The increasing trend to engage in sustainability reporting has attracted interest from research society (see Cho et al. 2015; Dienes et al. 2016; Hahn and Kühnen 2013; Parker 2005; Patten 2013). Research has primarily been focused on different perspectives on the adoption process of such practices (Adams and NcNicholas 2007; Bebbington et al. 2009; Prado-Lorenzo et al. 2009) and on determinants influencing different aspects on sustainability reporting (see Dienes et al. 2016; Hahn and Kühnen 2013). The value relevance of sustainability information has also attracted research attention (see Cahan et al. 2016; Dhaliwal et al. 2012), as well as, the puzzle of how the relationship between sustainability reporting, social performance and financial performance looks (see Behnam and MacLean 2011; Martínez-Ferrero and Frias-Aceituno 2015).

A Theoretical Background to Why Companies (Should) Engage in Sustainability Reporting

Reviewing the literature and the debate reveals that the arguments for providing sustainability reporting primarily have been for the sake of (i) gaining, maintaining and/or repairing legitimacy, (ii) improving stakeholder relations or (iii) decreasing information asymmetry. To some extent, these arguments and their underlying theories (legitimacy, stakeholder and information asymmetry) are viewed as both interrelated and include overlapping perspectives (see Gray et al. 1995b, 1996). In order to add to an enhanced understanding of how sustainability reporting has developed and what challenges this reporting practice faces, these arguments will here be further elaborated in a theoretical perspective.

The underlying idea of *legitimacy theory* is that it is vital for a company to be granted legitimacy in the form of a social contract or a social licence to operate (Dowling and Pfeffer 1975; Deegan 2002). Hooghiemstra (2000) argues that this implies that a company's success or even its survival in business society is dependent on the extent that the company are considered to operate within the norms of society (Brown and Deegan 1998). Thus, legitimacy theory suggests that no company has an inherent right to exist. Instead, every business operation is subject to the acceptance granted by society. Drawing on the ideas originating from Dowling and Pfeffer (1975), Hahn and Kühnen (2013) argue that this legitimacy is potentially threatened if society perceives that a company is *not* operating and conducting business in an acceptable manner. Legitimacy theory is often used to support the idea that sustainability reporting is a means for a company to gain, maintain or repair legitimacy (see de Villiers and Staden 2006; O'Donovan 2002). So, in order to understand not only why companies engage in sustainability reporting but also how they report on their sustainability activities, it is important to acknowledge that this practice is considered an important means aimed at securing legitimacy.

To be perceived as legitimate in society and accordingly receive the so fundamental social licence to operate is dependent on the perceptions that stakeholders have of the company and of its operations.

According to *stakeholder theory*, a company needs to take into account not only the perspectives and expectations of its various stakeholders as of today but also to be aware of shifts in these perspectives and expectations (Freeman 1984). The moral view of stakeholder theory proposes that those who are impacted by or impact a company's operations also have the right to be informed and to demand certain levels of performance (see Freeman 1984; Mitchell et al. 1997). This means that for a company to keep track of shifted perspectives and expectations, the management team must continuously analyse who its stakeholders are. The stakeholder salience framework (Mitchell et al 1997) offers a structured approach to identify the most prominent stakeholders by characterising them according to the attributes: *legitimacy*, *power* and *urgency*. Over the years, companies are found to provide accountability to their stakeholders (Mori Junior et al. 2014) by voluntarily report about their engagement in sustainability activities. Although it is not a typical two-way communication, sustainability reporting is often put forward as a dialogue between a company and its stakeholders (Edgley et al. 2010; Gray et al. 1995a). Considering the accentuated focus on stakeholder engagement and dialogue in the Global Reporting Initiative (GRI) G4 Guidelines, the dialogue perspective will probably be even more prominent in the years to come. Today, we often see arguments of the importance to involve stakeholders in the shaping of the sustainability discourse (Golob et al. 2017). Campbell et al. (2003) argue that sustainability reporting can be regarded as a means to shape the perceived legitimacy of a company. Thus, besides being assumed as a means to secure legitimacy, sustainability reporting is also claimed to be a stakeholder dialogue aimed at enhancing stakeholder relations.

The Nobel Laureate George Akerlof taught us already in the 60s and 70s that *information asymmetry* exists in situations where there is an asymmetric distribution of information between the parties involved (Akerlof 1970). Hahn and Kühnen (2013) argue that the sustainability performance of a company can be regarded as such asymmetric information. This is due to the difficulties for stakeholders outside the company to gain credible information on relevant aspects vital for assessing this performance. Following this line of arguing, proactively reporting on its sustainability-related activities in corporate reports might be an efficient way for a company to reduce this alleged information asymmetry. Several studies confirm that a company, which provides sustainability reporting, can decrease information asymmetries between itself and relevant stakeholders (see Montiel et al. 2012). Recent studies also ascertain a positive relationship between engaging in sustainability activities and financial performance (Cahan et al. 2016; Ramchander et al. 2012; Su et al. 2016), as well as a negative relationship with a company's cost of equity (Dhaliwal et al. 2014).

Sustainability Reporting: A Voluntary Reporting Practice Often Met with Scepticism

From the section above, we have gained better insights into the arguments underlying the corporate choice to engage in sustainability reporting. Besides being assumed an important means to secure legitimacy and a stakeholder dialogue, sustainability reporting is also supposed to be used as a critical means for decreasing asymmetric information by engaging in conveying credible information about its performance in the sustainability arena. Being acquainted with these underlying arguments that motivate companies to report on their sustainability activities probably makes it less astonishing to grasp that sustainability reporting primarily is a *voluntary* practice (see Searcy and Buslovich 2014). Until now, few countries mandate companies to report on how they perform in the sustainability arena. This is about to change as will be explored further in the coming sections. However, first we will learn more about *why* this voluntary reporting practice has been so criticised over the years.

Although sustainability reporting often is addressed as a new reporting phenomenon, we saw the first wave of corporate accountability in the form of these reports where environmental impact and social impact were at focus already in the 1970s in Europe and the USA (Kolk 2010). Around this time, there was a lot of scepticism towards why companies in the first place should engage in sustainability activities (see Andrews 1973; Levitt 1958). The most well-known argument *against* a corporate focus on a responsible business conduct is probably still the one posted in The New York Magazine in September 1970 by Milton Friedman who (soon to be Nobel Laureate) simply stated "...*there is one and only one social responsibility of business – to use its resources and engage in activities designed to increase its profits so long as it stays within the rules of the game...*". Hereafter, sustainability reporting lost momentum due to lack of institutionalisation (Kolk 2005; Dierkes and Antal 1986) and was only sporadically present in some industries and countries with companies particularly dedicated to the idea of sustainability reporting.

In the aftermath of the many corporate scandals taking place on the social, ethical and environmental arenas, e.g. Enron, WorldCom, gigantic bonuses, exploitation of child labour, increased pollution and CO_2 emission (see Arvidsson 2010), the opinion against a too strict focus on shareholder value grew stronger and resulted in a widespread mistrust against management teams (Ghoshal 2005; Gray et al. 2005; Kennedy 2000). Ghoshal (2005) claimed that the theory of shareholder value had contributed to short-sightedness and a lack of moral responsibility among management teams. All these corporate scandals with their origins in the social, ethical and environmental arenas provided a perfect hotbed for sustainability reporting, which at the time was put forward as an efficient means to decrease mistrust and also restore the so fundamentally important stakeholders' confident in management teams (see, e.g. SOU 2004a, b). Thus, around the turn of the century, we experienced a real shift in the perceptions and expectations among stakeholders, i.e. society, regarding what defines a socially acceptable business conduct. The corporate response to this shift was an increased focus to voluntarily develop their sustainability-reporting practices.

With the increasing trend among companies worldwide to report on their achievements in the sustainability arena (KPMG 2015), the scepticism changed from questioning the actual decision to engage in various sustainability activities to instead critique sustainability reporting per se for being insufficient, lack credibility, being a greenwashing activity, a PR invention or simply words not actions (Frankental 2001; Milne et al. 2009; Moneva et al. 2006; O'Dwyer et al. 2005). Gray (2010) claims that there is little hope that corporate sustainability accounting *ever* will be of much use. This notion, shared by several critical theorists (see Aras and Crowther 2009; Gray and Milne 2002; Welford 1997), is founded on the belief that the very definition of what is required for 'sustainability' is too ambiguous and obscure to be manageable in corporate reports (see Searcy and Buslovich 2014). In the next section, we will see how voluntary-sustainability standards have been developed to mitigate these alleged shortcomings with sustainability reporting by providing structure, principles, guidelines and certifications.

A Fierce Development of Voluntary-Sustainability Standards

There are some intriguing challenges related to sustainability reporting. This is due not the least to the lack of a uniform definition of sustainability and what it means to be a sustainable business. This renders difficulties for companies when it comes to decide on which sustainability activities they should engage in and how they should report on their achievements in the sustainability arena. In order to help companies to implement, manage and report sustainability activities, a new set of voluntary-sustainability standards has been developed (see Rasche 2009; Waddock 2008). Behnam and MacLean (2011) offer a well-established framework in which they categorise three types of standards; *principle-*, *certification-* and *reporting-based standards.*

The principle-based standards provide management teams with guidance on acceptable and unacceptable behaviours and practices. These standards can then be used by external stakeholders for assessing organisations' activities and commitment in the sustainability arena. The most prominent and world's largest voluntary citizenship is the principle-based standard United Nation Global Compact (UNGC) (Behnam and MacLean 2011; Waddock 2008), which focuses on, e.g. human rights, environmental sustainability and corruption (see Table 1).

This initiative was launched in 2000 by then UN Secretary General Koffi Annan. This was considered a bit controversial since it was the first time UN cooperated with *companies* directly instead of *countries.* It even resulted in some critique of 'bluewashing' suggesting that companies reported on sustainability under the UN flag (see Waddock 2008).

Table 1 The Ten Principles of UN Global Compact

Human Rights	
Principle 1:	Businesses should support and respect the protection of internationally proclaimed human rights
Principle 2:	Businesses should make sure that they are not complicit in human rights abuses
Labour	
Principle 3:	Businesses should uphold the freedom of association and the effective recognition of the right to collective bargaining
Principle 4:	Businesses should uphold the elimination of all forms of forced and compulsory labour
Principle 5:	Businesses should uphold the effective abolition of child labour
Principle 6:	Businesses should uphold the elimination of discrimination in employment and occupation
Environment	
Principle 7:	Businesses should support a precautionary approach to environmental challenges
Principle 8:	Businesses should undertake initiatives to promote environmental responsibility
Principle 9:	Businesses should encourage the development and diffusion of environmentally friendly technologies
Anti-Corruption	
Principle 10:	Businesses should work against corruption in all its forms, including extortion and bribery

While image gains still are considered a significant motivator for deciding to be signatories of UNGC, Arevalo et al. (2013) show that economic gains have emerged as an important motive for companies to apply UNGC. In 2015, a new set of elaborated principles saw the light when UN launched 17 Sustainable Development Goals, the so-called SDGs. These goals are aimed at ending poverty, protecting the planet and ensuring prosperity for all (see Fig. 1 and www.un.org/sustainabledevelopment/). The time period for the agenda for reaching these goals was set to 15 years, i.e. the Agenda 2030. Arvidsson (2017) confirmed that a great proportion of the largest Swedish companies already in their reports for the financial year 2015 started to accentuate their commitment to the SDGs. Also, this commitment has been criticised for being a commitment not integrated into organisational routines and

Fig. 1 The Sustainable Development Goals (SDGs)

processes and, thus, mere 'SDG-washing' (compare greenwashing and bluewashing).

The second type of standard is the so-called certification-based standards. They measure a company's sustainability performance by defining certain requirements (Behnam and MacLean 2011). Independent external auditors then certify the outcome of this assessment. These standards include different focus, e.g. environment (ISO14001), labour (Fair Labor Association's Code of Conduct) or social, environmental *and* economic issues (AA1000; SA8000; ISO26000). The AA1000 is a set of standards used to demonstrate leadership and performance in accountability, responsibility and sustainability (for further details see http://www.accountability.org/standards/). SA8000 was established by Social Accountability International in 1997 as a multi-stakeholder initiative. It measures social performance in eight areas important to social accountability in workplaces. (for further details see http://www.sa-intl.org/index.cfm?fuseaction=Page.ViewPage&PageID=1689). ISO26000 Social Responsibility was established by the International Organization for Standardization (ISO) with the aim of providing guidance on how businesses and organisations can operate in a socially responsible way (for further details see https://www.iso.org/iso-26000-social-responsibility.html). Although the meritorious contribution of all these sustainability standards when it comes to help companies to implement, manage and report sustainability activities, the voluntary nature of them is also viewed as rendering complications related to credibility, i.e. the risk of decoupling is imminently (Aravind and Christmann 2011; Vigneu et al. 2015). Since certification-based standards require evidence of compliance by a third party, they are argued to be less prone for decoupling compared to the other two categories of standards (Behnam and MacLean 2011).

Finally, the reporting-based standards offer a reporting framework for economic, environmental and social activities. Two of the most prominent in this category of standards are the integrated-reporting framework and Global Reporting Initiative (GRI) . The so-called <IR> framework (IIRC 2013) was developed to bring greater cohesion and efficiency to the reporting process and promoted an adoption of a more 'integrated thinking' where sustainability should not be an add-on but integrated into financial reporting (see chapter Rimmel Dumay). The adoption process of this integrative reporting approach has though been quite slow (KPMG 2015). GRI is the most implemented standard in this category (Behnam and MacLean 2011; Brown et al. 2009; Etzion and Ferraro 2010; IIRC 2013). It was initiated in late 1990s by the Coalition for Environmentally Responsible Economies (CERES) and UN Environment Programme (UNEP). An important objective was to allow not only cross-company but also cross-industry comparisons and this is why GRI is put forward as the global benchmark for standardised sustainability reporting. As such, it is aimed at being comparable to Generally Accepted Accounting Principles (GAAP) for financial reporting (Waddock 2008). Although the standard is widespread, Brown et al (2009, p. 197) already in 2009 argued that GRI has '…arrived at its maturation stage facing a plethora of challenges, many of which are grounded in the strategies adopted by its founder'. Roca and Searcy (2012) find that almost half of the examined corporate reports state that they use the GRI guidelines; however, less than one-third explicitly report on GRI indicators. They also find that there is an incredible diversity as to which GRI indicators companies include in their reports. This impairs comparability and the process of developing standard sets of indicators with broad acceptance among companies.

Mandatory Requirements: A Quick Fix?

Albeit the meritorious initiatives at corporate level to engage in sustainability reporting paired with the fierce development of voluntary-sustainability standards, the critique against sustainability reporting is still present. The critique is now primarily centred around the alleged lack of value relevant, credible and comparable sustainability information in the reports. In order to improve the credibility of sustainability information, sustainability assurance has become a widespread phenomenon within the sustainability-reporting sphere (cf. Faroq and de Villiers; Carrington). Mandatory requirements have been suggested as a broader remedy for these shortcomings. Some countries have started to mandate companies to provide sustainability information in their corporate report either by law (e.g. Nouvelles Régulations Économiques #2001-420 in France) or through de facto mandatory requirements through listing regulations (e.g. the Code of Governance in South Africa 2009 (King III)). However, empirical evidence reveals that not even mandatory requirements appear to be a quick fix when it comes to the alleged shortcomings with the information included in sustainability reporting. The informational quality is confirmed to be low (Chauvey et al. 2015; Larrinaga et al. 2002) even in those countries where companies are restricted by law to provide information about sustainability in their corporate reports. Yet, another problem is the low level of compliance with these laws. According to Bebbington et al. (2012), this depends on a lack of normativity, i.e. the degree to which management teams regard laws to be binding.

Sustainability Reporting and the Transformation Towards More Sustainable Businesses: A Financial Market Perspective

It is critical not the least from a financial market perspective that the informational quality of sustainability reporting is confirmed to be low also in settings where this information is required by law. A majority of stock market actors regard sustainability information so difficult to assess and benchmark that the usefulness of this information is reduced and not considered suitable for being included in investment analysis (Cho et al. 2015; Radley Yeldar 2012). Arvidsson (2014) finds that unstructured sustainability reports, which lack disclosing the value relevance of engaging in sustainability activities, might even be priced with a risk premium on the financial markets. Overall, this risks impairing the efficient allocation of capital on the financial markets. This is problematic since sustainability information is attracting more focus in corporate reports (KPMG 2015; Daub 2007).

Even though the interest in sustainability information has been tepid on the financial markets (Arvidsson 2003, 2014), efforts have been made to join forces in developing guidelines and structures aimed at finding a mutual ground or common language facilitating the process when management teams and actors on the financial markets communicate sustainability performance. Financial organisations like European Federation of Financial Analysts (EFFAS), Society of Investment Professionals in Germany (DVFA) and Swedish Society of Financial Analysts (SFF) have, for example, directed attention to examine the role sustainability information plays in a valuation context. This development is a reaction to the fact that the financial community experiences problems with understanding and evaluating this kind of information (see Arvidsson 2014). However, it is also triggered by stakeholders increased interest in safeguarding a sustainable development worldwide.

In the aftermath of the many corporate scandals around the millennium, stakeholders' interest in more sustainable businesses awoke. This was manifested in an increasing will to invest in companies categorised as being managed in a sustainable and responsible manner. In 2006, every one out of eight dollars invested in Europe and in the USA was subject to a social or ethical screen (Social Investment Forum, 2006). A direct outcome of this was the introduction of Dow Jones Sustainability Index, FTSE4GOOD Index and Ethibel Sustainability Index, which are all examples of indexes in which companies meeting globally recognised sustainability standards are included. In 2006, the U.N. introduced PRI—Principles for Responsible Investments. This is a guideline for how investors should include perspectives on environmental, social and corporate governance (ESG) issues when they make investments.

Until recently, sustainability rankings, indexes and funds have been viewed as a sub-market on the financial markets. However, the global sustainable investment market continues to grow and its share of professionally managed assets also grows. According to new statistics, there are now close to $23 trillion of assets being professionally managed under responsible investment strategies, which is an increase of 25% since 2014 (GSIA 2017). In relative terms, responsible investment now stands for 26% of all professionally managed assets globally (ibid.). Today, sustainable investing constitutes a major force across global financial markets. Already a decade ago, Waring and Edwards (2008) argued that the use of rankings and screens by fund managers to decide whether to invest in a company or not imposes considerable pressure on companies to provide attractive track records on the issues of importance to the fund.

Although it has been discussed for decades, it seems like neither management teams nor the actors on the financial markets have regarded the low informational quality of sustainability reporting to be enough critical or acute to really deal with until now. Today, we see an up-speeded transformation of our companies into more sustainable organisations resulting in a vigorous practice development. This is paired with forthcoming national and international regulation of different sustainability-related activities concerning, e.g. inclusion of sustainable perspectives on investment valuations, human rights, emissions, disclosure rules, tax transparency, compliance and anti-corruption. Together with an awaken interest of sustainability information from the actors on the financial markets triggered by a growing global sustainable investment market, the need to direct resources for establishing value relevant, credible and comparable information on how a company performs in the sustainability arena is now evident both to management teams and to the actors on the financial markets.

Enhancing Sustainability Reporting Through the New EU Directive (2014/95/EU)

When EU High Level Group on Sustainable Finance (HLEG) presented their final report in January 2018 (https://ec.europa.eu/info/sites/info/files/170713-sustainable-finance-report_en.pdf), they put forward some priority actions. These include establishing an EU sustainability taxonomy, clarifying investor duties to extend the time horizons of investment and bring greater focus on environmental, social and governance (ESG) factors into investment decisions and upgrading disclosures to make sustainability opportunities and risks transparent. The new EU Directive (2014/95/EU) (referred to as the Directive) transposed into national laws came into force financial year 2017. This is the first joint regulative effort that EU makes when it comes to upgrade the value relevance, credibility and comparability of sustainability reporting. The first reports in line with the Directive will be published in 2018, thus, covering the financial year 2017.

The Directive apply to large public interest companies with more than 500 employees. Approximately 6000 companies in the EU will be mandated to follow the Directive. The Swedish Government is one of few governments that decided to expand the number of companies mandated by the Directive to 1600 companies instead of 200 as the Directive stated. These so-called public interest entities will be:

a. Required to report on environmental, social and employee-related, human rights, anti-corruption and bribery matters;
b. Required to describe their business model, outcomes and risks of the policies on the above topics, and the diversity policy applied for management and supervisory bodies;
c. Encouraged to rely on recognised frameworks such as GRI's Sustainability Reporting Guidelines, the United Nations Global Compact (UNGC), the UN Guiding Principles on Business and Human Rights, OECD Guidelines, International Organization for Standardization (ISO) 26000 and the International Labour Organization (ILO) Tripartite Declaration.

The text under (c) above humbly suggests a set of voluntary-sustainability standards that the companies can rely on when structuring their reports; the text under (1) and (2) are more explicit. While the text under (a) requires the companies to focus their reports on certain sustainability-related topics, the text under (b) requires the companies to elaborate on the relation between the policies/achievements regarding the highlighted sustainability-related topics and organisational routines and processes related to business model, outcomes, risks and governance. Considering that sustainability reporting for decades has been criticised for lacking value relevance and credibility and been accused of being a PR invention not manifested in organisational routines and processes (ICGN 2016; Simnett et al. 2009), the focus of the Directive is indeed motivated. Although the Directive has been criticised for being too soft, it has been applauded for encouraging companies to focus their disclosures on explaining how their sustainability activities are manifested in organisational routines and processes (CSR Europe and GRI 2017; FAR 2017). Due to the soft tone in the Directive, several have questioned the actual effects the Directive will have on the informational quality of sustainability reporting and on the integration of sustainability activities into organisational routines and processes. To develop efficient regulations with high normativity, it is argued to be vital to examine the actual effects of the Directive (see CSR Europe and GRI 2017; Arvidsson 2018; Venturelli et al. 2017).

Concluding Remarks

This chapter has painted the picture of a fragmented transformation towards more sustainable businesses. A transformation was argued immensely vital already thirty years ago when the Brundtland Report was published in 1987. Today, there is a positive momentum worldwide for joining forces to promote a more sustainable development. When businesses increase their investments and engagement in sustainability activities, so does the need to provide their stakeholders with information on their sustainability performance. This means the developing of a new type of relevant corporate disclosure along traditional corporate financial information. Understandably, this poses new challenges to both companies that provide this information and stakeholders that will try to understand, assess and compare this new type of information, i.e. sustainability information. Unfortunately, the quality has been a problem and the scepticism and critique against sustainability reporting have not been subtle. As a response to this, many great initiatives, primarily of voluntary nature, have seen the lights and contributed to a fiercely development of sustainability-reporting practices. Today, management teams have become more proactive in making voluntary efforts to improve the quality of sustainability information. Triggered by a growing global sustainable investment market, the actors on the stock market have become less sceptic and more interested in trying to understand and integrate this type of information in their valuation processes. However, several challenges still line up the road ahead. These challenges relate to the need to enhance value relevance, credibility and comparability of information related to sustainability performance. This was also strongly accentuated in the final report from EU High Level Group on Sustainable Finance published in January 2018. The years to follow will reveal if the new EU Directive (2014/95/EU) has the potential to assist in improving the informational quality of sustainability reporting.

References

Adams, C. A., & McNicholas, P. (2007). Making a difference: Sustainability reporting, accountability and organisational change. *Accounting, Auditing & Accountability Journal, 20*(3), 382–402.

Akerlof, G. A. (1970). The market for “lemons”: Quality uncertainty and the market mechanism. *The Quarterly Journal of Economics, 84*(3), 488–500.

Andrews, K. R. (1973, May–June). Can the best corporations be made moral? *Harvard Business Review*, 57–64.

Aras, G., & Crowther, D. (2009). Corporate sustainability reporting: A study in disingenuity. *Journal of Business Ethics Supplement, 87*, 279–288.

Aravind, D., & Christmann, P. (2011). Decoupling of standard implementation from certification: Does quality of ISE 14001 implementation affect facilities’ environmental performance? *Business Ethics Quarterly, 21*(1), 73–102.

Arevalo, J. A., Aravind, D., Ayuso, S., & Roca, M. (2013). The Global Compact: An analysis of the motivations of adoption in the Spanish context. *Business Ethics: A European Review, 22*(1), 1–15.

Arvidsson, S. (2003). *Demand and supply of information on intangibles: The case of knowledge-intense companies.* Ph.D. dissertation, Department of Business Administration, Lund University, Lund University Press.

Arvidsson, S. (2010). Communication of corporate social responsibility: A study of the views of management teams in large companies. *Journal of Business Ethics, 96*, 339–354.

Arvidsson, S. (2014). Corporate social responsibility and stock market actors: A comprehensive study. *Social Responsibility Journal, 10*(2), 210–225.

Arvidsson, S. (2017). Sustainability disclosure in large listed companies: A longitudinal study on extent, content and structure (Working Paper). Lund University.

Arvidsson, S, (Ed.). (2018). *The 1st SUBREA conference report*, Media Tryck, Lund University.

Bebbington, J., Higgins, C., & Frame, B. (2009). Initiating sustainable development reporting: Evidence from New Zealand. *Accounting, Auditing & Accountability Journal, 22*(4), 588–625.

Bebbington, J., Kirk, E. A., & Larrinaga, C. (2012). The production of normativity: A comparison of reporting regimes in Spain and the U.K. *Accounting, Organizations and Society, 37,* 78–94.

Behnam, M., & MacLean, T. L. (2011). Where is the accountability in international accountability standards? A decoupling perspective. *Business Ethics Quarterly, 21*(1), 45–72.

Bondy, K., Moon, J., & Matten, D. (2012). An institution of corporate social responsibility (CSR) in multi-national corporations (MNCs): Forms and implications. *Journal of Business Ethics, 111,* 281–299.

Brown, N., & Deegan, C. (1998). The public disclosure of environmental performance information—A dual test of media agenda setting theory and legitimacy theory. *Accounting and business research, 29*(1), 21–41.

Brown, H. S., de Jong, M., & Lessidrenska, T. (2009). The rise of the global reporting initiative: A case of institutional entrepreneurship. *Environmental Politics, 18*(2), 182–200.

CSR Europe and GRI. (2017). *Member state implementation of directive 2014/95/EU: A comprehensive overview of how member states are implementing the EU directive on non-financial and diversity information*. Brussels: GRI.

Cahan, S. F., de Villiers, C., Jeter, D. C., Naiker, V., & van Staden, C. J. (2016). Are CSR disclosure value relevant? Cross-country evidence. *European Accounting Review, 25*(3), 579–611.

Campbell, D., Craven, B., & Shrives, P. (2003). Voluntary social reporting in three FTSE sectors: A comment on perception and legitimacy. *Accounting, Auditing & Accountability Journal, 16*(4), 558–581.

Chauvey, J.-N., Giordano-Spring, S., Cho, C. H., & Patten, D. M. (2015). The normativity and legitamacy of CSR disclosure: Evidence from France. *Journal of Business Ethics, 130,* 789–803.

Cho, C. H., Michelon, G., Patten, D. M., & Robets, R. W. (2015). CSR disclosure: The more tings change…? *Accounting, Auditing and Accountability Journal, 28*(1), 14–35.

Daub, C. H. (2007). Assessing the quality of sustainability reporting: An alternative methodological approach. *Journal of Cleaner Production, 15*(1), 75–85.

Deegan, C. (2002). Introduction—The legitimising effect of social and environmental disclosures—A theoretical foundation. *Accounting, Auditing & Accountability Journal, 15*(3), 282–311.

de Villiers, C., & Staden, C. J. (2006). Can less environmental disclosure have a legitimising effect? Evidence from Africa. *Accounting, Organizations and Society, 31*(8), 763–781.

Dienes, D., Sassen, R., & Fischer, J. (2016). What are the drivers of sustainability reporting? A systematic review. *Sustainability Accounting, Management and Policy Journal, 7*(2), 154–189.

Dierkes, M., & Antal, A. B. (1986). Whither corporate social reporting: Is it time to legislate? *California Management Review, 28*(3), 106–121.

Dhaliwal, D. S., Radhakrishnan, S., Tsang, A. H., & Yang, Y. G. (2012). Nonfinancial disclosure and analyst forecast accuracy: International evidence on corporate social responsibility disclosure. *The Accounting Review, 87*(3), 723–759.

Dhaliwal, D., Li, O. Z., Tsang, A., & Yang, Y. G. (2014). Corporate social responsibility disclosure and the cost of equity capital: The roles of stakeholder orientation and financial transparency. *Journal of Accounting and Public Policy, 33*(4), 328–355.

Dowling, J., & Pfeffer, J. (1975). Organizational legitimacy: Social values and organizational behaviour. *The Pacific Sociological Review, 18*(1), 122–136.

Edgley, C., Jones, M. J., & Solomon, J. F. (2010). Stakeholder inclusivity in social and environmental report assurance. *Accounting, Auditing & Accountability Journal, 23*(4), 532–557.

Etzion, D., & Ferraro, F. (2010). The role of analogy in the institutionalization of sustainability reporting. *Organization Science, 21*(5), 1092–1107.

EU Directive (2014/95/EU). (2014). *Directive on disclosure of non-financial and diversity information by certain large companies*. European Commission, Brussels, Belgium.

European Commission. (2013). *Report on corporate social responsibility: Promoting society's interests and a route to sustainable and inclusive recovery* (2012/2097(INI)). Brussels.

FAR. (2017). *FAQ Hållbarhetsrapportering enligt ÅRL*. FAR, Stockholm.

Frankental, P. (2001). Corporate social responsibility—A PR invention? *Corporate Communications: An International Journal, 6*(1), 18–23.

Freeman, R. E. (1984). *Strategic management: A stakeholder approach*. Marshfield, MA: Pitman.

Friedman, M. (1970, September 13). The social responsibility of business is to increase its profits'. *New York Times Magazine*, pp. 33, 122–26.

GSIA. (2017). *2016 Global sustainable investment review*. Bloomberg: Global Sustainable Investment Alliance (GSIA).

Ghoshal, S. (2005). Bad management theories are destroying good management practices. *Academy of Management Learning & Education, 4*(1), 75–91.

Golob, U., Verk, N., Ellerup-Nielsen, A., Thomsen, C., Elving, W. J., & Podnar, K. (2017). The communicative stance of CSR: Reflections on the value of CSR communication. *Corporate Communications: An International Journal, 22*(2).

Gray, R. (2010). Is accounting for sustainability actually accounting for sustainability…and how would we know? An exploration of narratives of organisations and the planet. *Accounting, Organizations and Society, 35*(1), 47–62.

Gray, K. R., Frieder, L. A., & Clark, G. W. (2005). *Corporate scandals—The many faces of greed*. St. Paul, MN: Paragon House.

Gray, R., Kouhy, R., & Lavers, S. (1995a). Methodological themes constructing a research database of social and environmental reporting by UK companies. *Accounting, Auditing & Accountability Journal, 8*(2), 78–101.

Gray, R., Kouhy, R., & Lavers, S. (1995b). Corporate social and environmental reporting: A review of the literature and a longitudinal study of UK disclosure. *Accounting, Auditing & Accountability Journal, 8*(2), 47–77.

Gray, R., Owen, D., & Adams, C. (1996). *Accounting accountability—Changes and challenges in corporate social and environmental reporting*. London: Prentice-Hall.

Gray, R., & Milne, M. (2002). Sustainable reporting: Who's kidding whom? *Chartered Accountants Journal of New Zealand, 81*(6), 66–74.

Hahn, R., & Kühnen, M. (2013). Determinants of sustainability reporting: A review of results, trends, theory, and opportunities in an expanding field of research. *Journal of Cleaner Production, 59*, 5–21.

Hooghiemstra, R. (2000). Corporate communication and impression management—New perspectives why companies engage in corporate social reporting. *Journal of Business Ethics, 27*(1), 55–68.

IIRC. (2013). *The international IR framework*. Available: http://www.theiirc.org/wp-content/uploads/2013/12/13-12-08-THE-INTERNATIONAL-IR-FRAMEWORK-2-1.pdf.

ICGN. (2016). *Feedback regarding draf 2016 code of corporate governance for publicly-listed companies*. London: ICGN.

Kennedy, A. A. (2000). *The end of shareholder value—Corporations at the crossroad*. Cambridge, MA: Perseus.

Kolk, A. (2010). Trajectories of sustainability reporting by MNCs. *Journal of World Business, 45*, 367–374.

Kolk, A. (2005). Social and environmental accounting. In C. Clubb (Ed.), *Blackwell encyclopedia of management accounting* (pp. 393–398). Malden, Oxford and Victoria: Blackwell.

KPMG. (2015). *KPMG international survey of corporate responsibility reporting*. Amsterdam: KPMG International.

Larrinaga, C., Carrasco, F., Correa, C., Llena, F., & Moneva, J. M. (2002). Accountability and accounting regulation: The case of the Spanish disclosure standard. *European Accounting Review, 11*(4), 723–740.

Levitt, T. (1958). The dangers of social-responsibility. *Harvard Business Review, 36*(5), 41–50.

Martínez-Ferrero, J., & Frías-Aceituno, J. V. (2015). Relationship between sustainable development and financial performance: International empirical research. *Business Strategy and the Environment, 24*(1), 20–39.

Milne, M. J., Tregidga, H., & Walton, S. (2009). Words not actions! The ideological role of sustainability development reporting. *Accounting, Auditing & Accountability Journal, 22*(8), 1211–1257.

Mitchell, R. K., Agle, B. R., & Wood, D. J. (1997). Toward a theory of stakeholder identification and salience: Defining the principle of who and what really counts. *Academy of Management Review, 22*(4), 853–886.

Moneva, J. M., Archel, P., & Correa, C. (2006). GRI and the camouflaging of corporate unsustainability. *Accounting Forum, 30*, 121–137.

Montiel, I., Husted, B. W., & Christmann, P. (2012). Using private management standard certification to reduce information asymmetries in corrupt environments. *Strategic Management Journal, 33*, 1103–1113.

Mori Junior, R., Best, P. J., & Cotter, J. (2014). Sustainability reporting and assurance: A historical analysis on a world-wide phenomenon. *Journal of Business Ethics, 120*, 1–11.

O'Donovan, G. (2002). Environmental disclosures in the annual report—Extending the applicability and predictive power of legitimacy theory. *Accounting, Auditing & Accountability Journal, 15*(3), 344–371.

O'Dwyer, B., Unerman, J., & Hession, E. (2005). User needs in sustainability reporting: Perspectives of stakeholders in Ireland. *European Accounting Review, 14*(4), 759–787.

Parker, L. D. (2005). Social and environmental accountability research: A view from the commentary box. *Accounting, Auditing & Accountability Journal, 18*(6), 842–860.
Patten, D. M. (2013). Lessons from the third wave: A reflection on the rediscovery of corporate social responsibility by the mainstream accounting research community. *Financial Reporting, 2*(2), 9–26.
Prado-Lorenzo, J.-M., Gallego-Alvarez, S., & Garcia-Sanchez, I. M. (2009). Stakeholder engagement and corporate social responsibility reporting: The ownership structure effect. *Corporate Social Responsibility and Environmental Management, 16,* 94–107.
Radley Yeldar. (2012). *The value of extra financial disclosure: What investors and analysts said.* Report commissioned by accounting for sustainability and the global reporting initiative. Retrieved from http://www.globalreporting.org/resourcelibrary/The-value-of-extra-financial-disclosure.pdf.
Ramchander, S., Schweback, R. G., & Staking, K. (2012). The informational relevance of corporate social responsibility: Evidence from DS400 index reconstitutions. *Strategic Management Journal, 33,* 303–314.
Roca, L. C., & Searcy, C. (2012). An analysis of indicators disclosed in corporate sustainability reports. *Journal of Cleaner Production, 20,* 103–118.
Rasche, A. (2009). Toward a model to compare and analyse accountability standards—The case of the UN Global Compact. *Corporate Social Responsibility and Environmental Management, 16,* 192–205.
SOU 2004:46. (2004a). *The Swedish code of corporate governance.* Stockholm: SOU.
SOU 2004:47. (2004b). *Näringslivet och Förtroendet* [Business Society and Trust]. Stockholm: SOU.
Searcy, C., & Buslovich, R. (2014). Corporate perspectives on the development and use of sustainability reports. *Journal of Business Ethics, 121,* 149–169.
Simnett; R., Vanstraelen, A. & Chua, W. F. (2009). Assurance of sustainability reports: An international comparison. *The Accounting Review, 53*(1), 94–111.
Su, W., Peng, M. W., Tan, W., & Cheung, Y.-L. (2016). The signalling effect of corporate social responsibility in emerging economies. *Journal of Business Ethics, 134,* 479–491.
UNWCED (United Nation World Commission on Environment and Development). (1987). *Report of the United Nation World Commission on environment and development 'our common future' (The Brundtland Report)* (Item 83, 42nd Session of the United Nations General Assembly).

Venturelli, A., Caputo, F., Cosma, S., Leopizzi, R., & Pizzi, S. (2017). Directive 2014/95/EU: Are Italian companies already compliant? *Sustainability, 9*(8), 1385.

Vigneu, L., Humphreys, M., & Moon, J. (2015). How do firms comply with international sustainability standards? Processes and consequences of adopting the global reporting initiative. *Journal of Business Ethics, 131,* 469–486.

Waddock, S. (2008). Building a new institutional infrastructure for corporate responsibility. *Academy of Management Perspectives, 22*(3), 87–108.

Waring, P., & Edwards, T. (2008). Socially responsible investment: Explaining its uneven development and human resource management consequences. *Corporate Governance: An International Review, 16*(3), 135–145.

Welford, R. (1997). *Accounting for common costs.* Center for International Education and Research in Accounting, Urbana-Champaign, II.

Integrated Reporting and Integrating Thinking: Practical Challenges

Matteo La Torre, Cristiana Bernardi, James Guthrie and John Dumay

Introduction

Integrated reporting (<IR>) is the latest attempt to counter alleged criticism of contemporary financial reporting that argues accounting no

M. La Torre (✉)
Department of Economic Studies, University "G. D'Annunzio" of Chieti-Pescara, Pescara, Italy
e-mail: matteo.latorre@unich.it

C. Bernardi
Lecturer in Accounting, Department for Accounting and Finance, Faculty of Business and Law, The Open University Business School, Milton Keynes, UK
e-mail: cristiana.bernardi@open.ac.uk

J. Guthrie · J. Dumay
Department of Accounting and Corporate Governance, Faculty of Business and Economics, Macquarie University, Sydney, NSW, Australia
e-mail: james.guthrie@mq.edu.au

J. Dumay
e-mail: john.dumay@mq.edu.au

S. Arvidsson (ed.), *Challenges in Managing Sustainable Business*,
https://doi.org/10.1007/978-3-319-93266-8_2

longer meets the information needs of stakeholders and, in particular, financial capital providers (e.g., investors and banks) (IIRC 2013; Lev and Gu 2016). As the International Integrated Reporting Council (IIRC 2013, p. 2) states, <IR> aims to "improve the quality of information available to providers of financial capital to enable a more efficient and productive allocation of capital". Integral to <IR> is *integrated thinking*, which is essential because the IIRC's "long term vision is a world in which integrated thinking is embedded within mainstream business practice in the public and private sectors, facilitated by Integrated Reporting (<IR>) as the corporate reporting norm" (IIRC 2013, p. 2). Thus, <IR>'s success as a reporting framework relies on embedding integrated thinking into organizations, with an integrated report being the final output of the process.

To assess <IR>'s success, in March 2017, the IIRC launched a global invitation for preparers and other interested parties, such as academics, to comment on the practical implementation of <IR> to identify enablers, incentives and barriers to its enactment (IIRC 2017). Overall, the consultation attracted more than 400 submissions and contributions from numerous stakeholders groups. As a result, the IIRC released a summary report entitled "International <IR> Framework Implementation Feedback" (IIRC 2017) that provides first-hand feedback and evidence of how <IR> and integrated thinking are developing in practice.

There is an escalating academic debate concerning <IR> that revolves around the challenges associated with the implementation of integrated thinking within organizations. The current literature suggests that integrated thinking is problematic in practice due to its ambiguity and lack of understanding of how it works (Dumay and Dai 2017; Feng et al. 2017). The recent feedback to the IIRC from stakeholders has led the IIRC to recognize that organizations are struggling with integrated thinking. Therefore, there is arguably a need to reflect on the future of <IR> in practice and how the next stage of academic research can help understand how integrated report preparers should implement integrated thinking.

Surprisingly, despite the extensive feedback received, the IIRC does not intend to make formal revisions to the <IR> Framework for the time being. According to the IIRC, "the feedback indicated that the Framework stands up well to the challenges of implementation". Nevertheless, the report concludes that (IIRC 2017, p. 3):

> There is clearly a choice to be made between giving sufficient time for companies to clearly implement the Framework without changes being made, and updating the Framework in the light of experience and external developments. We have carefully considered the small number of suggestions made in this exercise for Framework revisions, and concluded that none are of immediate concern to justify making those changes now. However, we undertake to consider those suggestions further, along with other feedback, as the IIRC implements the actions proposed in this report.

Rather than changing the <IR> Framework, the IIRC recognizes that it needs to focus on challenges related to <IR> implementation because there are several "opportunities to provide guidance and examples and take other actions to help report preparers and other stakeholders continue to tackle those challenges" (IIRC 2017, p. 3). However, even considering a strategic update in the next 12 months to support more companies adopting <IR> and issuing an integrated report, the IIRC does not expect to implement any change until 2019.

According to the feedback gathered by the IIRC, integrated thinking rises up as a substantial and practical issue of <IR>. In the call for feedback, the IIRC asked "*What is your experience with connectivity in integrated reports as an indication of Integrated Thinking and/or enabler of enhanced decisions?*" As we will detail later, the answers reveal practical concerns about integrated thinking and the connectivity as defined in the <IRF> (IIRC 2017, p. 6). Therefore, the concerns are the building blocks for researchers, practitioners, policymakers and the IIRC alike to develop insights into how to tackle the challenges for developing integrated thinking and for issuing integrated reports.

This chapter aims to analyse several practical challenges being faced by organizations in attempting to implement integrated thinking. In so doing, the chapter seeks to answer the question "how future research into <IR> and integrated thinking can be developed". We review the contemporary academic literature and use public available data (i.e., the <IRF> feedbacks and Google Trend data) to provide academics, practitioners and policymakers with insights into how to develop integrated thinking in practice. The chapter is structured as follows. Section "Challenges for Integrated Thinking" provides insights on the challenges impeding the implementation of integrated thinking and depicts avenues for future research and practical recommendations. Section "Conclusions and Implications for Research" provides the implications for future research and the overall conclusions to be drawn from our work.

Challenges for Integrated Thinking

Table 1 summarizes the main challenges for integrated thinking and <IR> in practice based on the "International <IR> Framework Implementation Feedback". The IIRC (2017) summarizes the key observations and issues brought up by respondents for each question posed. More specifically, the report highlights ten key observations (see, second column of Table 1) raised with respect to integrated thinking (IIRC 2017, p. 6). Since not all the submissions to the call have been published by the IIRC and, therefore, are not publicly available,[1] our analysis relies on the data provided by the IIRC's report, which summarizes the comments from all the responses.

We build Table 1 in accordance with the ten observations regarding integrated thinking made in the IIRC's report and classify them into five different groups representing the main challenges (first column) for implementing integrated thinking. The following sections discuss these challenges by aligning the IIRC's feedback on integrated thinking with contemporary literature on integrated thinking and <IR>. We then outline several avenues for future research about integrated thinking and<IR>.

Table 1 Challenges and key observations about integrated thinking

Challenges for integrated thinking	Key observations from the feedback
Understanding integrated thinking and connectivity	• Connectivity of information is a critical element of both integrated reporting and integrated thinking, but it is perhaps one of the least understood of the Framework's Guiding Principles
Connectivity and the incomplete space of accounting	• The Guiding Principle Connectivity of information suffers from implementation challenges in practice • Guidance and examples were requested on aspects of connectivity and integrated thinking
Integrated thinking vs <IR> internal practices	• Respondents reinforced the importance of experience as integrated thinking matures • Mature integrated thinking, demonstrated by effective connectivity, can lead to improved decision-making
<IR> form and substance	• Connectivity in a report may not always reflect the maturity of integrated thinking. In other words, the integrated report may be an imperfect proxy for integrated thinking • Some respondents argued for stronger IIRC focus on integrated thinking • Respondents also suggested collaborations with third parties and corporate reporting Dialogue attention to address connectivity of information and integrated thinking
Trust and credibility	• Respondents stressed the importance of senior management buy-into successful adoption of integrated thinking across an organization • Integrated thinking is supported as a core element of, and prerequisite for, effective integrated reporting. However, organizations appear to struggle with the foundational concept of integrated thinking

Source Adapted from the "International <IR> Framework Implementation Feedback" (2017)

Understanding Integrated Thinking and Connectivity

Integrated thinking is a fundamental concept, if not the core concept, underpinning the IIRC's agenda. The IIRC defines it as "the active consideration by an organization of the relationships between its various operating and functional units and the capitals that the organization uses or affects" (IIRC 2013, p. 2). Integrated thinking is meant to break down internal silos, thus reducing duplication and ultimately driving towards the creation of value over the short, medium and long term. Thus, according to the IIRC's view, integrated thinking is both the foundation, artefact and outcome of implementing <IR>.

Despite the pivotal role played by integrated thinking within <IR>, the <IRF> provides relatively limited guidance on integrated thinking. In fact, the IIRC emphasizes "the cycle of integrated thinking and reporting" (see, IIRC 2013, p. 2), but does not provide a straightforward explanation of the underlying causal nexus. In the IIRC's view, reporting and thinking constitute two sides of the same coin, as they both contribute to enhancing connectivity within the organization and ameliorating the communication on value creation to both internal and external stakeholders (IIRC 2016, p. 3), thus enabling a more efficient and productive allocation of capital. However, as it currently stands in the <IRF>, integrated thinking is an opaque concept broadly open to interpretation and, as a consequence, arguably represents a major challenge for those companies wishing to embark on the journey towards <IR>. Therefore, a first challenge for integrated thinking lies in its definition and practical understanding as there are different views about what it means.

The idea underpinning integrated thinking is that value creation is not only confined to the traditional boundaries of a company, rather it crosses organizational and geographical frontiers thus enabling the connection of various value drivers. Integrated thinking requires a thorough understanding of the company's business model (i.e., the process by which value is created), that in turn facilitates the identification of prospective risks and opportunities. In contrast with traditional business analysis, which has tended to focus on myopic short or medium time frame, <IR> encourages companies to embrace a broader understanding of the value creation process by providing, through a multi-capital lens, insights into business strategy. The assumption behind the multi-capital approach adopted by the <IR> is that financial value, although being relevant, is not sufficient for assessing value creation given that success for many organizations today depends on different resources (IIRC 2013).

As emerges from the feedback (see, Table 1), information connectivity is a critical element of the <IRF> but is still one of the least understood <IR> Guiding Principle. The low understanding is not surprising given that the connectivity principle is strictly related to the concept of integrated thinking, which is perceived as a potential impediment to the practical implementation of <IR>. Feng et al. (2017) identify three reasons for this lack of understanding. First, the integrated thinking concept as defined by the IIRC has no "clear precedents in reporting contexts" (p. 334). Second, "the IIRC has not fully defined and articulated the concept of integrated thinking" and, third, "there is no shared consensus among practitioners" (Feng et al. 2017, p. 330). Therefore, the ambiguity surrounding integrated thinking often leads practitioners to use their own definitions.

Connectivity and the Incomplete Space of Accounting

The lack of a clear definition for integrated thinking is connected with the lack of guidance about how to implement the Connectivity Guiding Principle in practice (IIRC 2017). <IR> defines *connectivity of information* as the capability to "show a holistic picture of the combination, interrelatedness and dependencies between the factors that affect the organization's ability to create value over time" (IIRC 2013, p. 16). It is argued that "the more integrated thinking is embedded into an organization's activities, the more naturally will the connectivity of information flow into management reporting, analysis, decision-making and integrated reports". Therefore, integrated thinking and connectivity depend on each other and represent a core aspect of <IR>. However, as outlined by the International <IR> Framework Implementation Feedback (IIRC 2017), interdependence represents a main challenge for implementing integrated thinking.

The <IRF> asserts that information should be connected, but little is known about how this can be achieved practically. The WICI's background paper explains the steps for connectivity (WICI 2013, p. 5). Nonetheless, the critical issues arising from the International <IR> Framework Implementation Feedback highlight that more guidance is needed to understand how connectivity works in practice. Although practitioners claim for more guidance on how to connect information, explaining how to implement connectivity is an ambitious task for the IIRC.

Connecting information is the prerogative of information users. It is the user who connects information by addressing his/her information needs. This can be demonstrated by referring to the Balanced Scorecard (BSC) within the management accounting research field. The BSC has been a management accounting innovation created to help organization link the factors underpinning value creation, explain their cause–effects relations and solving the need of causality (Cooper et al. 2017). However, recent studies demonstrate that the BSC's actual success and its practical outcome for businesses lie in its inability to represent a faithful and complete representation (Busco and Quattrone 2015, 2018). In essence, the BSC can be used to show the preparer's interpretation of what creates value, but the actual causes may be ambiguous (Dierickx and Cool 1989).

Busco and Quattrone (2015, p. 1253) describe the BSC as a "rhetorical machine" and outline that "it is this incompleteness that empowers the BSC's inscriptions and allows the process of interrogation and mediation to engage and unfold". Such an incompleteness is able to enact "in-tension" by pushing accounting information users to search for connections between information and enquire their logical meaning. Additionally, they argue that the "incompleteness of [the] BSC representations creates a theoretically infinite number of possibilities for imagining new and unforeseen relationships between key strategic imperatives, perspectives, and KPIs" (Busco and Quattrone 2015, p. 1253). Therefore, the power of accounting information does not lie in its "representational capability" (Busco and Quattrone 2015), but can be theoretically explained by the incomplete space generated by accounting inscriptions (reports) and performance measurement systems.

Similarly, if we translate the same theoretical explanation to <IR> and the Connectivity Guiding Principle, we can get an understating of the <IR> challenge of connecting information and demonstrate the difficulty of achieving connectivity in practice. The "incompleteness of accounting representations and performance measures" has an important function of "prompting and sustaining a continuous search for perfection which, however, is never achieved" (Busco and Quattrone 2018, p. 1). Thus, achieving connectivity in practice is arguably impossible, because it contrasts the nature and purpose of accounting information itself.

Sorting the pieces of the puzzle, representing the "big picture" is not a task for integrated reporters, but rather is a cognitive exercise for integrated report readers. Therefore, the implementation of the Connectivity Guiding Principle requires practitioners not to follow the compliance-driven approach that usually leads the adoption of a corporate reporting framework. Instead, when implementing <IR> and integrated thinking, practitioners need to shift the focus from producing an integrated report for external purposes to the internal business processes underpinning the use of its information. Even though it may be impossible to understand the direct cause and effect relationships between resources and value creation, by probing and attempting to discover these relationships, managers may reduce the ambiguity of value creation and accept that all the connections are impossible to discover (Dumay 2009).

Integrated Thinking Vs. <IR> Internal Practices

Respondents to the IIRC's call for feedback highlight the importance of experience as <IR> matures, and the need for understanding how integrated thinking can become part of improved decision-making as a result of <IR> internal practices. Overall, the feedback highlights how report preparers are still uncertain about integrated thinking, what it means and how it works. Not resolving how integrated thinking relates to practice arguably poses "potential reputational risk for the IIRC" (IIRC 2017, p. 6).

The feedback is mirrored in our research as it finds that integrated thinking is currently under the scrutiny of practitioners and academics alike, because of the growing focus on <IR>'s implications for internal practices and its voluntary nature (Dumay and Dai 2017; Guthrie et al. 2017; Oliver et al. 2016; de Villiers et al. 2017a). <IR> proponents claim that <IR> encourages integrated thinking, thus fostering connections and collaborations in "teams from across an organization, breaking down silos and leading to more Integrated Thinking" (Black Sun 2012, p. 4). In this respect, Ballou et al. (2012) assert that "accounting professionals are rarely involved in sustainability initiatives, but their involvement is highly associated with strategic integration", thus representing a counter to integrated thinking in practice. Additionally, <IR> early adopters demonstrate that <IR> does not stimulate "innovations in disclosure mechanisms" and radical changes, rather "incremental changes to processes and structures that previously supported sustainability reporting" (Stubbs and Higgins 2014, p. 1068). Furthermore, Dumay and Dai (2017) claim that existing management controls need to be deficient to allow integrated thinking to penetrate into the company, especially if a company does not see the need for change. Thus, major changes brought about by integrated thinking are not evident, and it seems more like business as usual from a reporting perspective.

According to Steyn (2014), in South Africa, where IR is more institutionalized due to the implementation of <IR> through the King III (IoDSA 2009) and King IV (IoDSA 2016) corporate governance guidelines, companies do not however perceive any promising internal outcome regarding business model innovation, sustainable product development and value creation assessment. Additionally, integrated thinking is costly to implement (Velte and Stawinoga 2017), and at present, little is known about its implications for top management thinking and internal transformations (de Villiers et al. 2017b).

In the same vein, McNally et al. (2017, p. 481) find that implementing <IR> in practice is not seen as a natural part of a business process, since it "is imposed on existing internal processes and reporting protocols which preclude a broad understanding of the purpose of <IR> and limit the development of management control systems". Additionally, as Guthrie et al. (2017) point out, implementing the <IRF> can sometimes lead to fundamental internal changes to organizations as management accounting tools and decision-making processes can change. However, organizational changes in reporting are usually incremental phases of previous reporting initiatives (Guthrie et al. 2017). Thus, even though many companies call their reports "integrated", the majority do not follow the <IRF> and thus the reports "lack both form and substance" (Guthrie et al. 2017, p. 467).

Under the <IRF>, managers are encouraged to engage with integrated thinking, which implies a more comprehensive approach to strategic planning and the development of new ways of reporting value outcomes. However, far from being solely an exclusive concept for senior managers, integrated thinking is required throughout the organization. This also implies that employees are expected to understand a matrix of considerations that combines each of the six capitals (i.e., financial, manufactured, intellectual, human, social and relationship and natural) and each functional unit (Dumay et al. 2017). Including all employees arguably represents a challenge because, whereas company managers by necessity have developed a knowledge of the organization over time, the employees capable of conceptualizing integrated thinking using such definition are few. Additionally, translating integrated thinking into action is not a trivial issue, since it requires reshaping existing organizational cultures which are neither readily nor easily replaced, especially if associated with past success (Dumay and Dai 2017).

By analysing integrated thinking as a cultural control, Dumay and Dai (2017, p. 574) demonstrate that it "clashes with the existing organizational culture rather than driving a new organizational culture". They argue that integrated thinking cannot break the silos if an organization does not suffer from managerial problems due to organizational silos. In this respect, they claim that existing management controls need to be deficient to allow integrated thinking to penetrate into the company, especially if a company does not see the need for change. Such findings question the main assumption supporting the claims about the need for integrated thinking: that organizations suffer from managerial control problems and have dysfunctional organizational silos. Therefore, integrated thinking is facing several challenges which refer to the existing internal precedents and structures, especially organizational culture, which consequently create a barrier to adopting <IR>.

<IR> Form and Substance

A main issue arising from the respondents is that connectivity in a report may not always reflect the maturity of integrated thinking. Organizations might in fact produce a highly integrated report but still suffer from weak internal integration. According to the feedback from the Chartered Accountants Australia and New Zealand, some organizations instead of applying integrated thinking to the decision-making process have delegated the production of integrated reports to the sustainability or communications team which tend to remain siloed from the rest of the business.[2] Furthermore, as Deloitte highlights, "for many organisations, in particular those just starting out with the Framework, the integrated thinking element does not come through strongly, perhaps as many organisations struggle to obtain the cross business engagement required to achieve it".[3] Thus, it is not always the case that <IR> is a proxy for integrated thinking.

According to Accountancy in Europe, the evidence on the adoption of the connectivity principle is mixed. Not all the reporters, in fact, provide detailed insights into the connectivity of factors affecting the company's value creation ability, properly adopt a forward-looking approach when discussing risks and opportunities that might affect the viability of the business or accurately describe the interdependencies among different capitals.[4] Thus, we argue there is a need to stress a focus on connectivity of information and integrated thinking as many companies are struggling with these concepts.

To overcome such perceived impediments, the IIRC seeks to promote leading practice examples that reflect connectivity of information with the IIRC technical team in charge of leading this ongoing action. Also, the IIRC proposes developing guidance on approaches to aid the practical implementation of integrated thinking. Given the criticality of the issue, the IIRC has planned to further clarify the concept of integrated thinking by providing case studies and examples from <IR> Business Network participants. The need for clarity testifies to the fact that the IIRC itself is aware there is considerable rethinking required. Therefore, in rethinking and clarifying integrated thinking, the IIRC needs to address two important issues: (i) the theoretical underpinnings of integrated thinking; and (ii) promoting the role of integrated thinking for implementing <IR>.

First, as demonstrated by Feng et al. (2017), integrated thinking lacks a common conceptualization and a theoretical base, even though there have been attempts to provide one. For example, Oliver et al. (2016) provide a theoretical explanation of integrated thinking through system thinking theory, but it is an explanation provided by academics with no direct connection to the IIRC. Arguably, the IIRC is attempting to establish the multiple capitals model of <IR> as a new theory of the firm. However, from a theoretical perspective <IR> appears to be nothing new because it mirrors what is already known that emanates from strategic management and intellectual capital (IC) research. Additionally, integrated thinking and the multiple capitals model can be positioned in the same theoretical stream as the Resource-Based-View of firm, which sees a firm as a blend of productive resources for creating value (Penrose 1959; Pike et al. 2005). Similarly, the multiple capitals model extends and remarks the same role and theoretical knowledge of IC's capitals (Petty and Guthrie 2000). Therefore, rethinking integrated thinking should build upon, rather than replace, previous managerial theories and their application in practice.

Second, as for the role of promoting integrated thinking, we observe that although <IR> has gained prominence as a novel form of external reporting, so far integrated thinking has not received as much attention and has been relegated to a marginal position in the corporate reporting landscape. Figure 1 shows the global interest in "integrated thinking" and "integrated reporting" from 2010, when the IIRC started using the two concepts (Feng et al. 2017), to 2017. Figure 1 is constructed using data collected from Google Trend, which estimates people's interest in particular concepts using an index (the y-axis) based on the number of times the terms appear in Google searches. As Fig. 1 shows, "integrated reporting" has constantly increased in popularity over time, while "integrated thinking" has received relatively scant attention and does not follow the same trend line. We argue this is because <IR> has been widely promoted as an external reporting tool rather than a managerial practice.

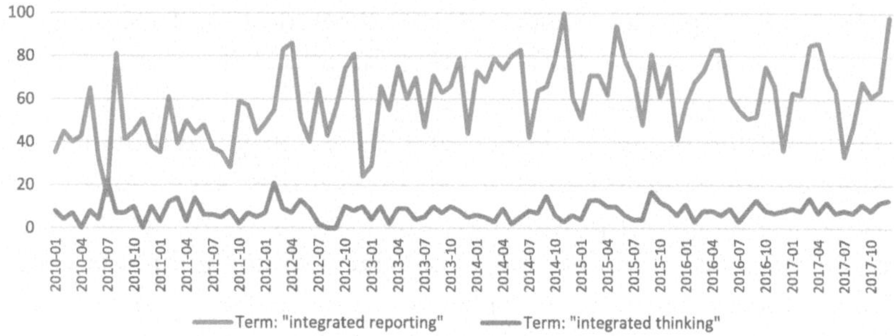

Fig. 1 Comparison between the global interest in IR and integrated thinking (*Source* Google Trend)

How <IR> is being promoted also relates to whether or not <IR> becomes regulated as in the case of South Africa where, imbued within the King IV corporate governance framework, listed companies are required to produce an integrated report on a "apply and explain" basis (IoDSA 2016). However, regulation or institutional pressures to comply with <IR> can be a double-edged sword in that it may encourage complying with the form of <IR>, while ignoring integrated thinking. Thus, the reports might not contain the substance that the IIRC seeks. As Dumay et al. (2017) identify, the lack of regulation is a barrier to implementing the <IRF>. Indeed, without regulatory and institutional forces <IR> is unlikely to become the corporate reporting norm (Flower 2015). Furthermore, it appears mandatory approaches to <IR> are preferred by investors, because they believe that regulation can lead to more substantial disclosure and reporting improvements compared to previous voluntary sustainability reporting practices (Stubbs and Higgins 2018). Nevertheless, the regulatory double-edged sword shows that regulation can contribute to the <IRF> institutionalization and widespread adoption, whereby under a regulatory approach companies would be encouraged to comply with <IR> rather than substantially disclose more relevant information for investors because there is no incentive beyond compliance. Thus, regulation might produce more form, but there is no guarantee of additional substance.

For example, in the European Union, the EU Directive represents a main regulatory action that may encourage further <IR> adoption (Dumay et al. 2017). To comply with the EU Directive, companies (undertakings) can use <IR> among other international frameworks and guidelines, as the <IRF> does not provide strict requirements about what information should be reported. As Flower (2015, pp. 9–10) observes, the <IRF> "leaves far too much discretion to the firm's management", and the form of an integrated report according to the <IRF> is "couched in very broad terms that impose no specific reporting obligations". Therefore, in pursuing compliance, companies may produce their reports according to the broad <IRF>, so to take a mere formal adoption of <IR> to comply with the EU Directive at the expense of its most substantial implications.

The implication is that regulatory pressures and the focus on reporting can undermine integrated thinking. As integrated thinking needs structural and cultural changes to the management decision-making (Dumay and Dai 2017), the risk of a "tick the box" approach undermines the potential for such a change. However, integrated thinking can be enacted in practice without any regulatory forces or even the need to follow a specific reporting framework. Therefore, we advocate that, to pursue integrated thinking, organizations need to free themselves from a compliance-driven approach to <IR>. Instead of being worried about how to comply with the <IRF>, companies need to abandon the aim of reporting and focus on the internal practices and governance mechanisms to overcome the "tick the box" trap. Only then <IR> will truly reflect how the organization is managed.

If history is a good judge, then we only need to look at how organizations have abandoned IC reporting after many years of its proponents trying to make IC reports part of mainstream corporate reporting (Dumay 2016). However, companies do not ignore IC because they find it more useful to understand its internal benefits rather than disclose how their organization works to external stakeholders and competitors (Schaper et al. 2017). Once companies understand better how they work, it is unlikely they will report these results to their competitors.

Trust and Credibility

Based on the responses to the IIRC's call for feedback (IIRC 2017), there is a wide acknowledgement that integrated thinking is a core element and prerequisite for effective <IR>. Yet, there is also the need for senior managers buy-into successfully implement integrated thinking (IIRC 2017, p. 6). In this regard, trust and credibility are crucial for <IR> to succeed because, without these, <IR> is doomed to be another idea that never took hold (Dumay 2016; Dumay et al. 2017). One key area of trust and credibility is that integrated thinking lies on the assumption that, because of the organizational silo problem, there is a need to strengthen the collaboration between departments within organizations, to foster awareness of the interconnections between different capitals. However, as Ballou et al. (2012) argue, there is a weak engagement of accounting expertise (e.g., risk identification and measurement, and financial reporting) into corporate social activities. One of the rationales of this is a lack of credibility of sustainability reporting (Boiral 2013).

However, research into <IR> practices finds that organizations prepare integrated reports in contexts where "reporting guidelines are used as disclosure checklists, stakeholder engagement is limited, systems are not always compatible, and data analysis is difficult" (McNally et al. 2017, p. 481). The authors conclude that "preparers are also unconvinced that integrated reports are taken seriously by investors, further limiting the interconnection between sustainability performance and integrated reporting" (McNally et al. 2017, p. 481). Integrated reporters are facing the challenge of credibility. They need to have trust in <IR> and convince others to take their reports seriously.

Chaidali and Jones (2017) demonstrate that the IIRC and <IR> suffer from a lack of credibility in the practitioners' eyes, a fact that negatively influences preparers' trust. The authors conclude that "preparers are often suspicious of the motives of the IIRC professionals and express concerns about the performance and appearance of the Integrated Report" (p. 1). Furthermore, they "are concerned about the credibility of a single report and seem uncertain of the benefits or the beneficiaries of IR" (Chaidali and Jones 2017, p. 1). By depicting the results of emerging research, Dumay et al. (2017, p. 473) argue that "the IIRC's rhetoric is persuasive but not convincing", as "it is grounded on few sound and rational arguments". Therefore, the challenge of credibility is a matter that requires the engagement of all the actors, but firstly originates from the IIRC's action and rhetoric. Accordingly, as long as integrated thinking is anchored to <IR>, its potential adoption will depend on <IR>'s credibility and the IIRC's ability to instil trust in the <IRF> to convince managers of its potential benefits.

Conclusions and Implications for Research

This chapter is motivated by the results arising from the IIRC's call for feedback on the <IRF> implementation, and focuses on integrated thinking as a substantial and practical issue of <IR>. Drawing upon our review and analysis of the feedback the IIRC received, integrated thinking does not stand up well from the <IRF> implementation. We demonstrate that understanding integrated thinking and connectivity, connecting information and resources, reshaping internal practices, overcoming the <IR> form and substance, and the IIRC' credibility represent the main challenges for integrated thinking. Next, we present our conclusions by offering a re-conceptualization of integrated thinking and introducing the new stage of <IR> research. Below, we summarize several challenges and offer avenues for future research.

Rethinking Integrated Thinking to Advance a Third Stage of <IR> Research

Despite the IIRC's conclusion, integrated thinking suffers from some important conceptual, theoretical and practical challenges, which obstruct the potential claimed benefits deriving from <IR>. The challenges integrated thinking is facing and the research questions below call for unveiling <IR> internal practices, rethinking the paradigm of integrated thinking and its position within <IR> by the IIRC.

To its credit, the IIRC does offer several prosed actions for improving "connectivity and integrated thinking" as outlined in Table 2. However, while we support future research, the responsibility refers to internal IIRC functions which generally preclude independent academic research. Most IIRC's research falls to these internal functions even though the IIRC claims it looks to include the "Academic Network or others". Thus, the role and involvement of academic research in those actions is not clear.

The main observation from Table 2 is that future research on connectivity and integrated thinking will mainly focus on internal organizational processes. Understanding internal practices implies the need to investigate organizations' business operations and their teleoaffective structure, acknowledging economic, social and environmental issues, the ethical values and principles associated with structures and processes (Lodhia 2015). A teleoaffective structure is "an array of ends, projects, uses (of things), and even emotions that are acceptable or prescribed for participants in the practice" (Schatzki 2005, pp. 471–472). Arhens and Chapman (2007, p. 8) observe that "understanding [how to do things], rules and the engagements of teleoaffective structure organize chains of actions" provides an understating of dynamics that make up practices. Therefore, to understand <IR> in action, future research on <IR> needs to move from analysing reporting outcomes to understanding internal practices, and the IIRC recognizes this need as Table 2 shows.

However, to foster new research and reduce ambiguity, we first need to redefine integrated thinking, so that researchers understand what they are researching and managers understand what they are implementing. In developing the new definition, we need to include the link between strategy, resources and teleoaffective structures. Hence, we redefine *integrated thinking* as:

> the collective ability of managers and employees to be aware of the company's strategy to create value and how it relates to their day-to-day and evolving functions, so that there is alignment between the overall strategy, available resources (capitals), and the decisions and actions made by managers and employees in the short, medium and long term.

Table 2 Connectivity and integrated thinking: issues and proposed action, responsibility and timing

Issue	Action	Lead (responsibility)	Timing
Promote meaningful leading practice examples that reflect effective integration of the capitals	Ensure that the <IR> Examples Database demonstrates integration of the capitals into integrated reports and addresses such aspects as measurement, trade-offs, connectivity between the capitals, and relationships between the capitals and stakeholders.	IIRC technical function	Ongoing
Revisit existing IIRC guidance on the capitals for potential update and reissue	Consider whether key elements of the 2013 Capitals Background Paper for <IR> should be updated and reissued, potentially as a Practice Note.	IIRC technical function	Q1 2018 (project proposal)
Research the relationship between connectivity of information and improved decision-making	Commission research into the extent to which connectivity of information improves decision-making.	IIRC technical function, Academic Network or others	Q4 2018 (project proposal)
Communicate how other corporate reporting developments can connect to or support the preparation of an integrated report	Identify and research corporate reporting developments—with a focus on prominent models and frameworks—for their alignment with integrated reporting. The scope might include, for example, the "Core and more" approach of Accountancy Europe and the Financial Reporting Council's Guidance on the Strategic Report.	IIRC technical function	Q1 2018

(continued)

Table 2 (continued)

Issue	Action	Lead (responsibility)	Timing
Promote leading practice examples that reflect connectivity of information	Ensure that the <IR> Examples Database demonstrates connectivity of information.	IIRC technical function	Ongoing
Clarify the IIRC's interpretation of integrated thinking and improve market understanding	Develop guidance on approaches to aid the practical implementation of integrated thinking. Draw on <IR> Business Network participants to demonstrate the concept of integrated thinking through case studies and examples.	IIRC technical and networks functions	Guidance: Q4 2018 (project proposal) Case studies: ongoing discussion with the <IR> Business Network

Source Adapted from the IIRC (2017)

In the natural world, an analogy would be the actions of worker bees in keeping the Queen Bee alive. The ultimate strategy is survival and sustaining the colony (or even creating new colonies). During their lives, worker bees progress through different roles, much the same as managers and employees progress through different functional silos and responsibilities. In their lifetime, a worker bee is a housekeeper, undertaker, nursemaid, attendant to the Queen Bee, nectar collector, temperature controller, wax producer and hive builder, and honey producer (Blackiston 2017). Thus, through each stage and function (silo) of a bee's life they work collectively towards executing the ultimate strategy of survival and sustaining the colony.

To motivate future research, lessons can be learned from a predecessor of <IR>, being the measuring, managing and reporting of IC. Similar to IC research, <IR> research is overcoming its "second stage" which is characterized by the focus on creating standards, guidelines and frameworks (Dumay 2013, p. 5) and evaluating the influence on financial outcomes (Dumay and Garanina 2013). As argued by Petty and Guthrie (2000, pp. 160–162), the second-stage research reflects the need of making something like IC visible, by addressing how it "should be measured and reported".

Arguably, research on <IR> and integrated thinking is moving to what is known as third-stage research, being a "critical and performative" assessment of <IR> in action (Dumay and Dai 2017, p. 597; Guthrie et al. 2012). The research questions we propose to address the challenges of integrated thinking invite researchers to abandon top-down ostensive research and embrace the praxis of integrated thinking and <IR> within organizations to provide insights into how the elements of integrated thinking actually work in practice. This means enquiring and critiquing the effects of integrated thinking and <IR> in action, by abandoning the "evaluatory trap" of top-down empirical assessments (Dumay and Garanina 2013, p. 20). Accordingly, we call for pragmatic and interventionist research that can improve the outcomes of reporting and address the challenges of integrated thinking and <IR> internal practice (La Torre et al. 2018). As Table 2 shows, the IIRC is also calling for future research on <IR> to shift the focus from reporting to its internal practices. The practice focus is already evidenced in the latest academic research (Dumay and Dai 2017; Feng et al. 2017; Guthrie et al. 2017; Maniora 2017).

Therefore, this chapter calls on <IR> researchers to participate in the evolving third-stage <IR> research, which focuses on critical research on the managerial implications of <IR> and integrated thinking using "bottom-up research as opposed to top-down" research (Dumay and Garanina 2013, p. 3). We outline these research implications next.

Research Opportunities Addressing the Challenges of Integrated Thinking

Understanding Integrated Thinking and Connectivity

Integrated thinking and the connectivity principle are widely misunderstood and arduously implemented in practice because of the lack of a clear conceptual and theoretical explanation. Accordingly, respondents to the IIRC's consultation call for a "stronger IIRC focus on integrated thinking" and request more examples of integrated thinking and connectivity (IIRC 2017, p. 6). However, despite the IIRC's declared future actions towards clarifying these concepts and providing more guidance for practitioners (IIRC 2017, p. 18), barriers to experiencing integrated thinking in practice will continue to persist as long as it will depend on the IIRC's action.

On the contrary, future research can also contribute to a pluralistic conceptualization of integrated thinking and explain its ontological base, by addressing the research questions below:

- How is integrated thinking understood and defined in practice?
- How do the differences between "talk" (understanding) and "action" (managerial practices) contribute to sense-giving of integrated thinking at a theoretical and conceptual level?
- How is integrated thinking dialogically constructed within organizations?

Connectivity and the Incomplete Space of Accounting

Another challenge for integrated thinking is the incompleteness of accounting representations and performance measures (see, Busco and Quattrone 2018), which makes achieving connectivity impossible in representing the value creation picture. The ambiguity behind accounting representations makes the relation between information and users (managers) a fascinating area to investigate. Thus, the following research questions can be worth investigating:

- How "are integrated reporting processes truly integrated and are these processes truly embedded in organisations' management control systems" (de Villiers et al. 2014, p. 1061)?
- How do managers use <IR>-related information for decision-making?
- How is the ambiguity of cause–effect relationships able to foster innovations, critical thinking and new avenues for creating value?

Integrated Thinking Vs. <IR> Internal Practices

The third challenge concerns the <IR> internal practices, as integrated thinking in practice has to face existing internal precedents and structures, especially organizational culture. This consequently creates a barrier to adopting <IR>. Since its inception, <IR> has been commonly identified as a new tool for external corporate reporting. As a result, it has gained the interest of the professional accounting associations (Flower 2015) and lobbying interest groups (Reuter and Messner 2015), which influenced its development. Instead, integrated thinking concerns internal processes such as information flows, improving information systems and internal reporting, and not just external reporting (IIRC 2013, p. 2). As Lodhia (2015, p. 597) asserts, "integrated reporting is a complex process involving a sequence of activities rather than merely an outcome in the form of an integrated report". Thus, the concept of integrated thinking reflects internal practices towards creating an integrated report, which are still widely unknown and rarely investigated (see, Dumay and Dai 2017). By focusing on the internal practices, managers can start discovering the cause–effect relationship between resources and value creation. This can allow discovering logical explanations to fill the incomplete space of accounting information, which we identified as a challenge to implement the connectivity principle.

Accordingly, to examine integrated thinking and internal practices, the questions below can inspire future research:

- Is integrated thinking able to reshape internal processes, structures and organizational culture?
- How can integrated thinking bring to radical or incremental changes to governance, strategic planning and decision-making?
- How and to what extent does integrated thinking penetrate organizations by influencing both managers and employees?
- As a result of integrated thinking, how do CEOs and CFOs "consider the direct and indirect negative influences their operations have on social and environmental (or human, social and relationship, and natural) capitals" (de Villiers et al. 2014, p. 1059)?

<IR> Form and Substance

Integrated thinking is undermined by the formal issues deriving from complying with the <IRF> and producing an integrated report. Although we agree that integrated thinking needs a better conceptualization and a strong theoretical base, our review advocates that integrated thinking is a managerial paradigm that cannot be anchored to a compliance-driven logic of external reporting. Similarly, since integrated thinking should result in structural and cultural changes to the management decision-making (Dumay and Dai 2017), regulatory pressures for adopting <IR> can undermine integrated thinking because of the "tick the box" trap. Therefore, when translating integrated thinking into action, practitioners need to shift the focus from producing an integrated report to reshaping internal business processes, governance mechanisms and organizational culture. As the form over the substance of <IR> represents a challenge for integrated thinking, integrated thinking needs to be observed in action and cannot be limited to the formal mechanisms of external reporting and its political pressures.

Accordingly, in investigating the form and substance of <IR>, the research questions below emerge:

- Are regulatory and institutional forces able to foster, or contrarily obstruct, integrated thinking in practice?
- To what extent does the form of implementing the <IRF> undermine the substance of <IR> and integrated thinking?
- Furthermore, by citing de Villiers et al. (2014, p. 1060), "whether senior executives endeavour to exploit social and environmental capitals or to ameliorate their influences, how will they go about balancing and weighing up the value creating and value destroying consequences of their proposed strategies?"

Trust and Credibility

Last, as integrated thinking belongs to the domain of <IR> and is dominated by IIRC's action, senior managers' engagement will depend on the IIRC's ability to be convincing about the benefits of <IR>. As argued, managers' trust in <IR> and the IIRC's credibility represent a challenge for promoting integrated thinking in practice. Therefore, future research can get some critical thoughts from the following research questions:

- Because the definition of integrated thinking is vague and the trust in and credibility of <IR> is questioned (Chaidali and Jones 2017; Dumay et al. 2017), why do (or should) practitioners and managers engage in embracing integrated thinking and <IR>?
- How can integrated reporters and practitioners be convincing enough so that report users take <IR> and integrated thinking seriously?
- Does integrated thinking actually need the IIRC's action and the <IRF> to be translated into practice?

Concluding Remarks and Limitations

To conclude this chapter, we want to emphasize that both our observations and the feedback to the IIRC show that integrated thinking still has considerable hurdles to overcome to be widely accepted as a fundamental principle that provides a foundation for <IR>. However, the feedback to the IIRC and their response appears to firmly ground future <IR> research on integrated thinking, to a practice perspective. We further call on the IIRC to ensure that this research is as much as practically possible, conducted by critical academics, unconnected to the formal IIRC's structure to ensure the independence and quality of the research. Not doing so will put further stains on the trust and credibility of integrated thinking and <IR>.

What we present in this chapter is a mix of our review of the feedback to the IIRC by its stakeholders and our current research into <IR>. As researchers who have followed <IR>, we observe how <IR> is developing, albeit not at the pace that the IIRC might like to achieve (e.g., see Dumay 2016). We see practice-based research into <IR> practice as essential for its continued future. Unless integrated thinking and integrated reporting can overcome the current challenges, then <IR> will struggle to find a home in most organizations. However, the findings are limited to the observations of four scholars, and other scholars examining the same evidence with different experiences may come to different observations and conclusions.

Notes

1. Only 63 submissions were published by the IIRC (see http://integratedreporting.org/submissions-for-ir-framework-feedback/).
2. http://integratedreporting.org/wp-content/uploads/2017/05/FFeedback17Response_28_Chartered-Accountants-Australia-and-New-Zealand.pdf. Accessed 14 December 2017.
3. http://integratedreporting.org/wp-content/uploads/2017/05/FFeedback17Response_48_Deloitte.pdf. Accessed 14 December 2017.

4. http://integratedreporting.org/wp-content/uploads/2017/05/FFeedback17Response_26_Accountancy-Europe.pdf. Accessed 14 December 2017.

References

Ahrens, T., & Chapman, C. S. (2007). Management accounting as practice. *Accounting, Organizations and Society, 32*(1–2), 1–27.

Ballou, B., Casey, R. J., Grenier, J. H., & Heitger, D. L. (2012). Exploring the strategic integration of sustainability initiatives: Opportunities for accounting research. *Accounting Horizons, 26*(2), 265–288.

Black Sun. (2012). *Understanding transformation: Building the business case for integrated reporting*. London, UK.

Blackiston, H. (2017). *Understanding the role of the worker bee in a hive*. Available at: http://www.dummies.com/home-garden/hobby-farming/beekeeping/understanding-the-role-of-the-worker-bee-in-a-hive/. Accessed 14 Dec 2017.

Boiral, O. (2013). Sustainability reports as simulacra? A counter-account of A and A+ GRI reports. *Accounting, Auditing & Accountability Journal, 26*(7), 1036–1071.

Busco, C., & Quattrone, P. (2015). Exploring how the balanced scorecard engages and unfolds: Articulating the visual power of accounting inscriptions. *Contemporary Accounting Research, 32*(3), 1236–1262.

Busco, C., & Quattrone, P. (2018). In search of the 'perfect one': How accounting as a maieutic machine sustains inventions through generative 'in-tensions'. *Management Accounting Research, 39,* 1–16.

Chaidali, P., & Jones, M. J. (2017). It's a matter of trust: Exploring the perceptions of integrated reporting preparers. *Critical Perspectives on Accounting, 48,* 1–20.

Cooper, D. J., Ezzamel, M., & Qu, S. Q. (2017). Popularizing a management accounting idea: The case of the balanced scorecard. *Contemporary Accounting Research, 34*(2), 991–1025.

de Villiers, C., Rinaldi, L., & Unerman, J. (2014). Integrated reporting: Insights, gaps and an agenda for future research. *Accounting, Auditing & Accountability Journal, 27*(7), 1042–1067.

de Villiers, C., Hsiao, P. K., & Maroun, W. (2017a). Developing a conceptual model of influences around integrated reporting, new insights and directions for future research. *Meditari Accountancy Research, 25*(4), 450–460.
de Villiers, C., Venter, E. R., & Hsiao, P.-C. K. (2017b). Integrated reporting: Background, measurement issues, approaches and an agenda for future research. *Accounting & Finance, 57*(4), 937–959.
Dierickx, I., & Cool, K. (1989). Asset stock accumulation and the sustainability of competitive advantage: Reply. *Management Science, 35*(12), 1504–1511.
Dumay, J. C. (2009). Intellectual capital measurement: A critical approach. *Journal of Intellectual Capital, 10*(2), 190–210.
Dumay, J. (2013). The third stage of IC: Towards a new IC future and beyond. *Journal of Intellectual Capital, 14*(1), 5–9.
Dumay, J. (2016). A critical reflection on the future of intellectual capital: From reporting to disclosure. *Journal of Intellectual Capital, 17*(1), 168–184.
Dumay, J., & Dai, T. (2017). Integrated thinking as a cultural control? *Meditari Accountancy Research, 25*(4), 574–604.
Dumay, J., & Garanina, T. (2013). Intellectual capital research: A critical examination of the third stage. *Journal of Intellectual Capital, 14*(1), 10–25.
Dumay, J., Bernardi, C., Guthrie, J., & La Torre, M. (2017). Barriers to implementing the international integrated reporting framework. *Meditari Accountancy Research, 25*(4), 461–480.
Feng, T., Cummings, L., & Tweedie, D. (2017). Exploring integrated thinking in integrated reporting—An exploratory study in Australia. *Journal of Intellectual Capital, 18*(2), 330–353.
Flower, J. (2015, March). The international integrated reporting council: A story of failure. *Critical Perspectives on Accounting, 27,* 1–17.
Guthrie, J., Manes-Rossi, F., & Orelli, R. L. (2017). Integrated reporting and integrated thinking in italian public sector organisations. *Meditari Accountancy Research, 25*(4), 553–573.
Guthrie, J., Ricceri, F., & Dumay, J. (2012). Reflections and projections: A decade of intellectual capital accounting research. *The British Accounting Review, 44*(2), 68–82.
Institute of Directors in Southern Africa (IoDSA). (2009). *King code of governance principles for South Africa*. Johannesburg: IoDSA.
Institute of Directors in Southern Africa (IoDSA). (2016). *King IV: Report on corporate governance for South Africa*. Johannesburg: IoDSA.

International Integrated Reporting Council (IIRC). (2013). *The international integrated reporting framework*. London: International Integrated Reporting Council.

International Integrated Reporting Council (IIRC). (2016). *Creating value: The cyclical power of integrated thinking and reporting*. London, UK.

International Integrated Reporting Council (IIRC). (2017). *International <IR> Framework implementation feedback*. London, UK.

La Torre, M., Valentinetti, D., Dumay, J., & Rea, M. A. (2018). Improving corporate disclosure through XBRL: An evidence-based taxonomy structure for Integrated Reporting. *Journal of Intellectual Capital, 19*(2), 338–366.

Lev, B., & Gu, F. (2016). *The end of accounting and the path forward for investors and managers*. Hoboken, NJ: Wiley.

Lodhia, S. (2015). Exploring the transition to integrated reporting through a practice lens: An Australian customer owned bank perspective. *Journal of Business Ethics, 129*(3), 585–598.

Maniora, J. (2017). Is integrated reporting really the superior mechanism for the integration of ethics into the core business model? An empirical analysis. *Journal of Business Ethics, 140*(4), 755–786.

McNally, M.-A., Cerbone, D., & Maroun, W. (2017). Exploring the challenges of preparing an integrated report. *Meditari Accountancy Research, 25*(4), 481–504.

Oliver, J., Vesty, G., & Brooks, A. (2016). Conceptualising integrated thinking in practice. *Managerial Auditing Journal, 31*(2), 228–248.

Penrose, E. (1959). *The theory of growth of the firm*. Oxford: Blackwell.

Petty, R., & Guthrie, J. (2000). Intellectual capital literature review. *Journal of Intellectual Capital, 1*(2), 155–176.

Pike, S., Fernström, L., & Roos, G. (2005). Intellectual capital: Management approach in ICS Ltd. *Journal of Intellectual Capital, 6*(4), 489–509.

Reuter, M., & Messner, M. (2015). Lobbying on the integrated reporting framework. *Accounting, Auditing & Accountability Journal, 28*(3), 365–402.

Schaper, S., Nielsen, C., & Roslender, R. (2017). Moving from irrelevant intellectual capital (IC) reporting to value-relevant IC disclosures. *Journal of Intellectual Capital, 18*(1), 81–101.

Schatzki, T. R. (2005). Peripheral vision: The sites of organizations. *Organization Studies, 26*(3), 465–484.

Steyn, M. (2014). Organisational benefits and implementation challenges of mandatory integrated reporting. *Sustainability Accounting, Management and Policy Journal, 5*(4), 476–503.

Stubbs, W., & Higgins, C. (2014). Integrated reporting and internal mechanisms of change. *Accounting, Auditing & Accountability Journal, 27*(7), 1068–1089.

Stubbs, W., & Higgins, C. (2018). Stakeholders' perspectives on the role of regulatory reform in integrated reporting. *Journal of Business Ethics, 147*(3), 489–508.

Velte, P., & Stawinoga, M. (2017). Integrated reporting: The current state of empirical research, limitations and future research implications. *Journal of Management Control, 28*(3), 275–320.

World Intellectual Capital Initiative (WICI). (2013). *Connectivity—Background paper for IR*. London, UK.

Human Capital Disclosures in Swedish State-Owned Enterprises—A Comparison of Integrated Reporting Versus Traditional Reporting

Gunnar Rimmel

Introduction

In 1987, the World Commission on Environment and Development (WCED) defined "Corporate Social Responsibility" (CSR) as "*the commitment of business to contribute to sustainable economic development, working with employees, their families, the local community and society at large to improve their quality of life*" and implicitly links human capital aspects to sustainability (WCED 1987). Sweden has a long tradition in sustainability and has been recognized to be among leading countries when it comes to sustainability reporting (Rimmel et al. 2017).

In Sweden, state-owned enterprises (SOEs) play an important role in sustainability reporting, as they should always be at the forefront of CSR to act as a role model to inspire other companies to follow their path (Swedish Government 2016). Human capital has an imperative part for SOE's value creation in three ways, to provide public wealth to

G. Rimmel (✉)
Henley Business School, University of Reading, Reading, UK
e-mail: g.rimmel@reading.ac.uk

S. Arvidsson (ed.), *Challenges in Managing Sustainable Business*,
https://doi.org/10.1007/978-3-319-93266-8_3

society and to their employees. Consequently, human capital disclosures in SOEs should aim to elucidate the value created for the company and to display the welfare of the employees and society.

A large stream of research on human capital reporting has been generated during the past two decades (Rimmel 2003; Rimmel et al. 2012). When the International Integrated Reporting Council (IIRC) developed the <IR> framework, human capital has been of specific focus, as the <IR> framework is based on six capitals: financial, manufactured, intellectual, human, social and relationship, and natural. These capitals are considered as stocks of value that the organization uses and transforms through its activities. The description of the interconnection between the different capitals provides a picture and understanding of the value-creation over time in an organization (IIRC 2013). Although the integrated reporting is a relatively new concept, its practice has rapidly spread in corporate reporting (de Villiers et al. 2014; Baboukardos and Rimmel 2016). Swedish SOEs have also started to apply integrated reporting in corporate reporting. Since the IIRC specifically put emphasize on human capital as one key capital of an integrated report, it is interesting to study how SOEs disclose human capital information. However, it has not yet been studied if there is a difference in human capital disclosure between companies that produce integrated reports and those that apply traditional annual corporate reporting.

Consequently, in this chapter the amount of human capital disclosure in Swedish state-owned entities' corporate reports is investigated. The aim of this chapter is twofold. First, to give an indication of how human capital may be disclosed in current sustainability reporting practice. Second, is there a difference in the level of human capital disclosure recognizable depending on whether applying traditional corporate reporting practice or integrated reporting. This chapter provides academics, regulators and reporting organizations with insights into human capital disclosure in different reporting traditions, which assist improvements in sustainability reporting practice. A key limitation is that it draws upon a synthesis of the existing literature which is at quite an early stage of development—but provides scope for considerable further development.

The remainder of the chapter is structured as follows. Section “Corporate Social Reporting in the Light of Global Reporting Initiative and Integrated Reporting” presents the development of corporate social reporting in the light of Global Reporting Initiative and Integrated Reporting. Section “Integrated Reporting's Revitalization of Human Capital Reporting” outlines Integrated Reporting's revitalization of human capital reporting. The progress of Swedish state-owned entities and corporate social reporting is presented in section “Swedish State-Owned Enterprises and Corporate Social Reporting”. Section “Studying the Level of Human Capital Disclosures in Corporate Reports” explains the disclosure scoreboard and collection of data for studying the level of human capital disclosures in corporate reports. Section “Empirical Findings on Human Capital in Swedish State-Owned Entities' Corporate Reports” presents the empirical findings on human capital in Swedish state-owned entities' corporate reports. In section “Conclusions”, the results are interpreted in the light of the increasing importance of disclosing information on human capital in integrated reports and constitute a contribution to the ongoing debate on corporate reporting practices.

Corporate Social Reporting in the Light of Global Reporting Initiative and Integrated Reporting

During the past 20 years, corporate social reporting has made a journey from being a niche reporting product by few green companies into the mainstream norm in corporate reporting, as more than 90% of all Swedish companies do report about sustainability. CSR reporting has evolved over time linking performance measurement with corporate reporting systems. This journey has developed from Balanced Scorecard, triple bottom line to frameworks such as the Global Reporting Initiative (GRI) and <IR> (de Villiers et al. 2014).

The Balanced Scorecard primarily processes internal performance by integrating internal financial measures and non-financial measures to achieve a holistic picture of corporate performance. At the end of the

1990s, the focus on external reporting gained in recognition regarding growing interest in CSR. In 1997, "the triple bottom line" was introduced by John Elkington and became the first widely used external reporting concept in CSR. The idea is that companies applying the triple bottom line should make external disclosures about three dimensions of their operations, providing social and environmental information along with financial performance (Elkington 1997). The triple bottom line concept lays the foundation to current external sustainability reporting (Milne and Gray 2013). It inspired especially the development of the GRI, which is today's most widespread sustainability reporting framework. The GRI's objective is to make sustainability reporting standard practice by providing guidance and support to organizations (Eccles and Serafeim 2011). Sweden was among the first countries that required SOEs to use the GRI guidelines.

GRI is an international and independent organization that issues guidelines for sustainability reporting in order to help organizations to understand and report about their impacts on the environment, society and the economy. It was founded in 1997 in Boston before it moved its headquarters to Amsterdam in 2002. GRI is cooperating with many organizations such as OECD, the UN Global Compact, UNEP and ISO (GRI 2017a). The GRI framework is built on guidelines, which have been continuously updated to reflect the developments in sustainability reporting. In October 2016, GRI issued new guidelines that are now referred to as GRI Standards and will replace the G4 guidelines (GRI 2017b). The new GRI Standards are quite similar to the G4 guidelines, with some new items to consider. However, the GRI G4 guidelines and the GRI Standards can be generally applied by all types of company sizes and industries around the world. GRI requires companies to disclose certain information, but leaves it to the discretion of the company to decide to report on Core or Comprehensive level (GRI 2015).

Companies applying GRI guidelines need to disclose all material sustainability issues or *Aspects* as they are referred to by GRI. The GRI G4 guidelines and GRI Standards divide aspects into *General Standard Disclosures* and *Specific Standard Disclosures.* The category General Standard Disclosures includes disclosures about the company that are of general nature on the overall reporting process. The category *Specific*

Standard Disclosures consists of specific indicators that should enhance comparison on material topics: economic, environmental or social. GRI encompasses disclosures on different human capital aspects (GRI 2015). GRI is recognized as the accepted international standard for reporting non-financial information (Solomon and Maroun 2012).

Parallel to the development of the GRI guidelines, GRI took together with organizations as the International Federation of Accountants and the Prince's Accounting for Sustainability Project (A4S) the initiative to establish the IIRC with the intention to create a globally accepted integrated reporting framework (Rowbottom and Locke 2016). A number of challenges arise from the nature of human capital when it comes to create connectivity between the financial and non-financial information of human capital, e.g. in traditional financial statements human capital is mainly accounted for as costs like wages or training costs. However, one challenge is to illustrate how human capital is contributing to the value-creation process of organizations.

Integrated Reporting's Revitalization of Human Capital Reporting

The IIRC approach to corporate reporting is different to the traditional corporate reporting. Traditional corporate reporting is primarily based on historic events that took place in the corporation during the year that has past. Non-financial disclosures are often disclosed in separated parts in the annual report or as stand-alone reports. This creates a lack of connectivity between financial disclosures and non-financial information. Therefore, traditional corporate reporting does not provide sufficient information about the interaction between the different business activities. The <IR> framework emphasizes on value creation over time, on short-, medium- and long-term by connecting different factors that are material for value creation (IIRC 2013). To deal with these issues, <IR> accentuates the interconnectedness between non-financial disclosures with the financial disclosures and how they affect each other. Thereby, a more holistic picture of the company is presented and how it creates value over time.

The IIRC described integrated reporting as in the following; "*An integrated report is a concise communication about how an organization's strategy, governance, performance and prospects, in the context of its external environment, lead to the creation of value over the short, medium and long term*" (IIRC 2013, p. 7). Furthermore, the IIRC (2011) describes integrated reporting as building on five guiding principles: (1) strategic focus, (2) connectivity of information, (3) future orientation, (4) responsiveness and stakeholder inclusiveness, and (5) conciseness, reliability and materiality. These principles should interconnect with six content elements: (i) organizational overview and business model; (ii) operating context, including risks and opportunities; (iii) strategic objectives and strategies to achieve those objectives; (iv) governance and remuneration; (v) performance; and (vi) future outlook. The International <IR> Framework was released in December 2013 (IIRC 2013) and is based on the existence of 6 different capitals: (1) financial capital, (2) manufactured capital, (3) intellectual capital, (4) human capital, (5) social and relationship capital, and (6) natural capital.

In the <IR> framework, the value-creation process is based on content elements to guide organizations on what to include in their integrated report. The content elements are not stand-alone objects but linked together and affect organizational performance. The content elements are organizational overview and external environment, governance, business model, risks and opportunities, strategy and resource allocation, performance, outlook and general reporting guidance. All content elements need to be included in the report. However, it might differ between companies how they are reported (IIRC 2013).

Apart from the content elements, the organization is also dependent on their resources, or capitals as referred to in the framework, to be successful. In the value-creation process, they are inputs to the organization's business model; they increase, decrease or transform through the business activities and finally end up as the output of the organization. The capital is divided into six categories: financial, manufactured, intellectual, social and relationship, natural and human (IIRC 2013).

By specifically addressing that human capital is one of the core capitals, the IIRC inevitably bring the reporting of human capital back on the agenda, as it had been relatively dormant since intellectual capital frameworks and models had highlighted human resources as a vital part for intellectual capital in the mid-1990s. To facilitate an enhanced evaluation of future performance, stakeholders demand non-financial disclosures about assets that are not captured on the balance sheet but still important for the success of the company, such as human capital (Amir and Lev 1996; Rimmel et al. 2012). The <IR> framework defines human capital as:

> ...people's competencies, capabilities and experience, and their motivations to innovate, including their alignment with and support for an organization's governance framework, risk management approach, and ethical values, ability to understand, develop and implement an organization's strategy, and loyalties and motivations for improving processes, goods and services, including their ability to lead, manage and collaborate. (IIRC 2013, p. 12)

The <IR> framework recognizes the importance of human capital for corporate performance and regards them as a resource rather than a cost. Although integrated reporting has found many supporters among listed companies, the <IR> framework may also be applied to the public sectors' reporting entities. The Swedish government encouraged their SOEs to issue integrated reports due to the concept of integrated thinking, as management need to face the challenge to constructively consider the trade-offs between capitals in order to keep a balance between corporate efficiency and broader societal health and well-being.

Swedish State-Owned Enterprises and Corporate Social Reporting

In a Swedish context, SOEs should always be on the forefront of CSR to gain confidence in society and to act as a role model in order to inspire public and private companies to conduct business in a sustainable way (Swedish Government 2016). Swedish SOEs play an important role in the market as they may act differently than private companies, as they often do have both a commercialized and public social mission

(Roper and Schoenberger-Orgad 2011). According to the Swedish government, SOEs should following the same notion as listed companies, but SOEs have the mission to become more transparent and to take responsibility for their actions. SOEs often operate as important social service providers and have responsibility to act in the best interest for society and to communicate their action to the citizens in order to gain legitimacy. In Sweden, SOEs play an important role on the domestic market and with over 137,000 employees; they can be considered as an important employer in Sweden (Swedish Government 2017).

Therefore, there it is of public interest in Sweden to know how SOEs treat their employees and what value employees account for. It can be argued that the state's interest in SOEs is twofold, the public wealth in the society and extra finance to the treasury. Consequently, human capital disclosures aim to both explain the value created for the company and display the welfare of the employees.

Some Swedish SOEs have started to apply integrated reporting in corporate reporting. Since the IIRC specifically put emphasize on human capital as one key capital of an integrated report, it is interesting to study how SOEs disclose human capital information. However, it has not yet been studied how SOEs disclose human capital. Consequently, this study aims to provide insight on how Swedish SOEs make disclosures about human capital in their corporate reports.

Studying the Level of Human Capital Disclosures in Corporate Reports

In the empirical part of this chapter, a disclosure scoreboard is used to quantify the amount of information regarding human capital included in corporate reporting. There is an extensive amount of accounting literature relating to the use of disclosure scoreboards to measure the amount of information that is contained in corporate reports.

For the quantification of human capital disclosure levels in Swedish SOEs corporate reports, this study applies a disclosure scoreboard. Disclosure scoreboard studies have developed since the 1960s and are quite common stream in accounting research (see Rimmel et al.

2017; Nielsen et al. 2015; Rimmel et al. 2009; Rimmel 2003). There is no standard disclosure scoreboards as they vary in type and numbers in order to fit the purpose of the study (Marston and Shrives 1991). Following this common tradition, the relevant human resource disclosure items for this study stem from the GRI G4 guideline. Since GRI is the most used sustainability reporting framework and contains specific disclosure items about human capital information, this found to be a good base for the disclosure index on human capital. From GRI G4 guideline, 66 human capital-related disclosure items were considered to be relevant. Based on the *aspects* in the GRI guidelines, the disclosure items were divided into five aspects: Employment, Labour/Management Relations, Occupational Health and Safety, Training and Education, and Diversity and Equal Opportunity. In each aspect, the items were divided into general and detailed disclosure. Consequently, this study applied a disclosure scoreboard consisting of 66 items, which were grouped into 5 different categories as illustrated in Table 1.

The disclosure scoreboard approach was specifically selected for this study, as a proxy for disclosure quality of human capital disclosures in corporate reports. In order to increase the reliability of the results and the objectivity of the study, the present study had clear instructions in the coding process. The coding was verified through separate coding by multiple researchers.[1] The content of each annual report was compared to the items on the disclosure scoreboard and coded as 1 or 0, depending upon whether the annual report contained or did not contain the item disclosure. The analysis of the disclosure scoreboard for this study is additive and unweighted following the path of the studies conducted by Rimmel et al. (2009, 2017), Rimmel (2003), Adrem (1999), Meek et al. (1995), and Cooke (1989). Hence, either a SOE discloses an item in its corporate report or not, which shows that the number of items measures the amount of disclosure. This procedure is verified by the criticisms examined in the study by Hackston and Milne (1996). It can be argued that the amount of disclosure might not be an exact indicator of disclosure quality (Rimmel 2016; Beattie et al. 2004). However, as this study is concerned with extent of disclosure, the disclosure scoreboard method fulfils these requirements satisfactorily.

Table 1 Disclosure scoreboard derived from GRI G4 guidelines

Items	ASPECT	GRI source	General items	Detailed items
19	Employment	G4-9	Total number of employees	
		G4-10		by gender
		G4-10		by employment contract (permanent/ temporary)
		G4-10		by age (group or average)
		G4-10		by employment type (full time/ part time)
		G4-10		by supervised workers
		G4-10		by region
		G4-10		by minority group
		G4-LA1	New employee hires during the reporting period	
		G4-LA1		by age group
		G4-LA1		by gender
		G4-LA1		by region
		G4-LA1	Total number of employee turnover during the reporting period	
		G4-LA1		by age group
		G4-LA1		by gender
		G4-LA1		by region
		G4-LA2	Benefits provided to employees	
		G4-LA3	Total number of employees that took parental leave	
		G4-LA3		by gender
3	Labour/management relations	G4-11	Total employees covered by collective bargaining agreements	
		G4-LA5	Number of weeks' notice prior to the implementation of significant operational changes	
		G4-LA5	Total number of grievances about labour practices filed through formal grievance mechanisms	
22	Occupational health and safety	G4-LA6	Types of injury	
		G4-LA6		by gender
		G4-LA6		by region
		G4-LA6	Injury rate	
		G4-LA6		by gender

(continued)

Table 1 (continued)

Items	ASPECT	GRI source	General items	Detailed items
		G4-LA6		by region
		G4-LA6	Occupational diseases rate	
		G4-LA6		by gender
		G4-LA6		by region
		G4-LA6	Work-related diseases (stress etc.)	
		G4-LA6		by gender
		G4-LA6		by region
		G4-LA6	Lost day rate	
		G4-LA6		by gender
		G4-LA6		by region
		G4-LA6	Absentee rate	
		G4-LA6		by gender
		G4-LA6		by region
		G4-LA6	Work-related fatalities	
		G4-LA6		by gender
		G4-LA6		by region
		G4-LA6	Disclosure of the system of rules applied in recording and reporting accident statistics	
12	Training and education	G4-LA9	Number of employees trained	
		G4-LA9		by gender
		G4-LA9		by employee category
		G4-LA9	Average hours of training by the employees	
		G4-LA9		by gender
		G4-LA9		by employee category
		G4-LA10	Programmes for skills management and lifelong learning	
		G4-LA10		type
		G4-LA10		scope
		G4-LA11	Regular performance and career development review	
		G4-LA11		by gender
		G4-LA11		by employee category
10	Diversity and equal opportunity	G4-LA12	Composition of the organization's governance bodies	
		G4-LA12		by gender
		G4-LA12		by age (group or average)

(continued)

Table 1 (continued)

Items	ASPECT	GRI source	General items	Detailed items
		G4-LA12		by minority groups
		G4-LA13	Ratio of the basic salary and remuneration of women to men	
		G4-LA13		by employee category

Table 2 Sample

Traditional corporate report		<IR> corporate report	
Company name	Sector	Company name	Sector
Systembolaget	Consumer staples	LKAB	Materials
ALMI	Financials	Vattenfall	Energy
Green cargo	Industrials	Svenska spel	Consumer staples
Teracom	Telecom services	SBAB	Financials

The focus of this study is on SOEs, which are companies that are 100% owned by the Swedish state. According to the Swedish government office, the state owns 49 companies in different sectors and sizes and 41 of those are wholly owned by the Swedish state (Swedish Government 2016). Three SOEs had not made the corporate reports available. Three SOEs provided separate reports (Annual Report and CSR report separately); 19 SOEs had traditional annual reports that contained CSR information (combined reports); 16 SOEs specifically mentioned that the applied integrated reporting with statements like the following: "*Vattenfall's Annual and Sustainability Report is an integrated report inspired by the Integrated Reporting Framework. The Non-Financial Information section is not a standalone report but rather provides additional explanation, context, and details on topics that have already been discussed in previous sections*" (Vattenfall 2017, p. 156).

Out of the 16 SOEs that state they have integrated reports as their 2016 annual report, 4 SOEs have been chosen randomly (see Table 2). These SOEs are LKAB (materials sector), Vattenfall (energy sector), Svenska Spel (consumer staples sector) and SBAB (financials sector). Out of the 19 SOEs that not mention to apply integrated reporting but combined reports, which mean that they publish their annual report and sustainability report in the same document. However, they do not indicate that the information is integrated. Out of these 19 SOEs, 4 SOEs have been chosen randomly. These SOEs are Systembolaget (consumer staples), ALMI (financials sector), Green Cargo (industrials sector) and Teracom (telecom services sector).

Empirical Findings on Human Capital in Swedish State-Owned Entities' Corporate Reports

In the empirical part of this chapter, the disclosure scoreboard is used to quantify the amount of information regarding human capital included in the 2016 corporate reports of the examined SOEs. In order to differentiate the companies, the first four SOEs, ALMI, Green Cargo, Teracom and Systembolaget, do use traditional corporate reporting, while the remaining four companies, LKAB, SBAB, Svenska Spel and Vattenfall, do issue integrated reports.

Figure 1 shows each company's total number of human capital disclosures, aggregating the scores from the five: Employment, Labour/Management Relations, Occupational Health and Safety, Training and Education as well as Diversity and Equal Opportunity. The maximum number of scores attainable for the total scoreboard amounts to a total of 66 items. Vattenfall's integrated report for the year 2016 achieved the highest total score of 22 items, which corresponds to 33.3% of the maximum score. Green Cargo's traditional corporate report had the lowest score with 9 items (13.6%).

SOEs that issued integrated reports disclosed more human capital items compared to SOEs with traditional corporate reports. In average, IR-companies disclosed information about 17.25 items, which would give a mean value of 26.14. The mean value for the traditional annual report companies is 20.45, which corresponds to an average disclosure score of 13.5 items. The level of detailed information items for companies with integrated reports is slightly higher (6.75 items on average per company) in comparison with the traditional reporting companies (6 items on average per company). The highest amount of disclosure was issued by Vattenfall with 12 general items out of the 23 possible general and 10 detailed items. Two detailed items that all companies disclosed

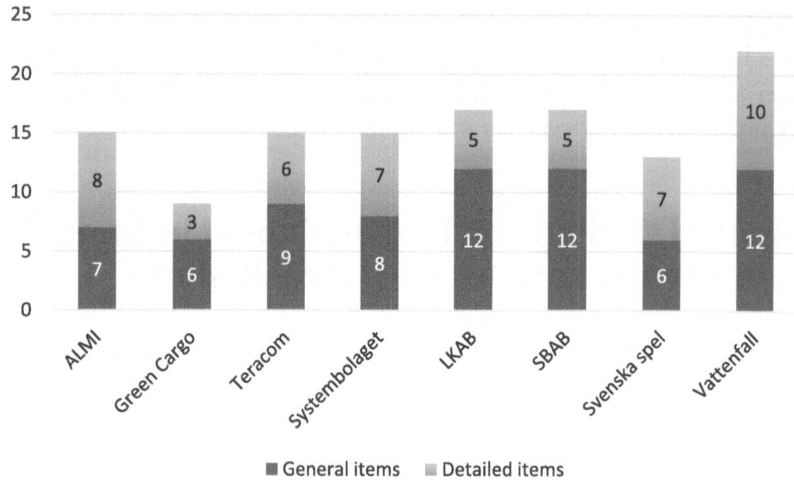

Fig. 1 Number of general and detailed disclosures

are "Total number of employees" and "Composition of the organization's governance bodies".

The human capital items in the GRI guidelines were grouped into 5 categories: Employment (19 items), Labour/Management Relations (3 items), Occupational Health and Safety (22 items), Training and Education (12 items), and Diversity and Equal Opportunity (10 items). The results from the scoreboard are illustrated in Fig. 2 in percent out of each category.

As Fig. 2 illustrates did the category Diversity and Equal Opportunity receive in traditional reports the highest level of disclosure with 43% of the maximum score. Even for integrated reporting SOEs, has this been the highest level of disclosure with 35%. The lowest level with 8% of the maximum was scored in the category Occupational Health and Safety by traditional reporting corporations. However, the integrated reporting companies disclose on average more information than the companies that report in traditional annual reports in the categories Labour/Management Relations, Occupational Health and Safety, and Training and Education. The category Labour/Management Relations had 25% for integrated reporting companies in comparison with 17% by traditional reporting companies. The category Occupational Health

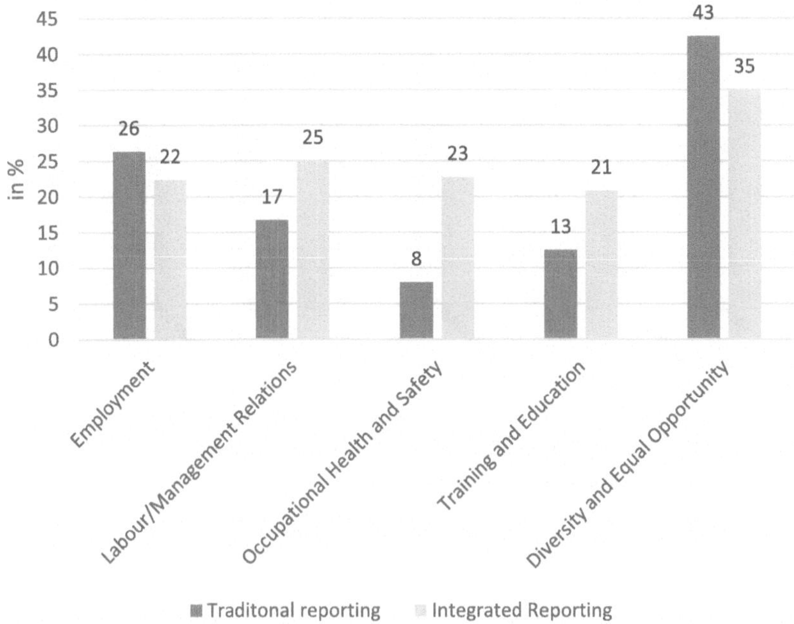

Fig. 2 Percentage of disclosed items per category

and Safety had 23% for integrated reporting companies in comparison with 8% by traditional reporting companies. The category Training and Education had 21% for integrated reporting companies in comparison with 13% by traditional reporting companies. The category Employment was disclosed more often by traditional reporting companies (26%) than by integrated reporting companies (22%).

The total disclosure with the disclosed items for all five categories is presented in Fig. 3. The first four SOEs, ALMI (ALMI 2017), Green Cargo (Green Cargo 2017), Teracom (Teracom 2017) and Systembolaget (Systembolaget 2017), do use traditional corporate reporting score lower than three of the integrated reporting SOEs, Vattenfall (Vattenfall 2017), LKAB (LKAB 2017) and SBAB (SBAB 2017).

Only Svenska spel (Svenska spel 2017), which issues an integrated report, is disclosing lower (13 items) than the traditional reporting companies, Teracom and Systembolaget, which disclosed 15 items each. Vattenfall had the highest disclosure level of all companies and scored in the

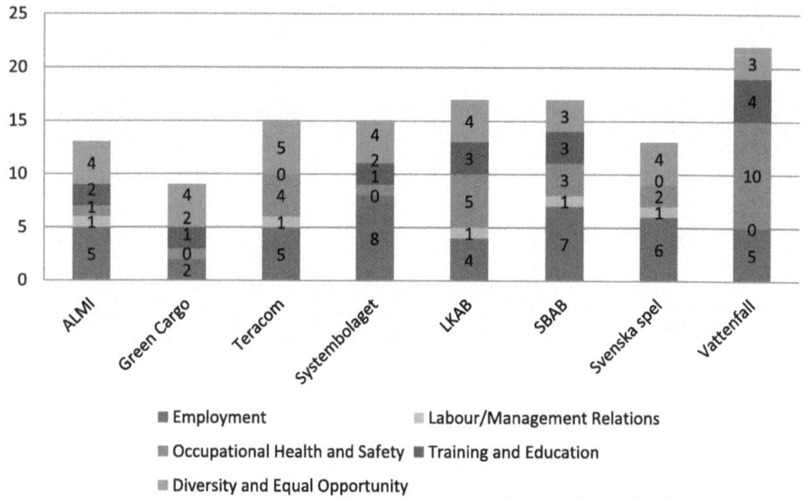

Fig. 3 Total disclosure with disclosed items per category

category Occupational Health and Safety the highest with 10 items, which is double to the second highest level in this category by LKAB (5 items). Systembolaget had the highest score of all companies in the category Employment (8 items). As already mentioned, SOEs that issued integrated reports disclosed more human capital items (17.25 on average) compared to SOEs with traditional corporate reports (13.5 items on average).

Conclusions

Integrated reporting has gained increased attention and it seems that Swedish SOEs have showed a positive attitude towards this comparatively corporate reporting concept. This could be seen in the response of the Confederation of Swedish Enterprises to the consultation draft of the <IR> framework. This positive attitude is motivated by the fact that 42% of Swedish SOEs issued integrated reports as their corporate reports.

Looking at the general empirical findings and the figures, the study above revealed that the level of human capital disclosure is on average higher than the level of human capital in traditional corporate reports.

Considering the overall level of disclosure in this study, there might be reflections possible that the overall level of disclosure might be low in relation to the total number of disclosures possible to score in the disclosure scoreboard. Nevertheless, the level of disclosure is fairly higher in comparison with disclosure scoreboard studies on human capital or intellectual capital (Rimmel 2003; Nielsen et al. 2015; Rimmel et al. 2009).

The finding of this study is quite interesting, as despite that there is little mandatory human capital reporting requirements existent there is an informative level of human capital disclosure noticeable in today's corporate reports, no matter if they are traditional reports or integrated reports.

Another thought-provoking result in this study is that human capital disclosures in integrated reporting companies do differ from companies that do not issue integrated reports. Examining documents from the IIRC's website, a presumption prevails that integrated reporting would result instantaneously in great differences to traditional reports. Hence, much higher human capital disclosure level should have been expected when comparing integrated reports with traditional reports. However, the disclosure scores in the study are not very greatly different at first sight. Looking at the figures tells a different story as it becomes apparent that the integrated reporting SOEs do provide a higher level of human capital disclosures. This finding is consistent with the aim of integrated reporting declared by the IIRC (2015).

Concluding this discussion, it must be taken into account that this study only examined 8 companies, which is a small sample. This small sample of integrated reporting companies can have an influence on the scores of human capital disclosures. Consequently, this study does not claim that there is a significant increase in the amount of human capital disclosures. Future studies could continue to look into these challenges, using the methodology outlined, and test on a larger number of companies. Furthermore, future studies could conduct complementary interviews for why companies disclose as they do. Integrated reporting is a rather recent reporting concept in Sweden. The Integrated Reporting Framework is not a comprehensive guide on how to use and implement integrated reporting in practice (Baboukardos and Rimmel 2016).

As a final point, no matter if companies do apply integrated reporting or follow traditional corporate reports, companies do report human capital. But it seems that integrated reporting has the potential to increase the level of human capital disclosures in corporate reports.

Acknowledgements The author is grateful to the Jan Wallanders och Tom Hedelius research foundation for financial support.

Note

1. The coding has been carried out by the author and his research assistants.

References

Adrem, A. H. (1999). *Essays on disclosure practices in Sweden: Causes and effects*. Sweden: Lund University Press.

ALMI. (2017). *Årsredovisning 2016*. Retrieved November 8, 2017, from https://www.almi.se/Aktuellt/Arsredovisning-2016/.

Amir, E., & Lev, B. (1996). Value-relevance of non-financial information: The wireless communication industry. *Journal of Accounting and Economics, 22*, 3–30.

Baboukardos, D., & Rimmel, G. (2016). Relevance of accounting information under an integrated reporting approach: A research note. *Journal of Accounting and Public Policy, 35*(4), 437–452.

Beattie, V., McInnes, B., & Fearnley, S. (2004). A methodology for analysing and evaluating narratives in annual reports: A comprehensive descriptive profile and metrics for disclosure quality attributes. *Accounting Forum, 28*(3), 205–236.

Cooke, T. E. (1989). Voluntary corporate disclosure by Swedish companies. *Journal of International Financial Management & Accounting, 1*(2), 171–195.

de Villiers, C., Rinaldi, L., & Unerman, J. (2014). Integrated reporting: Insights, gaps and an agenda for future research. *Accounting, Auditing & Accountability Journal, 27*(7), 1042–1067.

Eccles, R. G., & Serafeim, G. (2011). *Accelerating the adoption of integrated reporting*. Retrieved September 27, 2016, from http://papers.ssrn.com/sol3/papers.cfm?abstract_id=1910965.

Elkington, J. (1997). *Cannibals with forks: The triple bottom line of 21st century business*. Oxford: Capstone Publishing.

Green Cargo. (2017). *Årsredovisning 2017*. Retrieved November 8, 2017, from http://www.greencargo.com/globalassets/documents/hallbar-utveckling/resultat-och-rapporter/greencargo-ars--och-hallbarhetsredovisning_2017_sv.pdf.

GRI. (2015). *G4 sustainability reporting guidelines*. Amsterdam: Global Reporting Initiative.

GRI. (2017a). *Global reporting*. Retrieved November 7, 2017, from https://www.globalreporting.org/information/news-and-press-center/press-resources/Pages/default.aspx.

GRI. (2017b). *G4 sustainability reporting guidelines*. Retrieved November 7, 2017, from https://www.globalreporting.org/information/g4/Pages/default.aspx.

Hackston, D., & Milne, M. J. (1996). Some determinants of social and environmental disclosures in New Zealand companies. *Accounting, Auditing & Accountability Journal, 9*(1), 77–108.

International Integrated Reporting Council (IIRC). (2011). *Towards integrated reporting: Communicating value in the 21st century*. Retrieved September 12, 2016, from www.integratedreporting.org/wp-content/uploads/2011/09/IR-Discussion-Paper-2011_spreads.pdf.

International Integrated Reporting Council (IIRC). (2013). *The international <IR> framework*. Retrieved September 12, 2016, from www.integratedreporting.org/wp-content/uploads/2015/03/13-12-08-THE-INTERNATIONAL-IR-FRAMEWORK-2-1.pdf.

International Integrated Reporting Council (IIRC). (2015). *Creating value, integrated reporting <IR> and investor benefits*. Retrieved September 12, 2016, from www.integratedreporting.org/wpcontent/uploads/2016/01/1323_CreatingValue_No3_8a-1.pdf.

LKAB. (2017). *Årsredovisning 2016*. Retrieved November 8, 2017, from https://www.lkab.com/sv/Investerare/finansiella-rapporter/arsredovisning/.

Marston, C. L., & Shrives, P. J. (1991). The use of disclosure indices in accounting research: A review article. *The British Accounting Review, 23*(3), 195–210.

Meek, G. K., Roberts, C. B., & Gray, S. J. (1995). Factors influencing voluntary annual report disclosures by U.S., U.K. and Continental European multinational corporations. *Journal of International Business Studies, 26*(3), 555–574.

Milne, M. J., & Gray, R. (2013). W(h)ither ecology? The triple bottom line, the global reporting initiative, and corporate sustainability reporting. *Journal of Business Ethics, 118*(1), 13–29.

Nielsen, C., Rimmel, G., & Yosano, T. (2015). Outperforming markets: IC and the long-term performance of Japanese IPOs. *Accounting Forum, 39*(2), 83–96.

Rimmel, G. (2003). *Human resource disclosures: A comparative study of annual reporting practice about information, providers and users in two corporations.* Sweden: BAS Publishing House.

Rimmel, G. (2016). Kapitel5—Disclosureteorier (Chapter 5—Disclosure theory). In G. Rimmel & K. Jonäll (Eds.), *Redovisningsteorier* (*Accounting theories*) (pp. 77–88). Sweden: Sanomautbildning. ISBN: 978-91-523-1816-3.

Rimmel, G., Baboukardos, D., & Jonäll, K. (2017). Chapter 22—Revival of the fittest? Intellectual capital in Swedish companies. In J. Guthrie, J. Dumay, F. Ricceri, & C. Nielsen (Eds.), *The Routledge companion to intellectual capital.* Oxon: Routledge. ISBN 978-1-138228-214.

Rimmel, G., Dergård, J., & Jonäll, K. (2012). Human resource disclosures in Danish intellectual capital statements—Enhancing comparability of business models a decade ago? *Journal of Human Resource Costing & Accounting, 16*(2), 112–141.

Rimmel, G., Nielsen, C., & Yosano, T. (2009). Intellectual capital disclosures in Japanese IPO prospectuses. *Journal of Human Resource Costing & Accounting, 13*(4), 316–337.

Roper, J., & Schoenberger-Orgad, M. (2011). State-owned enterprises: Issues of accountability and legitimacy. *Management Communication Quarterly, 25*(4), 693–709.

Rowbottom, N., & Locke, J. (2016). The emergence of <IR>. *Accounting and Business Research, 46*(1), 83–115.

SBAB. (2017). *Årsredovisning 2016.* Retrieved November 8, 2017, from https://www.sbab.se/1/om_sbab/investor_relations/sbab-koncernen/finansiella_rapporter/sbab16.html.

Solomon, J. F., & Maroun, W. (2012, August). *Integrated reporting: The influence of King III on social, ethical and environmental reporting,* ACCA Research Report.

Svenska Spel. (2017). *Årsredovisning 2016.* Retrieved November 8, 2017, from https://om.svenskaspel.se/AnnualReport/2016/.

Swedish Government. (2016). *2016 annual report for state-owned enterprises.* Retrieved November 7, 2017, from http://www.regeringen.se/49e317/contentassets/2cf3908df4b240a4b2e28cf81d1739c6/2016-ars-redogorelse-for-bolag-med-statligt-agande-skr.-201516140.

Swedish Government. (2017). *Government policy for state-owned enterprises.* Retrieved November 8, 2017, from http://www.regeringen.se/regeringens-politik/bolag-med-statligt-agande/.

Systembolaget. (2017). *Årsredovisning 2016*. Retrieved November 8, 2017, from https://www.systembolaget.se/om-systembolaget/ansvarsredovisning_16/.

Teracom. (2017). *Årsredovisning 2016*. Retrieved November 8, 2017, from https://www.teracom.se/globalassets/finansiell-information/asredovisningar/teracom_ar16_sve_ny.pdf.

Vattenfall. (2017). *Årsredovisning 2016*. Retrieved November 8, 2017, from https://corporate.vattenfall.com/globalassets/corporate/investors/annual_reports/2017/vattenfall_annual_and_sustainability_report_2016_eng.pdf.

World Commission on Environment and Development. (1987). *Our common future*. Retrieved September 11, 2016, from http://www.un-documents.net/our-common-future.pdf.

Sense-Making and Sense-Giving: Reaching Through the Smokescreen of Sustainability Disclosure in the Stock Market

Susanne Arvidsson and Jeaneth Johansson

Financial Analysts Face a Smokescreen of Sustainability Information

Despite the increased focus on sustainability information in the information flow surrounding the valuation of companies, our knowledge is rather limited regarding how the financial analysts' sense-making and sense-giving of such information affect their work of interpreting, assessing and communicating value-added information to investors. This chapter sets out to enhance our knowledge in this vital area by exploring analysts' cognitive frames. We argue that the complex and

S. Arvidsson (✉)
School of Economics and Management, Lund University, Lund, Sweden
e-mail: Susanne.arvidsson@fek.lu.se

J. Johansson
Lulea University of Technology, Lulea, Sweden
e-mail: Johansson@ltu.se

J. Johansson
Halmstad University, Halmstad, Sweden

S. Arvidsson (ed.), *Challenges in Managing Sustainable Business*,
https://doi.org/10.1007/978-3-319-93266-8_4

ambiguous nature of sustainability information implies that the analysts are faced with a smokescreen challenging their sense-making and sense-giving processes (Weick 1995; Weick et al. 2005) of their important task to produce relevant and credible investment advices to their clients, i.e. the investors. In order to make informed investment decisions, investors need to be able to make appropriate valuations of companies and also understand their underlying value-creating mechanisms. Nevertheless, investors may not have time or competences to search for, evaluate and draw conclusions on potential investment opportunities. This is where professional financial analysts and management teams enter into the sophisticated exchange of corporate information. To enable efficient investment decisions and assessment of company potential, there is a need for relevant and credible information such as information on the company's operations, future strategies, risks, competitors, skills and patents. In this sophisticated exchange of corporate information, the management team is the core information provider or supplier of information to analysts (information intermediaries) and to investors (information demanders) (Arvidsson 2003; Johansson 1998, 2004). To understand the prerequisites for an efficient allocation of resources in the stock market, it is not only vital to acknowledge the roles of these key actors (management teams, financial analysts and investors). It is also important to identify different types of corporate information (financial information and non-financial information including sustainability information) and acknowledge the challenges that corporate information in general and sustainability information in specific mean in a transparency and information asymmetry perspective. Before we dig deeper into the analysts' sense-making and sense-giving processes and how they are affected by the increased focus on sustainability in corporate reports (sects. "The Cognitive Foundations: An Introduction to the Concepts", "Analysts' Cognitive Frames in the Early 2000s" and "A Shift Towards Enhances Cognitive Legitimacy in Sense-Making and Sense-Giving"), we will in the sections below, outline corporate information and corporate disclosure from a transparency and information asymmetry perspective.

Corporate Financial Information and Non-financial Information: The Birth of Sustainability Information

In all countries, there are laws and regulations requiring companies to disclose certain corporate to stakeholders such as investors and analysts. Corporate information is provided in corporate reports, i.e. the annual or integrated reports. We usually refer to this information as corporate *financial* information. It has a long tradition. The double-bookkeeping has roots in the thirteenth century when the monk Luca Pacioli invented this intriguing system for companies to keep track of their financial situation with help of the double-entry bookkeeping system.[1] Corporate financial information is a language of business; items and structure of the balance sheet, income- and cash-flow statements are familiar and understood both by management and by analysts. Also, the key performance indicators (KPIs) or financial measures like solvency, profitability and turnover are well-known and provide relevant information for assessing the performance of a company.

In 1987, the Brundtland Report entitled "Our common future" (UNWCED 1987) was published with the objective of drawing attention to the global need for sustainable development. The idea was to trigger companies to speed up their transformation of becoming more sustainable organizations. Consequently, companies started, however, quite slowly to disclose more information on how they performed on the sustainability arenas. This became a new type of non-financial information. A well-established definition of sustainability is that it includes information on social, environmental and economic aspects (UN 2018). Today, the integration of such sustainability information into corporate communication domain has become vital and is a topic high up on the agendas in politics, business society and the academia (Dameri and Ricciardi 2015, p. 861; Malmström et al. 2017). The environmental and social scandals taking place have served as triggers in establishing laws and regulations forcing companies to no longer merely consider economic aspects into measurement of performance (Massaro et al. 2018).

As discussed in chapter "An Exposé of the Challenging Practice Development of Sustainability Reporting: From the First Wave to the EU Directive (2014/95/EU)" in this book, there is an increasing corporate trend to engage in sustainability reporting, i.e. disclosure of sustainability information to external stakeholders. The soft information on social and environmental concerns has become more and more central, and specifically the integration of these aspects into business models and value chains (Foote et al. 2010; Wasiluk 2013). Studies show that companies integrating sustainability actions into the business model increase their reputation (Dutot et al. 2016), improve their image (Pedrini 2007) and enhance innovation capabilities (Chang and Chen 2012).

Sustainability reporting has also attracted interest from research society (see Cho et al. 2015; Dienes et al. 2016; Hahn and Kühnen 2013; Parker 2005; Patten 2013), for instance focusing on the value relevance of sustainability information (see Cahan et al. 2016; Dhaliwal et al. 2012).

Corporate Disclosure: A Remedy for Decreasing Information Asymmetry in the Information Flow

In the quest of decreasing information asymmetry (Akerlof 1970) and contributing to a fair valuation of the company, the management team provide corporate information to external stakeholders. Corporate information is primarily provided *indirectly* via, e.g. corporate reports, website, marketing materials, brochures and interviews. To a more limited extent, corporate information is disclosed *directly* to certain stakeholders (primarily analysts and investors) via private meetings, conferences and general annual meetings (Johansson 2004).

The management team is faced with a trade-off situation between disclosing and withholding information. Disclosing too much information might be unwise due for proprietary reasons and diminishing returns (Hallvarsson 2009; Johansson and Malmström 2013). However, the information flow between the insiders of a company and the outsiders, i.e. external stakeholders (including financial analysts), is characterized by asymmetric information (Akerlof 1970). This means that those outside the company, e.g. analysts and investors, are faced with a smokescreen regarding what is really going on inside the company. Thus, the presence of asymmetric information impairs the analysts' valuation process. The literature is full of examples of why a management team should try to decrease the level of asymmetric information in the information flow by disclosing information. According to empirical studies, the advantages with decreased information asymmetry are lower cost of equity (Dhaliwal et al. 2014), lower cost of debt, decreased risk-premiums due to lower bid-ask spreads and more accurate analyst forecasts (Dhaliwal et al. 2011). All these outcomes are highly desirable for management teams due to the positive effects these outcomes have on the bottom line.

Information about a company's sustainability performance is regarded as particularly asymmetric since it is difficult for stakeholders outside the company to gain credible information on relevant aspects vital for assessing how the company perform on the sustainability arenas (see Hahn and Kühnen 2013). The ambiguous nature of sustainability information adds to this complexity. Sustainability information is often criticized and questioned for being a PR invention rather than providing a true and fair view of a company (Frankental 2001). The limited credibility of sustainability may not only be caused by managements willingness to greenwash (bluewash and today even SDGwash) the company, it may also be due to management difficulties in "understanding," what sustainability is and how it should be measured, valued and assessed. Nevertheless, sustainability reporting receives criticism for its lack of value relevance and credibility. This impairs comparability and increases information asymmetry.

Previous literature even points to the fact that stock market actors claim that companies where the management team talk too much about sustainability without explaining its relevance to the value-creation process should be priced with a risk premium. Operationalization of sustainability information is challenging and results in a lack of reliable sustainability-related KPIs. Thus, there are substantial difficulties paired with trying to fit sustainability information into the analysts' excel sheets. The process of transforming our companies into more sustainable organizations will not slow down. Quite the opposite! Agenda 2030 and UN's Sustainability Development Goals (SDGs) clearly emphasize that sustainable businesses are the only way into the future.

This means that financial analysts need to understand, value and compare companies' sustainability performance. But how? How can they give and make sense of sustainability information? This is a great challenge! Until now, this problem has not been so acute and of need of urgent solutions. However, today it is a challenge that needs to be faced. Not the least due to the new EU directive (2014/95/EU) mandating the largest EU companies to disclose sustainability information. Furthermore, there is an increasing global sustainable investment market (Nilsson et al. 2014; Ramiah et al. 2016) that means that corporate-sustainability performance must be understood and assessed.

Financial Analysts Play a Central Role in Sustainability Reporting

The previous sections have highlighted the central role financial analysts' play in intermediating information on the stock market. We have also discussed how sustainability information adds to a new type of smokescreen. The analysts are viewed as core users and intermediaries of sustainability information. In this section, we will further our understanding of both the financial analyst's work per se and the roles that two core types of analysts, buy-side and sell-side analysts, have in the sophisticated exchange of information. The above will be outlined with respect to sustainability information.

The Financial Analyst's Work

Professional financial analysts need to be understood based on the context where they operate (Johansson 2007). In this case, as part of the value chain in the stock market, where they position themselves between the company and the investors and also as part of their own organizational setting, e.g. the investment bank. Researchers often consider analysts as proxies for investor beliefs in the stock market (Ivković and Jegadeesh 2004). Financial analysts are often appointed a critical role assuring information efficiency, an efficient allocation of finance, increased liquidity and investor confidence in the stock market (Johansson 2007; Beyer et al. 2010; Clatworthy and Lee 2018). They intermediate information between publicly listed companies and investors in a context characterized of high information asymmetry, where a company's management team has more information and knowledge about the company than the typical investors have. Recent findings point to the analysts' proactive role in addition to the traditionally merely passive role as intermediaries. The proactive role implies gathering and providing information and analyses contributing with enhanced information to investors beyond the information intermediated by companies (Salzedo et al. 2018). Thus, they contribute with value-added services.

There are different types of financial analysts operating in the stock market, fulfilling different roles with respect to investors. This chapter specifically deals with two types of financial analysts, i.e. buy-side analysts and sell-side analysts. These are presented further below.

Buy-Side Analysts—The In-House Generalist Group of Analysts

The buy-side analysts work for investment banks. They do not carry out the investments themselves, but they are responsible for internal investment advices in their *own* organizations, i.e. advices in-house to own fund managers (Brown et al. 2016). They support the fund managers with information, analyses and recommendations and decrease as such uncertainties and information asymmetry in fund managers' investment decision-making (see, e.g., Schipper 1991; Groysberg et al. 2011; Imam et al. 2008). Buy-side analysts are generalists, who covers a large number of companies and industries. In regard to use and communication of sustainability information, they collect, interpret and communicate value-added information to internal clients.

Sell-Side Analysts—The External Specialist Group of Analysts

The sell-side analysts are specialists, covering a limited number of companies typically within one or a few industries. They work at investment banks' equity research departments where they produce external recommendations and write analyst reports provided to their customers who are institutional investor organizations and brokerage houses. The sell-side analysts provide fund managers and buy-side analysts with information, analyses and recommendations and assist as such in decision-making. They primarily provide information to selected core customers, i.e. clients with a major part of their investments at the particular investment bank. They also produce written analyst reports with attached recommendations. Such analyst reports are available in different databases such as Investex and Bloomberg (Abhayawansa et al. 2017). The sell-side analysts' detailed coverage of listed companies and their industries decreases uncertainties and information asymmetry in the investors' decision-making process.

The Cognitive Foundations: An Introduction to the Concepts

In this section, we outline the conceptual framework of cognitive frames particularly the concepts of sense-making, sense-giving and legitimacy in general. When we discuss the concepts, we do so without reference to sustainability information and financial analyst. The sustainability and analyst perspectives are added in the following sections.

Sense-Making as a Concept

We apply a social-constructivist perspective in order to understand the underlying sense-making and sense-giving processes for use of sustainability information (Berger and Luckmann 1991). People in organizations try to clarify the situation by extracting and interpreting information in the organization, organize the information and try to make sense of what actually happens (Weick 1995; Weick et al. 2005). Sense-making is a social process where individuals construct their view of the world, a phenomenon, a situation, etc. They learn how to cognitively interpret the phenomenon or situation and how to behave and act in accordance with expectations (Weick 1979).

The sense-making process is considered as inherently social and discursive (Weick 1995; Weick et al. 2005). As such, "*Sensemaking is concerned with attempts to incorporate figural experiences into existing grounded institutional structures*" (Ifvarsson 2000, p. 102). The sense-making implies selectively organization and interpretation of information perceived as relevant for understanding the situation (Bean and Hamilton 2006). Tacit knowledge turns into more explicit knowledge throughout the sense-making processes (Weick 1995; Weick et al. 2005). Individuals react to the shaped environment at the same time as they also shape the environment. There are a dynamic creation and re-creation of meaning where individuals actively frame issues perceived as central while also reacting and modifying the view of, e.g., the situation at hand (cf. Gioia and Chittipeddi 1991; Weick 1993). It refers to "*the ongoing retrospective development of plausible images that rationalize what people are doing*" (Weick et al. 2005, p. 409). Nevertheless, we see this process as allowing for both retrospective (Weick 1995) and prospective processes (Gephart et al. 2010). The individuals' identity, and how individuals look at themselves, is central in the process of making sense (Weick et al. 2005). The sense-making process progresses through internal and external communication (Currie and Brown 2003).

The key themes of decision-making and change are common in the sense-making literature (Gioia and Thomas 1996; Rerup and Feldman 2011; Sonenshein 2010). Individuals face paradoxes in time when changes take place and managing change is thus much about managing these paradoxes (Nasim and Sushil 2011, p. 186). Sense-making allows for envision and revision of the meaning. There are also situations where individuals try to make sense of new, ambiguous and unclear situations that do not agree with expectations based on previous experience. There are tensions between the new and the old, involving needs of change causing uncertainty while a common way of dealing with uncertainty due to conflicting paradoxes is to strive towards order and stabilization and defending the old (Smith and Lewis 2011). As such, the sense-making process also touches on mechanisms of cognitive dissonance. When individuals perceive cognitive dissonance, they do not make sense of the situation or information at hand (Festinger 1962). Further, what is considered as cognitive dissonant is also considered as not legitimate.

Sense-Giving as a Concept

Individuals actively construct the framing in sense-giving, focusing on what is central for communication to external stakeholders (Gioia and Chittipeddi 1991). Individuals aim to make an impact on other individuals' behaviour through the sense-giving in communication. "*'Sensegiving' is concerned with the process of attempting to influence the sensemaking and meaning construction of others toward a preferred redefinition of organizational reality*" (Gioia and Chittipeddi 1991, p. 442). While sense-making refers to the *cognition*, sense-giving refers to the *acting*. Norms and behaviour are central in communication when aiming to influence another party (Gioia and Chittipeddi 1991). "*Sensegiving-for-others*" involves disseminating of new understanding in front of the audience in order to influence their "sensemaking-for-self" (p. 444). The sense givers aim to influence the perceptions, attitudes and beliefs of others. The initial view may change throughout the sense-giving provided. In order to bond with others and influence others, social skills are therefore central in the sense-giving process (cf. Rosen and Kuehlwein 1996, p. 507).

Sense-giving allows for signalling and energizing while individuals as receivers of the sense-giving may be cynical about communication from influencers who mount them (Bommer et al. 2005; DeCelles et al. 2013). Sense-giving further enables development and nurturing of relations between individuals (Bean and Hamilton 2006). Regular interaction may develop a sense of shared identity that also may reinforce their common key values and the business opportunities. The commitment to the sense-giving organization may be due to such relationships potentially embarking new directions of enthusiasm rather than resistance (Awamleh and Gardner 1999). Sense-giving is provided in a cognitive frame, i.e. an interpretative scheme (Burtunek 1984) aimed to agree with the followers' interest, values and beliefs as well as organizational activities, goals and ideology (Walsh 1995, p. 281).

Legitimacy as a Concept

The idea underlying legitimacy theory is that it is crucial for a company to be granted legitimacy in the form of a social contract often referred to a social licence to operate (Dowling and Pfeffer 1975; Deegan 2002). Hooghiemstra (2000) argues that this implies that a company's success or even its survival in business society is dependent on the extent that the company is considered to operate within the norms of society (Brown and Deegan 1998). With ongoing shifts in norms and expectations, the threshold for what is being regarded as legitimate in society also changes. Legitimacy constitutes a critical driving source in organizational behaviour (Oliver 1991). We distinguish between two types of legitimacy, i.e. *cognitive legitimacy* and *social legitimacy*. The cognitive legitimacy refers to the people or organization's own legitimacy, i.e. if it is legitimate for the people to use and communicate sustainability information. It may for instance touche upon the peoples' awareness and knowledge about the phenomenon, uncertainties in interpretation and understanding of what it implies (Scott 1994, 1995; Zimmerman and Zeitz 2002). High cognitive legitimacy implies that knowledge is taken for granted, considered as useful and displayed in daily routines and activities, e.g. by professionals or organizations (Scott 2014).

Social legitimacy touches upon acceptance and support of social norms, e.g. on what is acceptable, appropriate or proper. In order to convince others to engage in and increase awareness and interest, there is a need to legitimate the new assumptions made based on the value of the socially constructed norms and beliefs (Suchman 1995). High social legitimacy implies that a social norm is accepted and supported by a particular group or society; it might be an accepted opinion, an accepted acting, etc.

Analysts' Cognitive Frames in the Early 2000s

In this section and the following sect. "A Shift Towards Enhances Cognitive Legitimacy in Sense-Making and Sense-Giving", we continue to look into sense-making and sense-giving from the analyst's point of view but now explicitly with regard to sustainability information. We look into the analysts' cognitive frames also referred to as mental model, i.e. the cognitive meaningfulness and value attached to sustainability information (Schön and Rein 1994; Senge 1990). Much of the change occurs due to shifts in norms and expectation in society paired with changes in sustainability-reporting regulations. We characterize the early 2000s as the *voluntary-reporting period* (sect. "Analysts' Cognitive Frames in the Early 2000s") and the latter half of the 2010s as the more *regulatory-reporting period* (sect. "A Shift Towards Enhances Cognitive Legitimacy in Sense-Making and Sense-Giving") when it comes to sustainability reporting. We further look into the analysts' legitimation and the concepts of cognitive and social legitimacy of sustainability *before* the changes from voluntary reporting to more mandatory sustainability reporting not the least with the new EU directive (2014/95/EU). In sect. "Analysts' Cognitive Frames in the Early 2000s" and "A Shift Towards Enhances Cognitive Legitimacy in Sense-Making and Sense-Giving", we further apply an internal organizational perspective on the analyst's work in line with Gioia and Thomas (1996). We combine this with an external perspective on sustainability communication and reporting in line with Morsing and Schultz (2006).

Thus, we now further conceptualize the cognitive frames of sustainability information in decision-making processes and communication processes from the analysts' point of view outlining the core sequences of sense-making and sense-giving. In order to understand the analyst's sense-making and sense-giving, we need to take a step back to management teams' cognitive processes of sense-making and sense-giving and how these in a later stage impact and influence the analysts' processes. Corporate information deriving from management teams is a central part of the analyst's work when interpreting, assessing and communicating companies' investment potential. As such, the management team's sequences of sense-making and sense-giving contextualize the analysts' sequences of sense-making and sense-giving.

Our framework enables analyses of the analysts' interplay with management teams, the analysts' adoption of sustainability information into their own work and their communication of value-added information with their clients, i.e. the investors. The framework enables outlining of the gradual development of sustainability reporting into a global reporting practice directly affecting the analysts' everyday work. In order to understand the shift in analysts' cognitive frames and challenges due to their views of sustainability information, we start from a historical perspective a few years ago, then move further to the current state and start the conceptualization.

Social Pressure on Companies to Report on Sustainability Information

In a first step, companies make sense of the sustainability information themselves in order to interpret and transform the information in order to disclose a true and fair view of the company stakeholders, here financial analysts. Despite the fact that the sustainability debate gained momentum over 30 years ago with the Brundtland report (UNWED 1987), the ambiguous nature of sustainability information still means difficulties for companies to understand how it should be reported in a relevant and credible manner. Reporting on sustainability information has until the fiscal year 2017, when the new EU directive (2014/95/EU) came into force, primarily been a voluntarily reporting practice engaged in by companies. Regulation of sustainability information is new, and norms of what to measure, how to measure, what to communicate or not all remain uncertain. Companies struggle with making sense of the sustainability information in the jungle of voluntary frameworks, guidelines and standards available (<IR> framework, UN Global Compact, Global Reporting Initiative (GRI) and UN's SDGs, ISO 26000). The scattered reporting landscape renders many questions for management teams to acknowledge. What does sustainability imply for us? What is material sustainability information? To whom is it material? How can we understand and assess sustainability performance? How can sustainability information be connected to traditional financial corporate information? What consequences might be expected due to how sustainability information is reported, e.g. how does it affect the analysts' work and their views and valuation of the company.

A major shift took place for the companies in the early 2000s where expectations on companies to report on sustainability information increased in the aftermath of the many corporate scandals. This meant that the norms, values and expectations of what were considered legitimate (Dowling and Pfeffer 1975; Deegan 2002) in a sustainable, ethical and responsible context changed in society. This forced companies to develop their business conducts in a more responsible and sustainable way. To show their achievements and to be granted legitimacy, companies started to voluntarily engage in developing their sustainability-reporting practice (see Arvidsson 2010, 2011, 2012). It was at this point in time challenging for management teams to both make sense of sustainability information themselves and to give sense to this information to financial analysts. This implies that the management teams were not conscious, or at least unsure of what signals their sustainability reporting was sending to the financial analysts.

Cognitive Dissonance Due to a Lack of Cognitive Legitimacy

During the first decade of this century, when companies started to increase the focus on sustainability in their corporate reports, most analysts did not find this type of information neither relevant nor credible (Arvidsson 2014). Although management teams tried to convince the analysts and also their clients, i.e. the investors, of its value relevance, they were of the opinion that sustainability information was something that companies only provided for legitimacy reasons not for its relevance for corporate valuation. They did not seem to see a clear link between sustainability information and the corporate value-creation process. Nor did they seem to understand how sustainability fitted into business models, organizational routines and processes (Arvidsson 2014).[2] This led to scepticism towards the relevance of sustainability reporting and it was often considered a "greenwashing" and "bluewashing" reporting practice. Thus, the analysts were reluctant to make sense of the information and the information was not perceived as cognitive legitimate by the analysts. Analysts stated (Arvidsson 2014, p. 217):

> Management teams go on and on and on about their CSR [sustainability] activities.

> Neither me or my colleagues require CSR [sustainability] information.

Here, a situation of cognitive dissonance appears where the analysts kept to the well-known cognitive frame of reference of corporate *financial* information, implying a cognitive denial of sustainability information. The cognitive dissonance served as a gatekeeper for sustainability information and, therefore, hindered the analysts' sense-making of this information (cf. Festinger 1962). Analysts also stated (Arvidsson 2014, p. 217):

> The management teams talk more about CSR [sustainability] – but we do not listen.

This indicates that financial analysts reflect on the value of sustainability information and appear to find it of limited relevance for future value creation and, thus, not material in their work of interpreting, assessing and communicating corporate performance. As a consequence, they take at this stage a passive approach towards sustainability information, meaning that it is not actively included in their investment advices. This standpoint is further reflected in the following quotes (Arvidsson 2014, p. 217):

> The interest in CSR [sustainability] information from us financial analysts are and has always been extremely limited.

> The CSR [sustainability] information makes no difference and is of no interest to a financial analyst.

> Complete mumbo jumbo!

Here, we clearly see that the analysts due to the perceived lack of value did not cognitively legitimate sustainability information. They appear reluctant to make sense of the information. The cognitive frame of reference which still was centred around corporate *financial* information promotes this reluctant and passive behaviour. Probably, this was also reinforced by the fact that they regarded it challenging to understand sustainability information and that this prevented them from acting on this information (cf. Gioia et al. 1994). Difficulties in transforming the "soft" sustainability information into more "hard" financial information served as a barrier in the financial analysts' sense-making process.

The financial analysts appear to find sustainability information ambiguous and difficult to translate into monetary terms applicable in their Excel sheet context (Arvidsson 2014). The scattered reporting landscape resulted in an abundance of different ways to report on sustainability performance. This impaired the comparability of sustainability performance between companies, periods and industries. Considering the analysts' mission to generate profits for their investment bank, a consequence of the difficulties and ambiguity surrounding sustainability information appears to have made them hesitant to spend resources on actively engaging in the process of transforming sustainability information into more familiar type of information. Instead, they focused their sense-making efforts on traditional financial information, which they considered to be more meaningful when interpreting and assessing corporate performance and value.

At this time, there was a notion that companies primarily reported on information related to positive sustainability issues rather than negative (Emeseh och Songi 2014). However, the analysts appeared to be more interested in making sense of information related to incidents of *negative* sustainability character, e.g. pollution, use of child labour, unethical business conduct, violation against human rights and corruption. Already here, a gradual shift can be identified where analysts started to include sustainability information as part of their assessment of companies' risk profiles (Arvidsson 2014). The following quote (Arvidsson 2014, p. 218) reveals that a distinction is made between value creation and value destruction.

> CSR [sustainability] has more to do with avoidance of value destruction than value creation.
>
> CSR [sustainability] does not create value per se. It could, if handled correctly, assist in avoiding value destruction due to being caught in engaging in bad activities.

In this section, we outline how sustainability information in the first decade of the twentieth century affected the analysts' sense-making and sense-giving processes (Weick et al. 2005). The sustainability information is neither social legitimated nor cognitive legitimated by the analysts. Analysts' are unable to make sense of the ambiguous sustainability information; the information is not cognitively legitimated. The information is not social legitimate; it is not requested by the analysts' clients, not considered as value adding, not generating a pay-off and considered as purely a cost for the investment bank. The analysts face cognitive dissonance (Festinger 1962). They are unwilling to engage in sense-making activities and do not actively engage in sense-giving activities in front of clients.

A Shift Towards Enhances Cognitive Legitimacy in Sense-Making and Sense-Giving

We now look into more regulatory-reporting practice regarding sustainability reporting that characterize the latter part of 2010s. Here, we see a change in analysts' use and value attached to sustainability information, which we argue is caused by a shift in analysts' cognitive frames (Schön and Rein 1994; Senge 1990). Much of the change occurs due to shifts in norms and expectation in society paired with changes in sustainability-reporting regulations. On the one hand, there is now starting to be a societal pressure on management teams to run their business in a more sustainable manner and increase the quality of how they report on their sustainability performance. On the other hand, there is also a societal pressure on institutional investors to make sound investment decisions incorporating sustainability aspects. This societal pressure is paired with a changing reporting landscape towards more regulatory-reporting practices. We further look into the analysts' legitimation and the concepts of cognitive and social legitimacy of sustainability *after* the changes from voluntary reporting to more mandatory sustainability reporting not the least with the new EU directive (2014/95/EU). We continue to outline the analysts' core sequences of sense-making and sense-giving moving to the current state in the post-regulation period.

Increased Societal Pressure for More Sustainability Focus

The second decade of the twentieth century has been characterized by an increased societal pressure on companies to enhance the quality, relevance, credibility and comparability of sustainability information. Today, with Agenda 2030 and UN's SDGs we can conclude that sustainability is a topic high up on the agendas in politics, business society and academia. National and international regulations concerning, e.g. inclusion of sustainable perspectives on investment valuations, emissions, disclosure rules, tax transparency, compliance and anti-corruption are continuously taking a step forward. This imposes pressure on companies to provide structured and relevant information on these issues in their sustainability reporting. It also assists companies in sorting out what is relevant and material. A change is now taking place, which relates to sustainability information becoming more regulated and not only a voluntary-reporting practice. From the fiscal year 2017, the largest EU companies are mandated to disclose sustainability information in accordance with the EU directive (2014/95/EU).

The stakeholders harshly question and dislike companies that do not provide sustainability information or if they do not act in accordance with norms, values and expectations. Recently, HM was criticized for a racial tone in a sweater advertisement and for high risks of using child labour in their production (SvD 2018). Thus, sustainability issues have stepwise come to have an impact on share prices and, thus, corporate valuation particularly via news scandals (Aerts et al. 2008). In addition, Zhou et al. (2017) find that sustainability reporting by decrease the information asymmetry and reducing the information risk also decrease errors in analysts forecast and forecast dispersion.

There has been an increased pressure not only on management teams to engage in sustainability reporting but also on institutional investors to act and invest in accordance with sustainability criterion. The pressure on institutional investors primarily come from non-profit organizations (NPOs) and governments (Cornett et al. 2016). This is also illustrated through the following quotation by one investor in the study by Essland and Olausson (2018, pp. 20–21)[3]:

> It all started with the churches, and this was many years ago, they did not want their money to be invested in unethical industries such as pornography or tobacco. Later the municipalities started making the same requests due to political forces, and nowadays I do not believe we have a single institutional customer who do not demand certain restrictions in the investment universe.

The amount of capital invested in sustainable funds has extensively increased in recent years (Nilsson et al. 2014) and such investments expect to continue to increase in both relevance and numbers (Ramiah et al. 2016). Pension funds classified as environmental or ethical had over a period of five years shown lower fees and higher return on investments compared to other funds (Sievänen et al. 2013). Thus, sustainability has become a selling argument for investment funds. Sustainability information has thereby become value-added information and a natural part of the analysts' investment advices to clients.

Management and Institutional Investors Forced to Make Sense and Give Sense

Today, companies are forced by investors and analysts to become more transparent both in their communication of sustainability information and in acting in accordance with the norms of being a sustainable business. As such, management teams need to frame themselves as social legitimate both in reporting and in acting (Massaro et al. 2018). Company reports have traditionally focused merely on historical financial information while mandatory regulation now forces companies to integrate sustainability information, information capturing both the history and the future. Sustainability information has become central for companies' future performance and value (Eccles et al. 2014).

Management teams actively interpret, assess and communicate sustainability information, i.e. make sense and give sense to sustainability information. Institutional investors are now also pressured by actors such as NPOs and government to make sustainable investments (Cornett et al. 2016). Hence, they request sustainability information in order to signal their social legitimacy by investing in sustainable companies. For this, they need to make sense of and to give sense of sustainable investments. This is also illustrated through the following quotation by one investor in the study by Essland and Olausson (2018, p. 21):

> We have seen a tremendous increase in pressure from the surroundings when it comes to our sustainability screening and investment decisions. I believe

> that this pressure will continue, maybe even increase and that sustainable investments will be a hygiene factor rather than a differentiation factor.

There are a number of ongoing initiatives for instance an engagement programme by banks in Europe and USA, ShareAction, where small shareholders and institutional investors work together for taking an active standpoint and impact on the climate change (Share Action 2017: https://shareaction.org/in-the-news/boston-common-and-share-action-working-on-transatlantic-bank-engagement-on-climate-change/):

> Investors can protect themselves from stranded assets but they remain exposed to macro high-carbon risks. Banks are uniquely placed to influence actors across the emissions chain. By financing high-carbon, banks can contribute to temperature rises. Engaging with banks could avoid portfolio-wide exposure to climate risk.

The discussion above outlines the strategic change taking place where a vigorous practice for sustainability reporting is developing among companies and investors. This also affects the analysts' work with providing value-added information and, hence, also on the analysts cognitive frames regarding meaningfulness and values of sustainability information.

Analysts' Cognitive Frames: Sustainability Becomes Cognitive Legitimated

Operating within the norms of society is central for the analysts (cf. Brown and Deegan 1998) in order to assure for social legitimacy. There is an ongoing strategic change that takes place for analysts, transforming sustainability information into cognitive legitimate information. Analysts need transparency to surround corporate-sustainability information in order to evaluate potential and to assure for relevant and credible value-added advices to clients (Newell and Paterson 2009). In this process of starting to include a new type of information, i.e. sustainability information, there is a questioning of traditional norms and transformation into new norms values and believes (Suddaby and Greenwood 2005; cf. Gioia and Chittipeddi 1991).

A number of critical factors are involved in the process of decreasing the smokescreen of sustainability information. When sustainability reporting becomes more regulated, e.g. through the new EU directive (2014/95/EU), the sustainability information provided by companies opens up for less problems for analysts related to interpretation and valuation. This is due to increased transparency and also enhanced comparability. The financial analysts take a role as "meaning-makers" and want as such to influence their clients in order to achieve their organizational goals, i.e. generating businesses for the investment bank and for institutional investors to make beneficial investments. The analysts have an active role as facilitators, expected to have adequate competences to interpret, assess and provide relevant and reliable investment advices based on a mix of traditional financial information and sustainability information. When these prerequisites are achieved, analysts are ready to take an active part in the sense-making and sense-giving of sustainability information. The cognitive dissonance is no longer the problem hindering an active interpretation, assessment and communication. Through sense-giving, analysts influence and assist investors to better identify and understand investment opportunities.

However, empirical evidence reveals that not even mandatory requirements appear to be a quick fix when it comes to the alleged shortcomings with sustainability information in corporate reports. The informational quality confirms to be low even in countries with mandatory requirements on sustainability reporting (Chauvey et al. 2015; Larrinaga et al. 2002). This also received attention at the recent SUBREA conference (Arvidsson 2018), where it was highlighted that financial analysts *still* find it challenging to work with sustainability information. One critical barrier is the analysts' inability to make sense of this kind of new type of information (Abhayawansa et al. 2018). Efficient measurement techniques relevant for sustainability information are particularly requested by the analysts in order to deal with the ambiguity (Perez and Sanchez 2009). This is also illustrated through the following quotations from the study by Essland and Olausson (2018):

> I can measure a whole bunch of stuff, for example the 2 emissions from a company that manufactures cluster bombs, but that would not be that relevant, right? This is the hard part. (p. 23)

> Take the automotive industry, it is very problematic to evaluate regulatory risks. What will happen with diesel cars? Will there be tax reliefs for electric cars? We are not used to working with these potential changes in regulations. (p. 29)

This implies a pressure on analysts to engage in and actively integrate sustainability information provided through corporate reports despite the ambiguous nature of the information. The analysts' ability to interpret and assess sustainability information and hence their own sense-making processes become critical in order to provide value-added information and investment advice to clients. It is now to a greater extent *expected* of analysts to be able to provide this.

The relationships between management teams, financial analysts and investors become central in the sense-making and sense-giving processes of ambiguous sustainability information. Uncertainties are expected to be dealt with through the dual exchange of information between management teams, financial analysts and investors. Management teams play a central role in the analysts' sense-making efforts by actively engaging in sense-giving enabling analysts to provide relevant investment advices to their clients, i.e. the investors. As such, analysts' sense-making and sense-giving processes are closely intervened with sense-making and sense-giving by the management team. This also expects to be the case for the exchange between analysts and investors. According to a study by Abhayawansa et al. (2018), the main and preferred methods for analysts' gathering of information are through personal meetings with company management and conference calls. Sense-giving entails communication with management teams and clients via meetings and other types of direct and indirect communication and allows for interactively sense-making of corporate values. Direct contacts improve the potential for analysts' sense-making, especially when ambiguous information is at focus and, thereby, enables analysts to provide value-added investment advices to the investors (Johansson 2004, 2007). Although they rely on direct contacts, the analysts highlight the need for them to independently make sense of sustainability information. The independence does not exclude them from incorporating information from various corporate representatives with different types of informational input needed for them to make efficient investment advices. This is illustrated by the quotation by one analyst in the study by Abhayawansa et al. (2018, p. 24).[4]

> You can't collect information on that [i.e., strategic focus and future orientation]. You develop a view. Strategic focus is a means. You listen to what the CEO says - that's what's on the surface of it. You want to dig deeper than that. You want to speak to the guys who are technically involved in the company - not at the management level.

The analysts' sense-making and sense-giving processes appear to be iterative, sequential and mutual inclusive in nature involving a giving and taking between companies—analysts and investors (cf. Gioia and Chittipeddi 1991). The sequences involve the key actors *understanding* of the situation, i.e. the corporate value or potential, through sense-making and then *affecting* the investors' investments by *sense-giving* through relevant and credible investment advices. The analysts continuously interact with management teams and investors. They make sense of the situation; they revise their meaning and try to give sense of the information to investors by envisioning and energizing their standpoint. The analysts "sell" their investment advice, i.e. their view of a company's potential as an investment. These investment advices represent sense-giving while at the same time the analysts try to make sense *themselves* of the sustainability information at hand. The cycles involve as such both *cognition* and *action*.

Direct contacts may also allow for development of a *shared* framework of what is central when interpreting and assessing sustainability information. The sense-giving encapsulates social skills in the communication of the investment advices.

In this section, we have outlined how sustainability information in the latter part of the second decade of the twentieth century affected the analysts' sense-making and sense-giving processes (Weick et al. 2005). Sustainability information is now beginning to be socially legitimate and requested by the analysts' clients, i.e. investors. However, the complexity of the situation remains. This type of information is still not considered as cognitive legitimate due to the ambiguous nature, which renders difficulties for the sense-making and sense-giving processes. The information is not yet internalized into the analysts' cognitive frames, i.e. not taken for granted and integrated into the analysts' daily work (Scott 1994). Although analysts are still unable to make (perfect) sense of the ambiguous sustainability information, they are now willing to engage in sense-making activities due to the pressure of social legitimacy, i.e. investors expect this to be included in the analysts' value-added information. There appears to be a situation, which we refer to as a partial cognitive dissonance. Engaging in sense-making does no longer solely imply non-profit generating work, i.e. simple waste of resources. Engagement also generates pay-off since analysts' clients consider the information as value relevant and adding additional value to their investment decisions. In order to provide value-added information, analysts now need to be able to interpret both traditional financial information and sustainability information for making sense of what constitutes high potential investments (cf. Malmström et al. 2015). They are now expected to actively engage in *giving* sense of sustainability information to their clients. We have seen that the analysts' relationships with management teams and investors are central in their continuous sense-making and sense-giving of sustainability information. Efficient relationships enable analysts to decrease the perceived ambiguity and stepwise develop commonly accepted norms of sustainability information together with companies and clients (Scott 2014; Zimmerman and Zeitz 2002).

Cognitive Foundations and a Promising Future Ahead

In this chapter, adopted a sense-making and sense-giving perspective on how analysts work as information intermediaries and how an increased focus on sustainability information in corporate reports has affected their work. In particular, we wanted to highlight the challenges in sense-making and sense-giving to gain a better understanding of their interpretation, assessment and communication of sustainability information to their clients, i.e. the investors. This chapter problematizes the challenges due to *social legitimation* (i.e. investors' request of sustainability information) and *cognitive legitimation* (analysts' ability to understand the ambiguous sustainability information) and as a result, the hurdles of cognitive dissonance make analysts hesitant towards considering sustainability information in their day-to-day work. We develop a new perspective drawing on analysts' cognitive foundation underlying the smokescreen of sustainability information.

The discussion outlines changes in the analysts' cognitive frames from the first decade of the twentieth century to the second decade of the twentieth century. We argue that the first part of 2000s was characterized by cognitive dissonance due to both a low social legitimacy (sustainability was not yet requested by the investors to be attended to) and a low cognitive legitimacy (sustainability was regarded too ambiguous to be relevant for being considered in a valuation context). In the latter part of 2010s, we argue that there is only a partial cognitive dissonance. Now, sustainability information is beginning to be socially legitimate and requested by investors. However, the complexity of the situation remains. This type of information is still not considered as cognitive legitimate due to the ambiguous nature, which renders difficulties for the analysts' sense-making and sense-giving processes.

We can conclude that sustainability is largely about people, about the key actors in the stock market and their ability and willingness to make sense and give sense of sustainability information and to act in accordance with sustainability criterion. It is much about legitimate behaviour and accomplishes changes in values, norms and behaviour. Both cognition and action play vital roles in this process. In sum, we see a promising future ahead where sustainability information gradually is becoming (becomes?) more relevant, credible and comparable. The process of decreasing its ambiguous nature will result higher cognitive legitimacy of sustainability information. This will promote the integration of sustainability information in the analysts' work of providing efficient investment advices to investors. The findings have implications not the least in the ongoing quest of developing frameworks, standards and legislation (e.g. the EU directive (2014/EU/95)), that opt for improving the relevance, credibility and comparability of sustainability information. We finally conclude that:

In truth, the core nature of investment and return is not a trade-off between social and financial interest but rather the pursuit of an embedded value proposition composed of both. (Emerson 2003, p. 37)

Notes

1. *Reading tip*: Summa de arithmetica, geometria, proportioni et proportionalita by Luca Pacioli from 1492.
2. The semi-structured interviews in Arvidsson (2014) were conducted in 2010 with 17 financial analysts working at international investment banks. In this chapter, CSR is used as a proxy for sustainability.
3. The semi-structured interviews in Essland and Olausson (2018) were conducted in 2018 with 19 key actors in the stock market, primarily working at international investment banks.
4. The semi-structured interviews in Abhayawansa et al. (2018) were conducted with 23 analysts in the stock market, primarily working at international investment banks.

References

Abhayawansa, S., Bowden, M., & Pillay, S. (2017). Students' conceptions of learning in the context of an accounting degree. *Accounting Education, 26*(3), 213–241.

Abhayawansa, S., Elijido-Ten, E., & Dumay, J. (2018). A practice theoretical analysis of the irrelevance of integrated reporting to mainstream sell-side analysts. *Accounting and Finance, 57*(4), 38.

Aerts, W., Cormier, D., & Magnan, M. (2008). Corporate environmental disclosure, financial markets and the media: An international perspective. *Ecological Economics, 64*(3), 643–659.

Akerlof, G. A. (1970). The market for "lemons": Quality uncertainty and the market mechanism. *The Quarterly Journal of Economics, 84*(3), 488–500.

Arvidsson, S. (2003). *Demand and supply of information on intangibles: The case of knowledge-intense companies.* Ph.D. dissertation, Department of Business Administration, Lund University, Lund University Press.

Arvidsson, S. (2010). Communication of corporate social responsibility: A study of the views of management teams in large companies. *Journal of Business Ethics, 96,* 339–354.

Arvidsson, S. (2011). Disclosure of non-financial information in the annual report: A management-team perspective. *Journal of Intellectual Capital, 12*(2), 277–300.

Arvidsson, S. (2012). The corporate communication process between listed companies and financial analysts: A focus on trends and challenges. *Corporate Communication: An International Journal, 17*(2), 98–112.

Arvidsson, S. (2014). Corporate social responsibility and stock market actors: A comprehensive study. *Social Responsibility Journal, 10*(2), 210–225.

Arvidsson, S. (November 2018, forthcoming). *The 1st SUBREA conference report.* Media Tryck, Lund, Sweden.

Awamleh, R., & Gardner, W. L. (1999). Perceptions of leader charisma and effectiveness: The effects of vision content, delivery, and organizational performance. *The Leadership Quarterly, 10*(3), 345–373.

Bartunek, J. M. (1984). Changing interpretive schemes and organizational restructuring: The example of a religious order. *Administrative Science Quarterly, 29*(3), 355–372.

Bean, C. J., & Hamilton, F. E. (2006). Leader framing and follower sensemaking: Response to downsizing in the brave new workplace. *Human Relations, 59*(3), 321–349.

Berger, P. L., & Luckmann, T. (1991). *The social construction of reality: A treatise in the sociology of knowledge* (No. 10). London: Penguin UK.

Beyer, A., Cohen, D. A., Lys, T. Z., & Walther, B. R. (2010). The financial reporting environment: Review of the recent literature. *Journal of Accounting and Economics, 50*(2), 296–343.

Bommer, W. H., Rich, G. A., & Rubin, R. S. (2005). Changing attitudes about change: Longitudinal effects of transformational leader behavior on employee cynicism about organizational change. *Journal of Organizational Behavior, 26*(7), 733–753.

Brown, L. D., Call, A. C., Clement, M. B., & Sharp, N. Y. (2016). The activities of buy-side analysts and the determinants of their stock recommendations. *Journal of Accounting and Economics, 62*(1), 139–156.

Brown, N., & Deegan, C. (1998). The public disclosure of environmental performance information—a dual test of media agenda setting theory and legitimacy theory. *Accounting and Business Research, 29*(1), 21–41.

Cahan, S. F., de Villiers, C., Jeter, D. C., Naiker, V., & van Staden, C. J. (2016). Are CSR disclosure value relevant? Cross-country evidence. *European Accounting Review, 25*(3), 579–611.

Chang, C. H., & Chen, Y. S. (2012). The determinants of green intellectual capital. *Management Decision, 50*(1), 74–94.

Chauvey, J. N., Giordano-Spring, S., Cho, C. H., & Patten, D. M. (2015). The normativity and legitimacy of CSR disclosure: Evidence from France. *Journal of Business Ethics, 130*(4), 789–803.

Cho, C. H., Michelon, G., Patten, D. M., & Roberts, R. W. (2015). CSR disclosure: The more things change…? *Accounting, Auditing & Accountability Journal, 28*(1), 14–35.

Clatworthy, M., & Lee, E. (2018). Financial analysts' role in valuation and stewardship.

Cornett, M. M., Erhemjamts, O., & Tehranian, H. (2016). Greed or good deeds: An examination of the relation between corporate social responsibility and the financial performance of US commercial AMCs around the financial crisis. *Journal of Banking & Finance, 70,* 137–159.

Currie, G., & Brown, A. (2003). A narratological approach to understanding processes of organizing in a UK hospital. *Human Relations, 56,* 563–586.

Dameri, R. P., & Ricciardi, F. (2015). Smart city intellectual capital: An emerging view of territorial systems innovation management. *Journal of Intellectual Capital, 16*(4), 860–887.

DeCelles, K. A., Tesluk, P. E., & Taxman, F. S. (2013). A field investigation of multilevel cynicism toward change. *Organization Science, 24*(1), 154–171.

Deegan, C. (2002). Introduction: The legitimising effect of social and environmental disclosures—A theoretical foundation. *Accounting, Auditing and Accountability Journal, 15*(3), 282–311.

Dhaliwal, D. S., Li, O. Z., Tsang, A., & Yang, Y. G. (2011). Voluntary nonfinancial disclosure and the cost of equity capital: The initiation of corporate social responsibility reporting. *Accounting Review, 86*(1), 59–100.

Dhaliwal, D. S., Li, O. Z., Tsang, A., & Yang, Y. G. (2014). Corporate social responsibility disclosure and the cost of equity capital: The roles of stakeholder orientation and financial transparency. *Journal of Accounting and Public Policy, 33*(4), 328–355.

Dhaliwal, D. S., Radhakrishnan, S., Tsang, A. H., & Yang, Y. G. (2012). Nonfinancial disclosure and analyst forecast accuracy: International evidence on corporate social responsibility disclosure. *The Accounting Review, 87*(3), 723–759.

Dienes, D., Sassen, R., & Fischer, J. (2016). What are the drivers of sustainability reporting? A systematic review. *Sustainability Accounting, Management and Policy Journal, 7*(2), 154–189.

Dowling, J., & Pfeffer, J. (1975). Organizational legitimacy: Social values and organizational behaviour. *The Pacific Sociological Review, 18*(1), 122–136.

Dutot, V., Lacalle Galvez, E., & Versailles, D. W. (2016). CSR communications strategies through social media and influence on e-reputation: An exploratory study. *Management Decision, 54*(2), 363–389.

Eccles, R. G., Ioannou, I., & Serafeim, G. (2014). The impact of corporate sustainability on organizational processes and performance. *Management Science, 60*(11), 2835–2857.

Emerson, J. (2003). The blended value proposition: Integrating social and financial returns. *California Management Review, 45*(4), 35–51.

Emeseh, E., & Songi, O. (2014). CSR, human rights abuse and sustainability report accountability. *International Journal of Law and Management, 56*(2), 136–151.

Essland, C., & Olausson, A. (2018). *Barriers for responsible investments: Facilitating a greener economy—A multiple case study of asset management companies.* Master Thesis, Luleå University of Technology.

European Commission. (2014). *Directive on disclosure of non-financial and diversity information by certain large companies* (2014/95/EU). Brussels.

Festinger, L. (1962). *A theory of cognitive dissonance* (Vol. 2). Stanford, CA: Stanford University Press.

Foote, J., Gaffney, N., & Evans, J. R. (2010). Corporate social responsibility: Implications for performance excellence. *Total Quality Management, 21*(8), 799–812.

Frankental, P. (2001). Corporate social responsibility—A PR invention? *Corporate Communications: An International Journal, 6*(1), 18–23.

Gephart, R. P., Topal, C., & Zhang, Z. (2010). Future-oriented sensemaking: Temporalities and institutional legitimation. In *Process, Sensemaking, and Organizing* (pp. 275–312). Oxford: Oxford University Press.

Gioia, D. A., & Chittipeddi, K. (1991). Sensemaking and sensegiving in strategic change initiation. *Strategic Management Journal, 12*(6), 433–448.

Gioia, D. A., & Thomas, J. B. (1996). Identity, image, and issue interpretation: Sensemaking during strategic change in academia. *Administrative Science Quarterly, 41*(3), 370–403.

Gioia, D. A., Thomas, J. B., Clark, S. M., & Chittipeddi, K. (1994). Symbolism and strategic change in academia: The dynamics of sensemaking and influence. *Organization Science, 5*(3), 363–383.

Groysberg, B., Healy, P. M., & Maber, D. A. (2011). What drives sell-side analyst compensation at high-status investment banks? *Journal of Accounting Research, 49*(4), 969–1000.

Hahn, R., & Kühnen, M. (2013). Determinants of sustainability reporting: A review of results, trends, theory, and opportunities in an expanding field of research. *Journal of Cleaner Production, 59*, 5–21.
Hallvarsson, M. (2009). Rimliga Ambitioner Med CSR? [Reasonable Ambitions with CSR?]. In T. Borglund, H. De Geer, & M. Hallvarsson (Eds.), *Värdeskapande CSR – Hur företag tar socialt ansvar* (pp. 145–156). Stockholm, Sweden: Norstedts Aka- demiska Förlag.
Hooghiemstra, R. (2000). Corporate communication and impression management—New perspectives why companies engage in corporate social reporting. *Journal of Business Ethics, 27*(1–2), 55–68.
Ifvarsson, C. (2000). *Sensemaking and management: A theoretical discussion with research implications*. Doctoral dissertation, Luleå tekniska universitet.
Imam, S., Barker, R., & Clubb, C. (2008). The use of valuation models by UK investment analysts. *European Accounting Review, 17*(3), 503–535.
Ivković, Z., & Jegadeesh, N. (2004). The timing and value of forecast and recommendation revisions. *Journal of Financial Economics, 73*(3), 433–463.
Johansson, J. (1998). *Direct contacts between financial analysts and traded companies*. Licentiate dissertation, Luleå. Retrieved from http://urn.kb.se/resolve?urn=urn:nbn:se:ltu:diva-18509.
Johansson, J. (2004). *Recommendation changes in walls of glass: Perceived roles and relative importance of direct contacts*. Doctoral dissertation, Luleå tekniska universitet.
Johansson, J. (2007). Sell-side analysts' creation of value—Key roles and relational capital. *Journal of Human Resource Costing and Accounting, 11*(1), 30–52.
Johansson, J., & Malmström, M. (2013). The business model transparency paradox in innovative growth ventures: Trade-offs between competitive advantages and agency costs. *Journal of Entrepreneurship Research, 3*(2), 238–263.
Larrinaga, C., Carrasco, F., Correa, C., Llena, F., & Moneva, J. (2002). Accountability and accounting regulation: The case of the Spanish environmental disclosure standard. *European Accounting Review, 11*(4), 723–740.
Malmström, M., Johansson, J., & Wincent, J. (2015). Cognitive constructions of low-profit and high-profit business models: A repertory grid study of serial entrepreneurs. *Entrepreneurship Theory and Practice, 39*(5), 1083–1109.
Malmström, M., Johansson, J., & Wincent, J. (2017). Gender stereotypes and venture support decisions: How governmental venture capitalists socially

construct entrepreneurs' potential. *Entrepreneurship, 41*(5), 833–860. https://doi.org/10.1111/etap.12275.

Massaro, M., Dumay, J., Garlatti, A., & Dal Mas, F. (2018). Practitioners' views on intellectual capital and sustainability: From a performance-based to a worth-based perspective. *Journal of Intellectual Capital* (just-accepted), *19*(2), 367–386. https://doi.org/10.1108/JIC-02-2017-0033.

Morsing, M., & Schultz, M. (2006). Corporate social responsibility communication: Stakeholder information, response and involvement strategies. *Business Ethics: A European Review, 15*(4), 323–338.

Nasim, S., & Sushil. (2011). Revisiting organizational change: Exploring the paradox of managing continuity and change. *Journal of Change Management, 11*(2), 185–206.

Newell, P., & Paterson, M. (2009). The politics of the carbon economy. *The Politics of Climate Cchange: A Survey*, 80–99.

Nilsson, J., Jansson, J., Isberg, S., & Nordvall, A. C. (2014). Customer satisfaction with socially responsible investing initiatives: The influence of perceived financial and nonfinancial quality. *Journal of Financial Services Marketing, 19*(4), 265–276.

Oliver, C. (1991). Strategic responses to institutional processes. *Academy of Management Review, 16*(1), 145–179.

Parker, L. D. (2005). Social and environmental accountability research: A view from the commentary box. *Accounting, Auditing and Accountability Journal, 18*(6), 842–860.

Patten, D. M. (2013). Lessons from the third wave: A reflection on the rediscovery of corporate social responsibility by the mainstream accounting research community. *Financial Reporting, 2*(2), 9–26.

Pedrini, M. (2007). Human capital convergences in intellectual capital and sustainability reports. *Journal of Intellectual Capital, 8*(2), 346–366.

Perez, F., & Sanchez, L. E. (2009). Assessing the evolution of sustainability reporting in the mining sector. *Environmental Management, 43*(6), 949–961.

Ramiah, V., Gregoriou, G., von Müller, C., & Brieger, S. (2016). *Handbook of environmental and sustainable finance* (pp. 131–145). Amsterdam: Elsevier, Academic Press.

Rerup, C., & Feldman, M. S. (2011). Routines as a source of change in organizational schemata: The role of trial-and-error learning. *Academy of Management Journal, 54*(3), 577–610.

Rosen, H., & Kuehlwein, K. T. (1996). *Constructing realities: Meaning-making perspectives for psychotherapists*. San Francisco, CA: Jossey-Bass.
Salzedo, C., Young, S., & El-Haj, M. (2018). Does equity analyst research lack rigour and objectivity? Evidence from conference call questions and research notes. *Accounting and Business Research, 48*(1), 5–36.
Schipper, K. (1991). Analysts' forecasts. *Accounting Horizons, 5*(4), 105.
Scott, W. R. (1994). Institutions and organizations: Toward a theoretical synthesis. In W. R. Scott & J. W. Meyer (Eds.), *Institutional environments and organizations: Structural complexity and individualism* (pp. 55–80). Thousand Oaks, CA: Sage.
Scott, W. R. (1995). *Institutions and organizations*. Thousand Oaks, CA: Sage.
Scott, W. R. (2014). Institutions and organizations: Ideas, interests and identity.
Schön, D. A., & Rein, M. (1994). Frame reflection: Toward the resolution of intractable policy disputes.
Senge, P. M. (1990). The art and practice of the learning organization.
Share Action. (2017, February). *ShareAction, the UK-based campaign group, and Boston Common Asset Management, the US SRI specialist, are working together on a shareholder engagement programme with banks in Europe and the US on climate change*. https://shareaction.org/.
Sievänen, R., Rita, H., & Scholtens, B. (2013). The drivers of responsible investment: The case of European pension funds. *Journal of Business Ethics, 117*(1), 137–151.
Smith, W. K., & Lewis, M. W. (2011). Toward a theory of paradox: A dynamic equilibrium model of organizing. *Academy of Management Review, 36*(2), 381–403.
Sonenshein, S. (2010). We're changing—Or are we? Untangling the role of progressive, regressive, and stability narratives during strategic change implementation. *Academy of Management Journal, 53*(3), 477–512.
Suchman, M. C. (1995). Managing legitimacy: Strategic and institutional approaches. *Academy of Management Review, 20*(3), 571–610.
Suddaby, R., & Greenwood, R. (2005). Rhetorical strategies of legitimacy. *Administrative Science Quarterly, 50*(1), 35–67.
Swedish Pension Agency. (2016, September 23). *Statistik över hållbara fonder inom premiepensionssystemet*.
UN Sustainable-development-goals. (2018). https://www.un.org/sustainabledevelopment/sustainable-development-goals/.
UNWCED (United Nation World Commission on Environment and Development). (1987). *Report of the United Nation World Commission on*

environment and development 'our common future' (the Brundtland report). (Item 83, 42nd Session of the United Nations General Assembly).
Walsh, J. P. (1995). Managerial and organizational cognition: Notes from a trip down memory lane. *Organization Science, 6*(3), 280–321.
Wasiluk, K. L. (2013). Beyond eco-efficiency: Understanding CS through the IC practice lens. *Journal of Intellectual Capital, 14*(1), 102–126.
Weick, K. (1979). *The social psychology of organizing*. New York: McGraw-Hill.
Weick, K. E. (1993). The collapse of sensemaking in organizations: The Mann Gulch disaster. *Administrative Science Quarterly*, 628–652.
Weick, K. E. (1995). *Sensemaking in organizations* (Vol. 3). Sage.
Weick, K., Sutcliffe, K. M., & Obstfeld, D. (2005). Organizing and the process of sensemaking. *Organization Science, 16*(4), 409–421.
Zimmerman, M. A., & Zeitz, G. J. (2002). Beyond survival: Achieving new venture growth by building legitimacy. *Academy of Management Review, 27*(3), 414–431.
Zhou, S., Simnett, R., & Green, W. (2017). Does integrated reporting matter to the capital market? *Abacus, 53*(1), 94–132.

Changing Financial Firms Relative to ESG Issues

John Holland

Introduction

The aim of this chapter is to explore change in financial firms relative to environmental, social and governance issues (ESG). Many proposals have been made by external bodies and commentators to change financial firms (banks and other financial institutions) and their processes, behaviour, products and reporting. For example, the International Integrated Reporting Council has sought to develop guidelines (IIRC 2013) and encourage companies to report in a connected and integrated way on the role of intangibles in business models and value creation. Larsen and Tan (2015) and Larsen (2017) have explored how to develop integrated reporting <IR> in banking. The EU Directive on 'disclosure of non-financial reporting' (2017a) laid down mandatory rules requiring disclosure of non-financial and diversity information by

J. Holland (✉)
Adam Smith Business School, University of Glasgow, Main Building, Glasgow, Scotland, UK
e-mail: John.Holland@glasgow.ac.uk

S. Arvidsson (ed.), *Challenges in Managing Sustainable Business*,
https://doi.org/10.1007/978-3-319-93266-8_5

large companies including financial firms. The European Commission (2017a) also outlined non-mandatory guidelines on how companies can disclose 'relevant and useful information on environmental and social matters in a consistent and more comparable way'. The Financial Standards Board (FSB 2017) issued recommendations from its task force on 'Climate-related Financial Disclosures' (2017).

Bodies such as UNEP (2016) and authors such as Coleman and La Plante (2016) and Pavoni (2017) have also concentrated on the need for financial firms to be aware how climate change, associated economic, political and social issues can have an adverse impact on financial assets, liabilities and risks, customer exposures and financing products.

Finance theory such as agency theory and ideas of information asymmetry have had a strong focus on financial resources and have been used to explain their use and transformation in financial firms. However, Holland (2018) argued that this theory had insufficient explanatory power for banks and FIs. During the GFC, many of the economic problems faced by financial firms have been located in negative reciprocal interactions between their knowledge, social and financial resource factors. These led to major problems in decisions and reporting (Holland 2010).

This chapter argues, consistent with the IIRC (2013), and in response to problems revealed in the GFC and following decade, there needs to be a stronger focus on the whole financial firm, its combined use of intangible and financial resources, their connectivity, and for information on these issues to be disclosed. The chapter argues a 'behavioural theory of the financial firm' or BTFF is required to explain this phenomena. The next section shows how this can be based on empirical models about financial firms interpreted through theories of managerial behaviour, theories of the firm and organisational learning. The BTFF seeks to explain: how many intangible, technology and financial resource factors are integrated in the financial firm; how they are collectively used to transform financial capital and its risks; create value and achieve desired ESG outcomes; and how they influence disclosure on these matters. This creates a new focus to explore where ESG problems are in financial firms, and how they are connected. It provides means to explore how these issues change in the financial firm and can be managed and reported in an integrated way.

The development of a BTFF is intended to place more 'understanding power' in the hands of internal and external stakeholders concerning change in financial firms relative to ESG issues. The combination of BTFF analyses and enhanced reporting outcomes aims to improve dialogue between the company and its stakeholders (Gray et al. 1995), decrease information asymmetry and provide accountability to stakeholders. Improved understanding of financial firms, and enhanced connections between sustainability reporting and financial reporting, can increase the chances of financial firms being granted legitimacy (Etzion and Ferraro 2010) amongst stakeholders.

The first section discusses a brief outline of a 'Behavioral theory of the financial firm'. The second section investigates how the BTFF can be used to structure thinking and action in financial firms on ESG change issues. The third section explores how climate change can be used as an example of ESG issues and associated financial firm learning, design and use of resources. The fourth section discusses how problems and barriers to change in financial firms indicate that improved disclosure is required by citizens, regulators, legislators, policy advisory bodies and institutions. The BTFF can be used to provide clear structure to: co-ordinate thinking about existing external change pressures; overcome barriers; vigorously pursue desired ESG changes in financial firms; and improve the quality of disclosure on these matters.

'Behavioral Theory of the Financial Firm'

The BTFF concerns ideas of strategic dynamics and operational dynamics at all levels in the financial firm. It shows how many types of resources are used in transformation of financial capital and its risks in the financial firm. An embryonic BTFF is developed in Holland (2016, 2017, 2018) discusses how the BTFF differs from finance theory and how it can be used to develop conceptual connections to finance theory and concepts such as agency theory and information asymmetry. Holland (2017) uses the BTFF (as 'alternative theory') to explore the role of knowledge in financial firms. Holland (2016) uses fund management as an example of the BTFF. The BTFF will be briefly summarised in this section. It is used in the chapter as a conceptual frame to explore ESG issues.

Figure 1 illustrates a schematic view of the BTFF. In broad terms, the financial firm sought to understand external change, risk and uncertainty. **Learning** about change and the response of the firm to external change determined **strategic choices** about specialist financial functions, and specialist financial assets and liabilities. It determined how top teams constructed the firm, as a business made up of integrated internal and external intangibles (social, knowledge), to deliver these functions and products. The financial firm **mobilised** the chosen intangible resources to manage risk, respond to uncertainty, to deliver its specialist financial functions, and financial assets and liabilities to customers in markets. It did this to make a profit and achieve ESG aims. The firm used its understanding of the above for internal communications and to report on value creation and achievement of aims to stakeholders. This approach is consistent with satisfying European Commission (2011, p. 6), demands for firms, including banks and FIs to:

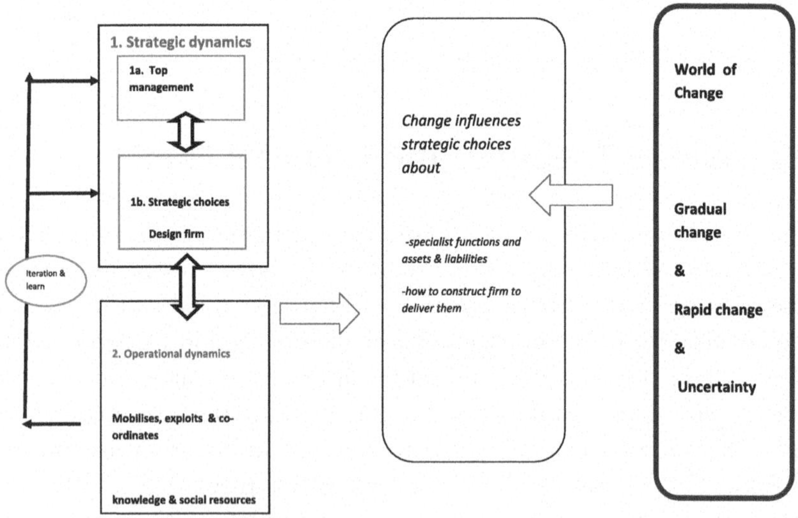

Fig. 1 BTFF structure and dynamics

> To fully meet their corporate social responsibility, enterprises should have in place a process to integrate social, environmental, ethical, human rights and consumer concerns into their business operations and core strategy in close collaboration with their stakeholders, with the aim of: maximising the creation of shared value for their owners/shareholders and for their other stakeholders and society at large; identifying, preventing and mitigating their possible adverse impacts.

Strategic dynamics involves top management learning and taking strategic actions in response to external change. Major external change factors such as: 'financialisation', securitisation, regulation, competition and technology lay behind change in statistical behaviour of financial resources and nature of financial firms (especially banks) in the period from 1980 onwards. In 2008, they contributed to the GFC (Holland 2010). Climate change and social responsibility issues have become important in driving change in the finance system and financial firms (Pavoni 2017).

Many field studies have illustrated *strategic dynamics* in the financial firm. They show how, in a world of change, learning by top management and other agents of bank and FI firms has led to new knowledge and capabilities. Research by authors such as Harris (2002), Antonacopoulou (2006), Shih et al. (2010), Holland (2010) and Chahal et al. (2015) illustrates how banks and FIs created knowledge-based intangibles or intellectual capital (Meritum 2002) of relevance to effective functioning of the financial firm.

These empirical models of financial firms are interpreted using, inter alia, theories of managerial behaviour (Cyert and March 1963), theories of the firm (Barney 1991) and organisational learning (Pedler et al. 1997). Many potential theories are available but a limited set have been chosen based on their relevance to empirical phenomena and from academic comments in conferences and during publication (Holland 2016, 2017, 2018). This approach connects the theories to the field studies and highlights the explanatory power of such theory for financial firms. The resulting BTFF creates a specialised conceptual frame to explain financial firms especially complex ongoing problems arising from joint misuse of intangibles and financial resources as revealed in the GFC and more recent cases such as Wells Fargo in 2016. This focused theoretical and empirical frame is required because of the significance of financial firms for the financial system, real economy and ESG issues.

The field studies revealed how board and top management teams in 'Learning organisations' (Pedler et al. 1997) exploited learning, to allocate resources in the design of the firm. They directed strategy, moulded and transmitted philosophy and culture and managed incentives and risk management ethos in the financial firm. They decided on the nature of resources *such as* organisation and hierarchy, external social networks, organisational processes, routines and technology. They designed organisational processes to create and exchange information, and control behaviour, in the hierarchy and market social networks. The organisational structures and processes were designed to transmit and exploit culture and knowledge in the firm and social networks. Choices were made by top management about the degree of autonomy of middle management and front-line staff in transacting and risk-taking. A trade-off was recognised between degree of control versus the creation of novel information and innovation (Holland 2016).

Top management learnt how to develop skills and capabilities of teams and individuals at all levels, as well as how to innovate in new products and services. They learnt how to develop their relationships, brands and reputation with customers and other external agents. The knowledge and social resources were strategically matched to the external environment, such as customer needs, market conditions, competition and technology change, and were designed to create a sustainable competitive advantage unique to each financial firm (Barney 1991).

Thus, top management and boards learnt, during historic mobilisation and use of resources, how to design a financial firm robust for varying circumstances. Many errors were made here in the GFC. The BTFF also illustrates how the above change processes created new conditions for operational dynamics. The latter has been illustrated in field studies including Coleman (2015) and Holland's (2016) research into fund manager firms; Chen et al. (2014) and banks, Chen et al. (2016) financial analysts; and Holland's (2017) 'market for information'. The studies showed how a combination of knowledge-intensive intangibles and tangibles was integrated in bank/FI business models and value creation chains (IIRC 2013). They were mobilised to maximise the financial benefits from financial resources during financial transactions and intermediation. They exploited bank/FI ability to overcome problems of information and behaviour, risk management, and to enhance production and sale of bank/FI products with customers. They were used to control adverse and risky behaviour in the firm and market social networks. They created superior information collection and evaluation capabilities in decision teams, about financial transactions and portfolios of transactions, and enhanced the transformation of financial capital and its risks.

Finally, it can be noted that BTFF, consistent with the IIRC (2013) approach, is a basis to develop a coherent narrative of value creation in the financial firm based on an integrated view of use of intangible and financial resources. This can aid internal communications and support effective mobilisation of resources. It also forms an explanatory structure for informing corporate financial reports, and public and private narratives (Holland 2005). Thus, the BTFF indicates how top management can inform their reporting frameworks in a way that explicitly considers strategic and operational decisions. It seeks to explain how they are conducted to achieve financial value, risk, ESG and climate change aims.

Influencing Financial Firms to Achieve ESG Outcomes

This chapter argues that given historic problems, 'top teams' in financial firms will have to improve their management of, and reporting on, the strategic and operational dynamics discussed in the BTFF. External agents such as regulators, legislators and advisory policy bodies must encourage this. Internal and external agents will have to make explicit how learning, design and mobilisation of resources in the financial firm are expected to lead to behaviour that is economically valuable and socially acceptable relative to ESG aims.

Influencing Learning and Strategic Dynamics to Reflect ESG Issues

The BTFF provides a structured way to think how financial firms can adapt strategic and financial aims to include ESG aims. A key risk has involved the capability to learn and adapt fast enough to respond to change (Holland 2010). A formal and explicit approach to active bank/FI learning is required to develop new ESG-based expertise, understand complex interactions, remove barriers to change and reduce possibilities of ongoing problems or repeat of historic problems.

Learning experiences can be enhanced by exploiting various literature sources, exemplary cases, social networks and local expertise. They can be stimulated by engagement with the proposals and rules from the IIRC (2013), FSB (2017) and European Commission (2017b). The chapter argues that dynamic learning processes, barriers and problems must be openly discussed and disclosed in bank and FI reports, to ensure that a public debate is informed on these matters. Reporting has to be about changing structure and process as well as outcomes.

For example, literature sources can help 'top teams' make learning issues explicit in the financial firm and in their reports. Pedler et al. (1997) discussed empirical findings and theoretical analysis concerning learning in large organisations. These could be the basis for: 'good practice' guidance concerning bank learning, and bank disclosure on learning; all relative to financial and ESG aims. Field studies by Harris (2002), Antonacopoulou (2006), Chivers (2011) and Royal et al. (2012) provide more specific guidance for understanding and actively managing bank learning. These authors noted many bank/FI problems with learning such as inability to learn from prior errors and inability to exploit prior knowledge.

Active management of learning is required to overcome barriers to developing knowledge and technical capabilities. Sims et al. (2017) in their NRDC report on developing 'green banks' noted that many barriers exist to developing technical expertise. Smallridge et al. (2013, p. 2) identified technical barriers as: lack of ability to identify and classify 'climate-relevant' projects, problems in assessing the risk (financial, technological and other risks) of projects and need for greater understanding of innovative financing structures for projects. Prior knowledge of such learning barriers can help agents overcome them and provide a basis to report on barriers and proposed solutions.

Engagement with the International Integrated Reporting Council (IIRC 2013), EU directive on non-financial disclosures (2017a), and proposals by the FSB's on climate change disclosures (2017) can stimulate learning in financial firms on how to manage ESG issues and how to disclose information. The FSB task force in climate-related disclosure (2017) recommended that firms disclose information on: Governance, Strategy, Risk Management, Metrics and Targets. These categories provide a focus for reporting how the firms have learnt about change in these areas, the problems they faced, and the outcomes of decisions.

However, the FSB guidelines and EU rules are somewhat static in nature. They rely on principles, empirical themes and categories, and list of key factors and issues, all derived from practice. The BTFF can provide the conceptual frame to aid the advisory policy bodies and legislators to learn about dynamic interactions between their chosen themed areas and principles and to demand enhanced financial firm disclosure on these matters.

There is growing evidence of learning and change occurring in banks and financial firms concerning sustainability actions. IISD (2013) noted that there is:

> '…integration of environmental and social considerations into product design, mission policy and strategies. Examples include the integration of environmental criteria into lending and investment strategy, and the development of new products that provide environmental businesses with easier access to capital'. … and this '…has the potential to influence business on a larger scale. By integrating sustainability into a bank's business strategy and decision-making processes, institutions can support environmentally or socially responsible projects, innovative technologies and sustainable enterprises'.

Larsen and Tan (2015) and Larsen (2017) in their analysis of integrated reporting (IIRC 2013) in banking noted that interactions involved learning about various forms of capital and trade-offs between them.

> Bank employees engage in corporate social responsibility activities and in doing so increase the social and relationship capital (e.g. brand) at the expense of financial and human capital (cost of time spent).

Larsen and Tan (2015) also argued there are problems in interactions between social, knowledge and financial resources and hence in learning how to adapt bank's financial decisions and <IRs> to ESG issues.

> Through its lending decisions, a bank can impact indirectly its surrounding environment. If a borrower uses its borrowed funds to negatively impact the environment, the bank may have increased its short term financial capital at the long term expense of its social capital and possibly eventually its financial capital if it leads to a negative reaction with existing or prospective customers.

Larsen (2017) also noted problems when banks seek to develop <IRs> to report on innovation. These problems arise from a limited awareness of dynamics between change, learning, strategic choice, innovation and mobilisation of resources in value creation. Financial firms have to develop formal processes to learn about these dynamic interactions, value/risk outcomes, ESG outcomes and hence develop their managerial expertise and reporting capabilities on these matters.

Finally, the chapter argues that regulators, advisory policy bodies, legislators and 'top teams' must address how learning and the construction of bank and FI structures can be conducted to achieve constrained shareholder wealth maximising aims such as Porter and Kramer's (2011) idea of 'shared value' or the 'Group of 300' (2017) (of worldwide investors) view that social responsibilities have to be included in investment decisions. This would involve external regulation, stakeholder pressure, shareholder consent and internal 'top team' action to modify shareholder wealth aims relative to ESG aims.

Climate Change as an Example of Learning and Financial Firm Redesign

In a world of climate change, financial firms have to learn about 'hard' risks (physical, financial) and 'soft' risks (with say knowledge and social structures) and how they interact. They have to learn how to respond to these risks via financial firm design, use of resources, and informed actions and transactions. They have to learn how to report this to stakeholders. Those financial firms that can learn and act fast enough and effectively enough in 'hard' and 'soft' risk areas and can clearly report this are likely to maintain their reputations and the confidence of finance suppliers and users. As Coleman and La Plante (2016) note.

> As public awareness grows and perceptions about climate change evolve, banks should expect that continued misalignment of their financing and investment practices with the transition to a low carbon economy will lead to increased reputational risks.

'Hard' Risks

Since 2000, climate change has become a major issue in driving change in the finance system and financial firms. The UN, EU, FRA, FCA and Bank of England have emphasised that financial firms in insurance, banking, pensions and fund management have to be aware about and learn how physical risk from climate change impacts on their financial resources and their risks and how this could create a new financial crisis. Pavoni (2017) noted that scenario analysis is threatening for financial firms.

> Experts say to reach the goals of the Paris Agreement, the world needs to decarbonise very rapidly over next 20 years, which involves huge structural changes to.....anything that is carbon intensive......Switching off the use of fossil fuels would also entail making the infrastructure supporting that production redundant ...Lenders and investors in those sectors risk seeing loans unpaid and assets' value plummet

Hence, financial firms have to learn about catastrophe modelling concerning the estimated impact of climate change on physical assets, owned, financed and insured by financial firms. They have to learn how climate change could affect stochastic behaviour of financial resources such as correlations, fat tails and tail dependence risks and how this could undermine risk estimation and conventional risk management methods such as diversification and risk spreading in the financial firm and its markets (Coleman and La Plante 2016). They have to learn how regulators are likely to respond and how regulatory risks will arise. They will have to understand transition risks or how effective the response of citizens, regulators, financial firms and corporate customers is likely to be when making the transition to a low-carbon economy. Financial firms that can learn how to minimise their exposure to such risks may be able to reduce the losses and risks they face from mistaken financial decisions and disclose this to stakeholders.

'Soft' Risks

Much of the above has a strong emphasis on change in financial assets and liabilities and their risks. However, the same climate change factors also drive changes in the nature of the financial firm and its intangibles. They drive 'soft' risks (with say knowledge and social structures) and how they interact with financial risks. The change factors have an effect on top management, strategic dynamics and their design choices in the firm. As a result, they must now learn how to redesign their traditional activities to include ESG issues such as climate change. The history of change in financial firms (Holland 2010) and the IIRC (2013) suggests they must learn how to change many financial firm factors in a connected and coherent way.

'Designing in' 'green' or environmental dimensions requires many connected changes to intangible resource factors *such as* organisation, culture and ethics, functions and products. They must develop expertise in new green functions and products; associated customer relations, trust and knowledge; and green financing. They must learn how to integrate these functions, products and capabilities within the firm and collectively reorient these intangibles around new markets for green financing and investing. They must learn how to exploit these intangible resources in the transformation of financial capital and its risks. They must learn how to report to stakeholders the nature of these firm design decisions and explain how 'soft' risks arise in connected intangible areas.

Expertise has to be developed in specialist teams operating in new functions in fund supply and use markets. This includes specialist knowledge of green projects and products and of green financing mechanisms. A conservative policy would involve marginal adaptations to existing products (Pavoni 2017). Mortgage valuations could use information on energy efficiency in houses to forecast lower costs and hence lower expected default. Corporate clients could be encouraged to improve their sustainability reporting and scores, lower their perceived risks and as result expect to be charged lower interest rates.

Close customer relationship with green fund user and suppliers must be established to develop conditions of trust and commitment for green finance raising and investing. Carbon exposure of customers (funds supply and use) must be understood and based on in-depth analysis of economic activities by individuals, social groups, firms and industries.

New forms of 'green' organisation have to be developed. Market-oriented teams (green funds supply and use) and their expertise can be connected via new internal integrating functions, where the analysis of green impact and financial impact can be assessed in decision-making that jointly pursues financial profit and desirable green outcomes. These are means to create the information-rich context about customer needs and risk with green asset and liability products and make green financial intermediation possible.

Such reorganisation and redesign of the financial firm have been associated with major 'soft' risks (Holland 2010). The history of change reveals possibilities of culture clashes in financial firms between 'finance and wealth oriented' functions and 'green oriented' functions say in bank lending. Incentives, commitment and understanding may vary between these agents. Traders may find ways to use new green products for risky trading and front-line agents may mis-sell green products to customers. These potential problems can combine with rapid change to exacerbate problems of integration and control in the firm. Financial incentives may create barriers to internal communication and external disclosure using guidelines such as the IIRC (2013). The latter problems may arise because new organisational forms, 'relations', knowledge and culture cannot adapt fast enough relative to rapid change, and top management does not provide strategic and ethical leadership. Being aware of such possibilities with ESG change can improve financial firm decisions and reporting content.

Current Problems

Problems of learning have already been encountered in managing climate change and in disclosing information about 'hard' risks. (Pavoni 2017) notes that financial firms have begun to disclose their own carbon footprints but:

> … we struggle to get a grasp of the carbon footprint of our clients…….. Data availability is poor … there's no globally agreed methodology to calculate risk in financial institutions, in banks,….It's a challenge as we have lots of loans not only to stock listed companies that may disclose their carbon footprint but also to unlisted companies that do not disclose it. This is why we supported the TCFD in its call for disclosure. We wouldn't mind it if that voluntary call got tightened a bit more

The European Commission (p. 16, 2017b) report on financing a sustainable European economy noted many 'soft' risks. Financial firms faced problems in learning, developing business models, incentives schemes and understanding customers and products. They faced problems in disclosing information on these matters.

> .. There remains a lack of common definitions and metrics. The levels and quality of disclosure are insufficient to enable informed decision-making and oversight. Financial incentives and the business models of intermediaries are not yet fully aligned with sustainable development… financial institutions need to understand better the sustainability expectations of individual savers and investors…levels of sustainability literacy and expertise along the investment and lending chain are often inadequate

The experience of specialised financial firms such as Green Investment Banks (GIBs) shows how conventional financial firms can, in part, overcome such problems and report this to stakeholders. The UK GIB illustrates how a financial firm can learn and develop new forms of organisation to deliver a range of equity and debt 'green' financing methods and advisory services. This can be achieved in firms when acting as a bank lender, investment bank equity provider, venture capital supplier and fund manager. The UK GIB 2016 report noted (p. 22):

> We have established a flexible Group structure which allows us to invest in different ways to maximise our direct impact and mobilise private sector investment in green infrastructure

The UK GIB has sought to develop its culture through a 'GIB Community' staff volunteering programme, a staff well-being and resilience lunch and learn programme, and by delivering company-wide training on unconscious bias. The plan for culture change is audited, and evidence is sought for progress and outlined in the financial report (2015–2106 report, p 28).

The experience of GIBs shows how financial firms can learn and develop technical expertise. Expertise included knowledge embodied in specialist investing routines, valuation methods, organisation process and culture for a 'green financial firms'. Lyon (2017) viewed the UK GIB as 'a cluster of expertise' with 'specialism, experimentation and rapid learning informing a range of finance forms' and forming 'Skills in due diligence in less well known sectors'. Networks such as the 'Green Bank Network' (2017) seek to accelerate learning about 'green financing' amongst members and,

> .. aims to 'collect, organize and share Green Bank know-how through virtual and in-person platforms to facilitate the exchange of information. .. GBN aims to .....driving standardization of deal structures, contracts and metrics; increasing visibility and transparency of Green Banks; and tracking progress made with key indicators....these activities will increase the scale, scope and efficiency of .. infrastructure finance

The OECD report (2016) noted that GIBs overcame barriers to learning, information and risk perceptions, by hiring financial professionals with local and national expertise;

> in low-carbon technologies, projects and investments, and an understanding of the specific risk-return appetites of local financial institutions and other investors such as institutional investors. This local expertise provides informational advantages that can be leveraged to overcome investment barriers, which are often location-specific

The above practices developed in GIBs could inform a model for change and learning in conventional financial firms seeking to develop ESG dimensions. Reporting practices in specialist green financial firms such as GIBs provide benchmarks for firms seeking to develop their own reports on 'hard' and 'soft' risks.

Influencing Operational Dynamics to Reflect ESG Issues

In terms of *operational dynamics* in the financial firm, the BTFF suggests new ideas about the nature of tangible and intangible resources and how they are mobilised in financial intermediation. For mobilisation to be effective, 'top teams', regulators and policy advisors must exercise influence: over key intangibles factors, how they are connected to each other, and their combined impact on how agents transact and behave. This includes using 'green oriented' organisational structures and processes to mobilise other intangible factors: *such as corporate governance mechanisms, green expertise and culture,* to achieve their desired and combined impact on front-line staff and customers. Such resource mobilisation has to be continuously driven by top teams through internal hierarchy and external networks, via processes for information production and control (Holland 2016). This can create desirable conditions (information, behaviour) for successful financial transacting and transformation of financial resources; consistent with desired 'green' outcomes; as well as for financial risk and value outcomes. The resource mobilisation process has to be a key part of firm reporting and has to be disclosed in an explicit, connected and integrated way as suggested by the International Integrated Reporting Council (IIRC) (2013). The following briefly explores these issues.

The GIB example illustrates how 'green' knowledge can be embedded in many aspects of the financial firm and mobilised in financial intermediation. Sims et al. (2017, p. 2) noted the central role of tailored knowledge in mobilising resources in GIBs. This illustrates how conventional financial firms can become ESG aware.

> Existing GIBs have demonstrated that a key to their success is having in-house dedicated technical expertise. This expertise has given them a

> fuller and deeper technical understanding of the attributes of new technologies, which… informs their approach to financing. Existing GIBs have used this strategy to increase understanding of the risks and opportunities presented by new mitigation technologies, such as residential solar, offshore wind, energy storage, and electric vehicles

Financial firms have historically mobilised social and knowledge resources in their financial transacting with 'relationship' customers. They have done this to reduce risk and improve financial performance and to maintain their relationship, trust, reputation and future business with customers (Holland 1993). In a world of increasing financial return and 'green' pressures, they have sought to reduce their exposure to liabilities arising from environmental risk problems, arising with their core customers (Pavoni 2017). For example, the IISD (2013) noted that banks sought to reduce financial exposure and improve risk management by looking closely at the environmental performance of their clients.

Financial firms have traditionally mobilised culture as major social resource: to influence internal norms, behaviours and actions and to enhance reputation with relationship customers. Trang (2016) notes that links exist between bank culture and performance and:

> Understanding .. linkages between strategy, structure and culture is key to top performance. Everyone must be familiar with the company direction, who does what and where as well as the values and beliefs to which employees must stay true….In light of technology and globalization, many banks implement new strategies and structures but ignore the cultural aspects, falsely believing culture will develop itself and align with business needs.

Bank 'Top teams', regulators and policy advisory bodies have historically been aware of the significance of financial firm culture and how changes can affect financial risk and performance. However, the GFC experience and increasing ESG pressures (especially climate change) have stimulated new demands to make explicit how culture is mobilised. Regulators such as the FCA (2015), BSB (2016) and G30 (2015) seek to influence and change existing bank culture and behaviour and its impact during ongoing transactions. They do so in the interests of fair dealing with customers and clients and effective functioning of markets. They seek to change culture with respect to ideas of perceived 'good practice', such as embedding desired values and ethics, adopting matching incentive schemes and using 'whistle blowing' methods. The focus of regulators is on bank boards and top management. The intention is that top teams promote desired culture norms to influence behaviour relative to ESG aims. The intention is that top teams will use culture to exercise the required influence on middle management and front and back offices, their incentive schemes, behaviour and actions. The intention is that they will generate full and complete disclosure on these matters.

The Need for Transparency

The chapter has noted the presence of historic and ongoing barriers to change in financial firms (Holland 2010, 2016). This suggests that barriers are likely to arise with proposed ESG change in financial firms and when reporting on these issues. Primary responses have to be improvements in understanding financial firms and in their transparency. The BTFF is intended to boost understanding. Improved understanding and transparency have been proposed by International Integrated Reporting Council (IIRC 2013), EU directive on non-financial disclosures (2017a) and the Financial Standards Board in their 'task force on climate related disclosure' (2017).

The BTFF and IIRC proposals are different but related approaches to understanding the role of intangibles in value creation in the firm and communication of this to stakeholders. They differ in their evidence sources and ways of constructing connected concepts. This creates opportunities to learn from each other. For example, Larsen and Tan (2015) have explored how to develop <IR> in banking. This work can provide new empirical insights to develop the BTFF. Larsen (2017) noted problems when banks seek to develop <IRs> ito report on innovation. The BTFF can provide the means to expand the conceptual frame to consider: the dynamics between change, learning, strategic choice, mobilisation of resources and their combined roles in value creation and innovation (Holland 2016).

Financial firms can use the BTFF as an alternative conceptual means to critically evaluate their integrated reports (Larsen 2017), to make explicit the nature of intangible resources, their interactions and use in financial intermediation for financial value and ESG outcomes. The UK GIB case illustrates how knowledge and social resources are used in green financing and reporting. These sources can be used by financial firms to support <IR> development to explain how resources are mobilised to reflect ESG and financial aims. Such adapted <IRs> could be used by financial firms to develop the content of their (mandatory) EU Directive reports on non-financial disclosures (European Commission 2017a). Bodies such as the IIRC (2013) and FSB (2017) could use the BTFF analysis of problems and barriers to change, as part of their critical frame when developing guidelines about bank/FI reporting, and when pressurising bank/FIs to change in the desired direction. Such combinations of law (EU), voluntary guidelines (IIRC, FSB) and theory (BTFF) have potential to strengthen disclosure activity when backed by strong desire to change.

Summary

This chapter sought to analyse ESG change issues in financial firms and propose a coherent response. The chapter used a 'Behavioral theory of the financial firm' (BTTF) to explore historic problems in banks and FIs and analyse current problems when implementing ESG changes. The chapter has illustrated how 'top teams', advisory policy bodies, legislators and regulators can use the BTFF to inform their actions and change proposals. This can support an integrated view of the financial firm and encourage a coherent pursuit of financial and ESG aims throughout the financial firm. Such actions should be adopted to match the needs of stakeholders, to improve reporting and hence improve legitimacy of the financial firm (DiMaggio and Powell 1991) with stakeholders (Guthrie and Parker 1990).

References

Antonacopoulou, E. (2006). The relationship between individual and organizational learning. *Management Learning, 37,* 455–473.

Barney, J. (1991). Firm resources and sustained competitive advantage. *Journal of Management, 17*(1), 99–120.

BSB. (2016, March). *Banking standards board.* Available at: http://www.bankingstandardsboard.org.uk/banking-standards-board-publishes-first-annual-review/.

Chahal, H., & Bakshi, P. (2015). Examining intellectual capital and competitive advantage relationship. *International Journal of Bank Marketing, 33*(3), 376–399.

Chen, L., Danbolt, J., & Holland, J. (2014). Rethinking bank business models: The role of intangibles. *Accounting, Auditing, and Accountability Journal, 27*(3), 563–589.

Chen, L., Danbolt, J., & Holland, J. (2016). *Analyst information intermediation and the role of knowledge and social forces in the 'market for information'.* Presented at APIRA Melbourne.

Chivers, G. (2011). Supporting informal learning by traders in investment banks. *Journal of European Industrial Training, 35*(2), 154–175.

Coleman, L. (2015). Facing up to fund managers: An exploratory field study of how institutional investors make decisions. *Qualitative Research in Financial Markets, 7*(2), 111–135.

Coleman, T., & La Plante, A. (2016). *Climate change: Why financial institutions should take note.* Global Risk Institute: Toronto. Available at: http://globalriskinstitute.org/publications/climate-change-why-financial-institutions-should-take-note/.

Cyert, R., & March, J. (1963). *A behavioral theory of the firm.* New York: Prentice-Hall.

DiMaggio, J., & Powell, W. (1991). Introduction. In W. W. Powell & P. J. DiMaggio (Eds.), *The new institutionalism in organizational analysis.* Chicago: Chicago University Press.

Etzion, D., & Ferraro, F. (2010). The role of analogy in the institutionalization of sustainability reporting. *Organization Science, 21*(5), 1092–1107. Available at: https://www.mcgill.ca/desautels/files/desautels/the_role_of_analogy_in_the_institutionalization_of_sustainability_reporting_0.pdf.

European Commission. (2011). *A renewed EU strategy 2011–2014 for corporate social responsibility.* Available at: http://eur-lex.europa.eu/legal-content/EN/TXT/PDF/?uri=CELEX:52011DC0681&from=EN.

European Commission. (2017a). *Guidelines on disclosure of non-financial information*. Brussels. Available at: https://ec.europa.eu/transparency/regdoc/rep/3/2017/EN/C-2017-4234-F1-EN-MAIN-PART-1.PDF.

European Commission. (2017b, July). *Financing a sustainable European economy, interim report*. By the high-level expert group on sustainable finance. Available at: https://ec.europa.eu/info/sites/info/files/170713-sustainable-finance-report_en.pdf.

FCA. (2015, July 7). *Senior bank management held accountable in responsibility area*. Available at: https://www.fca.org.uk/news/fca-publishes-final-rules-to-make-those-in-the-banking-sector-more-accountable.

FSB. (2017). *Recommendations of the task force on climate-related financial disclosures*. Basel: BIS. Available at: https://www.fsb-tcfd.org/wp-content/uploads/2017/06/Press-Release-FSB-Task-Force-publishes-recommendations-on-climate-related-financial-disclosures-29-June-2017.pdf.

Gray, R., Kouhy, R., & Lavers, S. (1995). Corporate social and environmental reporting. *Accounting, Auditing & Accountability Journal, 8*(2), 47–77.

Green Bank Network. (2017). Available at: http://greenbanknetwork.org/about-gbn/.

Group of Thirty (G30). (2015, July). *Banking conduct and culture*. Washington.

Group of 300. (2017). Available at: https://www.the300club.org/white-papers/.

Guthrie, J., & Parker L. (1990). Corporate social disclosure practice. *Advances in Public Interest Accounting, 3*, 159–173.

Harris, L. (2002). The learning organisation—Myth or reality? *The Learning Organisation, 9*(2), 78–88.

Holland, J. (1993). Bank-corporate relations—Change issues in the international enterprise. *Accounting and Business Research, 23*(91), 273–283.

Holland, J. (2005). A grounded theory of corporate disclosure. *Accounting and Business Research, 35*(3), 249–267.

Holland, J. (2010). Banks, knowledge and crisis: A case of knowledge and learning failure. *Journal of Financial Regulation and Compliance, 18*(2), 87–105.

Holland, J. (2016). A behavioural theory of the fund management firm. *European Journal of Finance, 22*(11), 1004–1039.

Holland, J. (2017). The market for information. *Qualitative Research in Financial Markets, 9*(3), 263–291.

Holland, J. (2018). A new approach to research and theory development for financial firms. *Journal of Financial Regulation and Compliance* (forthcoming).

International Integrated Reporting Council (IIRC). (2013). *The international integrated reporting framework*. London, UK: International Integrated Reporting Council.

International Institute for Sustainable Development (IISD). (2013). *Sustainable banking*. Available at: https://www.iisd.org/business/banking/sus_banking.aspx.

Larsen, M., & Tan, S. (2015, August). *Applying the integrated reporting concept of 'capitals' in the banking industry*. Published on behalf of Banking Network.

Larsen, M. (2017, March). *Innovation in banking—Are we communicating the value created?* Published on behalf of <IR> Banking Network.

Lyon, F., (2017), "*Filling the finance gap for sustainable prosperity: The challenge for green entrepreneurial finance*", 16th FRAP and 2nd SSFII, 25th Sept 2017, Hughes Hall, Cambridge University.

Meritum. (2002). *Guidelines for managing and reporting on intangibles* (Intellectual capital report). Tucson, AZ.

OECD. (2016). *Green investment banks*. http://www.oecd.org/environment/cc/Green-Investment-Banks-POLICY-PERSPECTIVES-web.pdf.

Pavoni, S. (2017, September 1). Will climate change cause the next financial crisis? *The Banker*.

Pedler, M., Burgoyne, J., & Boydell, T. (1997). *The learning company* (2nd ed.). London: McGraw Hill.

Porter, M., & Kramer, M. (2011, January–February). The big idea: Creating shared value, rethinking capitalism. *Harvard Business Review*.

Royal, C., & Rowley, C. (2012, May 22). *Knowledge acquisition in investment banking*. London: Cass Business School, City University.

Shih, K., Chang, C., & Lin, B. (2010). Assessing knowledge creation and intellectual capital in banking industry. *Journal of Intellectual Capital, 11*(1), 74–89.

Sims, D., Dougherty, S., & Bergöö, B. (2017). NRDC, *national development banks and green investment banks*. Available at: https://www.nrdc.org/sites/default/files/national-development-banks.pdf.

Smallridge, D., et al. (2013). *The role of national development banks in catalyzing international climate finance*. Washington, DC: Inter-American Development Bank.

Trang, D. (2016). *Has bank culture changed to ensure ethical behavior?* Seven Pillars Institute. Available at: http://sevenpillarsinstitute.org/case-studies/has-bank-culture-changed-to-ensure-ethical-behavior.

UK GIB. (2016). *UK Green Investment Bank plc, annual report and accounts, 2015–16*. Available at: https://www.gov.uk/government/uploads/system/uploads/attachment_data/file/537293/gib-annual-report-2015-16-web.pdf.

UN. (2015). *Trends in private sector climate finance*. Available at: http://www.un.org/climatechange/wp-content/uploads/2015/10/SG-TRENDS-PRIVATE-SECTOR-CLIMATE-FINANCE-AW-HI-RES-WEB1.pdf.

UNEP. (2016). *Greening the banking system—Taking stock of G20 green banking market practice*. Available at: http://wedocs.unep.org/bitstream/handle/20.500.11822/10604/greening_banking_system.pdf?sequence=1&isAllowed=y.

Part II

Sustainability Assurance

Sustainability Assurance: Who Are the Assurance Providers and What Do They Do?

Muhammad Bilal Farooq and Charl de Villiers

Introduction

Assurance is defined as "an engagement in which a practitioner aims to obtain sufficient appropriate evidence in order to express a conclusion designed to enhance the degree of confidence of the intended users other than the responsible party about the subject matter information" (IAASB[1] 2013, p. 7). The IAASB definition highlights the tripartite nature of assurance engagements, i.e. (1) a responsible party, (2) an assurance provider (independent expert), and (3) an intended user.

M. B. Farooq (✉)
Auckland University of Technology, Auckland, New Zealand
e-mail: muhammad.farooq@aut.ac.nz

C. de Villiers
The University of Auckland, Auckland, New Zealand
e-mail: charl.devilliers@auckland.ac.nz

C. de Villiers
University of Pretoria, Pretoria, South Africa

S. Arvidsson (ed.), *Challenges in Managing Sustainable Business*,
https://doi.org/10.1007/978-3-319-93266-8_6

Using the IAASB definition, Farooq and De Villiers (2017) define sustainability assurance as an engagement in which a third-party sustainability assurance provider (SAP) is recruited to undertake assurance over a sustainability report. The responsible party in this instance is the reporting organisation (or more specifically the board of directors[2]), and the intended users are the readers of the sustainability report. What this means is that the SAP is recruited to evaluate the sustainability report, which has been prepared by the board of directors, and to provide an opinion (an assurance opinion) on whether or not that sustainability report has been prepared according to an agreed criteria (e.g. sustainability reporting standards) to the users of the sustainability report. The SAPs opinion is designed to enhance the confidence (i.e. provide assurance) of the users of the sustainability report; i.e., users are provided comfort that the sustainability report is credible.

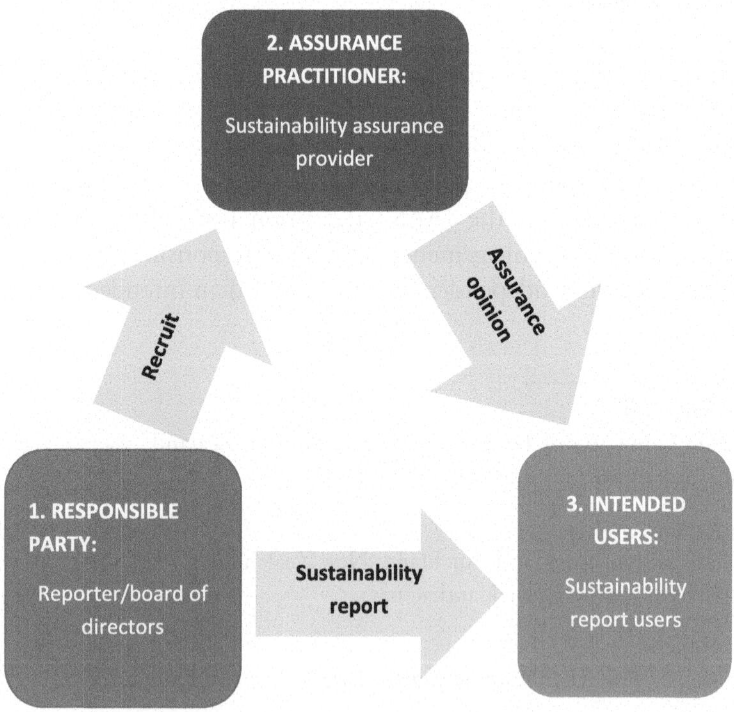

Fig. 1 The three parties involved in a sustainability assurance engagement

Figure 1 provides a summary of the relationship between (1) a responsible party, (2) an assurance provider (independent expert), and (3) an intended user in a sustainability assurance engagement.

However, sustainability assurance is still a voluntary undertaking in most jurisdictions, and the market is open to different types of SAPs who compete for a share of the market. As a result, there is no consensus on who should undertake sustainability assurance services or how (i.e. approach) the engagement should be undertaken. This gives rise to a number of challenges both for the field and assurance providers on the one hand, and organisations that seek to secure sustainability assurance services on the other (i.e. sustainability reporters). The following section examines these different types of SAPs, their competencies and the different approaches they use. The issues and challenges that are facing sustainability assurance providers and sustainability assurance seekers are also discussed.

Sustainability Assurance Provider Types

The market for SA is open to competition and as a result, a range of different providers are found competing for a share of the market. It is estimated that there are over 350 different types of SAPs operating in the market today (CorporateRegister.com Limited 2008). However, scholars and experts often categorise these SAPs into two broad groups comprising of accounting (ASAPs) and non-accounting SAPs (NASAPs) (Edgley et al. 2015; Manetti and Toccafondi 2012). ASAPs comprise of primary the big four accounting firms including PwC, E&Y International, Deloitte and KPMG. These accounting firms have traditionally focused on providing their clients with financial audit services.[3] However, facing an increasingly saturated financial audit market, which offers low growth potential and coupled with higher audit risk, financial audit firms are expanding their services and entering new assurance markets such as sustainability assurance (Ackers 2009; Wallage 2000).

The study by O'Dwyer et al. (2011) provides an interesting account of the types of strategies adopted by these accounting firms as they attempt to develop legitimacy for this new form of assurance amongst external stakeholder (i.e. users of sustainability reports and reporting organisations) and internal stakeholder (risk and quality control functions) groups. ASAPs attempted to demonstrate to client managers how sustainability assurance is a value-added service. With intended users, ASAPs highlighted how sustainability assurance was necessary in order to enhance the credibility of sustainability reports. Finally, with internal stakeholders, the aim was to demonstrate how the firm's exposure to reputational and legal risk was being minimised.

However, accounting firms traditional market base (i.e. financial audit services) is a highly regulated space. Accounting firms enjoy a monopolistic position protected by government regulation which prohibits anyone other than accounting firms from offering financial audit services (Elliott 1998). However, this is not the case with sustainability assurance, and accounting firms have found themselves facing tough competition from a range of assurance providers of a non-accounting background, i.e. NASAPs (Wallage 2000). Unlike ASAPs, NASAPs represent a more diverse group of assurance providers and include multinational engineering consultancies and certification providers, locally operated sustainability consultancies and other assurance providers[4] (CorporateRegister.com Limited 2008; Perego and Kolk 2012; Simnett et al. 2009).

However, ASAPs control a majority share of the sustainability assurance market. For example, the KPMG (2015) survey found that 63% (compared to 53% in 2013) of the world's largest 250 companies secured external assurance over their sustainability reports. The survey also examined sustainability assurance rates amongst the largest 100 companies in 45 different countries (referred to as N100 by KPMG) and found that on average 42% (compared to 38% in 2013) of these companies opted to secure external independent assurance. The report further shows that ASAPs dominate the market with 65% of the global 250 companies (down from 70% in 2013) opting to select an accounting firm for their sustainability assurance work. A similar situation exists amongst the smaller reporters with 64% of the N100 (down from 67% in 2013) opting to select an ASAP.[5]

Reviewing the literature on sustainability assurance, Farooq and De Villiers (2017) identify six areas where ASAPs and NASAPs are different. These are discussed below.

Knowledge of Assurance, Client Operations and Sustainability Reporting

Assurance providers must have knowledge and expertise of (1) assurance and assurance procedures, (2) their clients industry, business and operations, and (3) the subject matter of the assurance engagement, i.e. sustainability (Adams and Evans 2004). Scholars debate over which groups of SAPs have the required expertise (whether absolutely or relative to the other group) and should therefore be given preference over their rivals. However, it appears that neither ASAPs nor NASAPs tick all three boxes according to scholars. For example, while accountants are argued to have a relative expertise over NASAPs in the field of assurance, having acquired this expertise through years of providing financial audit services (Gray 2000), it is doubtful that they have the edge over NASAPs when it comes to knowledge over the subject of assurance, i.e. sustainability. Here, environmentalists, biologists, ethicists and sociologists (i.e. NASAPs) would have the edge over accountants/ASAPs (Gray 2000). Consequently, experts recommend that ASAPs employ non-accountants to fill this knowledge gap and to use multi-disciplinary teams of accountants and non-accountants on sustainability assurance engagements (Wallage 2000). In this way, the two groups can complement one another and better fulfil the requirements of the sustainability assurance engagement (Jones and Solomon 2010).

Elliott (1998) argues that in the long run accountants will need to acquire new skills to keep up with the changes in organisational reporting. To support the accounting profession in this area accounting academics in universities and colleges to update their curriculum in order to better prepare the accountants of tomorrow. These efforts are necessary if the accounting profession wishes to discard its old image of financial accountants and financial auditors to a new one which portrays accountants playing a broader role in organisations and society.

In terms of knowledge of the reporting entities industry, business and operations it is argued that ASAPs would have an edge over NASAPs. Since it is likely that ASAPs will also be employed to undertake the financial audits, ASAPs will have an edge over NASAPs in this regard. This argument is supported by Gillet (2012) who found that some reporters preferred to recruit an ASAP as the same ASAP (or accounting firm) was also engaged to undertake the financial audit and was thus already familiar with their reporters industry, business and operations (Gillet 2012). Consequently, many reporters prefer to not rotate that their SAP too frequently, and in many cases the SAP was engaged for more than 5 consecutive years (Park and Brorson 2005).

Size Advantage of ASAPs

The size of SAPs and the impact this has on the quality of sustainability assurance services offered has also been the target of much discussion. As Perego and Kolk (2012) point out, not all SAPs are of the size necessary to take on the assurance of large multinational corporations. Here, the big four accounting first (i.e. ASAPs), with their global presence, have an advantage over many NASAPs. These large assurance providers can use their size to their advantage by achieving economies of scale which can translate into lower assurance costs and thus lower fees charged to clients (Mock et al. 2013; Simnett et al. 2009). It is also argued that ASAPs can use their resources to invest in research and development, thereby contributing to new and innovative assurance technologies. However, many NASAPs, especially, large multinational engineering consultancies and certification providers argue that they too operate at a global scale and can achieve the same size advantages as those claimed by ASAPs.

Independence and Objectivity

As discussed in Section one, it is important for the SAP to be independent from the responsible party (i.e. reporting entity). A lack of independence will affect the SAPs ability to carry out the engagement in an objective manner thus compromising the quality of the work done and potentially issuing a misleading opinion to the users of the sustainability report. Some academics argue that given ASAPs experience with conducting financial audits, they have a better understanding of assurance and thus the need to maintain independence and objectivity than NASAPs (Gray 2000). Furthermore, ASAPs are members of a professional accounting body and will be aware of the need to ensure that they adhere to the requirements of a code of ethical conduct (Gray 2000). Such ethical codes clearly state the requirement for assurance providers to maintain their independence and to safeguard against certain threats which may affect their objectivity. However, the reputation of accountants as independent and objective assurance providers has been hurt by recent corporate accounting scandals such as the Enron and Arthur Anderson case (Dando and Swift 2003). Finally, scholars argue that ASAPs given their larger size, there is a less likelihood of them becoming dependent on any one client for their income (Perego and Kolk 2012; Simnett et al. 2009). Although there again, it must be remembered that some NASAPs are also large and have a diverse set of clients and are thus less likely to be dependent on anyone client for a major share of their income.

Stakeholder Perspectives on Sustainability Assurance Providers

Stakeholder views and perspectives on SAPs have also been examined within the academic literature. For example, Wong and Millington (2014) conducted a telephone survey in which 147 individuals[6] were asked a series of closed-ended questions on their preference towards SAP types. They found that these stakeholders leaned more towards NASAPs. When asked why two major reasons were identified. First, these stakeholders believed that it was important for an assurance provider to be independent and that ASAPs/accountants/accounting profession had lost their image of being independent assurance providers due to recent high-profile corporate scandals such as the Enron/Arthur Anderson incident. Second, these stakeholders placed a higher emphasis on knowledge over the subject matter of sustainability assurance (i.e. expertise in sustainability) than knowledge of how to conduct the sustainability assurance engagement itself (i.e. expertise in assurance procedures).

Interestingly, in a study by Jones and Solomon (2010), a different result was observed. Jones and Solomon (2010) interviewed managers responsible for preparing sustainability reports.[7] They found that these managers preferred to recruit an ASAP. The reasons for this preference were twofold. First, these managers believed that sustainability assurance is the same as a financial audit and thus it made sense to recruit an accountant to do the assurance work. Additionally, sustainability reporting managers believed that since the financial auditor/accountant had already studied their organisation, industry and operations as part of the financial audit, they would not need to do so again for the purpose of the sustainability assurance engagement. As a result, there would be benefits for the reporter in terms of lower assurance time and cost as well as an ease in terms of coordination (Huggins et al. 2011). These findings indicate that while internal stakeholders (i.e. sustainability reporting managers) prefer to recruit ASAPs, external stakeholders (such as those interviewed by Wong and Millington 2014) prefer to recruit NASAPs.

Impact on Sustainability Report Quality

The demand for sustainability assurance is a result of organisational stakeholders expressing scepticism over the credibility of published sustainability reports. However, does sustainability assurance actually improve the quality of published sustainability reports? Answers to this question can be found in a study undertaken by Moroney et al. (2012) who examine the quality of environmental reporting by Australian companies. They compared the quality of assured and non-assured environmental reports to assess if there were differences in the quality of disclosure. Their study indicates that assured environmental reports achieve a higher quality score than non-assured environmental reports. They also found that the quality of environmental reports improves over time; i.e., reporters learn and this learning is also partly responsible for improvements in quality.

However, they found that the SAP type had no impact on the quality of environmental reports. Although, environmental reports assured by NASAPs tended to have more soft/qualitative content then environmental reports assured by ASAPs. Moroney et al. (2012) speculate that this could be due to accountants training and traditional preference to assure only hard/quantitative data. Accountants are less comfortable providing assurance over the soft side of sustainability reports as this information is less easily verified. Thus, accountants appear to be adopting a more cautionary approach to sustainability assurance.

Approach to Conducting Sustainability Assurance Engagements

There are numerous standards available that provide guidance to SAPs on how to conduct the sustainability assurance engagement (Wallage 2000). This plethora of standards and guidelines are a result of the voluntary nature of sustainability assurance and indicate the lack of consensus on how sustainability assurance engagement should be undertaken (Dando and Swift 2003). However, as the field matures, there is a trend towards greater standardisation and consistency in approach to perform in sustainability assurance services. Over time, the use of internationally recognised sustainability assurance standards has increased from 18% in 2002–2004 to 45% in 2006–2007 while the use of national or local standards and guidelines decreased from 15.4 to 8% during the same period Mock et al. (2013).[8] These international sustainability assurance standards include the International Standards on Assurance Engagements (ISAE3000) and AA1000 Assurance Standard (AA1000AS)[9] (Kolk and Perego 2010; O'Dwyer and Owen 2005; Perego 2009). However, scholars argue that the scope of these two standards varies, and therefore these standards may be more complementary in nature than rival standards or substitutes for one another (Manetti and Toccafondi 2012; O'Dwyer and Owen 2007).

The former was developed by the International Audit and Assurance Standards Board (IAASB), an internal accounting body which develops audit and assurance standards for the accounting profession (Deegan et al. 2006a). Consequently, the standard draws heavily on financial auditing concepts, principles and procedures (O'Dwyer et al. 2011). However, ISAE3000 is a generic standard that has been developed for assurance engagements which do not involve an audit of financial statements (IAASB 2013; Manetti and Becatti 2009; Smith et al. 2011). The standard refers two types of assurance engagements. The first includes reasonable assurance engagements in which the SAP offers high level of assurance. The second includes limited assurance engagements in which a low level of assurance is provided to sustainability report users (Hasan et al. 2003). SAPs are also allowed to provide different levels of assurance for different sections of the sustainability report (Wallage 2000).

The second sustainability assurance, AA1000AS, was developed by AccountAbility a London-based global sustainability consultancy[10] (AccountAbility 2015). The AA1000AS is a specialist standard developed specifically for sustainability assurance engagements (Manetti and Becatti 2009; Perego and Kolk 2012). The standard distinguishes two types of sustainability assurance engagements, referred to as Type 1 and Type 2 engagements (AccountAbility 2008a). The scope of a Type 1 engagement is narrow, and the SAP provides assurance over both the SAP provides assurance over reporters application of the AA1000APS sustainability principles of inclusivity, materiality and responsiveness (AccountAbility 2008b). In comparison, Type 2 engagements are broader in scope, and the SAP assesses (and provides assurance over) both the reporters application of AccountAbility's sustainability principles as well as the credibility of the sustainability report (Table 1).

Numerous researchers have evaluated the quality of SAPs sustainability assurance statements against the requirements of the standards such as ISAE3000 and AA1000AS (Ball et al. 2000; Belal 2002; Cooper and Owen 2007; Deegan et al. 2006a, b; Gray 2000; Manetti and Becatti 2009; O'Dwyer and Owen 2005, 2007; Segui-Mas et al. 2015). Overall, the conclusion from these studies is that sustainability assurance statements suffer from poor quality and there is significant room for improvement. Additionally, the findings from these studies shed

Table 1 A summary of the six points from Farooq and De Villiers (2017)

Issue	ASAPs	NASAPs
Knowledge of assurance, client operations and sustainability	Because of their experience providing financial audit services, ASAPs are viewed as assurance experts Additionally, given that ASAPs audit the reporting entities financial statements, they acquire a detailed and comprehensive understanding of reporters operations which can beneficial in the sustainability assurance engagement	NASAPs have an advantage over accountants in that they have a better understanding of the subject of sustainability assurance, i.e. sustainability
Role of size	The big four accounting firms operate at a global level and can use their size to achieve economies of scale as well as investing in research and development in auditing	Most NASAPs operate at a local or national level and thus find it hard to compete against the big four. However, global certification providers and consultancies argue that they too operate on a global scale and can leverage similar benefits
SAP independence and objectivity	ASAPs argue that independence and objectivity are the hallmark of their profession, and they understand these issues better than NASAPs	NASAPs argue that accountants have tarnished their reputation in a post-Enron world and are unable to maintain their independence
Stakeholder perspectives on SAP types	Internal stakeholders view sustainability assurance as the same as or similar to a financial statements audit and thus the rightful role of accountants	External stakeholders prefer to recruit NASAPs because they believe that subject matter expertise is more important and that Enron type incidents reveal that accountants are not capable of maintaining their independence
Impact of SAP type on sustainability report quality	There is no evidence, as yet, to suggest that the type of SAP has any impact on the quality of sustainability reports published	Same
Approach to conducting sustainability assurance	ASAPs use ISAE3000 when conducting sustainability assurance engagements. This standard identifies limited and reasonable scope engagements	NASAPs use AA1000AS when conducting sustainability assurance engagements. This standard classifies sustainability assurance engagements into Type 1 and Type 2

Table 2 A summary of the key findings from the literature analysing sustainability assurance statements

Area examined	Findings
Who are the sustainability assurance statements addressed?	Interestingly sustainability assurance statements are addressed to the reporting entities management or board of directors. This is puzzling given that the sustainability report is designed for stakeholders and that sustainability assurance is designed to provide comfort to external stakeholders in the credibility of sustainability reports prepared by management or the board of directors
The scope and objectives of sustainability assurance engagements	A range of different engagements of varying scope and objectives are being undertaken. The most common objective is to simply verify the reliability of the content of sustainability reports and is popular amongst ASAPs. In such engagements, no assurance is given over the overall balance of these documents (i.e. do reporters provide information over material bad news?). However, NASAPs appear more willing to provide assurance over disclosure reliability and balance
Assurance over materiality	As discussed above, SAPs tend to focus more on assessing the reliability of sustainability report content and appear to shy away from offering assurance over materiality (including the reporting entities stakeholder engagement processes). This trend is more common amongst ASAPs than NASAPs
Assurance procedures undertaken	Some SAPs provide detailed information (e.g. one page) over the nature, timing and extent of audit and assurance procedures they undertake while others will simply provide a summary paragraph of the same. However, studies find that both ASAPs and NASAPs adopt relatively the same audit procedures to achieve their engagement goals

(continued)

Table 2 (continued)

Area examined	Findings
The use of an assurance standard	Interestingly, some sustainability assurance statements made no reference to a sustainability assurance standard. In other engagements, two or more standards were being used in combination. This indicates that ISAE3000 and AA1000 are perhaps more complementary in nature than substitutes
Assurance opinion expressed by the SAP	ASAPs assurance opinion used primarily the words accuracy and reliability of sustainability report content. In comparison, NASAPs assurance opinion used words like completeness and balance in addition to accuracy and reliability
The provision of recommendations	It is common for SAPs to issue recommendations within their assurance statements. This practice has generated criticisms as expert's comment that sustainability assurance is less assurance and more advisory in nature. However, this practice was more common amongst NASAPs than it was in ASAPs

light on the differences in ASAPs and NASAPs approach to sustainability assurance. These studies find that ASAPs prefer to use ISAE3000 while NASAPs lean more towards AA1000AS. Furthermore, ASAPs will tend to focus more on providing assurance over the reliability of sustainability report content while NASAPs appear willing to provide assurance over content reliability as well as the overall balance of the sustainability report.[11] However, the detailed assurance procedures used by ASAPs and NASAPs to achieve these objectives are broadly the same (Table 2).

Conclusion

In conclusion, the market for sustainability assurance is unregulated and as a result, a range of different sustainability assurance providers compete for work. These providers can be classified into accounting and non-accounting sustainability assurance providers. The literature in this field examines at least six areas/issues, including the knowledge requirements for sustainability assurance providers, the size advantage that some practitioners possess, the independence and objectivity of practitioners, internal and external stakeholder preferences for assurance provider, the impact of sustainability assurance on the quality of sustainability reporting, and practitioners approach to sustainability assurance. The discussion explores the differences and similarities between accounting and non-accounting sustainability assurance providers and the implications of this for both sustainability assurance providers and the sustainability reporting entities.

Notes

1. The International Audit and Assurance Standards Board (IAASB) is a sub body of the International Federation of Accountants or IFAC.
2. A board of directors would be the responsible party if the reporter's legal status is that of a company. However, if the reporter is a not-for-profit organisation (e.g. a university) the responsible party would be the board of trustees.
3. Financial audits are a type of assurance engagement in which the auditor provides an opinion on a set of financial statements.
4. The category of other assurance providers includes stakeholder panels, NGOs, academic institutions, individual auditors and experts and opinion leaders.
5. Junior et al. (2014) examine the sustainability reporting and sustainability assurance practices of the world's largest 500 companies. They note that ASAPs were more popular in Europe, South America and Russia. In comparison, NASAPs controlled 42% of the sustainability assurance market in the USA, India, China, Taiwan and Australia.
6. These individuals represented various stakeholder groups including procurement officers in public sector organisations, investment managers/analysts/researchers and managers in not-for-profit organisations (based in the UK only).
7. These managers were working in organisations based in the UK.

8. The study by Mock et al. (2013) involved the analysis of a random sample of 148 sustainability reports published during 2006–2007. The results from this study was then compared against those of an earlier study in which the sample covered the period 2002–2004 and was undertaken by Mock et al. (2007).
9. Although some studies (e.g. Perego 2009) identify the GRI as a set of SA standards, it is important to note that the GRI guidelines are primarily aimed at guiding reporters (Ackers 2009; Manetti and Becatti 2009). Thus, the GRI guidelines serve as a suitable criterion against which the sustainability report can be compared (Wallage 2000).
10. The standard is supported by a number of supplementary standards and guidance documents (AccountAbility 2008a, b, 2015).
11. The term reliability refers to content which can be verified, i.e. supported by evidence. The term balance refers to those sustainability reports which provide coverage over good and bad news.

References

AccountAbility. (2008a). *AA1000 AccountAbility Principles Standard 2008*. Available at: http://www.accountability.org/images/content/0/7/074/AA1000APS%202008.pdf. Accessed 17 Feb 2014.

AccountAbility. (2008b). *AA1000 Assurance Standard 2008*. Available at: http://www.accountability.org/images/content/0/5/056/AA1000AS%202008.pdf. Accessed 17 Feb 2014.

AccountAbility. (2015). *About us*. Available at: http://www.accountability.org/about-us/index.html. Accessed 25 Aug 2015.

Ackers, B. (2009). Corporate social responsibility assurance: How do South African publicly listed companies compare? *Meditari Accountancy Research, 17*, 1–17.

Adams, C. A., & Evans, R. (2004). Accountability, completeness, credibility and the audit expectations gap. *The Journal of Corporate Citizenship, 14*(Summer), 97–115.

Ball, A., Owen, D. L., & Gray, R. (2000). External transparency or internal capture? The role of third-party statements in adding value to corporate environmental reports. *Business Strategy and the Environment, 9*(1), 1–23.

Belal, A. R. (2002). Stakeholder accountability or stakeholder management? A review of UK firms' social and ethical accounting, auditing and reporting

practices. *Corporate Social Responsibility and Environmental Management, 9,* 8–25.
Cooper, S. M., & Owen, D. L. (2007). Corporate social reporting and stakeholder accountability: The missing link. *Accounting, Organisations and Society, 32*(7), 649–667.
CorporateRegister.com Limited. (2008). *Assure view: The CSR assurance statement report*. Available at: http://www.corporateregister.com/pdf/AssureView.pdf. Accessed 21 Aug 2015.
Dando, N., & Swift, T. (2003). Transparency and assurance: Minding the credibility gap. *Journal of Business Ethics, 44*(2), 195–200.
Deegan, C., Cooper, B. J., & Shelly, M. (2006a). An investigation of TBL report assurance statements: Australian evidence. *Australian Accounting Review, 16,* 2–18.
Deegan, C., Cooper, B. J., & Shelly, M. (2006b). An investigation of TBL report assurance statements: UK and European evidence. *Managerial Auditing Journal, 21,* 329–371.
Edgley, C., Jones, M. J., & Atkins, J. (2015). The adoption of the materiality concept in social and environmental reporting assurance: A field study approach. *The British Accounting Review, 47,* 1–18.
Elliott, R. K. (1998). Assurance services and the audit heritage. *Auditing: A Journal of Theory & Practice, 17,* 1–7.
Farooq, M. B., & De Villiers, C. (2017). The market for sustainability assurance services: A comprehensive literature review and future avenues for research. *Pacific Accounting Review, 29*(1), 79–106.
Gillet, C. (2012). A study of sustainability verification practices: The French case. *Journal of Accounting & Organisational Change, 8,* 62–84.
Gray, R. (2000). Current developments and trends in social and environmental auditing, reporting and attestation: A review and comment. *International Journal of Auditing, 4,* 247–268.
Hasan, M., Roebuck, P. J., & Simnett, R. (2003). An investigation of alternative report formats for communicating moderate levels of assurance. *Auditing: A Journal of Theory & Practice, 22*(2), 171–187.
Huggins, A., Green, W. J., & Simnett, R. (2011). The competitive market for assurance engagements on greenhouse gas statements: Is there a role for assurers from the accounting profession? *Current Issues in Auditing, 5*(2), 1–12.
IAASB. (2013). *International standard on assurance engagements 3000 (revised): Assurance engagements other than audits or reviews of historical financial information.* Available at: https://www.ifac.org/publications-resources/international-standard-assurance-engagements-isae-3000-revised-assurance-enga. Accessed 19 Feb 2014.

Jones, M., & Solomon, J. (2010). Social and environmental report assurance: Some interview evidence. *Accounting Forum, 34,* 20–31.

Junior, R. M., Best, P. J., & Cotter, J. (2014). Sustainability reporting and assurance: A historical analysis on a world-wide phenomenon. *Journal of Business Ethics, 120*(1), 1–11.

Kolk, A., & Perego, P. (2010). Determinants of the adoption of sustainability assurance statements: An international investigation. *Business Strategy and the Environment, 19,* 182–198.

KPMG. (2013). *The KPMG survey of corporate responsibility reporting 2015.* Available at: https://assets.kpmg.com/content/dam/kpmg/pdf/2016/02/kpmg-international-survey-of-corporate-responsibility-reporting-2015.pdf. Accessed 19 Oct 2017.

KPMG. (2015). *The KPMG survey of corporate responsibility reporting 2015.* Available at: https://home.kpmg.com/xx/en/home/insights/2015/11/kpmg-international-survey-of-corporate-responsibilityreporting-2015.html. Accessed 1 Jan 2018.

Manetti, G., & Becatti, L. (2009). Assurance services for sustainability reports: Standards and empirical evidence. *Journal of Business Ethics, 87,* 289–298.

Manetti, G., & Toccafondi, S. (2012). The role of stakeholder in sustainability reporting assurance. *Journal of Business Ethics, 107,* 363–377.

Mock, T. J., Rao, S. S., & Srivastava, R. P. (2013). The development of world-wide sustainability reporting assurance. *Australian Accounting Review, 23,* 280–294.

Mock, T. J., Strohm, C. J., & Swartz, K. M. (2007). An examination of world-wide assured sustainability reporting. *Australian Accounting Review, 17,* 67–77.

Moroney, R., Windsor, C., & Aw, Y. T. (2012). Evidence of assurance enhancing the quality of voluntary environmental disclosures: An empirical analysis. *Accounting and Finance, 52,* 903–939.

O'Dwyer, B. (2011). The case of sustainability assurance: Constructing a new assurance service. *Contemporary Accounting Research, 28,* 1230–1266.

O'Dwyer, B., & Owen, D. L. (2005). Assurance statement practice in environmental, social and sustainability reporting: A critical perspective. *The British Accounting Review, 37,* 205–229.

O'Dwyer, B., & Owen, D. L. (2007). Seeking stakeholder-centric sustainability assurance: An examination of recent sustainability assurance practice. *The Journal of Corporate Citizenship, 25*(Spring), 77–94.

O'Dwyer, B., Owen, D., & Unerman, J. (2011). Seeking legitimacy for new assurance forms: The case of assurance on sustainability reporting. *Accounting, Organisations and Society, 36,* 31–52.
Park, J., & Brorson, T. (2005). Experiences of and views on third-party assurance of corporate environmental and sustainability reports. *Journal of Cleaner Production, 13*(10), 1095–1106.
Perego, P. (2009). Causes and consequences of choosing different assurance providers: An international study of study of sustainability reporting. *International Journal of Management, 26,* 412–425.
Perego, P., & Kolk, A. (2012). Multinationals' accountability on sustainability: The evolution of third-party assurance of sustainability reports. *Journal of Business Ethics, 110*(2), 173–190.
Segui-Mas, E., Bollas-Araya, H.-M., & Polo-Garrido, F. (2015). Sustainability assurance on the biggest cooperatives of the world: An analysis of their adoption and quality. *Annals of Public and Cooperative Economics, 86*(2), 363–383.
Simnett, R., Vanstraelen, A., & Chua, W. F. (2009). Assurance on sustainability reports: An international comparison. *The Accounting Review, 84*(3), 937–967.
Smith, J., Haniffa, R., & Fairbrass, J. (2011). A conceptual framework for investigating 'capture' in corporate sustainability reporting assurance. *Journal of Business Ethics, 99*(3), 425–439.
Wallage, P. (2000). Assurance on sustainability reporting: An auditor's view. *Auditing: A Journal of Practice & Theory, 19,* 53–65.
Wong, R., & Millington, A. (2014). Corporate social disclosures: A user perspective on assurance. *Accounting, Auditing and Accountability Journal, 27*(5), 863–887.

A Critical Perspective on Sustainability Assurance

Thomas Carrington

Introduction

Sustainability reports are increasingly becoming not only accepted but also expected in a way that environmental reporting and the intellectual capital movement never were. The establishment of generally accepted reporting guidelines (principles) in the form of the global reporting initiative (GRI 2013a, b) is a testament to this success but also a strong driver for future acceptance. Sustainability reporting seems poised to claim a natural place among traditional financial reporting requirements for listed and other companies of importance. An important step in this direction is the changes made in 2014 (2014/95/EU) to the European Union's auditor's directive (2009/43/EU), entailing extended disclosure requirement of non-financial and diversity information.

The EU does not require a full audit of this information as they state that "[s]tatutory auditors and audit firms should only check that

T. Carrington (✉)
Stockholm Business School, Stockholm University, Stockholm, Sweden
e-mail: thomas.carrington@sbs.su.se

S. Arvidsson (ed.), *Challenges in Managing Sustainable Business*,
https://doi.org/10.1007/978-3-319-93266-8_7

the non-financial statement or the separate report has been provided. In addition, it should be possible for Member States to require that the information included in the non-financial statement or in the separate report be verified by an independent assurance services provider" (2014/95/EU, p. 16). Nevertheless, this is a move in the direction of more external assurance of reported sustainability information. And the EU rules notwithstanding, many companies voluntarily prepare and release sustainability reports that follow the GRI guidelines (KPMG 2017; Rao 2017). And many of these companies choose to have their reports assured by a third party (ibid.).

As shown by Farooq and de Villiers in a previous chapter in this volume, this demand has been met by a plethora of different sustainability assurance providers. What they all have in common, however, is that we label them sustainability *assurance* providers. But what do we mean by assurance in this context and how does assurance differ from other forms of external validation or control? Farooq and de Villiers make a distinction between accounting and non-accounting sustainability assurance providers and identify and discuss the similarities and differences in approach to sustainability assurance between the two groups. This chapter will return to some of these differences but only in the service of specifically focus on the meaning of "assurance" as applied to assurance reports. Because, although the meaning of "assurance" in sustainability assurance roughly corresponds to the everyday meaning of the word, when used in sentences such as "I assure you that…", it is also a word with a regulatory history, which prescribes a specific and particular interpretation of the term. As a large portion of the market for sustainability assurance is covered by the Big Four professional services firms (Deloitte, EY, KPMG and PwC) (O'Dwyer 2011), the meaning of assurance found in financial assurance and audit standards and the accountancy profession's translation of these meanings into the assurance domain is of particular interest (ibid.).

With this as a backdrop, the aim of this chapter is to critically examine the meaning of assurance in the context of sustainability reports and to trace the regulatory and etymological roots of assurance in the accounting profession. Because, although, as Farooq and de Villiers make clear, many assurance providers have a non-accounting background, they provide a service which itself, and the report (sic) which the assurance efforts are directed towards, are heavily clad in a language that to a large extent is derived from financial accounting. With this aim, the chapter will explore the historical and theoretical dimensions of the regulatory and etymological roots of assurance and auditing in order to be able to compare it with the particular configurations of these terms we find in current sustainability assurance standards and practice. To facilitate such a comparison, the chapter will, in addition to its theoretical explorations, examine two commonly used sustainability assurance frameworks: the AA1000AS and the ISAE 3000. The chapter ends with a concluding section followed by a final discussion of the challenges identified with sustainability assurance and how they can be met.

What Do We Mean by Assurance?

In general terms, sustainability assurance aims to provide credibility to the information published in corporate reports. For a fee, the assurance provider will make a review of the sustainability report to make sure that they, with a sufficient degree of comfort, can make their assurance statements. By adding a statement by an assurance provider, the propositions in the sustainability report become stronger (Hodge et al. 2009; IAASB 2017). The mechanism by which this confidence is, supposedly, produced is the willingness by the assurance provider to not accept errors which may harm their reputation and/or increase the risk of litigation they face for providing false assurance (Wallace 1980). See the chapter by Farooq and de Villiers for a more technical definition.

Sustainability assurance thus has many similarities with auditing (Power 1999), and the terms are often used interchangeably. According to the standards (and here we lean on the standards of the main accounting sustainability assurance provider standard-setter, the IAASB), an assurance engagement is, however, not necessarily an audit engagement. From a juridical perspective, this is an important distinction because an audit provides even stronger confidence, as the auditor then makes their statement with "reasonable assurance", while for other assurance engagements the assurance level can be lower[1] (ISAE 3000). Notwithstanding the level of assurance, audit is a form of assurance and hence theoretically the same. (More on this below.) From the perspective of the audit profession's assurance standards (IAASB 2017), assurance is thus the "wider" concept, of which audit is a specific form.

This is, however, only one of many possible conceptualisations of audit. Historically and etymologically, audit is the wider concept of which assurance is a particular instantiation. Historically, audits were judicial hearings where the person being held responsible got a chance to justify their actions in front of the auditors (Power 1999). Etymologically, this notion of audit can be derived from the Latin word *auditus* (Carrington 2014). This word in turn comes from *audire* which means "to hear" or "to listen" (ibid.). Hence, although this understanding of audit involves listening to the auditees' statements and propositions, it does not have to involve a report and neither does it have to be limited to these propositions as the aim is to get at what happened (i.e. the "truth" about the subject matter) (Power 1999). In this sense, there is considerable overlap with another important audit tradition.

In the Scandinavian languages, audit is etymologically related to another of the bodily senses. The word revision (revisjon) means to look back or to look anew (ibid.). Revision can also be traced back to a Latin origin: the word *revidere*, which means to revise or revisit (ibid.). The point of an audit (revision), in this sense, is hence not only to find out whether the report (or practice, if there is no report) is correct but also to find out whether things could have been done better. In many ways, the Scandinavian languages' meaning of audit (revision/revisjon) is closer to an inspection than the hearing of the English language meaning. This chapter will not go into detail about inspections or other forms of reviews and evaluations that lead to authoritative statements by a third party on the quality or performance of sustainability (or other) statements or practices. What is worth noting, however, is that sustainability assurance inherits a specific theory with a particular form of evaluating and making authoritative statements on sustainability practice.

Assurance as a Theory of Audit Practice: The Agency Theory Perspective

Although other theoretical influences can be found in assurance standards and national and EU law, assurance, such as it is prescribed in these standards, cannot be understood without at least a rudimentary understanding of agency theory. Agency theory shares many of the basic assumptions with contemporary economics, such as actors being rational and primarily interested in maximising their own utility. In addition to these basic assumptions, agency theory adds that relationships between actors are best understood as implicit (and sometimes explicit) contracts. In its most simple form, agency theory describes a situation with three main actors: the principal, the agent and the assurance provider (Jensen and Meckling 1976). The principal is, when describing financial auditing, a company's owners and investors. In the setting of sustainability assurance, the principals are whatever stakeholders we envision being in need of information to make decisions, which can but does not have to include the decision to hold the agent accountable or not.

The agent in agency theory is the company's management, in both a financial accounting and a sustainability reporting setting. The agent has information which the principal wants and, importantly, can only get with the assistance of the agent. Hence, agency theory speaks of an information asymmetry existing between agents (companies) and principals (stakeholders). This in itself is not problematic, but whenever the goals of the principals and agents diverge, there is a considerable risk that utility maximising parties will suffer from the information asymmetry between them. It is not hard to envisage how a principal (an investor or a different stakeholder in a sustainability setting) may come out disadvantaged from this relationship but agency theory, especially when retold in the context of explaining financial auditing (Jensen and Meckling 1976), shows how the agent also can lose in these situations.

As the reasoning goes, an owner can compensate their self for the risk that management will not act in their best interest by lowering the compensation (wages) to them. In this way, they may lose some due to (for the owners' utility) suboptimal decisions by management but will recover the losses by having to pay management less. (There are many problems with this line of reasoning but as a way to see why also an agent may lose in a situation characterised by information asymmetry it has its usefulness.) Hence, from this follow that it may also be in the agent's interest to do something about the information asymmetry. But what to do?

Unsurprisingly, the solution is to introduce the assurance provider to remedy the problem. But how may an assurance provider solve the problem? Theoretically, more than one solution present itself—such as acquiring the information the principal wants from the agent—and, in as much detail as possible, inform them. However, in the theory of the practice, only one solution is entertained: assurance. Assurance means that the assurance provider reviews a report that the agent prepares for the principal and checks that the propositions made are in correspondence with the reality it purports to represent. And, yes, according to some students of assurance (Power 1996), assurance/auditing comes first and the report/accounting only second, as a consequence of the needs of the assurance (setting). In short, assurance is a technique that alongside and to various extents in combination with the company board, the company's annual report and its annual general shareholder's meeting, function as control mechanisms to remedy agency problems.

Hence, assurance, as derived from agency theory, does not do anything about the information asymmetry between the parties. The value of assurance is that it does something about the problems following from the information asymmetry, and it adds credibility to the statements of the agent. In other words, sustainability assurance, if being true to its theoretical roots, will never have anything to do with what a company does in terms of sustainability, only what management says it does. There is value in this, but it is important to stress that it is this particular value, and nothing else, that sustainability assurance brings to the table. If this point is not stressed, sustainability assurance risks being marred with the same kind of expectations gap that has haunted (or served [Power 1999]) the financial audit profession for (at least) the last 40 years (Humphrey et al. 1992).

Moreover, the value of sustainability assurance must be specified further. Agency theory provides a foundation based on which assurance can be given a form as a particular configuration of review practices and authoritative statements on the quality or performance of statements. Agency theory does, however, not address the question of what good sustainability reporting performance (quality) is.

The Theoretical Value of Sustainability Reporting (Standards)

An often-quoted definition of auditing (and remember that auditing in the theory of the practice is a specific form of assurance) comes from the American Accounting Association.[2] It states that:

> Auditing is a systematic process of objectively obtaining and evaluating evidence regarding assertions about economic actions and events to ascertain the degree of correspondence between those assertions and established criteria and communicating the results to interested users. (American Accounting Association 1973, p. 7)

Firstly, this definition illustrates the transferability of assurance, because if the word "economic" were to be crossed out from the definition, assurance could, with the stroke of a pen, be applied to pretty much anything. And increasingly, it is (Pentland 2000; Power 1999, 2011). Secondly, and more important for the question at hand, it provides a clue to the answer to the question of what good sustainability reporting performance (quality) is. Because, if assurance is about "to ascertain the degree of correspondence between those assertions and established criteria" (American Accounting Association 1973) and "those assertions" are the sustainability report, then "established criteria" must be the answer we seek.

In other words, sustainability reporting performance (quality) is not decided by the assurance provider whose role is reduced to ascertain the degree of correspondence between the reports and the established criteria. (The established criteria are of course assurance standards.)

By a long, partly theoretical, detour, we can thus conclude that sustainability assurance provides confidence to the sustainability reports by making sure the reports comply with the standards they are purported to be prepared according to. This leads to some practical questions of which perhaps the most obvious is what the assurance provider shall do in those situations where the assurance report is not prepared according to a generally excepted reporting framework (standard)?

This question is far from hypothetical as, while the EU has made it possible for member states to require assurance reports to be verified by an independent assurance services provider, the EU does not specify a specific standard or framework which the assurance reports must comply with (2014/95/EU) (although they mention one EU framework—the Eco-Management and Audit Scheme (EMAS)—and six international frameworks—the United Nations (UN) Global Compact, the Guiding Principles on Business and Human Rights implementing the UN "Protect, Respect and Remedy" Framework, the Organisation for Economic Co-operation and Development (OECD) Guidelines for Multinational Enterprises, the International Organisation for Standardisation's ISO 26000, the International Labour Organisation's Tripartite Declaration of principles concerning multinational enterprises and social policy, and the Global Reporting Initiative—by name). Hence, if an assurance provider is asked or required to go beyond the mere identification that an assurance report exists (which is all that is required in at least one member state: Sweden) the assurance provider is faced with the challenging task to identify established criteria which the assurance report can be compared against, which in itself only makes sense if the report was prepared with these criteria in mind.

Over time, it seems reasonable to assume that assurance reporters that are required to have their reports assured but does not comply with a specific assurance standard or framework will start to do so. Because, as Michael Power has argued, auditability is not about whether things *are* auditable or not, the question is whether they *can be made* auditable (Power 1996), and if the demand for accountability is there, they often are made auditable (Power 1999). This leads to the question of which standard to choose, and as the main purpose of a reporting standard is to establish the meaning of "good" sustainability reporting, this is a question with some importance.

Deciding what reporting standard to compare the preparer's report with is however not the only standards-related challenge facing a sustainability assurance provider. Because, the assurance provider also has to face the quality question with regard to their own work. Hence, where the assurance standard tells us what sustainability is and how a proper report should be formed (e.g. GRI) other standards prescribe what good assurance is. This is yet another concern that must be dealt with if an assurance sustainability expectations gap similar to the expectations gap in financial auditing (Humphrey et al. 1992) is to be avoided.

Sustainability Assurance Standards

Assurance standards exist for much the same reasons that reporting standards do. The problem or question they seek to answer is, what is good assurance quality (performance)? This is useful for an assurance provider who wants to make an as good assurance review and report as possible, since a single reference for what is good and bad simplifies things. Assurance standards are however also useful for the assurance provider who is concerned with the opposite problem: How can an as efficient assurance as possible be produced? Because assurance providers are no different from any other businesses, they can only increase their profits in two ways; either they can increase the revenues, or they can reduce the costs. The easiest way for an assurance provider to lower the costs is to do less reviewing.

The reason why an assurance standard is useful in keeping costs down is that it—at least indirectly (and in the case of AccountAbility's AA1000AS directly and explicitly)—specifies the least an assurance provider has to do to provide a "good" (sufficient) assurance review. Because—and here we have to draw from the experience of financial assurance (auditing)—if the report turns out to be wrong and the preparers are held responsible, then the assurance providers are responsible only to the extent that they did not follow assurance standards (Carrington 2007, 2011). This is, arguably, the strongest concern with standards and the potential for an assurance sustainability expectation gap they create. In a less critical tone, the counterargument is that although standards may function as ceilings for good performance (quality), they also improve the possibilities to successfully sue a preparer or assurance provider that does not even raise to the bar set by the standard.

There are currently several competing sustainability assurance standards in use (Fuhrman et al. 2016; Rao 2017; Simnett et al. 2009). Some, such as the AA1000AS, is developed by consultancy firms, and others, such as the international ISAE 3000 and the local (Swedish) RevR 6, are developed by the (financial) assurance profession. GRI, the most widespread sustainability reporting standard, "recommends the use of external assurance for sustainability reports in addition to any internal resources, but does not require it" (GRI G4 implementation manual, p. 51). A further complication is that the application of sustainability assurance standards is not as straightforward as in the financial assurance world with more leeway for what to include in the assurance report or not (Rossi and Tarquinio 2017). Two standards dominate on the sustainability assurance market, International Standard on Assurance Engagements (ISAE) 3000, developed by the International Auditing and Assurance Standards Board, a sub-committee to the International Federation of Accountants (IFAC) and AA1000AS, developed by AccountAbility, a global consulting and standards firm.

As suggested in the chapter by Farooq and de Villiers, AccountAbility, the standard-setter behind the AA1000AS, is best described as a non-accounting sustainability assurance standards provider. Nevertheless, the AA1000AS standard is clearly modelled after a financial assurance (audit) engagement. The assurance engagements that results from compliance with the AA1000AS standard is visibly audit-like in their form. The standard, originally developed in 2008 is however considerably shorter, and hence less detailed, than an audit standard—the standard is only 28 pages in total, including forewords and appendices, plus an additional 39-page guidance manual—which allow for considerable variation from this auditing inspired core. In the standards own words, it "provides a platform to align the non-financial aspects of sustainability with financial reporting and assurance" (AA1000AS, p. 6) and to do so it "relies on mandatory reference to the AA1000 AccountAbility Principles Standard (2008)" (AA1000AS, p. 7).

In this way, the AccountAbility's standards closely follow the model for assurance set out in agency theory and described above. A further illustration of this is how the standard describes how an assurance engagement adhering to the standard provides conclusions on "the nature and extent of adherence to the AA1000 AccountAbility Principles, and where applicable the quality of publicly disclosed information on sustainability performance" (AA1000AS, p. 8). This quote also illustrates the two types of assurance engagements prescribed by this standard. An AA1000AS compliant engagement can either take the form of merely making authoritative statements on the extent of adherence to the AA1000 reporting standard or it can go beyond this and comment on the quality of the reported information, according to the same reporting standards.

An assurance provider (or the company hiring the assurance provider) can also choose between two levels of assurance (confidence), which can be high or moderate. An assurance engagement performed with the aim of making statements on the assurance reports with a high level of assurance will perform the engagement in such a way that it can make claims about reliability while the moderate form of assurance can only make claims about the plausibility of the reported information.

Similar to a financial assurance provider (auditor), the sustainability assurance provider following AA1000AS should be independent and impartial (p. 14) and also plan and document the engagement and gather evidence in a way a financial auditor would recognise as assurance. For instance, in order to produce a report with a moderate assurance level, the assurance provider must, at minimum, gather the following evidence:

- understanding and testing on a sample basis the processes used to adhere to and evaluate adherence to the AccountAbility Principles;
- inquiring of management, including senior management at executive and functional levels, and of relevant management responsible for the day to day management of sustainability, about the effectiveness of processes used to adhere to the AA1000 AccountAbility Principles;
- observing and inspecting management practices, process testing and evidence gathering across the organisation on a sample basis, and

- collecting and evaluating documentary evidence and management representations that support adherence to the principles. (AA1000AS, p. 18)

This, however, leads to the question of what it takes to produce a sustainability report with a high level of assurance. The answer, according to the standard, is that "[f]or a high level of assurance the assurance provider shall also seek more extensive evidence in all areas as well as corroborative evidence where available, including through direct engagement with stakeholders" (AA1000AS, p. 19). As mention above, the AA1000AS is not strong in details. The standard does however list what it takes to gather a minimum level of evidence for evaluating the reliability of "specified performance information at a moderate level of assurance" (AA1000AS, p. 19). This includes:

- understanding the management of specified performance information and information collection processes;
- reviewing the design of systems and processes for managing specified information;
- inquiring on a sample basis of individuals with overall responsibility for information measurement and collection (from source to aggregation) and reporting about the information collection processes;
- carrying out analytical procedures (e.g. trend analysis);
- observing and inspecting on a sample basis management practices, process testing and evidence gathering (from source to aggregation);
- limited testing of detail on a sample basis (e.g. re-performance of calculations);
- collecting and evaluating documentary evidence and management representations to support the assurance work undertaken, and
- confirming that what is disclosed is consistent with the findings of the assurance process. (A1000AS, pp. 19–20)

The standard also lists what the assurance report should include, as a minimum:

- intended users of the assurance statement;
- the responsibility of the reporting organisation and of the assurance provider;
- assurance standard/s used, including reference to the AA1000AS (2008);
- description of the scope, including the Type of assurance provided;

- description of disclosures covered;
- description of methodology;
- any limitations;
- reference to criteria used;
- statement of level of assurance;
- findings and conclusions concerning adherence to the AA1000 AccountAbility Principles of Inclusivity, Materiality and Responsiveness (in all instances);
- findings and conclusions concerning the reliability of specified performance information (for Type 2 assurance only);
- observations and/or recommendations;
- notes on competencies and independence of the assurance provider;
- name of the assurance provider, and date and place. (A1000AS, pp. 21–22)

Hence, the A1000AS standard in many ways can be described as a laundry list of minimum requirements rather than a cookbook full of recipes of how to review the sustainability reports produced by the reporting companies. In comparison, ISAE 3000 is a more extensive document than AA1000AS. (It is 83 pages long.) That does however not mean that it can be described as a collection of sustainability assurance recipes.

Different from the AA1000AS, ISAE 3000 is not a standard specific for sustainability assurance engagement but IAASB's general standard on assurance engagement other than audits or reviews of historical financial information. Thus, it is designed to catch all assurance engagement situations that are not financial audits or covered by other specific standards. If AA1000AS can be described as modelled on a financial audit, this description fits ISAE 3000 as well. However, it would be wrong to describe ISAE 3000 as a derivative of financial audit standards as the ISAE is part of the same family of standard as the International Standards on Auditing (ISA). The structure and form are thus similar to the ISA but even the content matter bears enough similarities that the differences with audit standards are better described in terms of scope and subject matter.

Since AA1000AS have many resemblances with an audit standard it would be repetitive to describe ISAE 3000 in a similar manner as AA1000AS was introduced above. Some differences are nevertheless worth pointing out. AA1000AS has two types of audits and two levels of assurance. Since ISAE 3000 is designed to cover a wider scope of assurance engagements than AA1000AS it similarly provides this kind of flexibility. The standard produced by IAASB makes the distinction between attestation and direct engagements where "attestation" is used synonymously with how "assurance" is used in this text. Direct engagements, however, are assurance engagements where the assurance provider prepares the report (makes the measurements) and evaluates this information against the established criteria. The introduction of direct engagements stretches the definition of assurance beyond its theoretical roots and seems difficult to apply in a sustainability reporting setting (as the whole point of a sustainability assurance is to bring confidence to the sustainability report) (GRI G4 Reporting principles and standards disclosures). Moreover, in ISAE 3000 itself, sustainability is mentioned as the first example of attestation engagements that can be performed under the standard (ISAE 3000, p. 161) and ISAE 3410 engagements on greenhouse gas statements, which may be used in the context of "a widely distributed sustainability report" (ISAE 3410, p. 327), is explicitly applicable only to attestation assurance engagements (ISAE 3410, p. 280). This information, in conjunction with the fact that an engagement may be either an attestation or a direct engagement, never both (ISAE 3000, p. 214), seems to considerably limit the possibility of using direct engagement in a sustainability assurance setting. Nevertheless, the inclusion of the theoretically dubious option of direct engagements in ISAE 3000 is an example of the flexibility of the standard.

Direct assurance engagements do not seem to have attracted the interest of the academic research literature, but the flexibility of the standards has given an imprint in the research results in form of an observed differentiation of reporting and assurance practices. The research on sustainability assurance is still nascent, but Rossi and Tarquinio (2017) summarise that "many differences in the assurance statements content in particular with reference to the criteria used, conclusive comments and recommendations" (p. 578) exist, and the differences seem to matter. Moreover, it seems that some patterns can be discerned in how the standards are applied, depending on who is providing the assurance (i.e. whether the assurance provider is a Big Four firm, or not) (Rossi and Tarquinio 2017—again, see also the chapter by Farooq and de Villiers for an explication of the differences between accounting and non-accounting assurance providers).

To sum up the argument, although considerable variation exists between sustainability assurance standards, prevalent assurance standards all have in common that they prescribe what is to be considered good assurance practices. This includes the description of a number of different techniques and procedures to assure that the sustainability reports are prepared in accordance with the often voluntary framework, if any, that the company follows in their preparation of its report. The differences between the standards (and in some cases between alternatives within a particular standard) primarily concern scope, objectives and levels of assurance and not the meaning of assurance as such.

What Assurance Is Not

Having established what sustainability assurance is, it becomes possible to say something about what sustainability assurance is *not*. Assurance is not an independent assessment of how sustainable the business is. This is perhaps obvious, but it is worth noting that making statements about specific or general sustainability concerns (or successes) is far beyond the scope of a sustainability audit. If we want a control of and statements on sustainability performance, assurance is not the solution. Neither is sustainability assurance an interpretation of or independent comment on the performed sustainability work. Assurance is always about providing confidence to the statements made by the company (the agent), and only in a partial and indirect way about what the company actually does. Because, the only times an assurance provider is concerned with what the company does (or do not) is when they, in their report, claim to do (or not do) something. In these cases, and only to the extent that the assurance standard requires it, must the assurance provider confirm that this is, in fact, the case. Hence, it is partial in the sense that what is not mentioned (directly or indirectly in the report) is not checked and indirect in the sense that the assurance provider does everything they do as a consequence of their aim to provide assurance to the report.

The only sense in which an assurance provider (maybe) can be said to not be indirect, and not only responding to the report, is when the sustainability reporting standard requires the company to disclose something that is not in the report and the assurance provider points this out. As outlined above, this is nothing that is peculiar to sustainability assurance but inherent to all forms of assurance and a consequence of its theoretical foundations. Assurance is always at least one degree removed from the practices it is assuring (Power 1999).

This does not mean that there is not value in assurance. The question is only, now that we now what assurance is (supposed to be), who this particular and specific value is for. It would be hard to argue that sustainability assurance does not have value for the organisation that prepares and publishes sustainability reports. Agency theory describes them as the ones in demand for assurance services and if assurance can provide confidence to the statements made in the sustainability reports, why shouldn't they be in demand? The market for sustainability assurance services seems to confirm this, with ever more companies deciding to hire an assurance provider (Farooq and de Villiers 2017). And why would a company, on an unregulated market, buy assurance services if they did not see value in sustainability assurance? However, as more and more markets become regulated this argument becomes decreasingly convincing.

The increase in regulation of sustainability reporting and assurance (e.g. 2014/95/EU) indicates that governments also see a value in sustainability assurance. This argument is less convincing as the legislative demands for assurance currently are not particularly extensive. Perhaps this hesitation to regulate comes from an uncertainty about who the reports, assured or not, are for? Previous research has lamented the absence of stakeholder involvement in assurance practice (O'Dwyer and Owen 2007), and there is not much evidence for a recent improvement (O'Dwyer and Unerman 2016). This leaves a big question mark around the question of whether there is value in sustainability reporting also for the stakeholder. The uncertainty is twofold: who are the stakeholders which the theoretical agents and actual companies should make their statements to and do these stakeholders, once identified, find value in current sustainability reporting and assurance practice?

Conclusion: The Challenge with Sustainability Assurance

The aim of this chapter has been to critically examine the meaning of assurance in the context of sustainability reports and to trace the regulatory and etymological roots of assurance in the accounting profession. It can be concluded that all studied sustainability assurance providers, regardless of whether they have an accounting or non-accounting background share a common foundation in assurance as envisaged by the financial accounting profession, and its standards and surrounding theorisation. In this sense, sustainability assurance is a member of the set of "assurance" which is a superset of (e.g. financial) auditing. The two forms of assurance differ considerably (as outlined here and in the chapter by Farooq and de Villiers) but they share some important family resemblances. Most notable from a critical perspective is how sustainability assurance, if true to its historical and etymological roots, always will be, at least, one degree distant from the sustainability practices it provides assurance about.

The historical and etymological examination of the words assurance and audit also, however, betrayed that assurance (also) can be a subset of audit, which is the considerably older of the terms. This opens up possibilities, which will be examined in the next and final—and more speculative—section of this chapter. What this, as a general observation, however reveals is the conclusion that perspectives matter. Sustainability assurance, in its current form, is an artefact of applying the perspective of assurance as a superset of auditing, which makes sustainability assurance and financial audit inherit many similarities. A perspective, in which assurance instead is a subset of auditing—a much more open and varied concept—allows for much more direct assessments aiming at ensuring that businesses operate in a way that is sustainable.

Meeting the Challenge: A Sustainability Audit Beyond Agency Theory

The value of assurance may be limited and in doubt in the sustainability setting but that does not mean it is not a net good in the world. An argument that claims that a world with sustainability assurance is better than a world without may be reasonable, because sustainability assurance does, after all, in some sense seek to validate the claims the company makes about its impact on social issues and the environment. However, for this to hold true in all cases we must introduce the restricting criteria that we live in a world with unlimited resources and attention. Because, if we do not, there is a distinct risk that assurance, while maybe being a net worth, crowds out other "solutions" to the sustainability problem. Because for agency theorists, as Roberts (2005) puts it, "ethics can only be ensured through external monitoring and controls" (p. 261). Self-interested opportunism ensures the prevalence of moral hazard and the best we can hope for is to constrain it (Roberts 2005; Roberts and Ng 2012). This troubling restriction notwithstanding, we must to meaningfully address the possibility of assurance being a net good however first better determine and specify what the problem is that companies and stakeholder are trying to solve with sustainability reporting and assurance.

The issue of sustainability can be traced back to many potential origins but a common and often referred to starting point in discussions about sustainability is the Brundtland Commission and report (Brundtland Commission 1987). In our common future (ibid.), as the report was called, a number of challenges were identified and goals for a sustainable future set for the year 2000 and beyond. The general problem behind these challenges can be described in terms of externality. A narrow hunt for short-term profitability excluded (and largely still excludes) other goals such as those related to social issues, long-term economic viability and the environment. The global reporting initiative (GRI) and other similar enterprises have since sought to bring more things in, as it were, in order to prevent them from becoming externalities.

It is in this light we must assess whether assurance is the best solution to the problem. The problem of externalities can be rephrased as a problem of perspectives. The problem in 1987 (and arguably still today) was the lens through which companies evaluated its business. It was too economic, too accounting focused. A good business is a business where revenues are high and costs are low or, even better, a business where shareholder value continues to climb. The question is whether sustainability reporting and assurance changes this lens. Granted, sustainability reporting and assurance let us see more and different things—such as pollution metrics and reports about work undertaken to avoid child labour in the so-called value chain—but does it allow us to see (things) differently?

Sustainable business is often portrayed as a win-win. A more efficient workplace is a workplace that consumes less energy and resources and causes less pollution as more of the material and energy put into the process is turned into sellable products resulting from the process. A decrease in work-related accidents leads to fewer interruptions of the production process, less hospital and rehabilitation costs as well as fewer hours spent on educatiing replacement workers. If child labour can be avoided, customers will be happier. And so on. And in many cases, this may be true. But in just as many (if not considerably more) cases the social, environmental and financial goals just cannot be reconciled. There is no ethics in place through which these issues can be addressed (Shearer 2002; Roberts 2005). Even worse, in many cases, social and environmental problems are not even identified because of the shift in perspective this would need. As a consequence, these externalities remain un-addressable unknown unknowns.

Framed in this way, it is not evident how adding confidence to management's assertions can make profound and lasting change. But, perhaps an audit could. If we return to the roots of auditing and define it as a hearing or tribunal (auditing: *auditus*, *audire*) or as a way to look back, redo and improve (revision: *revidere*); a practice of control resulting in authoritarian statements not just about management's statements about sustainability but about sustainability work and the sustainability of the business more directly, there just might be a chance to alternate between truly different perspectives rather than including those aspects from "the other" perspectives which fit, into the perspective of business profitability. Crucial, however, is that the audit that is invoked is not summoned in the service of agency theory. A sustainability audit should foster companies to take responsibility, not systematically hold them accountable (Bovens 1998). Any audit that draws on agency theory will find this difficult, because, "[o]ne of the dangerous sources of blindness in agency theory concerns its rather mechanical sense of causality. Because executives are greedy, therefore investors, regulators, etc. have no choice but to treat them with suspicion" (Roberts 2005, p. 261). It is simply difficult to find a place for ethics within agency theory (Shearer 2002; Roberts 2005). A sustainability audit free of agency theory could, however, together with the audited companies, perhaps, develop an ethics that includes social and environmental aspects rather than treating them as externalities.

Notes

1. An assurance statement can, according to ISAE 3000, be made with either reasonable or limited assurance. (AA1000AS speaks of high and moderate levels of assurance.) However, the guidance on how to reach these levels of assurance are much more specific in the case of financial auditing.
2. AccountAbility, a non-accounting sustainability assurance provider (see Farooq and de Villiers' chapter), similarly defines assurance as "the methods and processes employed by an assurance provider to evaluate an organisation's public disclosures about its performance as well as underlying systems, data and processes against suitable criteria and standards in order to increase the credibility of public disclosure. Assurance includes the communication of the results of the assurance process in an assurance statement" (AA1000AS, p. 22).

References

American Accounting Association. (1973). *Studies in accounting research No. 6: Statement of basic auditing concepts*. Sarasota, FL: Author.

Bovens, M. (1998). *The quest for responsibility: Accountability and citizenship in complex organisations*. Cambridge: Cambridge University Press.

Brundtland, G. H. (1987). *Report of the World Commission on environment and development: "Our common future"*, United Nations.
Carrington, T. (2007). *Framing audit failure: Four studies on audit quality discomforts*. Stockholm University School of Business.
Carrington, T. (2011). Ansvarsfullhet är viktigare än att följa regler. *Balans, 37*(1), 42–43.
Carrington, T. (2014). *Revision*. Stockholm: Liber.
Farooq, M. B., & de Villiers, C. (2017). The market for sustainability assurance services. *Pacific Accounting Review, 29*(1), 79–106.
Fuhrmann, S., Ott, C., Looks, E., & Guenther, T. W. (2016). The contents of assurance statements for sustainability reports and information asymmetry. *Accounting and Business Research, 47*(4), 369–400.
Global Reporting Initiative. (2013a). *GRI G4 reporting principles and standard disclosures*.
Global Reporting Initiative. (2013b). *GRI G4 reporting principles and implementation manual*.
Hodge, K., Subramaniam, N., & Stewart, J. (2009). Assurance of sustainability reports: Impact on report users' confidence and perceptions of information credibility. *Australian Accounting Review, 19*(3), 178–194.
Humphrey, C., Moizer, P., & Turley, S. (1992). The audit expectations gap—Plus ca change, plus vest la meme chose? *Critical Perspectives on Accounting, 3*(2), 137–161.
IAASB. (2017). *Handbook of international auditing, assurance, and ethics pronouncements*. New York: International Federation of Accountants.
Jensen, M. C., & Meckling, W. (1976). Theory of the firm: Managerial behavior, agency costs and ownership structure. *Journal of Financial Economics, 3*(4), 305–360.
KPMG. (2017). *The KPMG survey of corporate responsibility reporting 2017*. Retrieved April 12, 2018, from kpmg.com/crreporting.
O'Dwyer, B. (2011). The case of sustainability assurance: Constructing a new assurance service. *Journal of Corporate Citizenship, 28*(4), 1230–1266.
O'Dwyer, B., & Owen, D. (2007). Seeking stakeholder-centric sustainability assurance. *Journal of Corporate Citizenship, 25*(Spring), 77–94.
O'Dwyer, B., & Unerman, J. (2016). Fostering rigour in accounting for social sustainability. *Accounting, Organizations and Society, 49*, 32–40.
Pentland, B. (2000). Will auditors take over the world? Program, technique and the verification of everything. *Accounting, Organizations and Society, 25*(3), 307–312.

Power, M. (1996). Making things auditable. *Accounting, Organizations and Society, 21*(2), 289–315.
Power, M. (1999). *The audit society*. Oxford: Oxford University Press.
Power, M. (2011). Assurance worlds: Consumers, experts and independence. *Accounting, Organizations and Society, 36*(4–5), 324–326.
Rao, S. (2017, July). Current state of assurance on sustainability reports. *CPA Journal*, 52–57.
Roberts, J. (2005). Agency theory, ethics and corporate governance. In C. R. Lehman (Ed.), *Corporate governance: Does any sixe fit? Advances in public interest accounting* (pp. 249–270). Amsterdan: Elsevier.
Roberts, J., & Ng, W. (2012). Against economic (mis)conceptions of the individual: Constructing financial agency in the credit crisis. *Culture and Organization, 18*(2), 91–105.
Rossi, A., & Tarquinio, L. (2017). An analysis of sustainability report assurance statements. *Managerial Auditing Journal, 32*(6), 578–602. https://doi.org/10.1108/MAJ-07-2016-1408.
Shearer, T. (2002). Ethics and accountability: From the for-itself to the for-the-other. *Accounting, Organizations and Society, 27*, 541–573.
Simnett, R., Vanstraelen, A., & Chua, W. F. (2009). Assurance on sustainability reports: An international comparison. *Accounting Review, 84*(3), 937–967.
Wallace, W. (1980). The economic role of the audit in free and regulated markets. *Open Educational Resources*. 2. https://scholarworks.wm.edu/oer/2.

Part III

Sustainable Finance

Engagement Dialogue as a Nordic Sustainable and Responsible Investment (SRI) Strategy

Lars G. Hassel and Natalia Semenova

Background

Institutional investors incorporate environmental, social and governance (ESG) factors into their investment strategies in order to become more active in exercising their ownership rights in investee companies. As a corporate governance mechanism, active ownership can be used to improve companies' ESG performance and transparency and to hold management accountable for its long-term financial performance and impact on society. Successful active ownership can reduce the external risks of ESG factors, unlock hidden company market value, and enhance long-term financial returns.

L. G. Hassel
University of Gävle, Gävle, Sweden
e-mail: lars.hassel@hig.se

N. Semenova (✉)
School of Business and Economics, Linnaeus University, Växjö, Sweden
e-mail: natalia.semenova@lnu.se

S. Arvidsson (ed.), *Challenges in Managing Sustainable Business*,
https://doi.org/10.1007/978-3-319-93266-8_8

Sustainable and responsible investment (SRI) has grown rapidly in the last decade and has become integrated into the strategies of institutional investors and their advisors. According to Eurosif (2016, p. 9), SRI is defined as "a long-term oriented investment approach, which integrates ESG factors in the research, analysis and selection process of securities within an investment portfolio." SRI strategies include sustainability-themed investments, best-in-class investment selection, exclusion of holdings from investment universe, norm-based screening, integration of ESG factors in financial analysis, engagement and voting on sustainability matters, and impact investing. Many large owners have a fiduciary responsibility to address the ESG-related issues associated with their investments.

The country-specific context influences the exercise of the SRI strategy of active ownership (Bengtsson 2008; Eurosif 2016; Yamahaki and Frynas 2016). SRI is often included in traditional governance models that differ in practice around the world. In governance-related aspects, Nordic countries (i.e., Denmark, Finland, Norway, and Sweden) share similarities in cultural-ideological values and politico-economic institutions, combine economic competiveness with social welfare, and demonstrate high levels of commitment to the ESG concept at governmental and company levels (Bengtsson 2008; Gjolberg 2010; Scholtens and Sievänen 2013). The Nordic stakeholder-oriented corporate governance model is regarded as a specific model of governance that differs from the market model of Anglo-Saxon countries and the bank model of continental Europe (Poulsen et al. 2010; Thomsen and Conyon 2012). The Nordic model is characterized by active, long-term ownership, consensus-seeking dialogue, stakeholder value creation, employee representation at the board level, transparency, and relatively few agency problems (Poulsen et al. 2010; Thomsen and Conyon 2012).

Large Nordic owners tend to invest across the entire market index (also termed universal investors) and engage with global MSCI World companies. This chapter argues that Nordic institutional investors demonstrate a unique way of combining the features of the Nordic stakeholder model of governance with the SRI approach of active ownership. In particular, the chapter aims to illustrate engagement dialogue as an SRI strategy from the Nordic investor perspective. Engagement dialogue by Nordic institutional investors reaches out to global companies whose governance systems and types of relationships between owners and management can differ from the Nordic tradition. Global engagement brings additional challenges to the intensive engagement process for Nordic investors seeking to ensure sustainable value creation in investee companies in the long run.

The chapter examines a point-in-time record of 326 engagement cases with 267 MSCI World companies from 2005 through 2013, based on a data set that describes investor actions. A model for the engagement dialogue strategy of Nordic institutional investors is presented. The key feature of the model is its focus on a particular ESG incident related to a violation of norms on ESG issues by the company in which the owners have a stake. The identified ESG incident signals a higher level of investee company exposure to risk of unexpected negative ESG matters and a violation of ESG norms. The main elements of the Nordic model of private engagement dialogue, including an incident-based approach, norm-based compliance, small number of engagement cases, and long-term focus on risk reduction, are presented. In addition, the chapter conducts an extensive empirical analysis of the characteristics of target companies prior to engagement dialogue and the outcomes of successful engagement dialogue. Parallels are drawn with existing Anglo-Saxon studies regarding companies targeted by investor activism, the form of activism that takes place, and both financial and non-financial outcomes.

The chapter proceeds as follows. In the following section, the two principal forms of active ownership—private engagement dialogue and the filing of shareholder resolutions at an annual general meeting (AGM)—are presented. The chapter subsequently describes the details of the Nordic model of corporate governance and stakeholder capitalism as a basis for the engagement, the theoretical underpinnings of the empirical study, and prior empirical research. In the empirical section, the Nordic model for engagement dialogue is outlined. Next, the results of the descriptive analysis of company-specific drivers of engagement, and both the financial and non-financial outcomes of engagement, are presented. Before summarizing, the Nordic engagement model is placed in an Anglo-Saxon perspective.

Active Ownership

Active ownership is a corporate governance mechanism aimed at mitigating agency problems and information asymmetry between owners and management (Gillan and Starks 2007; Harris and Raviv 2010).

It comprises actions by which owners become involved with the company management (in particular the board of directors) in order to influence its activities, behaviors, and operations and to demand changes in the investee companies (Blowfield and Murray 2014; Goranova and Ryan 2014). Examples of traditional needs for active ownership, especially in the Anglo-Saxon model, include financial underperformance and concerns about corporate governance practices. The latter comprise confidential voting issues, executive compensation, company restructurings, board and committee independence issues, and the usage of antitakeover devices (Carleton et al. 1998; Gillan and Starks 2000). In the case of disagreements regarding the management of the company, active ownership stands opposite to departure from the company when owners sell their shares. Large, universal owners often exert their ownership power since they cannot sell shares of underperforming companies without experiencing a financial loss (Gillan and Starks 2000).

Regarding economic effects, successful active ownership needs to fulfill the condition of reaching two equilibriums. Active ownership implies equilibrium between the costs and benefits of a high degree of owner involvement in management and the costs and benefits of complete separation of management and ownership functions. The second equilibrium of active ownership is the balance between the relative costs and benefits of various means of exercising voice and the costs and benefits of departure through selling shares. If active owners are successful in reaching an agreement with the company's management, they restore confidence and trust in the investee company and its management. In addition, successful active ownership can lead to the potential benefits of greater long-term performance of portfolio companies (Gillan and Starks 2007). Active owners tend to analyze target companies' corporate governance practices in order to find the space to make value-enhancing improvements (Mallin 2016). Based on the best practices in corporate governance, active owners can suggest ESG improvements with high potential for increasing long-term market value.

Forms of Active Ownership

A range of approaches are used by active owners to influence company management (Bauer et al. 2015; Becht et al. 2009; Goranova et al.

2017; Yamahaki and Frynas 2016). According to the conceptual framework of Bauer et al. (2015), McNulty and Norberg (2016), and Goranova et al. (2017), the active owner approaches the company either publicly by filing a shareholder resolution or privately through engagement dialogue. Active owners generally practice a quiet, collaborative, informal, and friendly form of engagement dialogue with the target company (Carleton et al. 1998; Del Guercio and Hawkins 1999; Gillan and Starks 2000). For example, Carleton et al. (1998, p. 1335) state that "when an institution has an issue it is concerned about, it typically will contact a firm privately about the issue first." Engagement dialogue represents a sequence of interactions that can be conducted over the course of several years through different interaction channels such as letters, emails, telephone calls, and management meetings. Entering into engagement dialogue and reaching a private agreement with a company do not typically become public knowledge (Carleton et al. 1998). This form of active ownership is seen as the easiest and least costly approach to changing practices in the investee company (Poulsen et al. 2010).

Depending upon the company's response and the outcome of engagement dialogue, the active owner determines (1) not to pursue the specific issue further since the company has changed its practices, (2) to give up, or (3) to file a shareholder resolution in order to further pressurize the company's management. A formal shareholder resolution encompasses a public and reputation-threatening component of active ownership and may publicly signal a failure of behind-the-scenes engagement dialogue calling for changes (Carleton et al. 1998; David et al. 2007; Ferraro and Beunza 2014; Goranova et al. 2017). A shareholder resolution is often sent to the target company simultaneously with the effort to initiate or re-enter into dialogue at a higher-cost level (Carleton et al. 1998). Proposing a shareholder resolution is a public process (Reid and Toffel 2009). In addition, some owners or their agents who use this form of active ownership may provide public information about targeting and reaching agreements with companies. Active SRI owners have undertaken private engagement dialogue, shareholder resolutions, and voting at the AGM, in order to influence the company's ESG practices and improve ESG disclosure (Dimson et al. 2015; Grewal et al. 2016; Reid and Toffel 2009).

The Nordic Governance Model

The corporate governance practices of the Nordic region have attracted considerable interest owing to the growth of successful global companies with Nordic origins. Companies such as Novo Nordisk, Ikea, Stora Enso, Norsk Hydro, Novozymes, and Statoil have demonstrated long-term value creation for their companies and stakeholders (Strand 2014). The Nordic model of governance is characterized by the fact that large owners are able to control and take long-term responsibility for the companies that they own (Lekvall 2014). The model builds on self-regulations in the form of corporate governance codes and the generally accepted practice and traditions that exist in Nordic countries' welfare systems.

The model encourages large owners to play an active role in the governance of the investee companies in order to create value for the whole company. For example, a large owner can take seats on the board and be involved in its nomination committee. The Nordic model facilitates long-term ownership and ensures that the board is strictly accountable to company owners in order to incentivize regular dialogue between owners and company management, primarily through the chair of the board. Communication and dialogue between company managers and owners helps to ensure that the company's financial resources are used appropriately, and that the company continues to be competitive and create value (Mallin 2016). The Nordic model is based on the idea that an active owner is a more efficient and less costly monitor of management than are the financial markets, and embraces a shareholder-friendly governance system (Lekvall 2014). At the same time, the rights of minority owners are protected by the system of rules and practices that prevents the possibility of large owners extracting private benefits at the expense of minority owners. Given the tradition of negotiated compromises, the filing of shareholder resolutions outside the board and the nomination committee is quite rare (Poulsen et al. 2010). The nomination committee is elected at the AGM to monitor the board and to submit shareholder resolutions. As a result, the nomination committee facilitates active ownership and collaboration among owners and increases the power of active owners over company management. Overall, the key features of the Nordic governance model include importance of AGM for owners, shares with multiple voting rights, strong minority protection, effective individual shareholder rights, non-executive boards, use of board committees, auditors appointed by and accountable to the shareholders, an active governance role of major shareholders, and transparency to stakeholders (Lekvall 2014).

The Nordic stakeholder model of corporate governance differs from the market-oriented Anglo-Saxon model (Poulsen et al. 2010; Thomsen and Conyon 2012). The Anglo-Saxon governance model, used in, for example, the United States of America (USA) and United Kingdom (UK), relies on financial market mechanisms and places emphasis on short-termism, short-term returns, and financial incentives. Focus on the long-term perspective is limited, and considerations related to the expectations of the society in which companies operate can be disregarded because financial aspects are emphasized (Strand 2014). Other distinct elements of the Anglo-Saxon model comprise ownership dispersion, more serious agency problems, and strong managers and weak owners (Thomsen and Conyon 2012).

The Nordic model of stakeholder capitalism that encourages long-term relationships between companies and their stakeholders supports the Nordic corporate governance model. As such, the role of the company is embedded in the goals of the social system at large. In the early 1960s, the Swedish management strategist Eric Rhenman argued that the purpose of the company is to create value for stakeholders (Lekvall 2014; Strand 2014). The Nordic model has retained its strong focus on cooperation and compromise between companies and their stakeholders, a principle that Porter and Kramer (2011, p. 66) refer to as "creating shared value" (Strand and Freeman 2015). Based on companies' willingness and ability to cooperate with stakeholders, the Nordic model embraces the view that companies achieve a cooperative advantage in the form of value creation and long-term profitability. Stakeholders represent a broad range of groups within a society, including investors, employees, suppliers, government, media, consumers, the local community, industry bodies, and interest groups (Deegan 2015). Cooperation is deemed effective when it satisfies the demands of various powerful stakeholder groups. Powerful stakeholders (also called primary stakeholders) possess the power to impose constraints on company activities, since they are able to influence access to limited resources (finance and labor), shape consumption of the company's goods and services, access influential media, and impose legislation on the company (Henisz et al. 2014). The Nordic model of stakeholder capitalism builds upon the perspective that a successful company considers the interests of powerful stakeholders in order to transcend the interests of shareholders. The principles of stakeholder capitalism focus on the voluntary cooperation of individuals in order to create sustainable relationships that provide the opportunity for leadership and competitiveness (Semenova et al. 2010).

According to Strand and Freeman (2015), the Nordic model is based on three fundamental aspects of the company–stakeholder relationship: joint interests, cooperative strategic posture, and the rejection of a narrowly economic view of the company. Joint interests represent the emphasis of a company on creating greater value for a larger number of stakeholders, even where stakeholders pursue conflicting interests. Cooperative strategic posture refers to consideration of stakeholders as potential partners in cooperation. The rejection of a narrowly economic view of the firm is concerned with the adoption of value creation for the company's stakeholders, in addition to the interests of shareholders. The objective of large owners is to facilitate the investee company's social legitimacy and to prevent political intervention (Poulsen et al. 2010). Prior research has produced empirical evidence of the positive valuation consequences of cooperative relationships between company managers and stakeholders (Henisz et al. 2014). The particular mechanism of building cooperative relationships and achieving cooperative advantage is often company-specific and underrepresented in the research literature.

The Theoretical Underpinnings of Engagement Dialogue

The theoretical underpinnings of engagement dialogue are provided by agency theory, the theory of rational activism, and social movement theory. Agency theory describes the requirement for owners to ensure that the management of a company acts in the best interests of its owners (Goranova et al. 2017). Based on agency theory, this study argues that active owners seek to reduce agency costs by privately engaging in companies with ESG incidents in order to implement suggested improvements to manage risks.

Furthermore, the theory of rational activism claims that active owners engage with specific companies that are expected to adopt their recommendations for risk management and secure long-term financial returns (Smith 1996). Rational activists foresee the probability of successful engagement, thus increasing the expected benefits of activism. The theory of rational activism is embedded in this study in order to examine the company characteristics that determine the probability of being targeted by owners for engagement dialogue related to an ESG incident.

Finally, social movement theory argues that companies that are targeted by social activists (e.g., institutional investors, non-governmental organizations, and unions) respond to their social demands and align their business practices with the social movement, and change social expectations (Den Hond and de Bakker 2007). Social movement theory was adopted to account for the impact of greater confrontational external pressures of social activists in the form of boycotts, protests, lawsuits, campaigns, and shareholder resolutions, in order to stimulate companies to implement new social practices (Ferraro and Beunza 2014; Reid and Toffel 2009). By analyzing engagement dialogue, this study draws on the premise of social movement theory to argue that target companies will respond to the informal, unobservable pressures of social investors who ask them to address the ESG incident and to improve their ESG performance and transparency relative to pre-engagement levels.

Prior Empirical Activism Studies

Most prior research on active ownership has taken the perspective of the Anglo-Saxon countries, including the USA and UK (Bauer et al. 2013; Bauer et al. 2015; Becht et al. 2009; Dimson et al. 2015; Goranova et al. 2017; Smith 1996). These studies consistently report that active ownership by means of shareholder resolutions and related engagement dialogue results in changes to company practices. Earlier research on shareholder resolutions centers on corporate governance issues and the financial underperformance of target companies. These studies find evidence that submitting shareholder resolutions tends to positively affect short-term stock returns in the window of announcements (Del Guercio and Hawkins 1999), although the stock market's reactions can depend on the type of governance issue targeted (Carleton et al. 1998). Becht et al. (2009) find that the announcements of achieved objectives of activism are associated with positive abnormal returns at the announcement date. Furthermore, existing studies have examined the long-term effects of active ownership. However, research fails to document the positive influence of shareholder resolution activism and engagement dialogue on a company's financial performance (Carleton et al. 1998; Del Guercio and Hawkins 1999; Smith 1996). In terms of the success of voting on shareholder resolutions at the AGM, corporate governance resolutions receive most support from investors in the USA (Gillan and Starks 2000).

Recent studies have investigated the impacts of active ownership on ESG issues. Shareholder resolutions on ESG issues have increased significantly in recent years (Wang and Mao 2015), although they often do not receive majority voting support (Grewal et al. 2016). Companies tend to respond to shareholder resolutions on environmental topics by publicly disclosing information to the Carbon Disclosure Project (CDP) (Reid and Toffel 2009) and by participating in engagement dialogue on ESG issues (Bauer et al. 2013, 2015; Dimson et al. 2015; Rehbein et al. 2013). Some studies find that activism through shareholder resolutions reduces a company's social performance (David et al. 2007), and that companies can be reluctant to respond to social activists (Clark et al. 2008; Dimson et al. 2015). Another body of research reveals that shareholder resolution on material ESG issues increases the company's market value (Grewal et al. 2016). Successful private engagement dialogue results in positive abnormal returns beginning in the targeting year, and subsequently improved financial performance (operating performance, sales, and employee efficiency) and corporate governance (Dimson et al. 2015). In previous studies (Bauer et al. 2013; Dimson et al. 2015), engagement dialogue on ESG factors has addressed traditional governance issues, targeted financially underperforming companies that have the potential to improve, and focused on concerns pertaining to specific ESG themes, such as climate change, business ethics, and public health. Limited research exists that examines active ownership on ESG issues beyond the Anglo-Saxon countries and market models of corporate governance.

Analysis of Engagement Dialogue

This section introduces the study's methodology for analyzing engagement dialogue. The investigation subsequently disentangles the Nordic model for active ownership through forms of engagement dialogue triggered by ESG incidents. Exploratory evidence is provided regarding the characteristics and outcomes of successful engagement dialogue. The study draws on the argument that differences exist in the engagement approaches of SRI investors across jurisdictions. For example, US investors tend to exert active ownership by means of shareholder resolutions on ESG issues, and UK investors generally focus on themed-based engagement regarding ESG topics with companies on "focus lists" that underperform on the index, such as Standard and Poor's (Bauer et al. 2013, 2015; Dimson et al. 2015; Mallin 2016). The present study facilitates greater recognition and understanding of active ownership on ESG issues, especially among SRI investors, company managers, investor advisors, and professional service organizations, such as the United Nations (UN) Principles for Responsible Investment (PRI), the UN Global Reporting Initiative (GRI), and the UN Global Compact, by modeling the SRI strategy of engagement dialogue used by Nordic investors.

This study relies on the private database of 326 engagement cases constituting 3025 examples of engagement dialogue with 267 MSCI World Index companies between 2005 and 2013. A professional agent specializing in engagement as an SRI strategy provides the data on engagement dialogue. The agent has been a member of the UN Global Compact since 2004 and signed PRI in 2006. The agent analyzes MSCI World Index companies and provides institutional investors with a collaborative platform for an active ownership process. A dedicated global research team conducts dialogue with companies on behalf of institutional investors.

A detailed analysis is provided of the engagement dialogue between Nordic institutional investors and global companies targeted in connection with environmental, social and corruption risks. The analysis of engagement dialogue is built on the uniqueness of the Nordic case to develop a deeper understanding of its complexity. Given that details about engagement dialogue between the institutional investor and the company are unobservable and not usually made public, this study involves the revelatory case whereby the detailed electronic database of engagement dialogue and supporting data documents are made available for academic research (Bryman and Bell 2015).

The empirical part of analysis is based on descriptive and inferential tests. The descriptive tests provide summaries about private dialogue and successful engagement across ESG risks, and present quantitative descriptions of the financial and non-financial performance characteristics of companies in the pre- and post-engagement periods. The inferential tests are univariate parametric (nonparametric) *t*-tests in order to assess whether the means (medians) of two groups are statistically different from one another (Hair et al. 2014). Based on univariate *t*-tests, this study estimates the differences between target and non-target (matched) MSCI World companies and between pre-engagement and post-engagement period, to provide conclusions regarding the determinants and outcomes of engagement dialogue. The empirical approach and parameters' estimation in this study (i.e., two-tailed test and winsorizing) are consistent with prior research (e.g., Bauer et al. 2015; Becht et al. 2009).

The Process Model of Nordic Engagement Dialogue

Figure 1 displays a process model of Nordic engagement dialogue to provide a detailed analysis of the key aspects of engagement interactions. Engagement dialogue is an SRI strategy taken by Nordic institutional investors. It is based on the involvement of large, active owners in the external ESG risk management of the companies in which they invest. Constructive engagement dialogue is established with the target company when the increased financial risk resulting from an ESG incident is determined. The identified risk of an ESG incident is connected with companies that severely and structurally breach the ESG norms.

The Nordic model of engagement dialogue incorporates two facets of targeting: norms and incidents. ESG norms are established in international conventions and guidelines on the environment, human and labor rights, and corruption, such as the Organisation for Economic Co-operation and Development (OECD) Guidelines for Multinational Enterprises, the International Labour Organization (ILO) Tripartite Declaration of Principles concerning Multinational Enterprises and Social Policy, and the UN Global Compact. For example, the UN Global Compact has attracted the support of many Nordic SRI investors since its launch in 2000 (Bengtsson 2008). The Nordic model of engagement dialogue is based on the view that companies have a responsibility to comply with international norms on ESG issues, even though the norms only represent a soft law and so companies are not legally bound to comply. Company compliance with ESG norms has been the traditional focus of the Nordic SRI investors (Bengtsson 2008; Eurosif 2016; Scholtens and Sievänen 2013).

ESG incidents embody unfavorable public reports of alleged violations of ESG norms, revealed and reported by the media, consumer organizations, and non-governmental organizations. ESG incidents are analyzed by the systematic screening of companies regarding

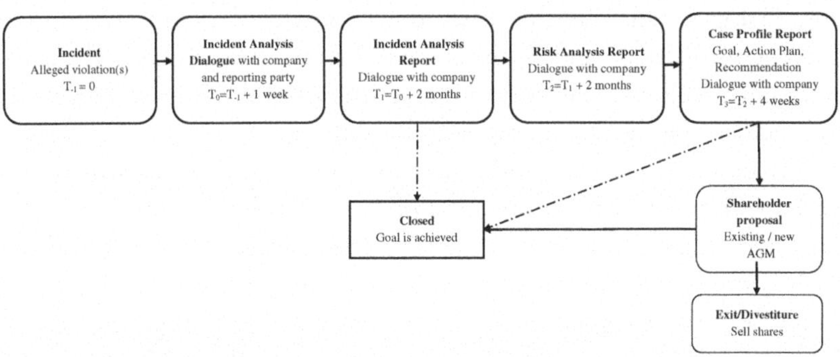

Fig. 1 The process model of Nordic engagement dialogue

their compliance with ESG norms. The historical development of SRI in the Nordic countries is related to specific incidents that spur investor attention to ESG factors (Bengtsson 2008). In previous empirical research, negative public ESG news has been found to result in a decline of the company's market value (Capelle-Blancard and Petit 2017; Kruger 2015). As such, an ESG incident exposes a company to risk, which can over time translate into financial risk for the company.

By attracting negative public exposure to company activities, ESG incidents may lead to the immediate exclusion or divestment of the portfolio company. The Nordic long-term approach is to engage in constructive dialogue with the company implicated in ESG incidents in order to mitigate the ESG risk by collaborating with and convincing the company management to make specific adjustments to ESG policy, performance, and transparency. Engagement dialogue related to an ESG incident seeks to ensure that the company accepts responsibility for compliance with ESG norms and takes appropriate actions to correct the reported violation and to avoid similar incidents in the future. It is also complemented by a risk analysis of the company's ESG performance in order to receive suggestions for improvements to company practices. Engagement dialogue is conducted via an intensive sequence of interactions, and it is defined as successful when the engagement goal is achieved and when the institutional investor decides not to pursue the dialogue further. If the company targeted for engagement does not agree with the suggested improvements of the investors and/or does not address the reported violation within a set period of time, the engagement dialogue fails. In this case, the company does not respond to engagement dialogue and/or display willingness to cooperate. The active owner may decide to continue approaching the company to address the ESG incident by filing a shareholder resolution.

Engagement dialogue under the Nordic model is classified into standard areas of corruption, environment, human rights, and labor rights, which are built into company relationships with key stakeholders. A company's compliance with ESG norms means that a company incorporates the accepted social norms into its relationships and cooperation with stakeholders. Traditionally, the most influential stakeholders of Nordic companies comprise the government, investors, employees, community, customers, and suppliers (Semenova et al. 2010; Vidaver-Cohen and Bronn 2015). Nordic investors and companies tend to reflect on and respond to the institutional environment, including advanced welfare government and strong legal institutions. For example, under a Swedish government directive issued in 2001, Swedish state pension funds (AP funds) are required to consider environmental and social aspects in investment decisions (Hamilton and Eriksson 2011). Nordic companies maintain relationships with labor unions and have employee representation on the supervisory board (Allen et al. 2007). Companies' preparedness to comply with labor standards includes policies on health and safety, diversity, working hours and wages, and child and forced labor. Support also exists for the perspective that responsible relationships with a company's suppliers and community are rooted in the company's compliance with human rights norms (Semenova et al. 2010). Examples include programmes on human rights in the supply chain, and community involvement policy and programs.

The Determinants and Outcomes of Nordic Engagement Dialogue

The chapter now turns to a descriptive analysis of engagement dialogue by Nordic institutional investors. Based on 326 engagements between Nordic institutional investors and companies during the period 2005–2013, Table 1 examines the typical areas and success of engagement dialogue. In 234 cases (71.78%), Nordic investors sought to decrease the risks related to social incidents (i.e., human rights and labor rights incidents) and achieved their engagement goals in 63 cases. Nordic investors also mitigated environmental risks in 68 cases (20.86%) and achieved their engagement objective in 26 cases. In 24 cases (7.36%), Nordic investors sought to reduce the corruption risk, and in 9 cases, the target companies agreed with the recommended changes.

Table 2 presents descriptive statistics and univariate tests by comparing the characteristics of target MSCI World companies and non-target MSCI World companies (matched sample) one year before the engagement

Table 1 Norm areas of engagement dialogue

Norm area	Num. of cases	% of sample	Num. of dialogues	Num. of successful cases
Environment	68	20.86	744	26
Human rights	131	40.18	1243	26
Labor rights	103	31.60	847	37
Corruption	24	7.36	191	9
Total	326	100.0	3025	97

dialogue. The group of non-target MSCI World companies consists of 2200 companies. The period of analysis is from 2002 until 2016.

The study employs the parametric *t*-test for differences in mean values of companies that are targeted and companies that are not targeted, and the nonparametric Wilcoxon rank-sum test that allows for different sample sizes in the distributions being compared. The univariate *t*-test for differences in the mean and Wilcoxon test for differences in medians consistently reveal that target MSCI World companies are significantly larger in size and have higher sales growth, return on assets, research and development (R&D) intensity ratio, ESG performance ratings, and ESG transparency ratings. The target companies are also younger than non-target MSCI World companies. The insignificant differences between the two groups of companies are associated with market value, leverage, cash holdings, and the dividend yield. The target companies hit by an ESG incident are generally outperforming their peers, and the agent wants to ensure that a private engagement will mitigate a further ESG risk.

Table 3 displays the outcomes of successful engagement dialogue on a company's financial and non-financial performance. This study compares the results of successful dialogue with the performance of a matched sample of non-target companies during the same time period. The outcome variables of engagement are market value, return on assets, ESG performance, and ESG transparency. Panel A and B of Table 3 provide the results of univariate test one year after being targeted for engagement dialogue and during the three-year period following the engagement. The findings of the univariate tests reveal that the target companies have, on average, higher subsequent return on assets, ESG performance, and ESG transparency than matched companies in the

Table 2 Characteristics of target companies relative to a matched sample one year before the engagement dialogue

Variable	Descriptive statistics			Univariate tests			
				t-test for diff. in means		Wilcoxon test for diff. in medians	
	Mean	Median	Num. of obs.	Mean diff.	*p*-value	z	*p*-value
SIZE	9.2754	9.5045	317	**8.9084**	**0.0000**	**8.155**	**0.0000**
AGE	19.7025	19.0000	326	**−2.8730**	**0.0041**	**−2.185**	**0.0044**
TOBINQ	39.9801	39.3380	317	−0.2282	0.8195	−0.121	0.9037
GROWTH	11.7282	10.62	322	**4.7244**	**0.0000**	**4.666**	**0.0000**
SALES_EMPL	65197.57	36616.67	298	1.0520	0.2928	**−1.772**	**0.0763**
LEVERAGE	23.8609	22.55	323	−1.1944	0.2323	−0.896	0.3705
CASH_HOLD	7.9922	5.5820	267	−0.5822	0.5605	0.436	0.6627
ROA	14.8223	13.6324	311	**5.8028**	**0.0000**	**5.490**	**0.0000**
CAPEX	0.5539	0.0649	317	**−2.4978**	**0.0125**	**2.337**	**0.0194**
DIV_YIELD	24.0766	19.4531	315	1.0570	0.2905	0.890	0.3736
RND	0.4877	0.0000	326	**4.0288**	**0.0004**	**4.028**	**0.0001**
TRESG_PERF	74.3523	87.16	253	**8.4771**	**0.0000**	**9.242**	**0.0000**
AESG_PERF	8.2035	9.0000	172	**7.9771**	**0.0000**	**7.833**	**0.0000**
TRANSP	73.6842	88.90	253	**9.0025**	**0.0000**	**9.294**	**0.0000**

The table presents descriptive statistics and univariate tests for target companies' characteristics one year before the engagement dialogue. Parameter estimates are reported with their *p*-values (2-sided). Significance at $p \leq 0.10$ is highlighted. All continuous variables are winsorized at the 1st and 99th percentiles. SIZE is natural logarithm of market value of equity. AGE is company age relative to the start date of the company in Thomson Reuters Datastream. TOBINQ is Tobin's Q calculated as (market value of equity + book value of debt)/(book value of equity + book value of debt). GROWTH is annual sales growth rate. SALES_EMPL is sales over employees, sales/number of employees. LEVERAGE is leverage that is book value of debt/(book value of debt + book value of equity). CASH_HOLD is cash holding, cash/total assets. ROA is return on assets that is earnings before interest, taxes, depreciation and amortisation (EBITDA)/total assets. CAPEX is capital expenditures/total assets. DIV_YIELD is dividend yield that is total dividends/(market value of equity + book value of equity). RND is research and development (R&D) intensity that is an indicator variable that equals one if company reports R&D expenditures. TRESG_PERF is aggregate ESG rating of Thomson Reuters. AESG_PERF is aggregate ESG rating of the agent. TRANSP is ESG transparency rating of Thomson Reuters

Table 3 The outcomes of successful engagement dialogue relative to a matched sample of MSCI World companies

Variable	Panel A: Univariate tests year +1				Panel B: Univariate tests year +3			
	t-test for diff. in means			Wilcoxon test for diff. in medians	*t*-test for diff. in means			Wilcoxon test for diff. in medians
	ENG=1	ENG=0	*p*-value	z (*p*-value)	ENG=1	ENG=0	*p*-value	z (*p*-value)
TOBINQ	37.5022	40.3017	0.2757	−0.964 (0.3349)	39.1480	40.3070	0.3688	−0.760 (0.4475)
ROA	16.6739	12.0743	**0.0000**	**4.472 (0.0000)**	15.4844	12.0491	**0.0000**	**7.070 (0.0000)**
TRESG_PERF	80.900	58.3469	**0.0000**	**7.297 (0.0000)**	80.6427	58.1372	**0.0000**	**14.627 (0.0000)**
AESG_PERF	8.0833	6.0669	**0.0000**	**4.639 (0.0000)**	8.3539	6.0403	**0.0000**	**10.157 (0.0000)**
TRANSP	79.0277	55.5775	**0.0000**	**6.775 (0.0000)**	78.3584	55.3645	**0.0000**	**13.224 (0.0000)**

The table presents univariate tests of the outcomes of successful engagement dialogue next year after targeting and during three years after targeting for engaged and matched MSCI World companies. Parameter estimates are reported with their *p*-values (2-sided). Significance at $p \leq 0.10$ is highlighted. All continuous variables are winsorized at the 1st and 99th percentiles. ENG is an indicator variable that equals one if the engagement dialogue is successful. TOBINQ is Tobin's Q calculated as (market value of equity + book value of debt)/(book value of equity + book value of debt). ROA is return on assets that is earnings before interest, taxes, depreciation, and amortisation (EBITDA)/total assets. TRESG_PERF is aggregate ESG rating of Thomson Reuters. AESG_PERF is aggregate ESG rating of the agent. TRANSP is ESG transparency rating of Thomson Reuters post-engagement period. The results hold when the study examines the three-year period following the engagement dialogue. The results are also consistent between the *t*-test for mean difference and the Wilcoxon test for median difference in the two groups of companies.

Table 4 provides the descriptive and univariate analysis of performance and transparency of the target companies before and after the successful engagements. The reported results of the univariate *t*-test calculate the differences between the mean value of analyzed variables in Year −1 and the mean value in Year +1, Year +2, and Year +3, correspondently. The results show that the mean and median market values of the target companies decline in Year +1 and then continue with a small increase from Year +2. The post-engagement levels of market value are not significantly different from those in Year −1. The mean and median levels of return on assets increase in Year +1, although they start to slightly decrease from Year +2. The *t*-test reveals the negative significant difference between the level of operating performance in Year +3 and Year −1.

Furthermore, Table 4 reports the ESG performance of the target companies. The levels of ESG performance ratings are slightly higher in the post-engagement period than in the pre-engagement Year −1. They slightly increase in Year +1 and Year +2 and decline in Year +3. The univariate test reveals the positive significant difference between the post-engagement ESG performance ratings in Year +2 and Year +3 and the pre-engagement ESG performance ratings in Year −1. The mean and median values of the ESG transparency ratings report small increases in levels of successful engagement after targeting, although they are insignificant in relation to the mean value of the ESG transparency ratings in Year −1.

The analysis reveals that target companies have higher pre-engagement ESG performance and ESG transparency ratings provided by Thomson Reuters than their counterparts, while the financial outcomes are, as might be expected, more volatile. Successful engagement can, in other words, improve the non-financial performance of leading ESG performers that are subject to an unexpected ESG incident. When an engagement process is brought to a successful conclusion, in the case of the Nordic model the objective has been to secure long-term value creation and not necessarily short-term profit maximization.

Table 4 Company performance of successful engagements in the pre- and post-engagement periods

		Pre-engagement period		Post-engagement period			
		Year −2	Year −1	Year 0	Year +1	Year +2	Year +3
TOBINQ	Mean	37.6560	38.2205	39.2059	37.5022	39.5674	40.4803
	Median	38.0889	39.1904	36.1684	35.9619	38.8612	39.4789
	Num. of cases	93	93	93	92	92	92
	p-value				0.8136	0.6593	0.4614
ROA	Mean	16.7216	16.9554	16.1415	16.6739	15.6108	13.3828
	Median	17.1553	15.8281	14.8228	15.8417	14.2974	13.6180
	Num. of cases	89	92	90	89	88	88
	p-value				0.8393	0.3189	**0.0063**
TRESG_PERF	Mean	77.0090	78.5779	79.6214	80.9000	81.2444	80.9244
	Median	89.285	90.6400	90.8600	90.9600	89.7600	90.9250
	Num. of cases	72	80	81	82	83	84
	p-value				0.5132	0.4433	0.4998
AESG_PERF	Mean	6.5556	7.2923	7.9091	8.08333	8.9706	8.5273
	Median	6.0000	7.0000	8.0000	9.0000	10.000	8.0000
	Num. of cases	63	65	66	72	68	55
	p-value				0.1659	**0.0022**	**0.0315**
TRANSP	Mean	70.7881	74.5010	75.6122	79.0277	79.0646	79.7361
	Median	89.6600	90.1450	91.2900	91.3850	90.41	90.8100
	Num. of cases	72	80	81	82	83	84
	p-value				0.2867	0.2829	0.2081

The table reports measures of financial performance, ESG performance, and ESG transparency of target companies for selected years in the pre- and post-engagement periods. All continuous variables are winsorized at the 1st and 99th percentiles. TOBINQ is Tobin's Q calculated as (market value of equity+book value of debt)/(book value of equity+book value of debt). ROA is return on assets that is earnings before interest, taxes, depreciation, and amortisation (EBITDA)/total assets. TRESG_PERF is aggregate ESG rating of Thomson Reuters. AESG_PERF is aggregate ESG rating of the agent. TRANSP is ESG transparency rating of Thomson Reuters

Nordic Engagements in an Anglo-Saxon Perspective

Nordic engagements in MSCI World companies are reactive actions by institutional investors driven by the financial risk inherent in ESG incidents. The focus of Nordic engagements is on the reduction of risk by suggesting improvements in a company's ESG performance and transparency. The Nordic model of engagement dialogue stresses the importance of company compliance with international norms on environment, human rights, and anti-corruption. The improvements made by target companies enable investors to expect that in the long run, the likelihood of future incidents is lower, and that the increased level of transparency will help to effectively manage ESG risks in investee companies. Engagement dialogue is seldom made public knowledge and does not impose a threat to the company's reputation. Neither Nordic investors nor their engagement agent publicly reports their involvement with company management. The Nordic model of engagement dialogue is consistent with the earlier observations of Bengtsson (2008) that Nordic SRI investors rely on dialogue, which is attributable to the tradition of consensus-seeking and a general preference for behind-the-scenes activity in business, as well as avoiding investing in companies that violate national and international law. In contrast, the Anglo-Saxon model of active ownership on ESG issues relies on a more formal, public means of engaging with the target company through shareholder resolutions. However, public shareholder resolutions can adversely affect managers' interests and the company's reputation, while informal private dialogue can require many interactions to reach an agreement. The Anglo-Saxon model of shareholder resolution can lead to a short-term immediate impact on the company's financial performance. Private engagement dialogue is expected to result in long-term improvements, but its impact on financial performance can be relatively small or insignificant in the short term. The challenge for the Nordic model is to create a relationship based on trust and shared values between the agent of the owners and the management of the target global company.

Nordic engagements are associated with target companies that outperform their counterparts on financial and ESG performance and ESG transparency before the engagement event. The view of Nordic investors differs from the Anglo-Saxon tradition in which poor financial performance and weak corporate governance drive engagement in the target companies. Nordic investors seem to try to challenge the existing practices of target companies, safeguard financial returns from unexpected incidents, and make recommendations that set the framework and facilitate company cooperation with key stakeholders. Nordic investors are involved in a small number of focused engagements in order to achieve a relatively high success rate. The main area of Nordic investors' ESG engagement pertains to social risk, followed by environmental and corruption risks. In the Anglo-Saxon model, active owners can influence the ESG practices of a larger sample of investee companies by focusing on a limited number of ESG themes that have potential to enhance market value. The outcomes of ESG engagement by Nordic activists indicate that target MSCI World companies continue to show high levels of operating performance, ESG performance, and ESG transparency over the one-year and three-year periods after being targeted for engagement dialogue related to incidents.

Chapter Summary

This chapter has aimed to highlight engagement dialogue as an SRI strategy from the Nordic investor perspective by generating an intensive and detailed examination of unique data on private interactions between Nordic institutional investors and the MSCI World Index companies in which they have a stake. This chapter extends the Anglo-Saxon SRI approach of exercising active ownership through shareholder resolutions by developing the Nordic model of engagement dialogue to study active ownership on ESG issues. The chapter reveals several distinguishing characteristics of the Nordic model for engagement dialogue and records results that are distinctive from previous US and UK literature on active ownership. First, the Nordic model of engagement dialogue builds upon external ESG risk management, which seeks changes in investee companies with ESG incidents that signal higher risk due to incident-related distance to ESG norms. Second, the Nordic practice of engagement is effective in conducting collaborative dialogue with a relatively small number of MSCI World companies and in providing focused suggestions for changes based on ESG information regarding the incident and company risk. Third, the majority of engagement dialogue cases pertain to social risks, including human rights and labor standards, rather than merely relying on traditional governance concerns like board changes and confidential voting issues. Fourth, target companies enjoy a relatively higher level of ESG performance, ESG transparency, and profitability than the other MSCI World Index companies in the pre- and post-engagement periods.

In sum, this chapter provides the first empirical analysis of the Nordic model for engagement dialogue and suggests that the SRI approach of active ownership and its outcomes are rooted in the Nordic corporate governance and stakeholder relationships model. It demonstrates that engagement dialogue regarding ESG risks has the potential to improve a company's ESG practices.

References

Allen, F., Carletti, E., & Marquez, R. (2007). *Stakeholder capitalism, corporate governance and firm value.* Retrieved from http://finance.wharton.upenn.edu/~allenf/download/Vita/JF-MS6731-Revision-corporate-governance-with-figures-16sep09-final.pdf.

Blowfield, M., & Murray, A. (2014). *Corporate responsibility.* Oxford: Oxford University Press.

Bauer, R., Clark, G. L., & Viehs, M. (2013). *The geography of shareholder engagement: Evidence from a large British institutional investor* (SSRN Working Paper). Maastricht: Maastricht University School of Business and Economics, Maastricht University.

Bauer, R., Moers, F., & Viehs, M. (2015). Who withdraws shareholder proposals and does it matter? An analysis of sponsor identity and pay practices. *Corporate Governance: An International Review, 23*(6), 472–488.

Becht, A., Franks, J., Mayer, C., & Rossi, S. (2009). Returns to shareholder activism: Evidence from a clinical study of the Hermes UK focus fund. *The Review of Financial Studies, 22*(8), 3093–3129.

Bengtsson, E. (2008). Socially responsible investing in Scandinavia—A comparative analysis. *Sustainable Development, 16,* 155–168.

Bryman, A., & Bell, E. (2015). *Business research methods.* Oxford: Oxford University Press.

Capelle-Blancard, G., & Petit, A. (2017). Every little helps? ESG news and stock market reaction. *Journal of Business Ethics.* Retrieved from https://doi.org/10.1007/s10551-017-3667-3.

Carleton, W., Nelson, J., & Weisbach, M. (1998). The influence of institutions on corporate governance through private negotiations: Evidence from TIAA-CREF. *Journal of Finance, 53*(4), 1335–1362.

Clark, G., Salo, J., & Hebb, T. (2008). Social and environmental shareholder activism in the public spotlight: US corporate annual meetings, campaign strategies, and environmental performance, 2001–04. *Environment and Planning A, 40*(6), 1370–1490.

David, P., Bloom, M., & Hillman, A. (2007). Investor activism, managerial responsiveness, and corporate social performance. *Strategic Management Journal, 28,* 91–100.

Deegan, C. (2015). *Financial accounting theory.* Sydney: McGraw-Hill.

Del Guercio, D., & Hawkins, J. (1999). The motivation and impact of pension fund activism. *Journal of Financial Economics, 52,* 293–340.

Den Hond, F., & de Bakker, F. (2007). Ideologically motivated activism: How activist groups influence corporate social change activities. *Academy of Management Review, 32*(3), 901–924.

Dimson, E., Karakas, O., & Li, X. (2015). Active ownership. *The Review of Financial Studies, 28*(12), 3225–3268.

Eurosif. (2016). *European SRI study.* Retrieved from http://www.eurosif.org/wp-content/uploads/2016/11/SRI-study-2016-HR.pdf.

Ferraro, F., & Beunza, D. (2014). *Why talk? A process model of dialogue in shareholder engagement* (SSRN Working Paper). Barcelona: IESE Business School, University of Navarra.

Gillan, S., & Starks, L. (2000). Corporate governance proposals and shareholder activism: The role of institutional investors. *Journal of Financial Economics, 57*(2), 275–305.

Gillan, S., & Starks, L. (2007). The evolution of shareholder activism in the United States. *Journal of Applied Corporate Finance, 19*(1), 55–73.

Gjolberg, M. (2010). Varieties of corporate social responsibility (CSR): CSR meets the "Nordic Model". *Regulation & Government, 4,* 203–229.

Goranova, M., Abouk, R., Nystrom, P., & Ehsan, S. (2017). Corporate governance antecedents to shareholder activism: A zero-inflated process. *Strategic Management Journal, 38*(2), 415–435.

Goranova, M., & Ryan, L. (2014). Shareholder activism: A multidisciplinary review. *Journal of Management, 40,* 1230–1266.

Grewal, J., Serafeim G., & Yoon, A. (2016). *Shareholder activism on sustainability issues* (SSRN Working Paper). Boston: Harvard Business School, Harvard University.

Hair, J., Black, W., Babin, B., & Anderson, R. (2014). *Multivariate data analysis*. Essex: Pearson Education Limited.

Harris, M., & Raviv, A. (2010). *Control of corporate decisions: Shareholders vs. management* (SSRN Working Paper). Chicago: University of Chicago Booth School of Business.

Hamilton, I., & Eriksson, J. (2011). Influence strategies in shareholder engagement: A case study of all Swedish National Pension Funds. *Journal of Sustainable Finance & Investment, 1*(1), 44–61.

Henisz, W., Dorobantu, S., & Nartey, L. (2014). Spinning gold: The financial and operational returns to external stakeholder engagement. *Strategic Management Journal, 35*(12), 1727–1748.

Kruger, P. (2015). Corporate goodness and shareholder wealth. *Journal of Financial Economics, 115,* 304–329.

Lekvall, P. (2014). *The Nordic corporate governance model.* Stockholm: TMG Sthlm.

Mallin, C. (2016). *Corporate governance*. Oxford: Oxford University Press.

McNulty, T., & Nordberg, D. (2016). Ownership, activism and engagement: Institutional investors as active owners. *Corporate Governance: An International Review, 24*(3), 346–358.

Porter, M., & Kramer, M. (2011). Creating shared value. *Harvard Business Review, 89,* 62–77.

Poulsen, T., Strand, T., & Thomsen, S. (2010). Voting power and shareholder activism: A study of Swedish shareholder meetings. *Corporate Governance: An International Review, 18*(4), 329–343.

Rehbein, K., Logsdon, J., & Van Buren, H. (2013). Corporate responses to shareholder activists: Considering the dialogue alternative. *Journal of Business Ethics, 112,* 137–154.

Reid, E., & Toffel, M. (2009). Responding to public and private politics: Corporate disclosure of climate change strategies. *Strategic Management Journal, 30,* 1157–1178.

Scholtens, B., & Sievänen, R. (2013). Drivers of socially responsible investing: A case study of four Nordic countries. *Journal of Business Ethics, 115,* 605–616.

Semenova, N., Hassel, L., & Nilsson, H. (2010). The value relevance of environmental and social performance: Evidence from Swedish SIX 300 companies. *The Finnish Journal of Business Economics, 3,* 265–292.
Smith, M. P. (1996). Shareholder activism by institutional investors: Evidence from CalPERS. *Journal of Finance, 51*(1), 227–252.
Strand, R. (2014). Scandinavia can be inspiration for creating shared value. *Financial Times*. Retrieved from https://www.ft.com/content/84bbd770-b34d-11e3-b09d-00144feabdc0.
Strand, R., & Freeman, R. (2015). Scandinavian cooperative advantage: The theory and practice of stakeholder engagement in Scandinavia. *Journal of Business Ethics, 127,* 65–85.
Thomsen, S., & Conyon, M. (2012). *Corporate governance: Mechanisms and systems*. London: McGraw-Hill Higher Education.
Vidaver-Cohen, D., & Bronn, P. (2015). Reputation, responsibility, and stakeholder support in Scandinavian firms: A comparative analysis. *Journal of Business Ethics, 127,* 49–64.
Wang, Y., & Mao, C. (2015). Shareholder activism of public pension funds: The political facet. *Journal of Banking & Finance, 60,* 138–152.
Yamahaki, C., & Frynas, G. (2016). Institutional determinants of private shareholder engagement in Brazil and South Africa: The role of regulation. *Corporate Governance: An International Review, 24*(5), 509–527.

Sustainable Business Practices—An Environmental Economics Perspective

Tommy Lundgren, Lammertjan Dam and Bert Scholtens

Introduction

According to conventional economic theory, society is organized on two pillars:

- The market and the "invisible hand" (Adam Smith in "The Theory of Moral Sentiments," 1759) ensures that the interests of consumers and businesses are controlled so that the outcome is effective;

T. Lundgren (✉)
Department of Economics, Centre for Environmental and Resources Economics (CERE), Umeå University, Umeå, Sweden
e-mail: tommy.lundgren@umu.se

L. Dam · B. Scholtens
Faculty of Economics and Business, University of Groningen, Groningen, The Netherlands
e-mail: l.dam@rug.nl

B. Scholtens
e-mail: l.j.r.scholtens@rug.nl

S. Arvidsson (ed.), *Challenges in Managing Sustainable Business*,
https://doi.org/10.1007/978-3-319-93266-8_9

- The government correct market failures[1] through market interventions as well as through distribution policies to redistribute income and wealth, as the distributions generated by the market are not always in line with those preferred by society.

Companies are governed by profit-maximizing shareholders and are influenced by other stakeholders, such as employees and customers and citizens in the surrounding community, which in turn are protected by various types of contracts[2] and government regulations. Most industrialized countries follow this basic recipe, although there are differences in the perception of when and to what extent the state should intervene. Based on this approach, it is primarily the state, and not individuals or companies, whose task is to correct market failures and equalize inequalities in income and wealth. Nevertheless, we see an increasing demand from society at large, and from regulatory authorities, that individuals and companies in particular should increase their social responsibility in addition to traditional utility and profit maximization (Bénabou and Tirole 2010).

As to the responsibility, we may differentiate between a legal, economic, and moral perspective. With the legal perspective of the firm's responsibility, one focuses on the situation that a firm has legally binding contracts with investors, suppliers, employees, and customers and is subject to a dense network of laws and regulation enforced by society. With the economic perspective, the focus is on the external effects on production and there are agency problems between investors, employees, customers, regulators, suppliers, and firm management. Then, there is a moral perspective. This holds that by its actions; the firm morally involves its stakeholders and makes them complicit in its behavior.

Since the Brundtland Report (The World Commission on Environment and Development 1987) was published in 1987, the concept of sustainable development has been discussed vigorously in the social and scientific debate, not least in terms of climate and whether human activities heat the earth. Part of this discussion has been devoted to what companies *voluntarily* can do—and actually do—to contribute to sustainable development that includes economic, environmental, and social development. Common to these companies is that they are in some way *socially responsible.* The phenomenon is commonly called *Corporate Social Responsibility* or simply CSR. Here, an issue is to demarcate to whom the corporations actually are responsible. Is it to their owners, their regulators, their stakeholders, or to society at large? The answer pertains in part to whether the firm has a legal, economic, or moral responsibility.

One of the challenges of discussing the concept of sustainable development and socially responsible companies is the definition of CSR itself. There are a variety of definitions that circulate in research and in the public debate, and most are ambiguous and perplexing.[3] We will use a definition that is simple and reasonable. According to conventional neoclassical economic theory, companies maximize profits under restrictions, and without regulations, there is a risk that companies, for example, release more carbon dioxide or have poorer working environment conditions than is socially optimal. Today, we see many companies that do more on the environment than they are required to do in accordance with laws and regulations. Even within other dimensions, such as working environment or human rights, some companies are doing more than they are legally required to do.[4] It is this type of voluntary self-regulation by companies that we define as CSR (see similar definition in, e.g., Hay et al. 2005). An advantage of explaining CSR as efforts beyond legal frameworks is that CSR becomes conceptually well-defined and unambiguous.[5] However, this does not mean that you get rid of the problem of measuring and quantifying CSR, more about this later.

The academic discussion about CSR seems to have begun in 1932 at a *Harvard Law Symposium* with the title of *Who are corporate managers' trustees?* (Dodd 1932). At this symposium, the discussion focused on whether it was even legal to use a company's earned profits and resources in the interests of society. Within economics, the debate took off in 1970 following Milton Friedman's article *The social responsibility of business is to increase its profits* in the *New York Times Magazine* (Friedman 1970). Friedman considered that charity should be managed by the individual while the company should concentrate on maximizing profits to its shareholders. But as we will see, profit maximization does not have to be in contrast to CSR, and in some cases, they go hand in hand.

Ever since Friedman's article 1970, the debate has continued and CSR has attracted considerable attention from researchers and society as well.

What is the role of companies in terms of increased social/environmental responsibility? Most agree that the companies should reasonably comply with acknowledged laws. But in addition to that, do companies have a further responsibility to transfer resources intended for profit generation to, for example, improve the environment? Much of what has been written in the area is confusing as it usually does not provide a well-structured basis for how to relate to CSR. In this chapter, we will discuss CSR from an *environmental economics perspective*. The discussion is based on the research available—mainly from economics—and aims to clarify some concepts and create an explanatory framework for understanding the corporate behavior economists refer to as CSR.

An adequate theory about CSR, we argue, would have to balance between personal taste and values, social norms, and market imperfections. To advance academic research about CSR, it is crucial to improve environmental accounting, especially at the firm level, as suggested already by Atkinson (2000). Thus, the system of double bookkeeping and national accounting needs to be accompanied by environmental, social, and material flows accounts in a more detailed manner than what we see today. Otherwise, any theory about CSR would run the risk of remaining sterile as it would be impossible to put it to the test.

The rest of the chapter is structured as follows. First, we describe possible reasons why companies engage in CSR. Then, we discuss the following relevant questions regarding CSR: *May firms sacrifice profits in the social interest? Is it economically sustainable that firms practice CSR? Should firms engage in CSR from a welfare point of view? Do we actually see that CSR is being practiced?* Thereafter, a selective inventory of empirical research on CSR is presented. We end with concluding remarks.

The Firm's Motivation for CSR

We rely on an economic definition of CSR and argue that CSR manifests itself in some observable and measurable behavior or output. The behavior of the firm in this respect exceeds norms and regulations or levels set by mandatory regulation or standards that are legally enforceable (Kitzmueller and Shimshack 2012). One can basically divide CSR into two different main types; *altruistic*[6] CSR and *strategic*[7] CSR. With altruistic CSR, we mean that the company "sacrifices" profits in community service, while strategic CSR means that the company basically profit maximize in traditional terms, but focuses on increased corporate social responsibility.[8] One can also imagine a difference where the motive for CSR is not strategic, but where the cost of CSR is offset by some of the revenue that is not foreseen. Or vice versa, the motive is strategic, but the cost of CSR is not offset by revenue. Our review below also covers these cases.

Even though altruistic CSR is not rewarded by the market, one can still imagine situations when it occurs; for example, when shareholders' preferences are characterized by environmental responsibility. If shareholders care about the environment beyond the law's domains, they may be willing to renounce a portion of the profit for CSR, or even a loss by using their influence as a way of rendering a kind of charity. Another motivation for altruistic CSR can be attributed to special preferences in terms of profit distribution, for example, that the shareholders prefer to spend more money on CSR than to increase bonuses (to new top levels) to their managers. This is particularly relevant now when bonuses and problems in the banking sector (the crisis that started in 2008), with state intervention as a consequence, are under the lap of society (Kitzmueller and Shimshack 2012).

A particular case discussed in the literature is CSR and the relationship between management (CEO, environmental manager, and others) and the owners. If we embrace Friedman's tight business paradigm—companies should maximize profits and not partake in charity—all types of altruistic CSR can be seen as a manifestation of principal-agent issues. This issue arises if there are conflicts of interests between company leaders and owners. CEOs or individuals in other senior positions (agents) in the company can use CSR to increase their own popularity and promote a personal agenda to other interest groups without the consent of the owners (principals). For a more detailed discussion of the principal-agent problem in relation to CSR, see, e.g., Kitzmueller and Shimshack (2012), or McWilliams and Siegel (2001).

Thus, the *agency cost view* implies that socially responsible behavior comes at the expense of shareholder value and might be exploited by managers to gain private benefits (e.g., improved reputation). Next to this agency perspective, the risk mitigation view is that CSR can be value-relevant by helping mitigate several stakeholder risks. As such, it may help reduce the probability and intensity of reputational damages, litigation, and costly regulatory requirements. For a discussion of the risk mitigation approach in relation to CSR, see Ferrell et al. (2016), or Fernando et al. (2017).

Market-driven CSR or CSR as a protection against future regulations or activism from interest groups is commonly called strategic CSR (more on this below). The term goes back to McWilliams and Siegel (2001) and Baron (2001). This behavior is basically profit-maximizing and driven by pressure on the company's demand side (customers) and from other interest groups such as employees, activists (NGOs such as the Nature Conservation Association and Greenpeace), and regulatory authorities.

To illustrate strategic CSR, we look at an example of a model of a profit-maximizing company with certain market power, i.e., the company has a certain influence over its product price. The model is described in detail in Lundgren (2011). A basic driving force for CSR in this model is goodwill or reputation. By investing in CSR measures, the company can build up a goodwill capital, as well as building up a capital stock with investments. The goodwill capital affects the company's profitability in different ways. A prerequisite for goodwill to be generated and beneficial to the company is that all CSR investments are adequately communicated to the market, which entails a cost beyond the investment itself (marketing, review of CSR actions in the annual report, and more). If the company signals CSR without actually doing something, it is called *greenwashing*,[9] which is likely to occur to some extent. However, it is excluded from the model.

Three main *positive effects of CSR* (benefit or income) can be identified:

- *The price effect.* Consumers/Customers reward CSR by being willing to pay a higher price or buy more at the same price. This is what economics theory calls price differentiation; by giving the product certain attributes that make it stand out from the competitors' products, the firm can enjoy a price premium.

- *Wage effect.* Employees are willing to accept lower wages to work in a CSR company or to work more productively at given market pay. This is based on the fact that the company can attract employees who sense a certain *warm glow*[10] feeling of working for a CSR firm.
- *Capital cost effect.* Capital costs can be reduced as the financial sector—banks, portfolio managers, private and public investors, etc.—attributes a lower risk to the CSR firm. The reason is that the likelihood of future conflicts with different interest groups is decreasing. For example, CSR can occur and prevent costly future regulations and/or improve the relationship with activist groups, and thus CSR becomes a kind of risk management.

The cost of CSR can also be divided into three main groups:

- *Investment cost.* There is always a direct investment cost of engaging in CSR.
- *Signaling cost.* If no one knows that the company has increased social responsibility, goodwill cannot be created, so companies must actively signal CSR to the market and interest groups, and this costs money in the form of marketing and/or other types of information campaigns.
- *Crowding out effects/costs.* Costs arise because resources are put on CSR that could have been used for potentially more productive investment alternatives (opportunity cost).

These costs and benefits are then built into a model of the firm. Note that this simple model refrains from including positioning and anticipation of firms here. A part of the theoretical literature on CSR looks specifically at strategic behavior and games, see, e.g., Arora and Gangopadhyay (1995) and Wirl et al. (2013). Continuing with our simple model, there can be different transmission mechanisms such as markets, policy, and norms. With markets, it is taste and incentives that drive the preferences of consumers and production costs. Both in factor and in product markets, accounting for responsibility can have an impact. Policy is an alternative pass-through to reveal preferences. Here, usually some policy threat is involved, be it a fine or public mentioning or increased monitoring. With social norms, there is an institutional environment with accepted norms/views/values that might discipline agents.

The main message here is that the firm that is in optimum will balance the marginal costs and benefits of investing in CSR. In other words, CSR is treated as an investment, costs are charged to income/benefits. The different results of the model can then be linked to many of the empirical observations and hypotheses contained in the CSR literature, such as whether CSR has a positive impact (or not) on the company's product price (*ceteris paribus*). The motive for developing such a model is that existing empirical research lacks a simple formal model to lean against in order to provide relevant hypotheses about CSR. See also McWilliams and Siegel (2001) for a similar but non-technical model. Also, an early—and somewhat overlooked—model of the "green firm" is found in Bergman (1995), in which CSR is also described in strategic terms as one of the firm's many investment decisions.

Now, we turn back to behavioral aspects of CSR. Altruistic and strategic CSR, and the preferences governing these behaviors, can be summarized in Fig. 1. The company's stakeholders are divided into shareholders and the market and other stakeholders (e.g., NGOs). Their preferences are then divided into social preferences and neoclassical preferences. Social preferences mean, for example, that customers value an eco-friendly product higher, or that the owners value the company's environmental work and may therefore refrain from yielding. What we can see is that if the owners have "classic" preferences and customers and other interest groups, then we end up in a situation with no CSR (Box 4). On the other hand, if the owners have social preferences and the market/stakeholders have classic preferences, we end up in Box 3, i.e., altruistic CSR with reduced profits. And if the owners have classic preferences and the market has social, we end up in Box 2, i.e., strategic CSR. Box 1 is altruistic CSR, but the effects on profit are either positive or negative depending on costs and revenues.

In this context, Dam and Scholtens (2015) show in a theoretical model that besides social preferences of shareholders potentially having a mixed effect on profits, higher average stock market returns may also no longer be associated with higher average profits. This result

		Shareholders	
		Social preferences (SP)	*Neoclassical Preferences (NP)*
The market and other stakeholders	*SP*	(1) Altruistic CSR Mixed effect on profit	(2) Strategic CSR Profit maximization
	NP	(3) Altruistic CSR Reduced profit	(4) No CSR Profit maximization

Fig. 1 Corporate CSR and the effects of different preferences at owners and market/stakeholders (*Source* Adaptation of Fig. 2 in Kitzmueller and Shimshack (2012))

highlights that confusion about the relation between CSR and financial performance can arise in empirical work.

In summary, preferences of the company's owners, the market, or other interest groups generate a certain behavior of the company that can be linked to profitability, thus qualifying CSR as part of the company's business model. This business model may mean that the company carries out altruistic CSR or strategic CSR, which depends on what motivates these commitments by the owners. This is the theoretical and conceptual framework we bring in the rest of the article.

In the next section, we specifically point to the four key issues that should be addressed in CSR, both altruistic and strategic.

CSR: Four Relevant Issues

There are four main issues that should be addressed when it comes to CSR and companies: *May firms sacrifice profits in the social interest? Is it economically sustainable that firms practice CSR? Should firms engage in CSR from a welfare point of view? Do we actually see that CSR is being practiced?* (Hay et al. 2005; Reinhardt et al. 2008). We will try to answer these questions separately to dispel some of ambiguities and confusion about the concept of CSR.

May Firms Sacrifice Profits in the Social Interest?

Is it allowed for management to use the company's resources, for example, environmental work that goes beyond what laws and regulations prescribe? The answer to that question can first seem apparent: Yes, why not? In the case when voluntary environmental effort has a positive impact on profit (or is profit neutral), for example, by investing in goodwill that attracts customers or increases customer loyalty, it is of course no problem; the company maximizes profit (strategic CSR). However, in the case of management failure, the answer is not as obvious (altruistic CSR).This means that those who own the company (shareholders) do not fully receive their eligible compensation as risk-takers. In the USA, there are examples of shareholders who have withdrawn management as they violate their powers, but it has not yet led to any convictions. It has been difficult to prove that specific voluntary environmental measures have been directly profitable. The USA can and should lead the business enterprise under the "commercial considerations" (the so-called *business judgment rule*), which gives them a relatively wide leeway in the use of company resources. This means that only in extreme cases CSR can be considered illegal (Elhauge 2005).

Is It Economically Sustainable That Firms Practice CSR?

Is it a sustainable strategy for a company to give up profits and engage in CSR, or will competition lead to the disappearance of such companies in the long term? Companies that have some degree of market power, including those who produce products for well-defined niche markets, may be able to transfer costs induced by CSR to their customers. But for the majority of companies operating in competitive markets with similar products, it is difficult to do so. Such companies must then somehow bear these costs, either in the form of lower profits and/or dividends, lower compensation to management, or lower wages for their employees. This implies that in competitive markets, CSR is not necessarily economically sustainable in the long run from the company's perspective, unless its shareholders or employees are willing to bear the costs. In light of this, one can also imagine a market in which the company is required to behave socially responsible, because all or most of the peer companies do so—driven by the demand for CSR from the market participants. In this case, CSR becomes a way of surviving in a market characterized by customers, shareholders, or employees, who value the social conduct of the firm and its products.

As mentioned earlier, CSR can also be motivated by the fact that companies anticipate stricter regulation in the future. By showing "good conduct," potentially expensive regulations and conflicts with different interest groups can then be avoided. If the risk of government intervention in any area or sector is high, companies in this area or sector are more likely to engage in CSR to prevent such interventions that may lead to increased costs in the future. Such behavior is therefore consistent with a "forward-looking" profit maximization under uncertainty. One can also think of situations when financially strong companies adopt CSR in order to push regulatory authorities to raise regulatory levels across the sector, which may result in financially weaker companies being forced out of the market. Both examples are situated in a gray zone between altruistic and strategic CSR. Both examples reflect a kind of game between the company and the regulator, implying that CSR is a profitable strategy in the long term, by either saving future costs or crowding out competitors. But in the short term, it might very well lead to additional costs without significant increases in revenues, which can be seen as altruistic CSR. However, in both cases, companies seemingly engage in altruistic and profit-impairing CSR, with the potential of this behavior to change into a profitable strategy in the future, depending on how the regulatory authority responds.

Should Firms Engage in CSR from a Welfare Point of View?

Even though companies may have certain incentives or motivations to engage in CSR, *should* they do so? Does such behavior lead to a more efficient use of society's common resources? To be more specific, under which conditions does CSR increase total welfare overall? According to

Paul Portney, this is only the case when companies engage in strategic CSR, that is, when it is economically profitable and when *green business* is *good business* (Portney 2005). The alternative, altruistic CSR is considered more costly and inefficient, since by definition it does not generate any value to, e.g., the consumers. In the case of altruistic CSR, consumers are not willing to pay a premium for green products.[11] From a welfare perspective, companies should invest in projects that generate the highest possible social welfare. This means that CSR is desirable if overall welfare is higher with CSR than without. For example, one can imagine that self-regulation by engaging in CSR might resolve environmental externalities or other undesirable market frictions.

Then, the question is whether companies should voluntarily regulate themselves, or whether the government is better at setting optimal regulation. It is unlikely that companies are always doing investments that maximize societal welfare. First, this is because CSR decisions are determined by a number of factors, many of which are not directly related to maximizing overall social welfare. Second, there is an obvious coordination problem between various firms to maximize overall welfare, in that it is not a priori clear to an individual firm how much it should contribute to achieve the collective goal. Individual companies probably have good knowledge of the individual economic impact of CSR, but the overall social welfare impact is much more difficult to estimate. This asymmetry can, for example, lead to an inefficient level of environmental protection (either too much or too little). In this case, centralized regulation by a government is more desirable.

But one can also think of situations where the company is better informed than a regulator. This applies, for example, to information about the company's current and future pollution, as well as costs for controlling these. With this type private or inside information, companies can make more informed and therefore better decisions regarding emission-enhancing business changes, compared to an authority that usually lacks this type of detailed knowledge about the company's technology. In such cases, CSR may defy regulation and lead to increased welfare when companies have more flexibility than under strict regulation. This applies of course to several types of environmental and social regulation.

CSR investments and commitments can be welfare-enhancing when the level of a centrally determined environmental regulation is set to "too low," that is, when the government fails to produce optimal regulation/policy (Reinhardt et al. 2008). For example, there may be welfare-increasing CSR aimed at mitigating environmental problems that are totally or partially unregulated; policies to tackle climate change suffer from failure of reaching international environmental agreements, for example. Another example is CSR that targets at improving working conditions in countries where regulations are non-existent or authorities do not enforce them.

Do We Actually See That CSR Is Being Practiced?

Do companies voluntarily go beyond the law and invest in CSR? There are a number of examples of voluntary commitments. In Sweden, for example, there is a furniture company in Malmö, which has a number of "climate-smart" products, waste sorting systems, biogas production (from food residues), environmental car parks with (free) electric power outlets, and own energy production (wind power and solar cells) where the surplus is sold in the energy market. These activities reflect of course largely voluntary commitments and can therefore be seen as CSR. More general examples of CSR are different types of environmental agreements between companies and governments, industry organizations or other community groups, or product certifications (such as forest products), and other environmental labeling of consumer goods such as the Swan or Good Environmental Choice (Svanen och Bra Miljöval). Entering these agreements is entirely voluntary and can reasonably be explained by the fact that companies believe that this type of behavior is in their self-interest, that is, the cost of changing the way of production is less than (or at least equal to) the revenue generated by the change.

A large number of environmental studies find that it is *generally* not possible to convincingly show that it is commercially profitable to be voluntarily "greener" than determined by law and regulations. However, in cases where the company can increase consumers' willingness to pay, reduce its costs, reduce risks, or preempt costly future regulation, it can be commercially viable to engage in CSR (Hay et al. 2005). There are companies that have successfully used CSR in their business model (e.g., Patagonia apparel company), but overall, it is difficult to find empirical support because strategic CSR generally means exploiting promising business opportunities and/or increased profitability. As such, the discussion about "true" CSR is sometimes clouded by semantics.

Empirical Research on CSR

As suggested in the previous section, empirical support for the claim that environmental CSR is profitable is not particularly convincing. What do we know about the profitability of CSR in general? We provide an overview of our current knowledge based on empirical studies in various areas related to CSR. The theoretical research on CSR is limited relative to the empirically oriented research. However, there are attempts to theoretically explain CSR in a strict model framework, such as McWilliams and Siegel (2001) and Lundgren (2011). For a compact review of theoretical modeling of CSR, see Lundgren (2011). This empirical review is based on a reasonably recent literature review in Kitzmueller and Shimshack (2012), with some additions from the Swedish perspective. We do not claim to be exhaustive in terms of referencing all relevant studies. Instead, we give some well-chosen examples within each sub-area of CSR research.

In early studies in the field of economics, CSR focused on the link between corporate social responsibility and financial performance, while recent research has focused on the mechanisms behind CSR. Understanding why companies engage in CSR and which stakeholders bear the cost of CSR are fundamental. Much of the empirical research on CSR in the field of economics is not explicitly presented under the label corporate social responsibility. Instead, scholars often adopt terminology such as *over-compliance*, *voluntary compliance*, *corporate philanthropy*, and *eco-labeling*.

CSR, Financial Performance, and Competitiveness

In the early and mid-1990s when Michael Porter at Harvard Business School launched his "Porter Hypothesis," a wave of empirical studies followed that examined the link between environmental regulation and competitiveness (Porter 1991; Porter and van der Linde 1995). Porter's hypothesis is based on a number of case studies that suggested that environmental regulation could create benefits/revenues from innovation and efficiency increases that neutralize or even outperform the cost of the regulation itself, i.e., the net profitability increases in the end. These empirical studies focus on mandatory regulation, such as taxes and fees, and not on voluntary self-regulation (CSR). It was a legal mandate that was the driving force of Porter's original argument. However, since Porter's logic can be applied to voluntary commitment as well, empirical studies related to the Porter hypothesis can shed some light on whether CSR has the potential to reduce costs and increase efficiency within the company. A number of review articles on the Porter hypothesis and its validity based on an empirical perspective have been published, and they show that there is no *systematic* evidence that changes in environmental performance due to stricter regulation urge innovation and lead to efficiency gains (see, e.g., Brännlund and Lundgren 2009).

However, it might be that voluntary self-regulation such as CSR implies that companies have more freedom in choosing appropriate measures themselves, such that these improve both environmental performance and economic performance. In this case, compulsory government regulation differs from CSR; regulations force the company to adjust, whether this is desirable or not, while voluntary CSR can be a deliberate strategic decision that is also profitable. Lundgren and Marklund (2014) investigate Swedish industrial data where environmental performance is divided into performance due to regulation (carbon dioxide tax) and voluntary or market-related causes. They show that environmental performance that can be linked to regulation has a neutral or negative impact on profitability. In other words, the Porter hypothesis can largely be rejected for most Swedish industrial sectors. However, voluntary improvements in environmental performance

(CSR) are positively correlated with profitability in most sectors, which would indicate that there is a degree of asymmetry in the impact on the profitability of regulation and self-regulation in Swedish industry; good environmental performance is good for profitability, unless it stems from regulation—in this case a carbon tax.

Within business economics and empirical financial economics, there are a large number of studies that analyze the general relationship between CSR and financial performance. Margolis et al. (2009) provide a review that extensively evaluates the research on this topic; they investigate 251 relationships from 214 studies between 1972 and 2009. One way of interpreting these studies is that they are an attempt to test the presence of altruistic CSR, that is, if CSR is costly without any measurable benefit. If this is the case, then the effect on financial performance is ultimately negative. In line with the previous discussion, we can identify two cases: (1) altruistic CSR resulting from management's preferences and/or private agenda (a principal-agent situation); (2) altruistic CSR that results from the owners' (shareholders') preferences who are willing to sacrifice profits in the interest of society as a whole. It turns out that there is no support for either type of altruistic CSR. Margolis et al. (2009) find a modest positive effect between CSR and financial performance for the entire time period and a very weak but positive effect over the last ten years. This result, that is, a small or, in many cases, no effect of CSR, could be interpreted as a manifestation of strategic CSR; companies invest in CSR up to a level where costs and revenue on the margin are equal. In this case, profitability is unaffected and CSR should not have a significant effect on financial performance.

However, a major problem with these studies is that is not clear how to appropriately measure CSR (this also applies to some extent to measures of financial performance). Most commonly, the empirical studies use performance indicators of various types created by consultancy companies (KLD, ASSET4, etc.). These measures will always contain a certain degree of subjectivity. Paul and Siegel (2006) note that most empirical studies that analyze CSR and financial performance are not particularly relevant from an economic perspective. They argue that the interesting relationship is between economic performance and CSR, where economic performance is based on company technology[12] and specifically taking into account the alternative cost for CSR. They also emphasize the importance of using objective and observable variables in studies on CSR, such as actual emissions to air/water/land, and not ratings by consulting firms that are difficult to translate into quantitative performance targets. Two studies that follow the advice of Paul and Siegel (2006) is Lundgren and Marklund (2014) and Lundgren and Wenchao (2017). These studies look specifically at changes in actual emissions, energy use and environmental management, and the effects on economic performance as measured by profit efficiency or productivity.

Another problem with studies looking at the relationship between CSR and financial performance is the causal relationship. As Margolis et al. (2009) suggest that the weak positive correlation (median correlation 0.09) can be explained either by causality from CSR to financial performance or vice versa. Attempts are made in the literature to adequately figure out the causal relationship, but at this stage there is no conclusive evidence. However, there are a large number of so-called event studies that examine both good and bad news (events) and how investors respond to them. In this case, causality is apparent; an oil spill is taking place today and the stock price moves tomorrow; or a company turns out to have a larger reduction in carbon dioxide emissions than expected, and as a result, the stock price increases. In this case, the causal relationship is clear. However, it is not easy to connect the response of financial markets to altruistic or strategic CSR as defined above. The seminal event study concerning CSR is Hamilton (1995). An example of an international study on more recent data is Lundgren and Olsson (2010).

Empirical Research and Strategic CSR

Contrary to empirical support for altruistic CSR and the Porter hypothesis (*win-win* regulations), the evidence on strategic CSR is somewhat more convincing. As discussed previously, the modest or no effect of CSR on financial performance can be interpreted as support for strategic CSR, i.e., costs and revenues of CSR are balanced. Who pays the cost associated with CSR? There are some answers in the literature, and we discuss a few studies in this context.

We first consider the labor market in the context of CSR. One of the cost-benefit considerations of CSR is that employees may be willing to work for lower wages or work more productively when a company engages in CSR. Empirical support for employees bearing the cost (or part of it) of CSR behavior through lower wages is relatively weak and more studies are needed (Kitzmueller and Shimshack 2012). However, there are few studies that demonstrate this effect—in particular the economic literature on compensating wage differentials[13]—for companies engaged in CSR (e.g., Bolvig 2005; Edmans 2011; Nyborg and Zhang 2013). Nonetheless, despite a few examples in the literature, there is currently no convincing evidence that workers generally accept lower wages or work more productively when employed socially responsible companies. The labor market does therefore not systematically provide incentives for companies to engage in CSR.

Responsible consumers (both end-users and consumers of intermediaries) and their demand for products with CSR attributes provide another explanation for the observed CSR behavior of companies. Indeed, a number of empirical studies suggest that this consumer demand-driven motive for CSR is at play. A study by Blend and Ravenswaay (1999) shows that consumers in USA are willing to pay a premium for certain kinds of organic apples. Kriström and Lundgren (2003) find that pulp mills' investment in environmentally friendly technologies can create goodwill, which has a positive effect on the price of pulp in the Swedish forest industry. A considerable amount of valuation studies shows that consumers are willing to pay more for food products from companies that adhere to local and/or organic production, or products with a *fair trade*-marking. In an econometric study, Eichholtz, Kok, and Quigley (2010) use data on commercial buildings in the USA and conclude that there is a price premium for "green" buildings. Mandell and Wilhemsson (2011) found similar results for Swedish households; they are prepared to pay a premium for "sustainable" housing. Many other examples of similar empirical results can be found in the literature. We can thus safely conclude that product markets in relation to different types of consumers/customers can potentially create incentives for strategic CSR, because some consumers are willing to take on all (or part of the) costs related to CSR.

Other interest groups than customers and employees may also to some extent drive CSR. Pressure from, and attitudes of activist groups, local community groups and regulatory agencies can influence CSR behavior. Arora and Cason (1999) show that the effect of social values and local attitudes toward a company's environmental behavior can be essential with respect to the level of contribution to CSR. A company operating in a local community where a large proportion of the population is politically and environmentally involved tends to have relatively better environmental performance compared to a similar company that faces less engaged residents. There is also empirical evidence that boycotts can have a significant effect on a company's share price. In sum, there is also evidence that other interest groups than customers and employees affect CSR, although the magnitude of such effects is not easy to quantify.

Khanna and Anton (2002) have asked a large number of American companies what affects their CSR behavior. They conclude that the decision to hire professionals with an environmental focus and internal environmental policy is greatly influenced by factors governed by regulation, while quality assurance and product development depend on market factors. Innes and Sam (2008) show that companies voluntarily reduce emissions in order to improve the relationship with the regulatory authorities and to avoid stricter future regulations. Companies subject to greater transparency from the regulator are more willing to engage in voluntary emissions reduction programmes. Empirical findings thus show that both private initiatives from various interest groups and public authority in terms of regulation or the threat of regulation may create incentives for CSR as we actually observe it.

Figure 1 above summarizes the interaction between the company's owners and various interest groups (*stakeholders*), such as customers, activists, regulators, and others, which in turn results in altruistic CSR, strategic CSR, or no CSR. We have discussed (a part of) the empirical research on CSR and its driving forces. There is little support for so-called altruistic CSR, i.e., the situation where the company voluntarily refrains from profits to benefit society as a whole. Even the so-called Porter hypothesis is difficult to maintain empirically. There is, however, support in the empirical literature for what we labeled strategic CSR, a kind of responsible *business as usual* where markets, stakeholders, and regulatory authorities play a crucial role in establishing corporate social responsibility.

In addition, Dam and Scholtens (2015) use a theoretical model to suggest a taxonomy of the empirical literature that links CSR to financial performance. The main takeaway of their research is that it matters how financial performance is measured in empirical work. The underlying reason is that in the valuation or measurement of the financial performance of firms, both (expected) cash flows and the cost of capital play a role. Since CSR can affect cash flows (through, for example, profits and/or costs), but also the cost of capital (through the discount rate induced by altruistic investor preferences), the net effect of these two mechanisms is not a priori clear and depends on the financial performance measure that is adopted. Their model predicts that accounting profits or market-to-book values of equity should show a positive association with CSR performance, whereas stock market returns should have an ambiguous relation with CSR performance. It turns out that the empirical findings in the literature are in line with these predictions.

Concluding Remarks

How should we think about companies with a social responsibility? Is CSR both economically and socially sustainable? If the company operates in a monopoly or a special niche market where they can overturn the costs of CSR in the market, this is more likely to be the case. Should companies engage in practices beyond statutory targets? Should companies sacrifice profits for the environment when the alternative is a more effective environmental policy designed and applied by a central regulator?

As indicated before, there are situations when it is feasible that CSR is welfare-enhancing. This applies primarily to strategic CSR directed against such environmental problems that are partly or entirely unregulated. An example of an environmental problem that in many parts of the world lacks adequate regulations is the increasing emissions of carbon dioxide and other greenhouse gases.

Another issue raised here is how to define and measure CSR. How to do this will be crucial for an evaluation or interpretation of a company's CSR. We have defined CSR as actions that go beyond and beyond laws and regulations, voluntary self-regulation. In that sense, our definition is clear and obvious. But it does not solve the problem of how to measure these measures quantitatively when we try observing CSR in the real world. It is often difficult to evaluate what the companies themselves call CSR. Much of what we see companies advertise as CSR will probably end up, according to our definition, in a "gray area". Thus, it is not straightforward to distinguish what is beyond the law and what is simply business as usual.

We argue that a theory about CSR would have to balance between personal taste and values, social norms, and market imperfections. An essential ingredient and the main challenge in advancing academic research about CSR would be improving environmental accounting frameworks—on both the firm and national levels—and insights in the interaction between the economy and the environment. Thus, the system of double bookkeeping (as suggested already by Atkinson 2000) and national accounting needs to be accompanied by environmental, social, and material flows accounts in a more detailed manner than what we see today. Otherwise, any theory about CSR would run the risk of remaining sterile as it would be impossible to test it appropriately.

It is tempting to attribute the growing interest in CSR as a new ethical thinking and a growing commitment to sustainable development of enterprises, and that they are willing to forego profits for this. But CSR is consistent with another explanation too, businesses and individuals to adjust their behavior in order to adapt to changes in their environment, such as changes in preferences, prices, and incomes. To a large extent, we can explain the observed CSR as a conventional economic adjustment to new market conditions. Thus, CSR is largely well-integrated with a strategy that characterizes most of the company's business model, profit maximization in the traditional sense.

Notes

1. Pollution is an example of a market failure and negative externality. An externality means that a company's production or a person's consumption affects other production and consumption without being reflected in current prices.
2. Examples are employment contracts and insurance.

3. There is no space in this paper to go into detail on all the different definitions that abound in various research and the media.
4. In this paper, I will mainly use examples related to the environment.
5. It should be emphasized that even companies that operate in the traditional sense, and comply with laws and regulations, provide a variety of useful and appreciated services by providing markets with products, paying salaries to employees and dividends to shareholders, and generating tax revenue to the state and municipalities. This is also an important "responsibility," but not the extended, voluntary social responsibility we associate to CSR in this chapter.
6. Altruism, compassion, selflessness (as opposed to egoism), is to help others without wanting anything in return.
7. Strategy is used here to illustrate the company's specific "tactics" (in this case CSR) that apply to their business model in order to maximize profits.
8. What determine whether CSR is altruistic or strategic are the owners' reasons for commitments.
9. Greenwashing means that a firm is trying to create an image of being environmentally friendly through misleading advertising.
10. Warm glow means that you feel good doing a voluntary responsible act.
11. If the green products also create a cleaner environment, then, from a societal point of view, you should take into account in the welfare assessment the net loss in consumer surplus *and* the value of improving the environment.
12. How inputs such as capital, labor, and energy are used within the firm to generate output.
13. One example is the miner that gets compensated for increased job risk (compared to a similar job above ground). In case of CSR, the interpretation is the reverse; the warm glow an employee experiences from working at a CSR firm could mean that he/she accepts a compensation reduction, thus a negative compensating wage differential.

References

Arora, S., & Cason, T. (1999). Do community characteristics influence environmental outcomes? Evidence from the Toxic Release Inventory. *Southern Economic Journal, 65,* 691–716.

Arora, S., & Gangopadhyay, S. (1995). Towards a model of over-compliance. *Journal of Economic Behavior & Organization, 28,* 289–309.

Atkinson, G. (2000). Measuring corporate sustainability. *Journal of Environmental Planning and Management, 43,* 235–252.
Baron, D. P. (2001). Private politics, corporate social responsibility, and integrated strategy. *Journal of Economics and Management Strategy, 10,* 7–45.
Bénabou, R., & Tirole, J. (2010). Individual and corporate social responsibility. *Economica, 77,* 1–19.
Bergman, L. (1995). Simple observation on the green firm. In R. Wolff & B. E. Ytterhus (Eds.), *Environmental management: Where do we stand?* Oslo: Cappelen Akademisk Forlag.
Blend, J. R., & Ravenswaay, E. O. (1999). Measuring the demand for eco-labeled apples. *American Journal of Agricultural Economics, 81,* 1072–1077.
Bolvig, I. (2005). Firm-provided social concerns? Just another compensating wage differentials story? *International Journal of Manpower, 26,* 673–704.
Brännlund, R., & Lundgren, T. (2009). Environmental policy without costs? A review of the Porter hypothesis. *International Review of Environmental and Resource Economics, 3,* 75–117.
Dam, L., & Scholtens, L. (2015). Toward a theory of responsible investing: On the economic foundations of corporate social responsibility. *Resource and Energy Economics, 41,* 103–121.
Dodd, M. (1932). For whom are corporate managers trustees? *Harvard Law Review, 45,* 145–163.
Edmans, A. (2011). Does the stock market fully value intangibles? Employee satisfaction and equity prices. *Journal of Financial Economics, 101,* 612–640.
Eichholtz, P., Kok, N., & Quigley, J. M. (2010). Doing well by doing good? Green office buildings. *American Economic Review, 100,* 2492–2509.
Elhauge, E. R. (2005). Corporate manager's operational discretion to sacrifice corporate profits in the public interest. In B. L. Hay, R. N. Stavins, & R. Vietor (Eds.), *Environmental protection and the social responsibility of firms: Perspectives from law, economics, and business.* Washington, DC: Resources for the Future.
Fernando, C. S., Sharfman, M. P., & Uysal, V. B. (2017). Corporate environmental policy and shareholder value: Following the smart money. *Journal of Financial and Quantitative Analysis, 52*(5), 2023–2051.
Ferrell, A., Liang, H., & Renneboog, L. (2016). Socially responsible firms. *Journal of Financial Economics, 122*(3), 585–606.
Friedman, M. (1970, September 13). The social responsibility of business is to increase its profits. *The New York Times Magazine.*
Hamilton, J. T. (1995). Pollution as news: Media and stock market reactions to the toxic release inventory data. *Journal of Environmental Economics and Management, 28,* 98–113.

Hay, B. L., Stavins, R. N., & Vietor, R. (Eds.). (2005). *Environmental protection and the social responsibility of firms: Perspectives from law, economics, and business*. Washington, DC: Resources for the Future.

Innes, R., & Sam, A. G. (2008). Voluntary pollution reductions and the enforcement of environmental law: An empirical study of the 33/50 program. *Journal of Law and Economics, 51,* 271–296.

Khanna, M., & Anton, W. Q. (2002). What is driving corporate environmentalism: Opportunity or threat? *Corporate Environmental Strategy, 9,* 409–417.

Kitzmueller, M., & Shimshack, J. (2012). Economic perspectives on corporate social responsibility. *Journal of Economic Literature, 50,* 51–84.

Kriström, B., & Lundgren, T. (2003). Abatement investments and green goodwill. *Applied Economics, 35,* 1915–1923.

Lundgren, T. (2011). A micro-economic model of corporate social responsibility. *Metroeconomica, 62,* 69–95.

Lundgren, T., & Marklund, P.-O. (2014). Climate policy, environmental performance, and profits. *Journal of Productivity Analysis, 44*(3), 225–235.

Lundgren, T., & Olsson, R. (2010). Environmental incidents and firm value—International evidence using a multi-factor event study framework. *Applied Financial Economics, 20,* 1293–1307.

Lundgren, T., & Wenchao, Z. (2017). Firm performance and the role of environmental management. *Journal of Environmental Management, 203,* 330–341.

Mandell, S., & Wilhemsson, M. (2011). Willingness to pay for sustainable housing. *Housing Journal of Research, 20,* 35–51.

Margolis, J. D., Elfenbein, H. A., & Walsh, J. P. (2009). *Does it pay to be good ... and does it matter? A meta-analysis of the relationship between corporate social and financial performance.* Available at http://ssrn.com/abstract=1866371.

McWilliams, A., & Siegel, D. (2001). Corporate social responsibility: A theory of the firm perspective. *Academy of Management Review, 26,* 117–127.

Nyborg, K., & Zhang, T. (2013). Is corporate social responsibility associated with lower wages? *Environmental & Resource Economics, 55,* 107–117.

Paul, C., & Siegel, D. (2006). Special issue on corporate social responsibility and economic performance. *Journal of Productivity Analysis, 26,* 207–287.

Porter, M. (1991, April). America's Green Strategy. *Scientific American*, p. 264.

Porter, M., & van der Linde, C. (1995). Toward a new conception of the environment-competitiveness relationship. *Journal of Economic Perspectives, 9,* 97–118.

Portney, P. R. (2005). Corporate social responsibility: An economic and public policy perspective. In B. L. Hay, R. N. Stavins, & R. Vietor (Eds.), *Environmental protection and the social responsibility of firms: Perspectives from law, economics, and business.* Washington, DC: Resources for the Future.

Reinhardt, F. L., Stavins, R. N., & Vietor, R. (2008). Corporate social responsibility through an economic lens. *Review of Environmental and Economics and Policy, 2,* 219–239.

Wirl, F., Feichtinger, G., & Kort, P. M. (2013). Individual firm and market dynamics of CSR activities. *Journal of Economic Behavior & Organization, 86,* 169–182.

World Commission on Environment and Development. (1987). *Our common future.* Oxford: Oxford University Press.

Will the Banker Become a Climate Activist?

Johan Henningsson

Introduction

As the transition toward a greenhouse gas constrained economy gains momentum (IEA 2016), a new business landscape gradually emerges. Commercial banks and other lenders increasingly have to take into account a scenario of new climate policies, low-carbon technology, and climate-aware consumers when assessing the ability of companies and projects to generate cash flows and to repay loans.

Bank loans will play an essential role in the transition to a low-carbon economy (OECD 2017). However, only a small fraction of banks have integrated climate-related factors into their credit decision process in a systematic way (GFSG 2017). Furthermore, business opportunities emerging from the investment needs in the world to fulfill the sustainable development goals (SDG 2015, Brookings 2016)[1] have not yet been addressed in large scale and in a systematic way by the sector. This indicates a view,

J. Henningsson (✉)
Örebro University School of Business, Örebro, Sweden
e-mail: Johan.Henningsson@sek.se

S. Arvidsson (ed.), *Challenges in Managing Sustainable Business*,
https://doi.org/10.1007/978-3-319-93266-8_10

still prevailing in the credit markets, that a changing business landscape toward a low-carbon economy would not affect business cash flows and debt valuations in the short term.

In contrast to this view, the emerging green bond market is recognized as an important financial tool to realize the Paris Agreement (SOU 2017). Investments in renewable energy make inroads in the energy mix of many developing countries, in particular solar energy commitments (World Bank Group 2015).[2] The OECD suggests that the 2020s could mark the beginning of the "golden years" for bond issuance in the low-carbon sector (OECD 2016). Furthermore, financial and economic systems are increasingly recognized as being overexposed to environmentally unsustainable assets (Caldecott et al. 2014). Subsequently, regulators require banks and other actors of the financial industry to align various stakeholder perspectives to better balance strategy, capital, and risk.

Banks appear to face difficulties in integrating sustainability and climate factors into credit decisions (HLEG 2017). Some efforts have been made by banking institutions to develop methods to assess financial impacts from environmental and climate-related factors (GFSG 2017), but the ability of the sector to incorporate climate-related factors into credit decisions has not changed significantly. Burdened by regulatory requirements since the global financial crises in the years of 2008 and 2009, the sector has become reactive. Furthermore, the idea of a broader risk concept creates rational logic resistance (Henningsson 2009) as climate-related financial risks and opportunities have not yet materialized in market prices.

In this chapter, I will discuss challenges for banks to integrate climate-related factors in their risk management practices.[3] The starting point for the discussion is seemingly increased pressure from regulators and credit agencies on banks to recognize climate factors as "material" for their credit and market risk assessments and risk profiles.

The questions raised in the chapter are: How can banks integrate climate factors into their risk management practices and what challenges will banks face in doing so?

In other words, will the banker become a climate activist?

How Climate Becomes Material for Banks

The concept of "materiality" is key in bank risk management and at the core of bank regulatory frameworks. The idea of materiality is used to identify relevant risks and opportunities emerging from bank businesses and once identified as material, risks and opportunities should be disclosed accordingly. The materiality of climate impact on businesses in general is becoming increasingly recognized by the business community but has not yet taken its proper form within the conceptual infrastructure of banking. There are still a diversity of views in the sector; if and how climate-related risks and opportunities could materialize into financial risks. A perceived long-term perspective of climate-related factors on businesses usually makes those factors fall outside the traditional horizon of bank risk management.

The Materiality Concept

The regulatory burden, put on the banking sector, has made corporate governance of banks increasingly an exercise to fulfill the requirements of regulatory bodies. The main purpose of these demands, since the global financial crises and before, has been to restore financial stability, which in itself is a pre-condition for developing an agenda for sustainable finance (HLEG 2017). It is then in light of financial risks historically exposed to banks we may understand how the concept of "materiality" traditionally has been used and interpreted by banks and regulators. But given a likely transition scenario toward a low-carbon economy, the concept of materiality in itself, as defined by regulators, should not prevent banks from including climate-related risks and opportunities as material factors in its bank businesses.

In the Capital Requirements Directive IV, an EU legislative package covering prudential rules for banks, materiality is defined as:

> Information in disclosures shall be regarded as material if its omission or misstatement could change or influence the assessment or decision of

> a user relying on that information for the purpose of making economic decisions. (CRD 2013, Article 432)

Furthermore, the European Banking Authority "believes that, when implemented adequately, 'materiality' refers to a sufficient level of detail for disclosures, including qualitative information" (EBA 2013, p. 8).

Thus, climate-related information, both quantitative and qualitative, should be regarded as material in a regulatory reporting context when such information could affect economic decisions. Given increased evidence that business as usual is not an option forward, we have to question why the banking industry still struggles to recognize transition risks and opportunities for businesses to a low-carbon economy, as material for economic decisions in larger scale.

The "Shadow Materiality" of Climate

A central problem would be the perceived "short termism" of financial markets, illustrated as a mismatch of time horizons between financial and climate-related factors across the investment and lending chain. A second problem is a too narrow concept of risk used by banks. These two problems are referred to as the problem of double compression in financial markets by the EU high-level expert group on sustainable finance (HLEG 2017).

According to the EU expert group (ibid.), when financial markets fail to deliberate itself from the problem of double compressions, long-term material climate-related factors are deemed to be assessed as non-material by financial markets. Instead, climate-related factors will take the form of "shadow materiality" making climate benefits and risks, for the society and the planet not properly translated into investment and lending decisions.

As the banking system is mainly structured around short-term funding needs of businesses, an insufficient demand for long-term risk analysis is prevailing. The mismatch of time horizons means that short-term performance has the priority over long-term opportunities and risks (ibid.).

Toward Increased Materiality of Climate

The Financial Stability Board (FSB) has recognized the materiality of climate-related risks for the financial stability both in short term and in the long term. The Chairman of FSB, Mark Carney, identifies three channels which climate change can affect financial stability. These are physical, liability, and transition risks. Physical risks are direct impacts from climate- and weather-related events on businesses and cash flows. Liability risks are risk insurance companies, and businesses will face as future claims for compensation raised by parties who have suffered losses or damages from the effects of climate change. Lastly, transition risks are changes in policy, technology, and physical risks prompting a reassessment of a large range of asset values (Carney 2015).

In response to an increased awareness of climate risks, the level of activity of stock exchanges and financial market regulators to develop sustainability reporting instruments worldwide has been noteworthy. In 2016, these two groups together represented almost one-third of all sustainability reporting instruments (KPMG, GRI, UNEP, & CCGA 2016).

Furthermore, the EU high-level expert group on sustainable finance (HLEG 2018) discusses possibilities to define "green" and "brown" asset classes in order to apply differentiated capital requirements in the future. The expert group urges banks to ensure that their assessment of material risks covers financial and non-financial risks through models and forward-looking perspectives. Too much reliance on historical data would not properly include exposures to future stranded assets, due to climate factors (ibid.).

As a first mover in Europe, France has recently passed a law introducing mandatory extensive climate change-related reporting for asset owners and asset managers. The reporting obligations set out under Article 173 in the French Energy Transition Law addresses publicly traded companies, banks and credit providers, asset managers, and institutional investors, with various degree of reporting obligations. As an example, institutional investors are required to report on the integration of both physical risks and transition risks caused by climate change on their activities and assets.

The same development is noted in the Netherlands, where the parliament has agreed on a bill which requires transparency on the role of banks in supporting the Paris Climate Agreement. The bill calls for:

- An agreement on how Dutch banks will contribute to the Paris Climate Agreement.
- An agreement on disclosing the carbon intensity of the loan portfolios of Dutch banks.

Accordingly, the Dutch Central Bank (DNB) promotes transparency regarding carbon footprint of companies and calls upon financial institutions to take carbon risk into account in credit risk models.

Also, rating agencies are starting to recognize how climate policy risk for companies can quickly transfer as credit risks to banks. Standard & Poor's (S&P) released an outline of the long-term consequences of climate change for banks which include increases in bad loans, falling asset values, as well as additional regulatory costs and increased reputational risks. S&P argues that the financial sector has a key role to play in the transition to a low-carbon economy, which if not actively filled, may compel regulators to act. Subsequently, the most tangible financial impacts for banks are likely to be impaired asset values, for example, if the valuation of a fossil fuel company reserves cannot be realized. While these impacts may be low in the short term, S&P expects them to grow. The rating agency also sets out indicators, which will increasingly be used to identify financial services companies that are likely to be hardest hit by climate change. In this way, banks, exposed to climate-related risks, could suffer lower credit ratings in the future.

In a similar manner, Moody's highlights the potentially material role of technology risks and opportunities in the way environmental factors affect credit quality. They maintain that policies to reduce carbon emissions are now changing the dynamics of some sectors, such as the coal and power generation industries, and may dramatically transform the dynamics of other sectors, such as automobiles as well as oil and gas, over the next five to ten years. Technological solutions, such as carbon capture storage, renewable energy, and electric batteries and storage, will materially influence these dynamics. This process will create winners and losers in certain sectors, depending on an institution's business and financial flexibility or ability to develop, or adapt to, technological innovation (Moody 2015).

Integrating Climate in Bank Risk Management

Once climate impacts become recognized as material, potentially affecting credit and market risks of banks, the European capital requirements directive (CRD 2013, Article 432) call for those factors to be addressed and disclosed by banks. If the bank is exposed to climate-related financial risks, the bank would need to set aside enough capital to protect the solvency and assets of the bank and in the end to protect the financial system. When climate-related factors are integrated into bank risk management structure, these factors become, as a consequence, part of the activity to define bank risk profile and risk appetite. In this section, I will discuss how these two concepts could relate to climate impacts and how climate factors could then be translated into credit quality. I start by defining what debt capital is and how credit risk due diligence could be performed in practice by a bank.

Debt Capital

Debt capital is a loan with a commitment to repay the principal capital borrowed plus an interest. Debt capital can be raised publicly by issuing a bond on the public bond markets, or by a commercial bank providing a loan, normally called a bilateral loan. A group of banks can provide a syndicated loan where the risk is distributed among the lenders.

Any financing has some elements of risk. In the case of debt, it is the risk that some or all of the principal capital and interest committed will not be repaid. Banks mostly function as financial intermediaries that channel funds between lenders and borrowers. Accordingly, banks often act as both providers of capital (lenders) and underwriters of securities that are purchased by investors.

A bank risk profile is an evaluation of a bank's willingness to take risks, as well as the threats to which the bank is exposed. Main risks assessed by banks are credit and market risks but other types of risks are also assessed. Those are normally operational, compliance, legal, reputational, and strategic risks.

Loans entail different forms of credit risks depending on the type of lending. For instance, "corporate lending" is a type of debt financing generally used by mature companies with stable, reliable cash flows from business operations. Lenders generally assess borrowing capacity based on the strength of a company's balance sheet and other financial performance indicators. In a corporate loan, and in the case of bonds, credit ratings by third-party agencies are often used. Analysts, within the bank, looking at the credit risk of bonds are mainly focused on the issuing firm's capacity to repay the borrowed funds and thus focus on short-term financial buffers rather than medium-term cash flows. These are key factors feeding into a bond-rating decision.

Project finance, on the other hand, is a type of loan where the debt capacity is assessed and repaid through cash flows generated by a project often structured as a project company. Project finance is typically used for large infrastructure projects and other large assets. The loan is generally longer term. This requires higher levels of due diligence on project-level risks and strong involvement of sponsors and project developers to make the project commercially and financially viable.

To conclude, when credit risks are evaluated, banks use a variety of tools and the level of due diligence varies according to the type of underlying asset being evaluated. Climate-related factors will thus be dealt with on different analysis depths by the bank accordingly.

How Climate Materializes into Financial Risks

According to capital requirement regulations, banks are obliged to disclose their overall risk profile of their businesses and implement practices to manage those risks and according to a defined risk appetite. The terms risk profile and risk appetite are interlinked as the former expresses risks emerging from a bank's business activities and the latter expresses how the bank intends to deal with and mitigate those risks. By doing these two definition exercises, a bank defines indirectly the scope of the concept "risk" that will govern its day-to-day business and credit decisions in practice.

The Bank of International Settlement (BIS) defines risk profile as

> Point in time assessment of the bank's gross (i.e. before the application of any mitigants) or, as appropriate, net risk exposures (i.e. after taking into account mitigants) aggregated within and across each relevant risk category based on current or forward-looking assumptions. (Basel Committee on Banking Supervision 2015)

Risk appetite is defined as:

> The aggregate level and types of risk a bank is willing to assume, decided in advance and within its risk capacity, to achieve its strategic objectives and business plan. (ibid.)

Climate-related risks (often also referred to as carbon risks) represent the risk that loans to carbon assets do not financially perform as expected, because of new policy, economic, market, and social trends that emerge within a global greenhouse gas constrained economy (WRI and UNEP FI 2015).

Climate-related risk factors might then pose risks to financial assets of a bank. Such factors may include the direct risks such as physical impacts of climate change to real economic assets, or indirect risks posed by policy and market responses to environmental factors as stated above. Notable in this respect are transition scenarios, which simulate how a transition to a low-carbon economy could play out across different sectors and countries. If firms are unprepared for either the physical impacts or for the low-carbon transition, they can be faced with credit, market, business, and legal risks (GFSG 2017).

Climate-related factors may thus materialize as a variety of financial risks to the bank. A common tool used by banks to understand if and how risks in general could transform into different financial risks would be the method of stress testing.

Translating Climate Factors into Credit Quality

When analyzing the credit impacts of climate-related factors on assets, banks would need to apply the materiality concept. This would help the bank to focus on only those climate-related impacts that are reasonably likely to affect the financial performance or operating condition of a company and therefore affecting its credit quality (SASB 2016). Moody's also stress the importance of consider only material credit implications of ESG considerations in their rating methodology of sectors and debt issuers (Moody's 2017).

To translate climate-related factors into credit quality of assets, the bank needs them to combine two elements in the risk analysis: climate-related factors and credit risk tools. Starting with climate-related factors, SASB (2016) identifies three climate risk categories (which cohere with definitions made by the FSB above):

1. Physical effects: Climate change has a range of current and projected acute and chronic effects on the physical environment, leading to risks and opportunities for business entities. The probability, magnitude, and timing of these impacts remain uncertain and may be influenced by geographic location, industry, political response, and capacity for adaptation.
2. Transition to a low-carbon resilient economy: Transition risks relate to the market-based need to transition to a low-carbon economy, including development of, and investment in, new technologies and services that support this transition. Specific activities comprise the mitigation of carbon emissions and/or adaptation to be resilient against climate change.
3. Climate regulation: Regulatory risks resulting from climate regulation include a range of legal, regulatory, policy, and liability issues associated with climate change. This encompasses all international, national, and subnational targets, mandates, legislation, and regulations to address climate change. It also includes those issues that establish a price for carbon emissions and compliance with policy-driven responses to climate change. This category also encompasses a range of potential impacts that may occur due to legal actions against issuers in response to climate change.

Climate-related factors have to be assessed in quantitative measures of credit quality in a way that informs the bank risk management.

According to SASB methodology (ibid.), financial implications of climate-related factors for firms could channel to revenue impacts, cash flow and operating impacts, asset valuation impacts, and financing impacts. Based on such analysis, positive and negative outcomes of climate to a business, commercial banks will have to judge whether climate-related factors affect the credit quality of the entities to which they lend. In this way, climate-related risk factors become an addition to credit risks that analysts evaluate during credit due diligence of an individual credit.

The next step would be to determine whether climate-related factors translate to potential financial risk for the bank. In the analysis, three concepts and tools already used by banks (Basel Committee on Banking Supervision 2015, p. 25) become important. These are "climate scenario analysis," "stranded assets," and "stress testing."

Scenario analysis is an effective approach to consider the business risks associated with a two-degree climate scenario because it allows for a multitude of considerations of a wide range of factors that may have an influence on the business environment under a global climate accord. A climate scenario analysis involves using a climate policy framework to forecast potential future outcomes under a range of different assumptions. Stranded assets are economically under-performing assets, at the extreme fully written down. In the case of climate analysis, these effects would appear due to new policy, economic, market, and consumer behavior trends within a global GHG-constrained economy. Stress testing is a method of assessing how certain factors or changes could affect the financial performance of an asset or company.

According to WRI and UNEP FI (2015) define a "two degree scenario":

> The 2°C Scenario (2DS) is the focus of Energy Technology Perspectives. The 2DS describes an energy system consistent with an emissions trajectory that, recent climate science research indicates, would give an 80 percent chance of limiting the average global temperature increase to 2°C. It sets the target of cutting energy-related CO2 emissions by more than half in 2050 (compared with 2009) and ensuring that they continue to fall thereafter. Importantly, the 2DS acknowledges that transforming the energy sector is vital, but not the sole solution: the goal can be achieved only if GHG emissions in non-energy sectors are also reduced. The 2DS is broadly consistent with the World Energy Outlook 450 Scenario through 2035.

For a commercial bank, two-degree scenario analysis and stress testing would be used to assess how climate-related risk factors might evolve over time and what the financial impact on the bank assets could be. Such analysis can be performed in two ways: at the company level and at a financial portfolio level, focusing on how risk factors affect a diversified portfolio of assets. The company approach applies scenarios to companies and their physical assets, testing the potential financial impact on assets as measured through valuation methods like discounted cash flows (ibid.). At this level, governance structures, operational management, capital expenditure, and capital management impacts are all relevant. A top-down, portfolio-level approach would also be relevant for lenders. Risk factors are then identified from scenario analysis and used to measure the overall portfolio exposure.

The time perspective of climate-related factors becomes critical in a two-degree scenario analysis. Many of the scenarios on global energy are based on long-term horizons. However, some of the scenarios have shorter pathways, which is important given that most debt financing are relatively short term. The question of time horizon becomes therefore a critically important one to disclose and explain.

Based on the climate scenario analysis and the prevailing maturity of a credit or a portfolio of credits, the bank could now migrate current credit ratings of specific loans in a variety of scenarios and demonstrate how financial risk patterns change and affect the solvency of the bank, should the two-degree scenario materialize.

Climate Becomes Market Risks

One of the main risks assessed by banks is market risks. As discussed previously in the chapter, banks and regulators have not yet properly integrated climate-related factors in risk management practices. This way of systematically excluding climate risks in risk assessments and credit decisions, in combination with the risk of fossil assets becoming stranded assets, could potentially create a sudden market movement, referred to as a "climate Minsky moment." Such movement would emerge from a change in systemic logic, in a similar way as the revaluation of sub-prime loans in the years of 2008 and 2009.

Stranded Assets

Caldecott et al. (2014) define stranded assets as assets that have suffered from unanticipated or premature write-downs, devaluations, or conversion to liabilities. They can be caused by a range of environment-related risks. These risks are arguably poorly understood and regularly mispriced, which has resulted in a significant overexposure to environmentally unsustainable assets throughout our financial and economic systems (ibid.). Environment-related factors are already stranding assets in different sectors of the economy. This trend looks to be accelerating, which could represent a major discontinuity, able to profoundly alter asset values across the global economy.

The Climate Minsky Moment

A Minsky moment is a sudden major collapse of asset values which is part of the credit cycle or business cycle. Such moments occur because long periods of prosperity and increasing value of investments lead to increasing speculation using borrowed money. In the case of climate impacts, we could argue that a Minsky moment could emerge from a speculative reliance on "business as usual."

Climate-related risks could then be materialized as a financial risk when financial markets discount a potential massive revaluation of assets that will not generate cash flows in a low-carbon environment. Such market movement could potentially become a "climate Minsky moment," a significant change in financial market valuations of certain assets.

Mark Carney refers a second climate paradox as that success is a failure. That is, a too rapid a movement toward a low-carbon economy could damage financial stability.

> A wholesale reassessment of prospects, as climate-related risks are re-evaluated, could destabilize markets, spark a pro-cyclical crystallization of losses and lead to a persistent tightening of financial conditions: a climate Minsky moment.

On a speculative note, I would argue that debt incurred in financing investments in "business as usual" could lead to cash flow problems for investors and affect credit quality. In such a scenario, cash generated by such assets may no longer, at the extreme, be sufficient to pay off the debt they took on to acquire them. Losses on such high carbon assets or companies that are not equipped for a low-carbon economy would prompt lenders to call in their loans and investors to sell bonds. A spiraling market effect on debt leads to further collapse of asset values, a climate Minsky moment.

Increased Demand for Corporate Climate Information

An increased awareness from investors and lenders about the link between climate-related factors and financial risks creates an increased demand for corporate information on climate impacts on a strategic level. Such information would help financial market participants make a market in climate-related financial risks. Static disclosures of current carbon footprints of companies would not be sufficient to reveal a company's climate-related financial risks. Investors and lenders need to know the strategic issues as well as the static ones (WRI and UNEP FI 2015).

In his speech at Lloyds in the year 2015, the Governor of Bank of England, Mark Carney, states that…

> a framework for firms to publish information about their climate change footprint, and how they manage their risks and prepare (or not) for a 2 degree world, could encourage a virtuous circle of analyst demand and greater use by investors in their decision making. It would also improve policymaker understanding of the sources of CO2 and corporate preparedness. (Carney 2015, p. 13)

In late 2015, at the request of G20 leaders, the FSB established an industry-led Task Force, under the leadership of Michael Bloomberg. The purpose was to develop recommendations for voluntary, consistent, comparable, reliable, and clear disclosures around climate-related financial risks for companies. The main reason was to provide information to lenders, insurers, investors, and other stakeholders.

In their final report, the Task Force recommends that preparers of climate-related financial disclosures provide such disclosures in their mainstream annual financial filings. As an argument, the Task Force refers to the fact that in most G20 jurisdictions, companies with public debt or equity have a legal obligation to disclose material information in their financial filings—including material climate-related information (TCFD 2017). The Task Force believes climate-related issues are or could be material for many organizations, and its recommendations should be useful to organizations in complying more effectively with existing disclosure obligations.

In practice, the recommendations will provide firms with a framework to disclose a mix of forward-looking, qualitative, and quantitative information in order for stakeholders to get a real insight into how climate-related risks and opportunities may impact a firm's existing and future business lines. This could include information on governance and the management of such risks, and on a firm's mitigation strategy and its financial planning, including capital expenditures and research and development (R&D). The robustness of a firm's strategy and targets could be further illuminated through scenario analysis.

For lenders to evaluate climate-related credit risks and opportunities correctly, they need to weigh firms' strategies against plausible public policy developments, technological advances, and evolving physical risks. In practice, a full exploration of transition risks may require consideration of credit risks and opportunities under several scenarios.

Concluding Discussion

In this chapter, I have discussed how climate factors are becoming a growing concern bank regulators and rating agencies. This development put pressure on banks to integrate climate factors into their risk management practices. Even though banks currently lack proper understanding and incentives to manage climate-related factors and translate such risk metrics and methods into strategic decisions (HLEG 2017), potential scenarios for this to change were highlighted.

Firstly, the materiality of climate-related factors in bank risk management is now recognized by the FSB and regulators within the EU. Rating agencies are developing methodologies to effectively integrate climate factors into banks' credit decision process, using well-tested financial tools that can be adapted to take into account climate-related factors. Driven by regulators and rating agencies, lenders become more concerned consumers of corporate climate information. In such a scenario, the bank risk concept could gradually be broadened to include climate-related financial risks.

On a speculative note, I argue that as climate-related metrics and models are being applied in the banking industry and among other financial market participants, an increased awareness of climate-related financial risks could in itself develop a "climate" market risk, putting assets not generating cash flows in a low-carbon environment at risk. In this scenario, banks will become exposed to market risks, generated by climate-related factors, which, under the new regime of IFRS 9, could have an immediate effect on the bank solvency.[4] When long-term climate risks in this way translate into short-term market risks, the problem of time horizon could be solved but also potentially create new problems for banks and financial stability.

What challenges could bank face to better integrate climate factors in risk management practices? Firstly, banks face practical challenges when combining approaches to assess climate-related risks which could become problematic. The first one is to seek to understand how climate factors may pose risks to financial assets and liabilities. The second is to translate climate risk factors into quantitative measures of financial risk that can, in turn, inform risk management and credit decisions (GFSG 2017). Possibly, the investor community could lead the way. Investors within the UNEP Finance Initiative have taken important steps to include climate factors into investment decisions and to implement decarbonization strategies across their portfolios (UNEP FI and CDP 2017). Lenders could be inspired to the same development and for the sector to adapt. Given the close relationship between banks and small and medium-sized corporates, a change, in line with investors, could make a significant difference for the financial industry contribution to a transition towards a low-carbon economy.

Secondly, the current lack of relevant corporate information will create a challenge for banks. However, recent initiatives to improve corporate disclosures of climate-related risks and opportunities will provide banks with better information on how businesses could be affected in a low-carbon environment (TCFD 2017).

Lastly and more generally, the changes required of the financial industry to accept broader risk concepts could create strong resistance on a psychological level. From a sociocultural perspective, the financial industry could be regarded as heavily influenced by the strong logic of financial models created in the 1960s and onward. For an industry which usually relies on financial outcomes in markets as some kind of financial "truth," stabilizing the storytelling between financial actors (Henningsson 2009), climate-related risks, and opportunities not yet materialized in market prices would pose a rational logic type of problem for the banking-sector business model.

To conclude, banks are still subject to short-term market and regulatory pressures in their credit decisions, restraining them from providing credits to long-term projects and long-term risk materialization. However, an increased awareness of climate-related risks is gradually built up in the banking industry, mainly driven by regulators and rating agencies. Changes in day-to-day credit risk management practices and regulatory disclosures to better include climate-related factors could eventually change and broaden the risk concepts as perceived by the banking industry. The drivers for systemic change to solve the problems of time horizon and the too narrow risk concept (the double compression) will thus come from outside and not inside the banking sector. However, as noted by Mark Carney (2015) "By managing what gets measured, we can break the Tragedy of the Horizon."

Finally, will the banker become a climate activist? Yes, but collectively, involuntarily so.

Notes

1. The yearly investment needs to fulfill the sustainable development goals (SDGs) are estimated to USD 5–7 trillion (UNCTAD 2014). The world bank estimates the total investment needs in order to fulfill the SDGs by the year 2030 of 20 developing countries to amount to USD 21 trillion (IFC 2016).

2. At US$9.4 billion, commitments in solar energy in 2015 were 72% higher than the five-year average of US$5.5 billion (2010–2014). South Africa alone secured US$2.4 billion in solar deals.
3. I recognize the importance of the development of a green bond market for banks to manage their climate-related opportunities. Green bonds will, however, not be included in the discussion of this chapter.
4. Under IFRS 9, changes in market valuation of a financial asset (a credit) would directly affect the capital situation of a bank. If the credit risk of a financial asset increases to the point that it is considered credit-impaired, interest revenue is calculated based on the amortized cost (i.e., the gross carrying amount less the loss allowance) (IFRS 9 2014).

References

Basel Committee on Banking Supervision. (2015). *Corporate governance principles for banks.* Retrieved from https://www.bis.org/bcbs/publ/d328.pdf.

Brookings. (2016). *Links in the chain of sustainable finance. Accelerating private investments for the SDGs, including climate action* (Global Views, No 5). Washington.

Capital Requirements Directive IV, CRD/2013/36/EU.

Caldecott, B., Tilbury, J., & Carey, C. (2014). *Stranded assets and scenarios—Discussion paper* (Stranded assets programme). Oxford.

Carney, M. (2015). *Breaking the tragedy of the horizon—Climate change and financial stability.* Retrieved from https://www.bankofengland.co.uk/speech/2015/breaking-the-tragedy-of-the-horizon-climate-change-and-financial-stability.

Carney, M. (2016). *Resolving the climate paradox.* Retrieved from https://www.bis.org/review/r160926h.pdf.

European Banking Authority. (2013). *Guidelines on materiality, proprietary and confidentiality and on disclosure frequency under articles 432(1), 432(2) and 433 of regulation (EU) 575/2013.*

G20 Green Finance Study Group. (2017). *G20 Green Finance Synthesis Report.*

Henningsson, J. (2009). Fund managers as cultured observers. *Qualitative Research in Financial Markets, 1*(1), 27–45.

High-Level Expert Group on Sustainable Finance. (2017). *Financing a sustainable European economy* (Interim report). Retrieved from https://ec.europa.eu/info/sites/info/files/170713-sustainable-finance-report_en.pdf.

High-Level Expert Group on Sustainable Finance. (2018). *Financing a sustainable European economy* (Final report). Retrieved from https://ec.europa.eu/info/publications/180131-sustainable-finance-report_en.

IFC. (2016). *Climate investment opportunities in emerging markets.* Washington.

IFRS 9. (2014). Retrieved from http://www.ifrs.org/issued-standards/list-of-standards/ifrs-9-financial-instruments/.

International Energy Agency (IEA). (2016). *World energy outlook 2016.* Paris.

KPMG, GRI, UNEP, & CCGA. (2016). *Carrots and sticks: Global trends in sustainability reporting regulation and policy.* Retrieved from https://home.kpmg.com/content/dam/kpmg/pdf/2016/05/carrots-and-sticks-may-2016.pdf.

Moody's. (2015). *Environmental risks heat map shows wide variations in credit impact across sectors.*

Moody's. (2017). *Environmental, social and governance (ESG)—Global: Moody's approach to assessing ESG in credit analysis.*

OECD. (2016). *A quantitative framework for analyzing potential bond contributions in the low carbon transition.* Retrieved from www.oecd-ilibrary.org/environment/mobilising-bond-markets-for-a-low-carbon-transition/a-quantitative-framework-for-analysing-potential-bond-contributions-in-a-low-carbon-transition_9789264272323-6-en.

OECD. (2017). *Investing in climate, investing in growth—A synthesis.* Retrieved from https://www.oecd.org/environment/cc/g20-climate/synthesis-investing-in-climate-investing-in-growth.pdf.

SASB. (2016). *SASB technical bulletin 2016–01—Climate risk* (Working Draft). San Francisco.

SOU. (2017:115). *Att främja gröna obligationer.* Stockholm: Norstedts Juridik AB.

TCFD. (2017). *Recommendations of the task force on climate-related financial disclosure.* Retrieved from https://www.fsb-tcfd.org/.

UNCTAD. (2014). *World investment report 2014—Investing in the SDGs: An action plan.*

UNEP FI, & CDP. (2017). *Portfolio investment in a carbon constrained world* (The third annual report of the portfolio decarbonization coalition).

UN Sustainable Development Goals. (2015). Retrieved from http://www.un.org/sustainabledevelopment/development-agenda/.

World Bank Group. (2015). *Project PPI database.* Retrieved from http://ppi.worldbank.org/~/media/GIAWB/PPI/Documents/Global-Notes/Global2015-PPI-Update.pdf.

World Resources Institute, & UNEP Finance Initiative. (2015). *Carbon asset risk: Discussion framework.* Retrieved from http://www.unepfi.org/fileadmin/documents/carbon_asset_risk.pdf.

Investing in Sustainable Infrastructure

Tessa Hebb

Introduction

When thinking about sustainable businesses, it is essential to also look at the underlying infrastructure on which these businesses depend. Roads, buildings, energy grids, sewers, airports, and telecommunications are all vital components of sustainable business going forward. Yet everywhere our infrastructure is crumbling. It has been estimated that $94 trillion will be needed globally in infrastructure investment by 2040 (Reuters 2017). Clearly, governments acting alone do not have the necessary resources to meet these needs. Private investment will be required. But how can we ensure that private investment is directed to infrastructure projects that meet the high environmental, social and governance (ESG) standards that we need to ensure sustainability and resilience going forward?

T. Hebb (✉)
Carleton Centre for Community Innovation, Carleton University,
Ottawa, ON, Canada
e-mail: tessa.hebb@carleton.ca

S. Arvidsson (ed.), *Challenges in Managing Sustainable Business*,
https://doi.org/10.1007/978-3-319-93266-8_11

Sustainable infrastructure is defined as infrastructure that integrates ESG aspects into a project's planning, building, and operating while ensuring resilience in the face of climate change or shocks (Egler and Frazao 2016). Sustainable infrastructure can include natural or green infrastructure that incorporates natural ecosystems to address problems such as stormwater management or climate change risk in infrastructure development.

This chapter explores the shift toward greater consideration of sustainability issues and ESG in infrastructure investment. It seeks to understand the motivations propelling investors in this direction. It examines the implications both in the short term and long term when taking ESG into account in this asset class. It details new financial instruments emerging in the sector such as Green Bonds and CBP3s. The chapter concludes with an examination of some of the challenges institutional investors face as they seek to incorporate ESG in their infrastructure portfolios.

A variety of pressures are driving the shift toward sustainable infrastructure. Given the magnitude of many of these infrastructure projects, societal pressure increasingly seeks to raise the standards embedded in these projects. Communities large and small are demanding greater consultation in how infrastructure projects are built and managed. One need only to reflect on the public reaction to ill-thought-out hydroelectric dams or pipeline construction to see the role community engagement now plays in these massive projects.

The effects of environmental degradation are being felt around the world. Whether the infrastructure project is in Brazil, Africa, India, or North Dakota, concern for the health and safety of our planet is growing. Environmental sustainability is essential for infrastructure projects to be viable.

Climate change is another major driver of increased investment in sustainable infrastructure in the near future. In recent years, we have seen dramatic warming of our atmosphere (IPCC 2014) resulting in increasingly volatile weather patterns. As weather volatility continues, current infrastructure may not be viable and may need to be replaced. Direct rebuilding costs following Hurricane Sandy totaled $50 billion in the US east coast alone (Rand 2014). One can only imagine the magnitude of investment that will follow the dramatic weather events of 2017.

We are beginning to see an intersection between private investment and sustainable infrastructure. There is a growing movement of both responsible investors and impact investors who have pledged to take ESG factors into account in their investment decision-making. In fact, the UN-backed Principles for Responsible Investing (PRI) represents signatories with over $60 trillion of assets under management. Increasingly, these large mainstream asset owners and asset managers are applying ESG considerations to their ever-growing infrastructure portfolios. Impact investors go a step further by actively seeking positive environmental and social impacts together with financial return in their investments.

In the past, infrastructure investment was guided by initial lowest cost. This often ruled out high ESG considerations, as many sustainable infrastructure projects face high costs at the outset. However, measured over the full life cycle of the infrastructure project, these costs are reduced when sustainable systems are in place. Savings are generated through more effective and efficient use of resources over time. These savings range from reduced energy and maintenance costs to increased productivity. In addition, taking ESG into account can greatly reduce risk in infrastructure investment by ensuring greater community acceptance, reducing potential environmental damage, and raising operating standards over time.

New innovative financing mechanisms are increasingly directing capital investment into much-needed sustainable infrastructure projects around the world. This includes the burgeoning field of Green Bonds, growing from a $4 billion market in 2010 to $155 billion in 2017. Green Bond investment is explicitly directed at environmentally beneficial infrastructure offerings. These often include renewable energy projects, transportation, and climate change adaptation. Green Bonds have been issued by countries, regions, cities, and financial institutions. Issuers range from China, the largest issuer in 2017 at US$17 billion, to Lithuania, one of the smallest country issuers at US$370 million. Other new financial innovations in infrastructure investment include Community Benefit Public Private Partnerships (CBP3s), real asset credit markets, mitigation banks, pay–for–performance, and environmental impact bonds (EIBs). This chapter will examine these new investment opportunities in more detail.

But integrating ESG in infrastructure investment is not without its challenges. There are significant hurdles to overcome in order to integrate high ESG in infrastructure portfolios. Institutional investors face tensions embedded in the fiduciary duty they owe to their beneficiaries. In the past, this duty was interpreted to mean simply maximizing profits. Increasingly integrating higher ESG standards that reduce risk in investment is recognized as a core component of fiduciary duty. This allows institutional investors to take into account short-term higher costs that pay off over time.

Other challenges have also been identified in sustainable infrastructure investment (Egler and Frazao 2016). Pension funds and other institutional investors tend to be risk averse and shy away from investment in risky and uncertain alternative assets. There is a lack of a transparent and bankable project pipeline. In many cases, project originators tend to be small, local governments that lack the capacity to develop and structure investment opportunities that would be attractive to large institutional investors. As a result, these deals often tend to be too small to be of interest to institutional investors. Investors also face unfavorable and/or uncertain regulatory environments that create perceptions of undue risk in these projects. Another challenge is a shortage of data on the performance of infrastructure projects generally and sustainable infrastructure projects specifically. A final barrier to investment in sustainable infrastructure projects is the political risks these projects face. Designing the supports to overcome these challenges will be key to unleashing the potential of private capital to deliver the much-needed infrastructure our businesses, communities, countries, and indeed planet will need going forward.

The next section of this chapter describes the rise of responsible and impact investment. The chapter goes on to review the intersection between these investors and the sustainable infrastructure market. It provides an in-depth look at the new financial offerings detailed above and their impact on investment in sustainable infrastructure. The chapter closes with a deeper examination of the challenges that investors face in investment in sustainable infrastructure.

Responsible and Impact Investors

Responsible investment (RI) has been a growing phenomenon since the early 2000s. Over the last twenty years, it has grown from a niche investment approach to a mainstream understanding. Large institutional investors have declared that they will take ESG factors into consideration in their investment decision-making. Responsible investing signatories to the PRI now account for over two-thirds of all investable assets in the world (PWC 2017).

ESG factors used to be considered non- or extra-financial, meaning that they did not influence the financial valuation of the investment offering (whether equity or debt). But it has been shown that taking these factors into account can play a large role in reducing investment risk and may enhance financial performance over time (Clark et al. 2014). Given that these investors are long term, such risk and return potential has been seen as important in their investment selection. The tech bubble crash of 2001 and the subsequent 2008 Global Financial Crisis added momentum behind the realization that ESG factors should indeed play a role in investment selection.

An earlier antecedent of RI is socially responsible investment (SRI), also termed ethical investment, double- and even triple-bottom-line investment. Though this investment approach shares similar concerns to RI, its origins and motivation are not identical. While SRI is concerned with ESG, it also includes an ethical dimension that is absent in most RI portfolios. Ethical investment decisions are usually associated with individual investors rather than institutional investors who owe a fiduciary duty to their beneficiaries.

Initially responsible investors only considered ESG in their public equities portfolios, focusing on company-level standards to enhance financial performance and reduce risk over time. But over time these investors began to address ESG in their fixed income investments. Recently, many realized their alternative assets including their infrastructure portfolios should also be subject to the ESG lens they apply to other asset classes. This shift parallels their increased investment in infrastructure assets over the past ten years. It is estimated that globally \$3.5 trillion of pension fund assets is invested in infrastructure debt and equity (PWC 2017).

Given the proximity of infrastructure to community, its long-term nature, and dependence on revenue streams underpinned by defined cash flows, it stands to reason that ESG factors should play a role in this asset class. It is well recognized that 'what gets measured gets managed' (Drucker 1954). This holds as true for increased sustainability in infrastructure development as it does for other aspects of our economy.

A recent report from the PRI (2018) demonstrates how ESG factors in infrastructure investment are material for investors.[1] They detail twenty reasons for why these are important considerations, including: "maintaining social licence to operate; health and safety standards (pre- and post-commercial operation date); biodiversity impacts; alignment of interest with shareholders; stakeholder management and community relations; labour standards; land rights, indigenous rights; accessibility and social inclusion; service reliability; climate change impact and additionality; resource scarcity and degradation; extreme weather events; supply chain sustainability; accountability; board independence and conflicts of interest; management and board oversight of ESG; bribery and corruption; tax policy; cyber security; diversity and anti-discrimination."

Investors have the ability to demand higher environmental and social standards in infrastructure projects and are increasingly using their influence to raise these standards. This trajectory is similar to that of the LEED[2] standard in real estate, where investors demanded higher environmental standards and the industry delivered. All too often without the demand for higher ESG standards, infrastructure project originators fall into the trap of short-term thinking and lowest cost delivery, without the long-term asset management these investors are seeking.

Increasingly large institutional investors are seeing direct investment in sustainable infrastructure as a key component of their investment portfolio. As early as 2012, the French Caisse des Depots touted their investment in renewable energy, public transportation, and affordable housing. CalPERS, the large California pension plan, is a joint partner with the State of California on investment in water infrastructure, providing access to water in some of the State's most drought-prone regions (CalPERS 2018).

In 2014, a group of large institutional investors came together to begin measuring the ESG in their infrastructure portfolios. Under the banner of GRESB Infrastructure, twenty of the world's largest institutional investors (including CalPERS, Dutch PGGM, and Canadian Ontario Teachers Pension Plan) began measuring the ESG performance of both infrastructure funds and their underlying assets. GRESB Infrastructure uses eight categories by which to assess infrastructure investments: management, policy and disclosure, risks and opportunities, implementation, monitoring and EMS, performance, certifications, and stakeholder engagement. They have developed thirty-two indicators by which to rate and rank both infrastructure assets and funds. By 2017, GRESB Infrastructure covered sixty-four funds and 160 individual assets using their ratings. GRESB's 2017 report indicates a marked overall improvement in both ESG standards and reporting among the funds and assets covered, reflecting the ability of large institutional investors to raise awareness and ESG standards in their investments.

Within the infrastructure field itself, a variety of standards for measuring sustainability of have emerged including the SuRe Standard developed in partnership between the Global Infrastructure Basel Foundation and Natixis, a subsidiary of the French Groupe BPCE (the second largest banking group in France). This Standard measures sustainability and resilience in infrastructure using fourteen themes across sixty-one ESG criteria. This Standard has been used since 2012 in over 150 infrastructure projects.

Envision provides yet another sustainability rating system for infrastructure. Developed by the Institute for Sustainable Infrastructure, Envision employs sixty sustainability indicators across environmental, social, and economic impacts. These criteria are placed in five categories: Quality of Life, Leadership, Resource Allocation, Natural World, and Climate and Risk.

Large infrastructure fund managers such as Canadian-based Brookfield Asset Management ($250 billion of assets under management) are using ESG measurement within their holdings. Brookfield states, "Strong ESG principles benefit the environment, our communities, stakeholders and investors while also significantly boosting the potential for higher investment returns. The bottom line is that it reduces risk and increases value (Brookfield 2017)."

Responsible investing is now a mainstream activity for most institutional investors. However, a newer approach is also on the rise, impact investing. While responsible investing seeks to reduce risk and may add financial value through ESG integration, impact investing seeks to achieve measurable positive social and environmental impact together with financial return. Investors' intentionality to achieve impact is key to this investment approach. Initially, such investment was conceived on a very small scale, with micro-loans and direct investments in social enterprise as primary mechanisms used to achieve these results. While this approach attracts high net worth individuals, family offices, foundations, and endowments, it leaves large-scale institutional investors on the side lines. But in the past two years we have begun to see large investment managers engage in impact investing. This includes one of the world's largest investment managers, BlackRock, with $6 trillion of assets under management (*NY Times* 2017).

To date, the RI and impact investment worlds have remained in separate silos, each pursuing their goals through different investment lens and mechanisms. However, with the arrival of these big asset managers, new avenues for impact investing are opening up. This includes the infrastructure asset class, with its ability to make significant positive contributions to the communities in which it is built, while being an asset class that attracts large institutional players.

Impact investment in infrastructure should be considered in its broadest context, encompassing large-scale public systems, services, and facilities of a country or region that are necessary for economic activity. It includes investment in renewable energy, affordable housing, public transportation, water and waste water, and other systems necessary for vibrant, dynamic, and healthy communities. It provides positive economic, social and/or environmental impact, in addition to job creation, community resiliency, and financial return. Rather than seeing impact investing as a small niche investment approach, it should be embraced at this scale enabling investment in sustainable infrastructure to deliver positive impacts for communities around the world.

Investment Opportunities in Sustainable Infrastructure

It is estimated that there is currently $50 trillion of investment in infrastructure worldwide (Egler and Frazao 2016). To date, most of that investment has been made by governments, with emerging market governments such as China investing 8.5% of GDP in infrastructure annually, while OECD countries manage a much smaller 3%. Private investors own about 25% of all infrastructure assets (ibid.). Of this, 60% is held as equity investment and 40% as debt. The vast majority of equity ownership is through publicly listed entities such as the Australian asset manager Macquarrie, Canadian Brookfield Asset Management, and US-based Global Infrastructure Partners, who are the three largest of these firms globally (Infrastructure Investor 2018). The split between public ownership and private ownership, direct and indirect, debt, and equity make the infrastructure asset class hard to quantify. Kaminker (2016) suggests that infrastructure assets can be classified into nine different investment classes.

Increasingly large asset owners such as pension funds, sovereign wealth funds, and insurance companies are seeking to invest directly in infrastructure rather than through asset managers, where private equity fee structures make such investment costly. Given the long-term nature of these investments together with stable, inflation-linked returns, direct investment in large infrastructure opportunities is on the increase for these funds. These investors, with their commitment to responsible investing and ESG integration, have the potential to move the market toward greater sustainable infrastructure investment (Fig. 1).

Egler and Frazao's 2016 report on this topic provides a good overview of the infrastructure investment instruments available to large institutional investors (Fig. 2).

While public investment and ownership of infrastructure remain the primary source for funding infrastructure globally, we are seeing increased use of both private investment and public–private partnerships (commonly called P3s and discussed in more detail below). However, debt remains the most common instrument with 70–90% of most infrastructure projects financed through debt (McKinsey 2013).

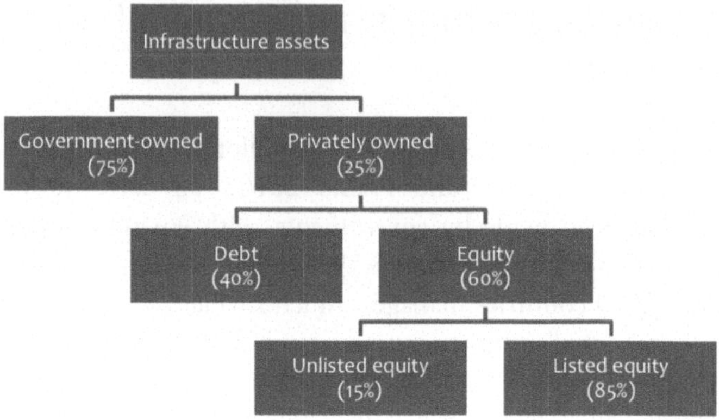

Fig. 1 Global ownership of infrastructure assets (*Source* Egler and Frazao 2016)

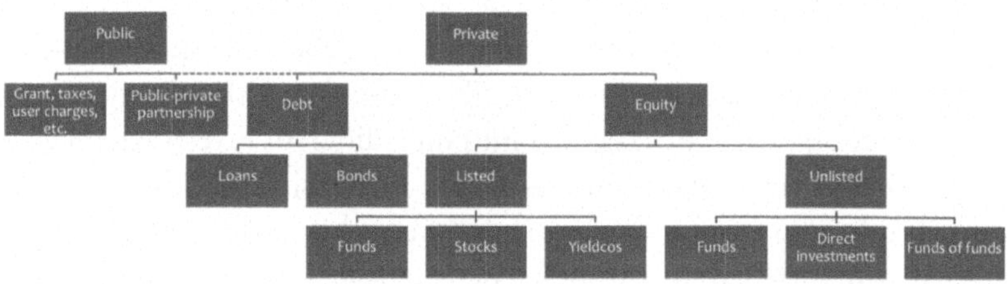

Fig. 2 Instruments for infrastructure investment (*Source* Egler and Frazao 2016)

Green Bonds

One area of rapid growth for institutional investment in sustainable infrastructure is through investment in Green Bonds. Green Bonds are fixed income securities issued by governments, development agencies, and corporates where the use of the funds is explicitly designed for projects with positive environmental impact (Climate Bond Initiative 2018). In most cases, these bonds adhere to a set of Green Bond Principles (2017) that detail the way in which the proceeds from the Green Bond issuance will be used. There are four core components to the Green Bond Principles: use of proceeds; process for project evaluation and selection; management of proceeds; and reporting.

The Green Bond market has grown from $4 billion issuance in 2010 to $155 billion in 2017 and is projected to reach $300 billion in 2018 and $1 trillion by 2020 (Climate Bond Initiative 2018). Most Green Bond offerings are purchased by institutional investors and are often fully subscribed within twenty-four to forty-eight hours after their issue (Fig. 3).

Renewable energy is the most common use of Green Bonds with $51 billion or approximately 1/3 of the proceeds directed to these projects. Energy efficiency and low-carbon buildings account for $45 billion of this investment. Low-carbon transport accounts for $24 billion in investment, and sustainable water management $20 billion (ibid.). Institutional investors are attracted to Green Bonds as a part of their fixed income portfolios, as the rates of return are comparable to other similar bond offerings with the added benefit of the environmental impact they generate. In a few cases, Green Bonds are issued for a lower cost of capital, as the increased environmental standards are seen to lower the risk of the bond defaulting.

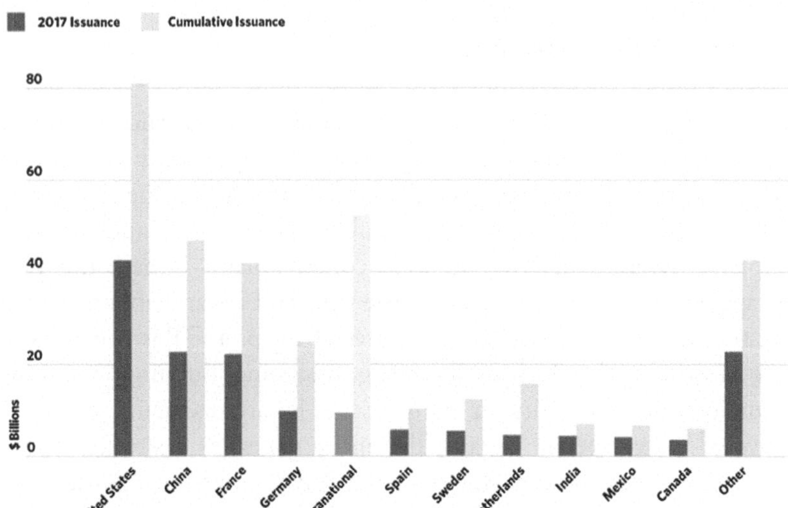

Fig. 3 Green Bonds issuers (*Source* Climate Bonds Initiative)

The financial performance of Green Bonds can be measured using the Bloomberg Barclays MSCI Global Green Bond Index Total Return (US$ unhedged) established in 2014. This fund uses MSCI ESG data to establish inclusion of the bond in the index. MSCI uses four criteria that reflect the Green Bond Principles established by the International Capital Market Association. MSCI evaluates Green Bonds on the basis of the use of proceeds; the process for green project evaluation and selection; the process for management of proceeds; and the commitment to ongoing reporting of the environmental performance (MSCI 2018). The use of proceeds must be directed to one or more of the following: alternative energy; energy efficiency; pollution prevention and control; sustainable water; green building; and climate adaptation.

When measured against a comparable benchmark, the Bloomberg Barclays Global Aggregate Index Total Return (US$ unhedged), the Green Bond Index lagged in 2015–2017, but by 2018 the financial performance of the two funds was comparable with the Green Bond Index outperforming, with a one-year return of 10.46% (as of April 9, 2018) while the Global Aggregate Fund had a one-year return of 6.71% (as of the above date) (Figs. 4 and 5) (Bloomberg 2018).

Private–Public Partnerships

Public–Private Partnerships (P3s) are another infrastructure investment on the rise. These too can provide an opportunity for sustainable infrastructure investment. A public–private partnership is "a legally binding contract between a public sector entity and a private company—typically referred to as a concessionaire—where the partners agree to share some portion of the risks and rewards inherent in an infrastructure project (Sabol and Puentes 2014, p. 4)." P3s encompass a range of options that include financing, designing, building, operating, and maintaining the entity. In many cases, a P3 arrangement can include all five of these aspects. Usually, the entity generates a stream of revenue that provides the repayment to the private investor. Common P3 projects include toll roads, bridges, airports, and water delivery systems. Investors generally participate through an equity rather than debt investment, in either listed or unlisted funds or funds of funds (see Fig. 2).

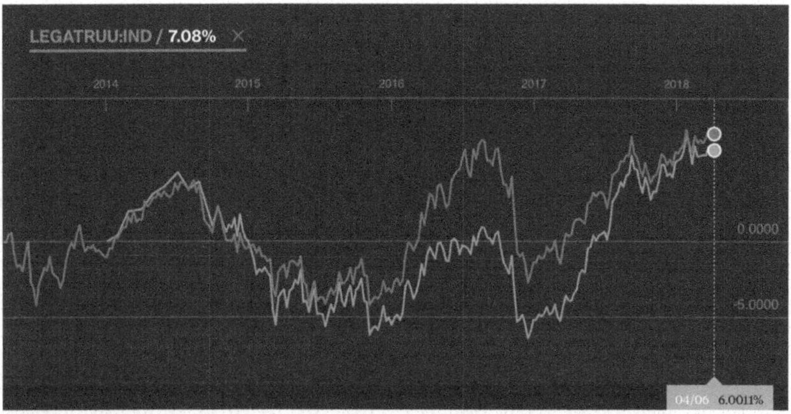

Fig. 4 Bloomberg Barclays Global aggregate index total return five-year performance measured against benchmark (*Source* Bloomberg)

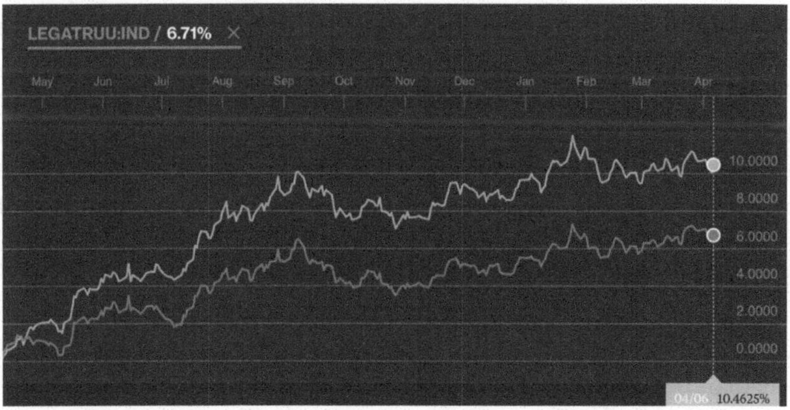

Fig. 5 Bloomberg Barclays Global aggregate index total return one-year performance measured against benchmark (*Source* Bloomberg)

In the past, large institutional investors engaged in this market as limited partners (LPs) within an infrastructure fund that is managed by a general partner (GP). A well-known example of this type of arrangement is Macquarrie Funds. Many of these offerings are structured as private equity arrangements, where the GP earns 'two and twenty', a standard term for a private equity arrangement where the GP who manages the fund is paid 2% per year on the assets under management and 20% of any profit generated above a minimum threshold. Increasingly large, sophisticated institutional investors such as pension funds and sovereign wealth funds have gained the knowledge and tools required to make direct investments in P3 infrastructure opportunities, much as we see in project finance, and hold the asset directly in their portfolios. This shift is important for ESG integration in these investments, as large institutional investors are able to demand higher ESG standards in projects that they invest in directly. They are also able to actively seek out investments in sustainable P3 offerings.

P3s have often been viewed unfavorably by the general public. They have been associated with governments off loading their obligations, privatization of public services, and increased costs to the general public. The US Skyway and Indiana Toll Roads, and Chicago's parking meter privatization, stand as cautionary tales as to how these projects can go wrong (Long 2014). Many of these controversies involve what has become known as 'asset recycling', a term coined by the Australian Government. Here, the infrastructure asset already exists, paid for through public expenditure, and is to be sold to the private investor, thus generating additional funds for governments to invest in new infrastructure. These sales have been perceived as generating windfall profits for private investors at the expense of the general public. Given the controversies that often surround P3s, institutional investors are more willing to invest in these opportunities outside their own country. For example, significant capital has been invested in UK infrastructure by Canadian pension funds (who along with Australian pension funds have led in private infrastructure investment) including airports, water systems, and shopping centers.

Although P3s have been viewed negatively, they can provide an interesting opportunity for institutional investors to integrate higher ESG standards in these offerings. In essence, P3s represent a nexus of contracts. As a result, investors can leverage their position to demand increased sustainability standards in the infrastructure asset. Additionally, institutional investors can specifically target their investment in areas such as renewable energy, mass transit, green infrastructure, and affordable housing that generate positive environmental and social impacts. While the ESG component in infrastructure may not necessarily deliver additional financial returns to the investor, these raised standards can significantly reduce risk in infrastructure investments, particularly given their long-term nature. Additionally, these considerations can also contribute to much-needed social license to operate that are embedded in these deals.

Innovative Infrastructure Financing Models

A new form of P3 is taking root, Community-Based Public Private Partnerships (CBP3s). CBP3s are partnerships between government and private entities that leverage large infrastructure projects to deliver on a range of policy goals and objectives over the life cycle of the asset. These goals are delivered using community-centered metrics, such as local employment and training opportunities, economic development, and/or positive environmental impacts, that are major components of the contract with the private partner. Key progress indicators (KPIs) are established and tracked to ensure the delivery of these objectives by the private partner. This type of P3 contract is often called a Community Benefit Agreement or CBA. CBAs have been implemented in many regions including the UK, USA, Australia, and Canada. In 2013, the UK government passed the Public Service Social Value Act (2012) establishing "an Act to require public authorities to have regard to economic, social and environmental well-being in connection with public services contracts; and for connected purposes." It encourages project commissioners to embrace a range of social value through public purchasing of goods and services including infrastructure. In 2017, the Province of Ontario introduced the use of Community Benefits Agreements in its long-term infrastructure plan (2015, 2017).

The US Environmental Protection Agency (EPA) promotes the use of CBP3s for stormwater management and green infrastructure development across the USA. Green infrastructure "uses vegetation, soils, and natural processes to manage water and create healthier urban environments" (US EPA 2017). They suggest that over the full life cycle of the asset, governments see significant savings when installing stormwater abatement mechanisms such as permeable pavement, sponge parks, and tree soil cells. While green infrastructure can be costly in the short run, over time they save money and are environmentally beneficial. The EPA notes that these interventions may be too expensive for local and regional governments to implement. By using alternative financing mechanisms, investors absorb some of the risks of these newer innovations while providing much-needed access to capital. Investors are paid out by government as a stream of revenue partially generated from the savings generated (ibid.).

There are additional investment opportunities emerging in storm water and wastewater. For example, credit markets are developing across a number of infrastructure opportunities. Stormwater retention credits (SRCs) allow for trading allowances. One example is Washington, DC, where property developers are required by the municipality to meet a runoff retention standard. Developers are allowed to buy credits when their projects do not comply with the limit. Project originators are able to sell credits when they reduce stormwater runoff. Much as we see in the carbon credit market, this creates an opportunity for investors to "make the market" between buyers and sellers of stormwater credits through direct or indirect investment in the "Exchange." While this market has been implemented on a small scale in Washington, the number of credits issued and the value of those credits have been growing exponentially, providing investment opportunities going forward (Table 1).

Environmental Impact Bonds (EIBs) provide another new investment opportunity. These structures are similar to Social Impact Bonds (SIBs) and are sometimes referred to as 'pay for performance' contracts. EIBs are of particular interest to impact investors, who actively seek positive environmental and/or social impacts together with financial return. They are not typical bonds as such. The investor agrees to make the investment with a repayment of principal and return if a certain agreed upon objective is met. The government pays the investor from the savings generated from the social or environmental intervention. If the targets are not met, the investor does not receive any financial return. As a result, the risk of innovation is transferred from government to the private investor. SIBs have become very popular in the UK, Australia, USA, and Canada.

Table 1 Value of stormwater credits Washington, DC

Year	SRCs traded	Value of SRC trades	Average price
2018 (YTD[a])	32,456	$77,591.45	$2.39
2017	108,537	$218,912.70	$2.02
2016	24,972	$46,284.40	$1.85
2015	11,013	$20,924.70	$1.90
2014	11,013	$25,000.00	$2.27

[a]To March 31, 2018
Source US Dept. of Energy and Environment stormwater database

In 2016, this model was used in Washington, DC in the first EIB issued in the USA. The Calvert Foundation and Goldman Sachs invested in a 25-year tax-exempt municipal bond (with a mandatory tender in year five) for $25 million directed to green infrastructure within the $2.6 billion DC Clean Rivers Project. This bond will pay an additional $3.3 million after 5 years if agreed upon targets for stormwater runoff are met. If the targets are not met, the investors will pay DC Water $3.3 million (Goldman Sachs 2018) (Table 2).

Financial Returns from Infrastructure Impact Investment

Investors intentionally seeking both positive social and/or environmental impact together with financial return in the infrastructure asset class have primarily invested in renewable energy portfolios. For a number of reasons, the renewable energy field has not generated strong returns to date. Several factors have come into play including the flooding of the market with relatively inexpensive solar panels from China, the increased use of natural gas made more readily available through fracking, and inefficient energy grids and other infrastructure to support the renewable energy field (particularly in solar energy). The S&P Global Clean Energy Index is a common benchmark in this field and is comprised of 30 international companies involved in clean energy-related businesses. It's inception date was 2007, and while its 1- and 5-year annual rates of return have been positive (14.71 and 3.54%, respectively, as of April 16, 2018), it's 10-year annual return was −15.71% having dropped 73% of its value during the 2008/2009 financial crisis that it has yet to recover.

Table 2 Washington, DC. EIB contingent payment

Performance tier	Outcome ranges	Contingent payment
1	Runoff reduction>41.3%	DC water will make an outcome payment to investors of \$3.3 millions
2	18.6%<=R runoff reduction<=41.3%	No contingent payment due
3	Runoff reduction<18.6%	Investors will make risk share payment to Dc water of \$3.3 million

Source Goldman Sachs fact sheet: DC water environmental impact bond

A recent study by Cambridge Associates and the Global Impact Investment Network surveyed seventeen impact infrastructure funds, investing primarily in renewable energy, climate change mitigation, and water resource management with vintage years 2005–2014. The average size of these funds was \$1.4 billion. They found that "The top fund produced a net IRR over 29% since inception to June 30, 2016, and nearly one in four funds generated a net IRR greater than 10%. However, three funds had returns below -15%, so the overall pooled net IRR was 0.3% and median IRR, 2.5%." These financial returns are low when compared to a conventional infrastructure benchmark pooled net IRR of 6.6% through this same period (Cambridge and Associates/ GIIN 2017).

Challenges to Investment in Sustainable Infrastructure

Institutional investors seeking to integrate high ESG standards in their infrastructure portfolios face a number of challenges. Egler and Frazao (2016) identified five major hurdles for institutional investors to integrate high ESG in their infrastructure portfolios. The first is a lack of a transparent and bankable project pipeline. Given that the current need for infrastructure investment is projected at over \$1 trillion dollars annually, this lack of a deal pipeline demonstrates the gap that exists between project originators and investors. In many cases, project originators tend to be small, local governments that lack the capacity to develop and structure investment opportunities that would be attractive to large institutional investors. These deals often tend to be too small to be of interest to institutional investors. Additionally, government officials often lack the capacity to communicate the social and environmental benefits of these opportunities (Cambridge and Associates/GIIN 2017). Bankable projects require sufficient collateral, future cash flows, and a high probability of success if they are to be of interest to institutional investors.

The second hurdle is unfavorable and/or uncertain regulations such as the capital requirement rules put in place after the 2008 Global Financial Crisis. These rules require financial institutions to hold additional capital against riskier investments and can cause a restriction in the availability of debt and equity financing for large infrastructure projects. The third barrier is restrictions on pension investment itself. Pension funds tend to be risk adverse, which means they continue to invest most of their portfolio in public equity, fixed income, and cash rather than take on risky and uncertain alternative assets.

The fourth challenge is a shortage of data on the performance of infrastructure projects generally and sustainable infrastructure projects specifically. Both financial data and ESG standards and performance metrics are still under development (Environmental Defense Fund 2017). Because this world has been dominated by private infrastructure funds, there is limited information available to investors. This is exacerbated by the sheer number of asset types found in infrastructure projects (see Fig. 2 on this point).

The final barrier to investment in sustainable infrastructure projects is the political risks these projects face. Because these projects have multiple stakeholders including the communities in which they reside, they are subject to political pressures that can sideline and even derail infrastructure projects. "Closely related to the political and regulatory risks, is the non-transparent disclosure risk. Due to the extremely complex structure and delivery process of infrastructure projects as well as the interaction between all the stakeholders, projects are exposed and highly sensitive to corruption and mismanagement (Egler and Frazao 2016, p. 21)."

Conclusion

Despite the challenges that private investors face when investing in sustainable infrastructure, there has been a steady increase in these investments globally. With over a $1 trillion dollars in infrastructure investment needed annually, it is evident that governments acting alone do not have the necessary resources required to meet current needs. Yet without robust, resilient, and sustainable infrastructure underpinning our economies, we cannot meet the business demands needed in the future.

The United Nations Secretary General declared when launching the Sustainable Development Goals (SDGs) that $3–5 trillion of private investment would be needed worldwide if we are to achieve these goals by 2030. Yet to date private infrastructure investment remains in the billions rather than the trillions needed. A recent report, "Better Business, Better World" by the Business and Sustainable Development Commission (2017), estimates that achieving the SDGs could open up $12 trillion of market opportunities in food and agriculture, cities, energy and materials, and health and well-being. They estimate this market could create 380 million new jobs by 2030. To date, it is largely untapped.

The question remains: Can we adequately link institutional investor's investment requirements with the growing need for new sustainable infrastructure and create a win/win scenario? Investors need long-term, stable, revenue streams generated by large-scale opportunities with high ESG consideration and minimum risks over time. The challenge to governments is to provide these opportunities and facilitate the flow of capital.

Until very recently, infrastructure has been delivered as a public good. There are significant implications of the shift to private markets providing the underpinnings of our economy and indeed society. Citizenry often react negatively to the incursion of user fees and private ownership in realms that have always been provided freely via the tax system. Private investors seek out the strongest financial returns for their investment, leaving whole swaths of the economy unserved. Such a shift can exacerbate the growing inequality in our societies, favoring those who have access to capital to pay for much-needed services. Conflicts between the rights of one group versus another are hard to settle without recourse to democratic institutions.

But these negative forces can be mitigated when infrastructure projects are embedded with high ESG standards. Such standards can reduce the conflicts detailed above through community consultation, sustainable practices, and sensitivity to all stakeholders including the environment. When investors use a sustainability lens in their infrastructure investments, they reduce risk in their portfolios and may add to their financial return. Additionally, when they intentionally seek positive social and environmental impact, they actively contribute to addressing many of societies' most pressing problems. These include the need to shift to a low-carbon economy through investment in renewable energy systems, the provision of clean water in drought stricken regions, and the creation of affordable housing in our communities.

Investment in sustainable infrastructure through well-structured partnerships between government and institutional investors can provide the much-needed underpinnings for business and indeed the global economy going forward. But to achieve its desired ends, such investment must incorporate high ESG standards in the long run if it is to serve all our needs and help create the world we want to live in.

Notes

1. "Materiality is the principle in accounting that trivial matters are to be disregarded, and all important matters are to be disclosed. Items that are important enough to matter are **material items**. United States GAAP, for instance, states that items are *material* if 'they could… influence the economic decisions of [financial statement] users…'. In other words, materiality errors can *mislead* decision makers" (Business Encyclopedia 2018).
2. Leadership in Energy and Environmental Design.

References

Bloomberg. (2018). *Bloomberg Barclays MSCI Global Green Bond Index Total Return Index*. Retrieved from https://www.bloomberg.com/quote/GBGLTRUU:IND.

Brookfield. (2017). *ESG at Brookfield*. Report. Toronto.

Business Encyclopedia. (2018). Retrieved from https://www.business-case-analysis.com/materiality-concept.html.

Business and Sustainable Development Commission. (2017). *Better business, better world*. Report, p. 12.

CalPERS. (2018). *California investments*. CalPERS Newsroom. Retrieved from https://www.calpers.ca.gov/page/investments/investment-manager-engagement-programs/california-investments.

Cambridge and Associates and Global Impact Investment Network. (2017). *The financial performance of real assets impact investment*. Report.

Clark, G., Feiner, A., & Viehs, M. (2014). *From stockholder to stakeholder*. Arabesque Partners, Report.

Climate Bond Initiative. (2018, January 2018). *Green Bond highlights 2017*. Report. Retrieved from https://www.climatebonds.net/files/reports/cbi-green-bonds-highlights-2017.pdf.

Drucker, P. (1954). *The practice of management*. New York: Harper Business.

Egler H. P., & Frazao R. (2016, June). *Sustainable infrastructure and finance*. Report for Designing of a Sustainable Financial System (Inquiry Working Paper 16/09).

Environmental Defense Fund. (2017). *Unlocking private capital to finance sustainable infrastructure*. Report. New York.

Goldman Sachs. (2018). *DC water environmental impact bond fact sheet*. Retrieved from http://www.goldmansachs.com/media-relations/press-releases/archived/2016/dc-water-environmental-impact-bond-fact-sheet.pdf.

GRESB. (2017). *2017 GRESB results, fact sheet*. Retrieved from http://gresb-public.s3.amazonaws.com/2017/Public%20Results/2017_INF_Global_Results.pdf.

Infrastructure Investor. (2018). *Review*. Retrieved from https://www.infrastructureinvestor.com/ii-50/.

IPCC. (2014). Fifth Assessment Report (AR5). Report. International Panel on Climate Change.

Kaminker, C. (2016). *Mobilising flows of institutional investment for sustainable energy*. Ph.D. thess, School of Geography and the Environment, Oxford University.

Long, C. (2014). *Are private toll roads a losing idea?* Muniland Blog, Reuters. Retrieved from http://blogs.reuters.com/muniland/2013/01/19/are-private-toll-roads-a-losing-idea/.

McKinsey. (2013, January). *Infrastructure productivity: How to save $1 trillion a year*. McKinsey Global Institute.

MSCI. (2018). *Bloomberg Barclays Green Bond Index*. Retrieved from https://www.msci.com/documents/10199/242721/Barclays_MSCI_Green_Bond_Index.pdf/6e4d942a-0ce4-4e70-9aff-d7643e1bde96.

NY Times. (2017). *BlackRock the $6 trillion money manager*, January 12, 2018.

PRI. (2018, January 17). *Primer on responsible investment in infrastructure*. Principles for Responsible Investment.

PWC. (2017, June). *Asset management 2020: Taking stock, asset & wealth management insights*. Report. London, UK.

Rand Corporation. (2014). *The Hurricane Sandy rebuilding task force's infrastructure resilience guidelines*. M. L. Finucane, N. Clancy, H. H. Willis, D. Knopman. Report. Rand Corporation.

Reuters. (2017, July 25). World will need $94 trillion spent on infrastructure by 2040. *Business News*. Retrieved from https://www.reuters.com/article/us-global-infrastructure-report/world-needs-94-trillion-spent-on-infrastructure-by-2040-report-idUSKBN1AA1A3.

Sabol, P., & Puentes, R. (2014). *Private capital, public good drivers of successful infrastructure public–private partnerships*. Report. Brookings Metropolitan Infrastructure Initiative.

US EPA. (2017). *What is green infrastructure?* Website. Retrieved from https://www.epa.gov/green-infrastructure/what-green-infrastructure.

Part IV

Anti-corruption and Business Ethics

Anti-corruption: Who Cares?

Steven Sampson

Introduction: Against Corruption!

Everyone is against corruption. Unlike other issues, such as climate change, global trade, or immigration, where there may be two sides to an issue (left/right; liberal/conservative; pro/contra), corruption does not cleave into pro-corruption versus anti-corruption forces. Corruption, everyone agrees, is bad (Bukanovsky 2006). It has been bad since ancient times, when it connoted a description of a collapsing, putrid society (Buchan and Hill 2014). Modern corruption fighting has been on the global agenda for about twenty years, notably since the famous 'cancer of corruption' speech from World Bank president James Wolfensohn in 1996. (Before that, the bank called corruption 'the C word'.) So fighting corruption, raising awareness about corruption, and preventing corruption have come to be a desirable thing, a good thing. There is so much agreement about fighting corruption that

S. Sampson (✉)
Department of Social Anthropology, Lund University, Lund, Sweden
e-mail: steven.sampson@soc.lu.se

S. Arvidsson (ed.), *Challenges in Managing Sustainable Business*,
https://doi.org/10.1007/978-3-319-93266-8_12

anti-corruption conferences tend to take on a ritualized content: one speaker after another—government ministers, NGO activists, corporate executives—recites the mantra about all the bad things that corruption does—that corruption is an extra tax on the poor, that corruption undermines trust in government, that corruption distorts and dilutes development aid, that corruption discourages business investment, etc. Hearing such speeches, one begins to wonder why the disease of corruption, like smallpox or polio, has not been eradicated long ago. Perhaps this fight against corruption is not so self-evident as we think. Perhaps there indeed are some 'pro-corruption forces' out there that we do not understand. Perhaps we have to rethink what we are doing when we say that we will all come together to fight corruption. Perhaps we have to think not just about the rhetoric we use, but about the motivations of and social forces behind corrupt actors. Indeed, we need to think about WHO CARES about fighting corruption, WHY they care, and HOW they translate care into action. Analyzing who cares should not just be limited to taking a hard look at the business community, government programs, or international organizations to measure whether their commitment is real. We also need to look more closely, even critically, at the anti-corruption NGOs, the so-called moral entrepreneurs. For it is manifestly obvious that even anti-corruption NGOs have their own organizational interests. The world of anti-corruption, what I have called the 'anti-corruption industry' (Sampson 2010a), is thus more complex than we might think. It is a world dominated by what I call 'anti-corruptionism'. Those concerned with sustainability and sustainability reporting are now part of this anti-corruptionist discourse (Sampson 2005, 2009, 2010a, b, 2015b).

To examine anti-corruption 'critically' raises a red flag. In academia, the word 'critical' or 'critique' tends to have a negative, destructive, more cynical connotation. Sometimes this critique takes on a moral tone, as a critique of power, a rhetoric of 'speaking truth to power'. But this tone tends to be self-righteous and counterproductive. Other times the critique is too abstract: it deconstructs, or destructs, but fails to offer practical solutions. Small wonder that a critique of the anti-corruption industry may be marginalized as purely 'academic' or simply ignored. Here I would propose a critical view of anti-corruption as more self-critical or even 'reflective'. After all, we have spent millions of dollars and thousands of hours and mobilized thousands of ordinary people and consultants in the 'struggle against corruption'. Here in the wake of yet another scandal, the Paradise Papers, it's time to think about what we have to show for it. We might even turn things upside down and ask whether anti-corruption might have come into the scene even if the so-called anti-corruption movement were not with us. This is not the place to record the history of anti-corruptionism. Yet, it is clear that anti-corruption campaigns in places like Saudi Arabia, China, or Russia are not the result of World Bank loan pressures, EU accession conditions, or advocacy campaigns by local NGOs; something else is going on that these countries suddenly decide to 'fight corruption'.

In this presentation, therefore I want to reflect on what is actually going on when we talk about and perform fighting corruption. When you fight something you have an enemy. Who exactly is the enemy when we are fighting corruption? How do we envision this enemy? Is it the lowly bureaucrat or traffic cop who just cannot resist that extra cash tip? Is it the unscrupulous official or government minister in a developing country who demands a 'facilitation payment' from a pressured sales representative and then deposits the funds into his Swiss bank account? Is the enemy the international corporation whose agents will do ANYTHING to get that pharmaceutical sale or infrastructure project, including bribes, free trips, commissions, and hiring the minister's daughter? Is the enemy the bribe giver or the bribe taker? Is it the simple citizen who unhesitatingly bribes the doctor in a Romanian hospital to care for his elderly father? Or is it the Romanian doctor or government official who takes the money (Stan 2012, 2018)? Is it the unscrupulous sales rep out in the field, or is it the manager back home who knows that his field staff are making facilitation payments? Who, indeed, are the corruption fighters fighting against?

I am an anthropologist. We anthropologists study culture. The cultures we study can be far away, in a mountain herding village or in a tropical forest among swidden farmers; or the cultures can be close by, as when we study an organization and they explain to us 'this is the way we do things around here'. I myself have studied corruption and civil society in many settings. I have studied planning and improvisation in socialist Romania. I have been an NGO project consultant for governments, organizations and consulting companies (Sampson 1996). I have worked in the government of Romania trying to make administrative reform. I have studied anti-corruption initiatives in the Balkans. And I have recently studied ethics and compliance in private firms by attending ethics training courses and conferences (Sampson 2016). I have learned, for example, that in each of these settings, the 'enemy' and the definition of corruption are different. In the ethics and compliance field, which is largely a field for private firms created in the wake of the Enron scandal, there are no evil or corrupt employees. Bad guys are supposed to be weeded out in the hiring process. There are only 'good people doing bad things'. But wait a minute. Why do the good people do so many bad things, you might ask? Well they didn't know they were bad. In the ethics and compliance field, the task is to teach employees that this or that kind of behavior is not just unethical or immoral, but worse: it is bad for the company—that giving a bribe or fixing a bid might end up costing the company a lawsuit, criminal charges, and it might damage its reputation so badly that sales and profits suffer.

Now I give this example because I think that we need to understand more fully the relation between corrupt practices and the anti-corruption landscape that all of us now operate in. This includes those who are pursuing the sustainability project, which, under the slogan of transparency, includes sustainability reporting and accountability. So let me begin by describing two worlds: of corruption and anti-corruption, and then provide some suggestions about what we need to reflect upon in trying to understand them. I will not touch on sustainability reporting per se. But I will argue that much of what I present about the anti-corruption industry can be transferred to sustainability reporting regimes, transparency regimes, CSR, and other self-evident ethically highlighted practices that are now part of business life and of the work of many public organizations.

The World of Corruption and Anti-corruption

Let me begin by presenting the two views of what is going on in the corruption universe. We might call them the optimistic view and the cynical view. The optimistic view sees a widespread anti-corruption movement that has taken off in the last 15 years, a movement that has made a deep impact in fighting corruption, reducing corruption, and preventing corruption. It is a view based on the idea that were it not for this coalition of enlightened civil society activists, international organizations, committed governments, and progressive private firms, that corruption would be much worse. The optimistic narrative is promoted in the many conferences and program declarations that take place almost weekly in some form, where aid organizations, government agencies, ethics officers from firms and NGOs participate. As a result of this frenetic activity, organizations, governments, firms, and the public are now more aware of corruption. This awareness is hyped by incessant demands for transparency, more audit systems, expert monitoring, public reporting, and more incentives to employee whistleblowing. In this view, the anti-corruption movement has led to real progress (Sampson 2010a, 2015a). By 'progress' is meant less corrupt firms or less corrupt bureaucracies, less bribery and nepotism, more corruption being identified and caught earlier, more effective corruption prevention programs, and more firms having anti-corruption initiatives and programs within their CSR or Ethics and Compliance office. 'Progress' in anti-corruption means that through various auditing mechanisms and coalitions of business, government and civil society actors, 'we' are on the way to some kind of 'society without corruption'. The fight against corruption is supposed to mean that things are getting better and that the bad guys increasingly have 'no place to hide'. I have called this package of anti-corruption practices and discourses 'anti-corruptionism' (Sampson 2015b). Like other such 'packages' or 'industries', such as human rights, good governance, gender mainstreaming, climate change action, or sustainability reporting, anti-corruptionism is now part of our everyday organizational life. The concrete manifestations of anti-corruptionism are everywhere: UN and OECD conventions, new or enhanced anti-corruption laws in the USA, the UK and other countries, anti-corruption initiatives, budget lines, agencies and programs, anti-corruption conferences and training, anti-bribery investigations, corruption diagnostics and surveys, an ISO anti-bribery standard, and even Master's degrees and certification in corruption and governance studies. The anti-corruption industry is established indeed.

Integrity warriors are everywhere. One of these days, you might think, there will be no corruption. It will be eradicated, like polio or smallpox.

Contrasting this optimistic, even heroic vision, there is a darker view: that petty and grand corruption continue to occur; that countries and sectors that were profoundly corrupt remain corrupt; that corrupt practices have now simply become more sophisticated due to electronic money transfers, global connections, and tax havens; that all the anti-corruption conferences, declarations, programs, standards, the awareness raising, Global Compact initiatives, and integrity systems have not had much effect. This darker view is confirmed by the major corruption scandals that appear every day, such as the Panama Papers; FIFA; Volkswagen; GSK in China; Siemens; Petrobras, Brazil; FCPA judgments; the UK Serious Fraud Office raids; and the many accusations levelled at accounting firms such as KPMG and PWC, who while training firms to become more ethical are at the same time caught in gross financial and bribery violations (see the FCPA blog or fcpaprofessor.com). This darker vision is marked by spectacular accusations, impressive fines, deferred prosecution agreements, reputation scandals, and the chain of apologies by firms who insist that 'we are changing our culture' and that 'it won't happen again'. These declarations last until the next scandal or the next leak of incriminating mails from WikiLeaks or the Paradise Papers. The anti-corruption dynamic also has its brakes, such as the Trump administration's effort to water down enforcement of financial irregularities. In Scandinavia as well, we have had our share of corruption scandals (the largest FCPA penalty ever, 966 million dollars, belongs to the Swedish telecom Telia). Most corruption scandals involve some kind of subversive cash payment. But here in the north, our corruption may be more sophisticated than cash under the table. It may be the kind of networking that has a dark side: fixing of public bids or contracts, free trips given to public officials, hiring former politicians as consultants or their children as interns, making sure your best friend finds out about a job or contract, or as recently occurred among politicians in Copenhagen, getting free use of the city hall to hold your private wedding reception. Here in Scandinavia, it's not called corruption. It's networking run amok. It may be called abuse of power, or conflict of interest (Swedish: *jav*) or bad management. From a Scandinavian perspective, 'corruption' is something that takes place far away, to the south or east. Yet, it is certainly one example of the darker scenario of persistent corruption. Nevertheless, the continued corruption scenario is illustrated by the numerous examples in Asia, Africa, and Latin America, where corruption scandals (both financial and political) occur with stunning regularity and involve those in the very highest offices.

It is not my intention to say that one of these scenarios is more valid than the other. Perhaps we can say that anti-corruptionist progress discourse and the reality of rampant corruption exist in two parallel universes. They influence each other, to be sure, but the presence of anti-corruptionism does not necessarily entail the reduction in corruption (this is hardly unusual, think of the relation between trafficking and anti-trafficking initiatives, between drug abuse and antidrug campaigns, between campaigns against sexual harassment and pervasive sexual harassment in Hollywood, business, academia, and elsewhere). Further, with so much funding available for anti-corruption programs and campaigns, it would be no accident to find corrupt anti-corruption organizations, which has in fact been the case. This has led Transparency International to develop a sophisticated monitoring, certification (and re-certification) regime for its affiliate national chapters, all in order to safeguard 'the brand'.

Why Care About Corruption?

If my hypothesis about parallel universes is true, how do we explain it? One possible answer is that those in the 'anti-corruption community' are just hypocritical and insincere—that fighting corruption is nothing more than hollow piety. That it's just window dressing or PR façade, and that firms are pursuing business as usual. We might call it 'anti-corruption washing'. It might be, as some critics have asserted, that all the corruption awareness-raising seminars and ethics and compliance initiatives are only therapeutic, a kind of PR initiative, or a disguise by which neoliberalism penetrates the third world (Ochunu 2016; Bedirhanoğlu 2016). However, this PR explanation would be all too easy. There are people who sincerely want to stop the abuse of power we call corruption, and who have seen what even minor corruption can do in Scandinavia and in developing countries around the world. Peter Eigen and his international development colleagues, who founded Transparency International in 1994, were some of these dedicated people. Their tactic was to get businesses and especially the World Bank 'on board' (Eigen himself had previously resigned from his position at the Bank). For Transparency International, anti-corruption became 'coalition-building' among elites and interest organizations rather than a grassroots, radical social movement. Attending the World Economic Forum in Davos was more important than the World Social Forum in Porte Alegre, or marching in the streets. Getting project grants was more important than the kind of social mobilization that might antagonize government elites or potential donors.

If we examine anti-corruption from a managerial standpoint, we can see that while corruption can overcome certain bureaucratic barriers (the 'lubrication' thesis, via speed payments), paying bribes and patronage also involves certain risks (financial/legal/reputational). In this sense, pursuing an anti-corruption strategy presents a series of business-related 'opportunities': what Burritt and Schaltlegger (discussing sustainability reporting) list as 'reputational opportunities, competitive opportunities, political opportunities and also market opportunities' (2010, p. 5). With these opportunities, let us assume that there really are people within firms who care about fighting corruption. The question, then, is whether the individual people's commitment to fighting corruption can be elevated to some kind of organizational commitment. From the firm's perspective, fighting corruption need not be simply an ethical or moral mission. There is a practical side: acting corrupt may be bad for business, especially in the Instagram age, where a single embarrassing post might ruin a firm's reputation. On the positive side, promoting anti-corruption may actually be good business (at least in some sectors). The idea that a nonbusiness aspect of firm behavior is ULTIMATELY GOOD FOR BUSINESS is invoked for other issues as well: climate change, sustainable development, sustainable development reporting, etc. In fact, there seems to be an entire industry trying to convince businesses that transparency, honesty, anti-corruption, climate awareness, CSR, and sustainability reporting are as important for the firm's bottom line as sales and financial accounting. Firms are encouraged to be proactive: grabbing the opportunity before some kind of anti-bribery law or sustainability reporting standard is thrust upon them, or before a scandal occurs and a naming and shaming event takes place. For business, then, the issue is whether to come forward on their own initiative and exert a bona fide ethics and compliance management, or to wait and see if a scandal might occur.

Acknowledging that there are indeed people in the business world who sincerely want to reduce or prevent corruption also entails some qualification. Organizations being what they are, not everyone in the firm will share the same beliefs, attitudes, or priorities. More likely, there are groups within the firm, such as the ethics and compliance department or the CSR unit, who genuinely care about fighting corruption. It is this group who are most aware of the nonfinancial risks. In contrast, other sections of the firm might see anti-corruption as a necessary component of doing business but nothing more. Finally, the marketing and sales force, operating under other incentives, might view ethics, compliance and anti-bribery regulations as an impediment, or even straitjacket, to their work. The task for the ethics officer would be to get the sales force 'on board'. For this, one needs the proverbial 'tone at the top', such that anti-corruption becomes a priority in the organization. The problem is that companies are not ethical actors as such. Unlike NGOs, they do not have a moral project. Firms do not exist to be good. They exist to make money, as Milton Friedman famously reminded us. Businesses use ethics as an instrument. They are ethical only in so far as they believe that ethics is good business. Businesses respect those ethical, legal, and moral bounds because transgressing these might make their operations too risky due to legal penalties, regulatory surveillance, whistleblowing risks, or swindle by clients. If businesses care about corruption, it is a conditional sort of caring. If we operate with this assumption, that business' caring about corruption is conditional, then perhaps several basic concepts about corruption, as well as accepted measures of fighting corruption, need to be reconsidered. Let me summarize some of these reconsiderations.

The Definition of Corruption

In the ancient world, corruption was a social state that characterized an entire society. It connoted a weakness or decay in the social order (Buchan and Hill 2014). We still use the word *korrumperede* in Germanic/Nordic languages when we talk about this kind of societal decay. Today, however, our definition of corruption is more limited. Corruption is defined as 'the abuse of public office for private gain'. It is this 'bad bureaucrat' definition that we find in major policy documents by international institutions and aid donors. Transparency International, in the post-Enron era, later extended this definition of 'bad bureaucrats' to 'the abuse of *entrusted power* for private benefit'. The 'trust' in this 'entrusted power' definition could be conferred (or abused) not just in a bureaucracy, but in a private firm or an NGO. And the 'benefit' need not be a bribe but could also be favoritism, nepotism, or party political advantage. This expanded definition of corruption, however, is in fact the result of a hotly contested political struggle between first and third world that took place decades earlier (Katzarova 2017). It constructs first world companies as victims of venal third world bureaucrats, and it downgrades the active use of bribes and abuse byu corporate powers in the global economy, not to mention tax havens, etc. We now know that the corporate bribe givers are not just innocent victims. We are now seeing these abuses with the Panama and Paradise Papers. But perhaps we need to view corruption not as something extraordinary, as an isolated practice or set of practices, but as a daily, routine practice in the basic operation of some of our most established corporations, financial institutions, and accounting firms, as well as in many bureaucracies (Ochunu 2016 for Nigeria). Investigations into tax swindles, offshore tax shelters, or fixed public bidding contracts reveal hundreds of small decisions made by these firms and by those accountants, executives, and advisors entrusted with power. Tax evasion, tax shelters, umbrella holding companies, pervasive secrecy, secret oral agreements, shredded correspondence, and various other maneuvers resemble the very kind of corruption that these very companies—most of them signatories to the Global Compact—say they are fighting. Anti-corruption declarations aside, it seems that corruption is embedded in even the most routine business practices, in much the same way that it is embedded in so many bureaucratic offices in developing countries (typically customs, police, healthcare, contracting, etc.). If this is true, then what would 'fighting corruption' look like? It would be combatting routine practices.

What Is 'Corruption Fighting'?

Over the years, we have seen various methods of fighting corruption. These campaigns have begun with 'raising awareness'. Transparency International's Corruption Perceptions Index and Bribe Payers Index are two examples of these awareness-raising campaigns. The 'I paid a bribe' sites (India) also work this way, as a kind of naming and shaming enterprise. They shine a light on corrupt practices and are meant to make publicity and then mobilize people to 'do something'. But who exactly does something? In fact, as many observers have pointed out, this awareness-raising project is now completed. We have a UN anti-corruption convention, an ISO anti-bribery standard, and all the rest. What is needed are various measures to actually reduce or prevent corrupt practices, to enforce anti-corruption laws. 'Good governance' in public administration and codes of conduct in the private firm are the mantras here. The measures involved are combinations of carrot and stick, incentives and penalties, plus measures to improve governance so that opportunities for bribes and favoritism become more difficult. Since corrupt practices are human activities, preventing corruption requires a combination of social psychological and sociological approaches. Do we try to make people better, make them more ethical? (education) Do we try to improve *structures* so that people to do not feel the *need* to be corrupt? (carrot and stick). Do we assume that people 'need' to be corrupt, and if they were not compelled to take bribes that they wouldn't? Or do we try to reformulate the contexts, making it *more costly* to be corrupt (Lenin: 'Trust is good, but control is better'). In the present fad of nudging, can we nudge people to be more honest? I am not sure. What we do know is that people act differently once they feel outside a community. You do not cheat your friends or your family, or those to whom you feel attached (your mates, team, or gang). But you *can* cheat a faceless bureaucracy for whom you have no loyalty, or clients whom you will not see again and to whom you owe nothing. So perhaps fighting corruption is really about something much larger. Perhaps it is about how people, including ourselves, relate to institutions and communities. Perhaps it is about attachment, the attachment we now call 'trust'. Let's turn Lenin upside down, to fight corruption, trust is good, control is worse.

Deciding Which Corruption to Fight

Since abuse of power, including the abuse of power that we call corruption, is undesirable, and since there are so many kinds of corruption, we face a dilemma in deciding which kinds of corruption we should fight. If we examine debates and controversies about corruption, there seem to be two basic targets against which corruption fighting is directed: greedy officials in bureaucracies and unscrupulous international corporations. The officials may be bribe takers, or they may be pressuring clients or local/foreign companies for bribes to fulfill tasks that the official should do anyway. The corporations may be abusing their influence by paying for positive decisions, or by manipulating prices or using secret contacts to win lucrative contracts. Fighting these kinds of corruption requires more than just naming and shaming. Both the greedy officials and the unscrupulous corporations are quite aware that corruption is bad.

Fighting such corruption requires a theory of human behavior. Social science has tried to categorize types of behavior and types of influences on our behavior. Psychology, sociology, social psychology, anthropology, economics and political science try to understand why people do some things, and why they refrain from doing other things. I think it comes down to three basic explanations. First, people do things because they *want to.* That is, they have values which they act out in practice. For example, no one forces me to buy a birthday present for my daughter. I just do it. Second, people do things *because they have to.* There are structures and incentives which dictate that the benefits gained from doing something are higher than the costs of not doing something. I buy a birthday present for my boss because my chances for promotion are better if he remembers me. Buying the present for him is the sensible thing to do. And since everyone else is doing it, it would be awkward if I did not. Finally, we do things *because other people are doing them* and we want to stay in the community. I watch football with my friends or go with my street gang and fight another gang to show my loyalty. In this third type of motivation, we act because it gives some kind of meaning to be a member of a group or community. So we have these three kinds of human behavior. The social sciences articulate these three types of behavior in different ways: as theories of motivation, as social capital, as interest groups, as power, as agency, as kinship obligations, or as community solidarity. But regardless of terminology, I think human behavior (voluntary, forced, or nudged) comes down to these three factors. Now, what if we applied these factors to ethics and compliance and to anti-corruption (Sampson 2014)? Since people are often resistant to change, we need to ask: Which kind of behavior is most difficult to change? I am not sure I have the answer, but I think all of us would agree that changing people's basic values is difficult, and it is a long-term project. Values tend to be deeply embedded; we are emotionally attached to them; values are part of our very self. It is easier to change the structures and incentive systems that affect people's actions, and it is also easier to affect communities, to build teams to make meaning, or to create conditions whereby people find their team or gang unfulfilling. In practice, this means that fighting corruption entails a process of deciding what kinds of behavior we should fight, and then identifying why people act corrupt: why they achieve their goals by giving bribes, why they accept bribes, why they encourage or tolerate nepotism, why they falsify records and conspire to cheat the state, their firm, or their community. A full understanding of corrupt practices also means recalling that people may not even view their behavior as corrupt or even wrong. Corrupt behavior may even be considered a kind of social obligation, or a kind of reaction or revenge to abuses by the system, as a means of asserting one's right to common goods. If this is true, 'awareness raising' about corruption is a blind alley.

Rethinking Transparency

Many anti-corruption and governance initiatives place their faith in illuminating information and procedures, invoking the trope of transparency. Hence, if we only make all bids for government contracts public, if we allow people access to information, if everything becomes digitally accessible, then nepotism and corruption will be limited or disappear. This idea of transparency involves an assumption of pervasive openness. It also assumes that corruption invariably involves some kind of secrecy. Various 'sunshine laws', forcing companies and public actors to show their financial affairs, to disclose their CSR initiatives, or to submit sustainability reports, are viewed as measures that will magically stimulate firms to act better. These transparency mandates have given rise to all kinds of reporting regimes and associated monitoring systems of firms and organizations. Through transparency, firms commit themselves to ethical or moral projects such as the Global Compact, sustainability, diversity, Global Reporting Initiative, or various anti-corruption standards. With transparency and reporting comes the inevitable monitoring bureaucracy of periodic updates, statistics, and deadlines. We academics experience this kind of monitoring in terms of our 'productivity', which is followed by statistics on number of downloads of our articles, amount of grants we receive, and the measurement of the impact of our work. Firms and organizations experience the same thing. Such reporting regimes consolidate what anthropologist Marilyn Strathern (2000) called 'audit culture' and what Michael Power (1997) called 'rituals of verification'. The unintended by-product to all this, which all of us know but often ignore, is that every move toward transparency involves hiding something. Every disclosure creates its own shadow (Han 2015). Every demand for standardization creates a path around it. Every raised bar allows someone to slide under it undetected. We academics know how to manipulate the publication statistics. And firms now hire experts, lawyers, accountants, and consultants, to ensure that even under the strictest of transparency regimes, certain practices can be hidden, statistical categories can be made confusing, disasters are made to look like glitches, and crises are now reconfigured as 'challenges'. Like the Kremlinologists who analyzed the Soviet Union, we need new skills to interpret reports generated under transparency regimes. We need to do more than just read between lines. We need to truly translate what is being said. Take a look at World Bank anti-corruption reports, Council of Europe corruption monitoring reports, the sustainability reports of private firms, and other such documents. The most impressive fact about them is how few people actually download them, much less read them closely! The reports *perform* transparency, yes, but the performance is a pure ritual. Apparently, not many people care. If no one cares about transparency, if those decision-makers who matter do not care, then the chances of transparency as a solution to corruption become that much less. Transparency regimes alone do not necessarily generate the kind of commitment—the kind of CARING—required to pursue anti-corruption. With more transparency and more data, there are fewer people to read them and make judgments. More transparency, more reporting about more things is not the magic bullet. What is missing in this kind of fetish of reporting, auditing, and self-auditing was highlighted by Michael Power in his book, *The Audit Society* (1997) 20 years ago. This something is called 'judgment'. Judgment involves decisions and risks. It involves taking responsibility. It involves CARING about what you are doing. And in much of the CSR, sustainability, and anti-corruption reporting regimes, with its mandatory categories, metrics, protocols, and systems, judgment is somehow set aside. Judgment becomes suspect. How regrettable, since judgment, like corruption, is human behavior. Like human behavior, judgment articulates a set of values. Judgment articulates a community, and such communities can resist the pressure for easy, or illicit, or corrupt solutions. Academia, my community of meaning, is a community of judgment. We are now being increasingly subordinated to audit, metrics, and productivity indices (Strathern 2000). But none of us like it. Protest is useless. So what do we do? We PLAY ALONG. And I suspect that much organizational reporting on ethics, compliance, anti-bribery, anti-corruption, CSR, and sustainability is also affected by playing along, that is, by a calculation of the costs of not participating versus the benefits of playing along. So let us not delude ourselves about the magic bullet of transparency. Regardless of transparency, we still need to make judgments: about what to report, when to report, how to report, to whom to report, and especially why we report. WE NEED TO CARE ABOUT IT. Transparency regimes are regimes of power. Somebody is compelling someone else to act in a certain way. We may appreciate producing reports and manipulating statistics, we may get well paid to do them, but behind the reporting effort lies compulsion. It is a compulsion to put away our judgment tools and to play along.

We thus need to rethink the performance of transparency and to rethink what all this disclosure is leading to. We need to rethink what it means to actors to make certain kinds of information (in certain forms) 'public'. Most such reporting, including sustainability reporting, can itself become corrupted; any statistician knows how to do this. Transparency and disclosure can be manipulated, contested, or passively accepted as the lesser of evils. There is a politics of transparency and a politics of disclosure that we need to understand. More is not always better. The transparent report becomes a dead exhibit, a fetish to be waved around, as so many reports are nowadays. We wave it, but don't read it! We put it up on our Web site, but no one downloads it.

Conclusions: Caring About Corruption

Management is about deciding on purposeful action to achieve results. Deciding that anti-corruption or sustainability are important goals, and that reporting on these goals is good for the firm and for society are management decisions. Management decisions should be translated into purposeful action. Like management experts, we social scientists also study purposeful action. But we also study *why* people think a specific course of action is purposeful, *how* this course of action was chosen over others, and what are the *unintended consequences* of such actions. The word 'unintended' also needs specification: unintended by whom, about what? Abuse of power exists in firms, organizations and societies, and some of these abuses have come to be called 'corruption'. Everyday actions of corporations and bureaucracies may also be abuses of power but these are called 'business as usual', 'how we do things around here' or 'just how the system works'. Anti-corruption, transparency, and sustainability initiatives, including the associated reporting regimes, certainly have an impact on how power is exercised and how power is abused. But this does not necessarily mean that these kind of initiatives have reduced or prevented these abuses, or reduced corruption. This is because anti-corruptionism also has its own dynamic, including its own potential for abuse. We might therefore conclude that anti-corruptionism has made corruption more sophisticated, and therefore harder to fight, in the same way that modern computer systems make it easier for us buy online, while also enabling hackers to empty our bank accounts.

In particular, we need to assess whether all this anti-corruptionism, with its many programs, with its awareness raising, the conventions, the laws, the regulations, the ethical finger pointing, the training, the seminars, and agencies, whether it makes a difference in how power is exercised and how it is abused. We need to figure out *who really cares about preventing corruption, why they care, and how. Ultimately, we need a theory of engagement.* Business is most effective when it engages with customers to find out what they think, or how to market a product in a new country. There is some kind of commitment from the executive, in the marketing and sales force. Can anti-corruption, ethics, and compliance not mobilize the same commitment? If we can figure this out, then maybe we can take the first steps toward eliminating the kind of impunity, the kind of abuse of power, and the perversion of trust that characterizes corruption. We need to share our knowledge about corruption and anti-corruption, so that we can understand who really cares about corruption.

References

Bedirhanoğlu, P. (2016). Corruption of anti-corruption: Deconstructing neoliberal good governance. In J. A. Scholte, L. Fioramonti, & A. Nhema (Eds.), *New rules for global justice: Structural redistribution in the global political economy* (pp. 57–70). London: Rowman and Littlefield.

Buchan, B., & Hill, L. (2014). *An intellectual history of political corruption.* London: Palgrave.

Bukanovsky, M. (2006). The hollowness of anti-corruption discourse. *Review of International Political Economy, 13,* 181–209.

Burritt, R., & Schaltegger, S. (2010). Sustainability accounting and reporting: Fad or trend? *Accounting, Auditing & Accountability Journal, 23,* 829–846.

Han, P.-C. (2015). *The transparency society.* Stanford: Stanford University Press.

Katzarova, E. (2017, December). From global problems to international norms: What does the social construction of a global corruption problem tell us about the emergence of an international anti-corruption norm. *Crime Law and Social Change.* https://doi.org/10.1007/s10611-017-9733-z.

Ochunu M. E. (2016). Bring back corruption: A critique of neoliberal anti-corruption rhetoric. *Pambazuka News,* September 8. www.pambazuka.org/democracy-governance/bring-back-corruption-critique-neoliberal-anti-corruption-rhetoric.

Power, M. (1997). *The audit society: Rituals of verification*. Oxford: Oxford University Press.

Sampson, S. (1996). The social life of projects: Importing civil society to Albania. In C. Hann & E. Dunn (Eds.), *Civil society: Challenging western models* (pp. 121–142). London: Routledge.

Sampson, S. (2005). Integrity warriors: Global morality and the anti-corruption movement in the Balkans. In D. Haller & C. Shore (Eds.), *Corruption: Anthropological perspectives* (pp. 103–130). London: Pluto Press.

Sampson, S. (2009). Corruption and anti-corruption in Southeast Europe: Landscapes and sites. In L. de Sousa, P. Lamour, & B. Hindness (Eds.), *Governments, NGOs and anti-corruption: The new integrity warrior* (pp. 168–185). Abingdon: Routledge.

Sampson, S. (2010a). The anti-corruption industry: From movement to institution. *Global Crime, 11*, 261–278.

Sampson, S. (2010b). Diagnostics: Indicators and transparency in the anti-corruption industry. In S. Jansen, E. Schröter, & N. Stehr (Eds.), *Transparenz: Multidisziplinäre Durchsichten durch Phönomene und Theorien des Undurchsichtigen* (pp. 97–111). Wiesbaden: VS Verlag für Sozialwissenschaften.

Sampson, S. (2014). Culture and compliance: An anthropologist's view. *Compliance & Ethics Professional*, June, 35–39 (Society of Corporate Compliance and Ethics). http://www.corporatecompliance.org/Portals/1/PDF/Resources/Compliance_Ethics_Professional/0614/scce-cep-2014-06-Sampson.pdf and www.corporatecompliance.org. Republished in *Ethikos: The Journal of Practical Business Ethics, 29*(2), March/April 2015, 8–12.

Sampson, S. (2015a). The audit juggernaut. *Social Anthropology, 23*, 80–82.

Sampson, S. (2015b). The anti-corruption package. *Ephemera: Theory and Politics in Organization, 15*(2), 115–123.

Sampson, S. (2016). The 'right way': Moral capitalism and the emergence of the corporate ethics and compliance officer. *Journal of Business Anthropology, 5*(3), 65–86.

Stan, S. (2012). Neither commodities nor gifts: Post-socialist informal exchanges in the Romanian healthcare system. *Journal of the Royal Anthropological Association, 18*, 65–82.

Stan, S. (2018). Neoliberal citizenship and the politics of corruption: Redefining informal exchange in Romanian healthcare. In J. Carrier (Ed.), *Economy, Crime and Wrong in a Neoliberal Era*. Oxford: Berghahn Books.

Strathern, M. (Ed.). (2000). *Audit cultures: Anthropological studies in accountability, ethics, and the academy*. London: Routledge.

Rationalizing Deviances—Avoiding Responsibility

Tomas Brytting

...it is necessary to know well how to disguise this (hypocritical) characteristic, and to be a great pretender and dissembler; and men are so simple, and so subject to present necessities, that he who seeks to deceive will always find someone who will allow himself to be deceived. (Machiavelli 2006)

We are born with the ability to deceive, and it is a highly useful capacity. It is usually used in relatively harmless contexts such as playing, gaming, acting on stage. Making jokes, ironizing, diverting attention, using under—and overstatements and special lingo—only understood by initiates, these are everyday examples near the boundaries of the deceptive. Enthralling and deceiving are rather similar phenomena but with completely different moral loadings. One amuses and fascinates. The other offends us. Admiring and pursuing the former, condemning and avoiding the other is something that

In this article, I develop ideas that were introduced in Brytting, T. (2013) and in Brytting, T et al. (2011).

T. Brytting (✉)
Ersta Skondal Bracke University College, Stockholm, Sweden
e-mail: tomas.brytting@moralspace.se

S. Arvidsson (ed.), *Challenges in Managing Sustainable Business*,
https://doi.org/10.1007/978-3-319-93266-8_13

most of us can manage, but not everyone. Deception, fraud and in more general terms corruption and irregularities, abound.

In 1995, after his unauthorized financial speculations led to the collapse of the over 200-year-old Barings Bank, Nick Leeson was quoted saying: "Somebody should have stopped me!". Bernard Madoff said something similar, addressing the banks, when the unimaginable SEK 500 billion (USD 65 billion) had disappeared from his Ponzi scheme. In addition to the moral dubiousity of their efforts to abdicate from their role as responsible actors, one must also question Leeson's and Madoff's reliance on the surveillance systems ability to detect fraud. Although these systems seem to be increasingly efficient in recent years, the organizations' own security controls—internal and external audits and IT controls—only detect one in five instances of fraud (ACFE 2016). Internal audit detected 16.5%, External audit 3.8% and IT Controls 1.3%. The majority—81%—of the fraudsters being insiders is a fact that might explain the difficulty in stopping them with internal measures (The Economist 2016).

Improved administrative measures are of course important, but psychological and cultural factors should not be underestimated. In this article, I will treat fraud, corruption, discrimination, theft, cheating, etc.—in one word: *deviances*—as a social and psychological problem. I will argue that *rationalizations* both from the fraudsters' and the bystanders' side are one important factor to understand if these kinds of deviances are to be prevented. I will also propose that these rationalizations can be interpreted as a kind of perverted modern virtues. Being in line with virtues might just explain their persuasive power.

The Construction of Social Facts

What does it take, more precisely, to create a common understanding of deviances in organisations and to get a common consensus around the importance of detecting and preventing them? Rubington and Weinberg (1968) use the following explanatory model:

> For deviance to become a social fact, someone must perceive an act, situation or event as a departure from social norms, must categorize

> that perception, must report that perception to others, must get them to accept this definition of the situation, and must obtain a response that conforms to their definition. Unless all these requirements are met, deviance as a social fact does not come into being.

The requirements mentioned in this quote could just as well be reformulated in a way that describes what is needed in order to detect and fight deviance successfully:

- *Knowing norms*; acquaintance with relevant social norms.
- *Knowing the facts*; the possibility and ability to know about the devious act, situation or event. (Deviances are special in the sense that they are hidden.)
- *Judgemental ability*; the capability to categorize these acts, situations or events not only as departures from relevant social norms and values but also as morally reprehensible.
- *Communication*; being able to formulate and report that judgement to others and getting the others to accept the definition of the act, situation or event as reprehensible.
- *Mobilisation*; obtaining adequate action from, or together with, others.

And, just as the quote said "Unless all these requirements are met, deviance *as a social fact* does not come into being"—meaning: deviance will not be adequately detected and dealt with. The fact that deviances are so common could therefore be understood as a failure to construct them as social facts. The presence of *rationalizations* can explain this failure. They tend to de-construct deviances into something rational (Fig. 1).

Criminologists often explain white-collar crime with what is called the fraud triangle. Experienced needs of, for example, more money combined with an opportunity for theft, bribes or fraud is not enough. The actor/criminal also has to perceive the crime as acceptable, in one way or the other. He has to be able to integrate the crime with his self-perception as being a rational creature. If that is not possible, the crime will not take place, even though both need and opportunity may be in place.

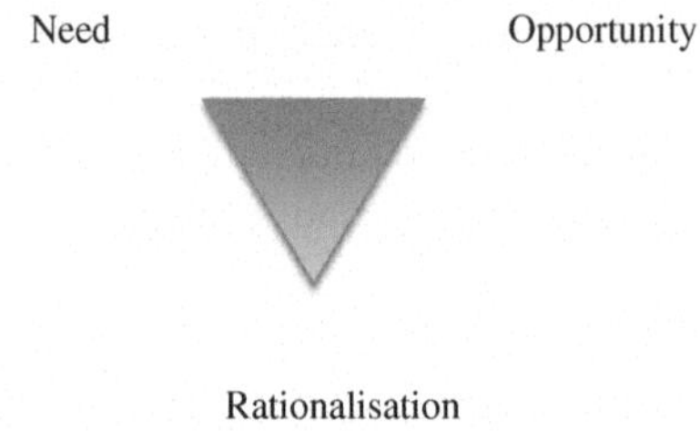

Fig. 1 The fraud triangle

Much of the work currently being undertaken to reduce fraud and corruption, etc. has been focused on minimizing *opportunities* for crime. Developing administrative safety routines, more accurate monitoring systems and more rigorous spot-checking are examples of this. Such measures risk creating costly and ineffective bureaucracy. And as we have seen, they have their own inherent limitations.

Perceived *need* for more money or higher status in the organization is often looked upon not as part of the problem but rather as an important driving force for both managers and employees. On the contrary, it seems as if the linking of financial targets to variable remuneration have increased both in scope and size. It is therefore highly doubtful to attack corruption by attempting to influence, i.e. reduce, the perpetrators perceived needs. Getting the boards to set lower financial goals would mean asking owners and investors to invest their money elsewhere. At the individual level, one can imagine that the perceived need for more money can be reduced, but only on a voluntary basis. It is only when the individual perceives his need as obsessive or as a barrier to a more rich personality development that some form of reorientation can take place. However, that requires self-awareness and free will. I will return to this problem.

By picturing The Fraud Triangle as unstable, with its tip down, I want to point out that rationalizations—the balance point—is something that can dynamically be adapted to maintain the fraud, at least in the perpetrator's eyes. In the moment of temptation—when needs and opportunity coincide—one can imagine the potential perpetrator trying out different rationalizations to see whether or not the crime can be legitimized, after all. The same goes, I think, if we speak about deviances more generally.

Rationalizing Deviance

There seems to be an infinite number of rationalizations and, interestingly enough, they reflect and cancel out each other (See also Taro Lennerfors article in this volume). Appropriate excuses are available for every conceivable occasion:

- *Everyone is doing it*, but on the other hand…
- *Others are much worse*
- *This is how things work here*, but on the other hand…
- *This is an exception*
- *I have no choice*, but on the other hand…
- *It is for a good cause*
- *It is probably OK*, but on the other hand…
- *I will never get caught*
- *It's just a loan and I'll pay it back*, but on the other hand…
- *They don't mind*
- *Take from the rich and give to the poor*, but on the other hand -
- *I've (they've) earned it*
- *No one is hurt*, but on the other hand -
- *It's only fair*
- Etc.…

The actors involved are probably well acquainted with current norms. They also know how to act deceivingly. They feel the tension between these deviant acts and the norms, but they allow one or more rationalization to blur out their judgemental ability. Moreover, the power of rationalizations is underestimated if the bystanders are not included in the discussion. They also often engage in such unreasonable delusions in order to avoid being involved and having to do something about it.

One can organize the rationalization of deviances into four basic forms depending on whether the perpetrator deceives with or without intent and how tolerant people are surrounding him.

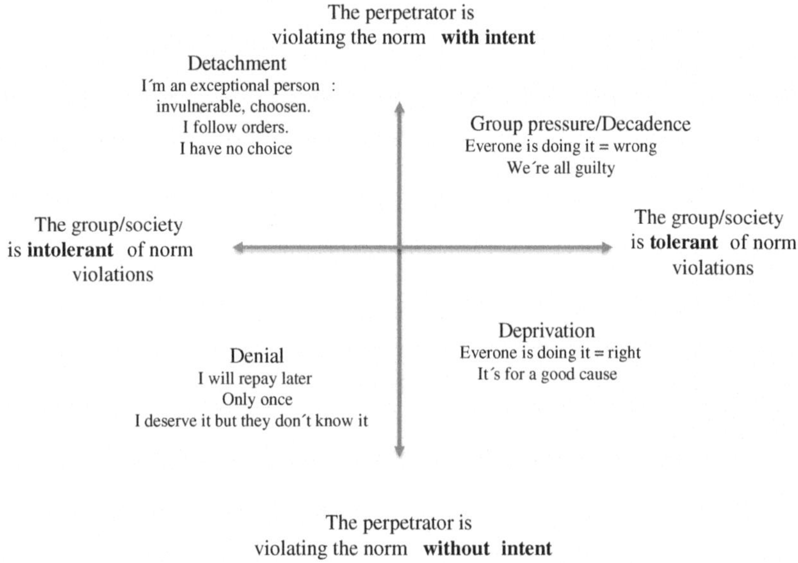

Fig. 2 Four ways of rationalizing deviances

Being in the first category—*Group pressure/Decadence*—does not mean that the perpetrator thinks that violating the norm is totally acceptable. It may, in fact, only be done after a painful emotional struggle and under great mental strain. The psychological mechanism is partly a strong impulse to adapt oneself to the behaviour of one's own flock, partly diluting one's sense of responsibility for the act by spreading responsibility to the whole group.

The last impulse is not as irrational as it might seem at first. Suppose the alternative choices of action in a situation are unclear: what's right and what's wrong? Looking to see how others seem to evaluate the situation can provide reasonable information. Several individuals together probably have more experience than a single one, and together they may therefore make a more accurate evaluation. A moral issue only occurs when the group's influence is so strong that it prevents the individual from taking a position that is the most reasonable from his own convictions but divergent from the group's.

The group's tendency to share and thereby dilute one's sense of responsibility seems to be based on a subconscious mindset were responsibility is treated as a zero-sum game (Latané and Darley 1970). The situation is perceived as sharing 100% responsibility between those involved. If, e.g., 100 individuals are involved, psychologically speaking just one percent responsibility falls on each one of them. That fraction is often not enough to trigger a sense of personal responsibility and responsible action. If the individual was alone, his own sense of responsibility would be much profoundly felt. This idea gets an even greater apologetic power if it is combined with the feeling of being in a decadent environment where others commit offenses much worse than what the individual is conceiving. In other words, group pressure as a rationalization category means that the perpetrator consciously engages in what is perceived as wrongdoings because he thinks everyone else is doing it.

In the second category—*Deprivation*—the perpetrator does not fully realize that his own and the bystanders violations of norms are in fact morally reprehensible. Here, the individual finds the environment's apparent tolerance supportive. Their behaviour is taken as evidence of what is to be perceived as right and wrong. The perpetrator does not experience any wrongdoing because "what's normal can't be wrong". In this way, the difference between "norm" and "normality" is being confused.

Another variation of deprivation is when the perpetrator lets the ends justify the means. If this also seems to be the view taken by the surrounding group, the perpetrator experiences social support or at least social acceptance for his behaviour. If nothing but the purpose or consequences of the action is being evaluated, the act itself will of course not be subject to any moral reflection at all. Then the actor and other involved individuals can be said to be devoid or deprived of moral denouncement.

In the third rationalization category—*Denial*—the perpetrator does not regard the denunciatory attitude taken by the environment as relevant and sees the violation of norms as a kind of exception. The perpetrator can accept the norm as a relevant principle but at the same time fail to recognize it as applicable or relevant in the specific situation. An action that others would call a theft the fraudster can perceive, e.g. as a loan or as a fair compensation for an extraordinary effort. Then the deceiver will not perceive the act as a violation of norms, norms which he under other circumstances would endorse: "It may seem like theft, but I do not see it that way—neither would you, if you knew what I know".

The fourth category—*Detachment*—is probably the one that demands the most of the perpetrator in terms of self-delusion. Detachment implies both finding an apology in one's own eyes—the perpetrator is deliberately violating norms that he thinks are valid even in the actual situation at hand—*and* an explanation of why the group's or society's condemnations should not be decisive. The sense of being forced, of having no other choice, can fill both needs. Being entirely without choices, the individual has no moral responsibility for his actions. "I had no choice" or "I only followed orders" serve as a kind of whitewash in order for the perpetrator to perceive himself both as just and at the same time knowingly violating the norm. In both cases, the moral responsibility for the act taken is being placed elsewhere or with someone else.

A variant of detachment is the delusions narcissistically disturbed people may suffer: "megalomania" or "grandiose delusions". Such a perpetrator sees himself as a superior being—or "Übermensch" in Nietzsche's sense. The norm in question is perceived as applicable to all other humans but not to the perpetrator himself and neither to a few selected others of a similar exceptional sort. People of this superior standard are not bound by ordinary rules. They are chosen by God, destiny or cosmic forces to play a special role in the world. They may even sense a kind of almost divine protection; i.e., they will never be caught. In this distorted perception of reality, breaking norms can even be perceived as a good thing—among the few chosen ones. In a less extreme wording, detachment means that the perpetrator believes that "the norms do not apply to me - at least not at the moment".

A Vicious Circle?

One can in fact imagine an increasingly corrupt process beginning with *group pressure*, turning into *deprivation* which through *denial* ends in a total *detachment* from norms. Such a development is certainly not bound to take place, but the dynamics could be inherent and those working against corruption should be aware of what can happen if rationalizations are allowed to flourish without proper countermeasures.

As the figure above is drawn, it has a social dimension that deals with the environment's acceptance or condemnation. The other dimension is the individual's and describes whether violations of norms occur consciously or not. Using that structure, I will now move on and look for the deeper origins of these rationalizations and for suggestions for cures both at the cultural and the individual level.

Cultural Explanations

The fact that deviances are relatively common in all sorts of organizations suggests that a cultural analysis at a general level could be useful in understanding the phenomena and finding remedies. In other words, such an analysis focuses on the horizontal dimension in the figure above.

Obviously, if the environment tolerates deviances—or if the perpetrator believes this to be the case—then an important antidote to norm violations fails; social condemnation. It is even worse, of course, if the surrounding group or society appreciate or even rewards such behaviour.

When PriceWaterhouseCoopers (2003) some years ago conducted an international study of fraud in which senior executives were interviewed, the investigators drew the following conclusion:

> Criminological research indicates that most fraudsters tend to be risk-takers, decisive, extroverted, career or success-oriented individuals. Paradoxically, it is precisely these traits that are also highly prized in management recruitment.

Over-ambitious financial targets in combination with substantial bonus systems, not only drive unhealthy levels of risk in financial terms. They also risk supporting dysfunctional rationalization processes in which increasingly desperate business leaders might perceive violation of norms—e.g. tax evasion, paying black money, inflate sales figures, bribing, making fake forecasts—as the most rational solution.

In an international survey by PriceWaterhouseCoopers (2009) conducted during the recent financial crisis, 68% of respondents indicated that the reward systems and increasing performance requirements were the main reasons behind managerial fraud. In addition, it appears that reward systems with a high-performance-based share—more than 50%—increased the likelihood of fraud.

In other words, seeing economic growth as something good is not the problem. However, exaggerated growth expectations, i.e. ever-growing market shares and profit levels, in combination with "risk-taking, decisive, extroverted, career or success-oriented managers" may form a dangerous blend. The problem must be termed "social" or "cultural" because it is very difficult or even self-destructive for an individual company on its own to deviate and reduce these expectations to more realistic levels.

Something similar applies to other strong social expectations of, for example loyalty, social competence, self-confidence and flexibility. They may put the individual actor under highly normative pressure from both within and without, at the same time if they are exaggerated.

From a cultural perspective then, one might hypothesize that the rationalizations enabling deviances simply express strong prevailing cultural ideals—albeit in a strained or perhaps even corrupt form. For example, for most of us "social competence" implies an ability to engage in small talk; to listen to the viewpoints of others; to be seen as pleasant, trustworthy, loyal, easy-going and fun. Another example: we live in a society where success is measured in financial terms. Your employer has set numerical goals and if you reach them you will receive financial rewards. Reaching for more money is the right thing to do… never mind what it takes. These examples seem to be anything *but* descriptions of deviant behaviour. However, they might also depict a weak personal character being caught up in a corrupt subculture, unable to realize moral autonomy. Your loyalty has turned into weakness and your ambitions into what Solomon (1992) called "abstract greed": greed without realism, passion, and understanding of effort or purpose. You have been corrupted by the same virtues that were supposed to turn you into a moral role model for others.

The problem of deception is then not so much about the perpetrator lying to herself or being irrational. Rather, the problem is that

Table 1 Rationalizations and corresponding cultural ideals or virtues

Type of rationalization	Example	Corresponding cultural ideals or virtues
Group pressure/ Decadent	Everyone is doing it=wrong We are all guilty	It is commendable to be part of and loyal to one's own community
Deprivation	Everyone is doing it=right It's for a good cause	It is commendable to be responsive and open to other's point-of-view, to show social competence, to be flexible and pragmatic Economic incentives are rational
Denial	Only once I will repay later I deserve this	It is commendable to grasp opportunities, to be creative and to solve problems as they come
Detachment	(a) I have no choice I followed orders (b) I'm an exceptional person	(a) It is commendable to be realistic and avoid wishful thinking It is commendable to be loyal (b) It is commendable to have ambitions and self-confidence, to overcome resistance and setbacks

she is *too* eager to fit in, too compliant and, with a weak sense of autonomy, is acting rationally within *apparent* or very local norms. This line of reasoning may enlighten also the other forms of rationalizations presented above; they all rely on social ideals and virtues (i.e. commendable personality traits) (Table 1).

There is a pattern here that together with a common cultural background forms a strong normative context in which, e.g., egoism, economic rationality, pragmatism, social compliance and flexibility are norms which takes on a matter-of-fact quality. In and by themselves, these norms do not explain all forms of deviances. They do after all also form a list of modern virtues. What is also needed in order to rationalize serious deviances is a certain kind of unbalanced interpretation of these virtues. Those interpretations we might find on the individual level.

Individual Explanations

My hypothesis is that by being aligned with virtues these social norms (egoism, economic rationality, pragmatism, social compliance and flexibility) are set in practice and seen as commendable, sometimes in an uncritical way. When that happens, in more or less extreme cases, they may develop into a kind of exaggerated or corrupt (distorted) thinking that ends in irresponsible action. This idea is outlined by adding a column to the table above:

Table 2 Rationalizations, virtues and corrupt thinking

Type of rationalization	Example	Corresponding cultural ideal or virtue	Corrupt thinking
Group pressure/ Decadent	Everyone is doing it = wrong We are all guilty	It is commendable to be part of and loyal to one's community	The individual can no longer realize fully what it means to act against one's own consciousness
Deprivation	Everyone is doing it = right It's for a good cause	It is commendable to be responsive and open to other's point-of-view, to show social competence, to be flexible and pragmatic Economic incentives are rational	The individual can no longer oppose others and/or expose his/her own self. Other people or "the cause" has taken over The ends justify the means
Denial	Only once I will repay later I deserve this	It is commendable to grasp opportunities, to be creative and to solve problems as they come	The individual can no longer plan or control his/her own life

(continued)

Table 2 (continued)

Type of rationalization	Example	Corresponding cultural ideal or virtue	Corrupt thinking
Detachment	(a) I have no choice I followed orders (b) I'm an exceptional person	(a) It is commendable to be realistic without wishful thinking It is commendable to be loyal (b) It is commendable to have ambitions and self-confidence, to overcome resistance and setbacks	(a) The individual escapes from freedom and responsibility (b) The individual over compensate low self-esteem = develops narcissistic traits

If corrupt thinking is the case: What then is the remedy?

"Moral Space" as a Solution?

Obviously, we need common values and norms in order to function as human beings. Taylor (1991) adds to this that in order to avoid a trivialization of our lives, these values and norms must concern "significant" issues. The most significant ones are connected to *moral* claims originating from something more general and enduring than our own whims or feelings:

> Only if I exist in a world in which history, or the demands of nature, or the needs of my fellow human beings, or the duties of citizenship, or the call of God, or something else of this order matters crucially, can I define an identity for myself that is not trivial.

And determining what "matters crucially" is not up to each individual to decide. Originality is not equivalent with significance. The individual finds herself "in a world in which history, or the demands of nature…etc. … matters crucially" and has to relate to that world—like it or not. Taylor pictures a stable "moral space" in which one's identity has to be defined and defended against accusations of being dysfunctional or trivial.

It is not freedom then, but restrictions—e.g. moral duties or prohibitions stemming from a social moral discourse—that render our lives significance. We exist as selves in a "moral space" that is made up of what society has found to be "crucial matters" reaching far beyond ourselves.

This is something else than social compliance; what I called loyalty, responsiveness and flexibility in the tables above. Taking a stand-in moral space is something fundamentally different. It implies investing in and, even more importantly, being able to do defend deeply held convictions. In contrast to this, rationalizations in the form of what I called corrupt thinking imply that nothing seems to matter crucially, nothing but getting away with deviances. There is definitely nothing infinitely valuable at stake in the latter, quite the opposite. Rationalizations facilitate violations of important norms. They serve a deceptive cause.

In summary, based on a cultural analysis fighting deviances would imply taking—or returning to—a position, I would like to call conservative. Modernistic claims of constant change and pragmatism need to be restrained by respect for the fairly inflexible nature of basic ethical norms. Schematically, it can be said that several of the features of modern culture need to be balanced or even replaced by some kind of counterforce, for example:

- Materialism needs to be balanced by humanism
- Individualism becomes unsustainable without solidarity
- Pragmatism should never override honour
- Flexibility must be combined with respect for approved practices
- Short-term goals and behaviours must not endanger long-term consequences

In particular, it is important to understand the functioning of basic, common moral values and norms setting limits to what we ought to do.

Self-Analysis as a Solution?

The vertical dimension of Fig. 2 describes whether the perpetrator acts with or without intent, i.e. if she fully wants to violate norms and what that means. This dimension makes us look for *individual* cures.

Fighting irregularities on the individual level—i.e. the perpetrator's own level—is then obviously about reaching self-awareness and self-understanding. But what if the perpetrator is deceiving herself? How can you discover your own unawareness? How do you know if the risk of becoming a perpetrator yourself has increased?

In order to protect ourselves, we should take a close look at the column *Corrupt Thinking* in Table 2 and ask: is there a grain of truth in these statements? Do they apply to me? In that way, by critically examining ourselves and our rationalizations, we learn not only more about ourselves. We can also regain control of action patterns that have become compulsory and destructive both for us and for others. Self-analysis is thus a way to become more consistent in one's actions and a way to avoid lack of logic in one's own reasoning.

For each kind of rationalization, a self-analysis might look like this:

1. What is my reason for questioning this particular norm—i.e. what rationalization am I using?
2. What does this rationalization say favourably about my personality—if I translate it into a cultural ideal?
3. To a personal virtue?
4. What happens if I consider the virtue as a psychological problem instead? Do I recognize that it has an influence in my life?
    a. Do I have obsessive thoughts?
    b. Do I often feel jealous of my colleagues?
    c. Do I feel stressed often? Chronically tired?
5. Do I have full control over my own actions in tempting situations?
6. Do I have financial problems?
7. Am I willing to see my actions on the front-page news?

The goal of such self-analysis could, in a slightly provocative way, be to develop something we may call "healthy narcissism". It is about finding a controlled balance between megalomania and self-extinction. Everyone benefits from feeling special but not necessarily chosen; strong but not above law and morality; ambitious but not perfect; flexible but not coward; benevolent but not seductive; powerful but not brutal; goal-focused but not parasitic; and observant but not paranoid.

The Deceived Crowd

Deviance exists not only because an individual is deceitful. It is also imperative for individuals and organizations to perceive these irregularities as so-called social facts. Fighting deviances is therefore also about changing the perceptions of managers, colleagues and other bystanders. Here, no more than the contours of such an effort can be outlined.

The public goes to a theatre because they want to be deceived and wrapped into a false reality. The reality at the stands and stalls meets the play on stage, but the audience wants to be fooled by it. A good performance is something that moves us into another time and space. Actors are therefore a kind of skilled and accepted fraudsters. In real life, outside the theatre, the ones who deceive are often at least as skilled as the actors on stage, but those who are deceived are ignorant and have not given their permission (Brytting et al. 2011) (Table 3).

Because deviances often take place in an unprepared environment, it is far from obvious that the involved individuals will understand what it is going on. Returning to the beginning of this article, they will neither perceive the deviances nor the deceptions as *social facts*. Thereby, it is even less likely that they will do something about it. All warning signs may exist, but the organization will not be able to stop it.

Once again, we might use the model proposed by Rubington and Weinberg (1968):

Table 3 The differences between acting on stage and fraud

Acting	Fraud
Acting takes place on an artificial stage	Action takes place in real life
The actor is a third party	The deceiver is one of us
Plays a fantasy	Delivers a lie
A play to entertain and stimulate	Creates confusion
Follows a script	Delivers a lie
The audience expects a fantasy	Diverts from correct conclusions
A short presentation	A long-term habit or plan improvised script
The audience observe	The bystanders participate themselves
The interest of the other is in focus	Egoistic motives at the centre

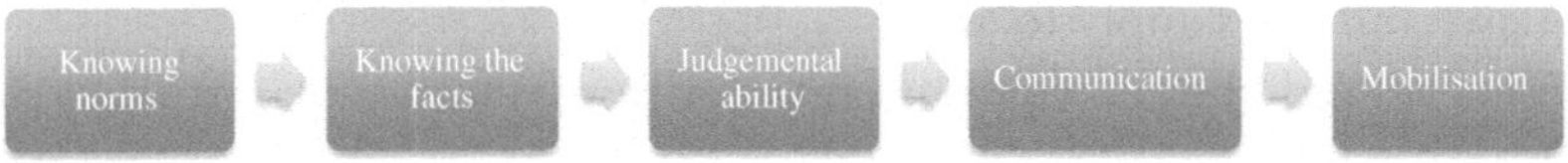

Fig. 3 The construction of deviance as a social fact, according to Rubington and Weinberg (1968)

> For deviance to become a social fact, someone must perceive an act, situation or event as a departure from social norms, must categorize that perception, must report that perception to others, must get them to accept this definition of the situation, and must obtain a response that conforms to their definition. Unless all these requirements are met, deviance as a social fact does not come into being.

I also transformed this lengthy and somewhat tortuous sentence into a sequential list of prerequisites required to fight irregularities (Fig. 3).

In each step, there are powerful mechanisms that prevent awareness and concrete countermeasures: e.g. ignorance, fear, wishful thinking, group pressure, power play and, not least important, the environment's own delusions, which in many ways resemble the perpetrators'. In other words, it is a lot that unites the deceiver and the deceived. In that sense, they are all human.

Entertaining Doubts

In his contribution to this volume, Taro Lennerfors presents four "subject positions" when it comes to anti-corruption measures: anxiety, superego, courage and justice. Unable to dwell deeply into this here (for details I refer to Taro Lennerfors article), I interpret these subject positions as four ways of entertaining doubts, as the individuals' efforts to turn and twist their predicament in order to avoid the easy way out.

I have my own ideas of how that can be achieved that might fit alongside Lennerfors'. The following advices may be helpful to those who want to examine others' rationalizations critically and counteract their intentions to deceive:

- Laws and rules apply to all.
- Thieves and cheaters are not creatures from another planet. They are like us but live partly in delusions.
- That something is common does not mean that it's OK.
- Examine critically claims about corrupt culture:
  - Is it true that everyone is doing it?
  - Do managers really have a right to special treatment?
  - Is everyone else so much worse?
  - Was it really a one-off-a-kind event?
  - Are we really forced to take shortcuts?

If something looks mysterious, take that mystification seriously. Something may in fact be seriously wrong.

References

ACFE (Association of Certified Fraud Examinators). (2016). *Report to the nations on occupational fraud and abuse.* Austin: ACFE.

Brytting, T. (2013). Chefen som bedragare. In T. Brytting (Ed.), *Chefsarbetets etik* (pp. 176–207). Lund: Studentlitteratur.

Brytting, T., Minogue, R., & Morino, V. (2011). *The anatomy of fraud and corruption—Organizational causes and remedies.* New York: Gower Publishing.

The Economist/Kroll. (2016). *Global fraud report—Vulnerabilities on the rise.* New York: Kroll.

Latané, B., & Darley, J. (1970). *The unresponsive bystander: Why doesn't he help?* New York: Appleton-Century-Crofts.

Machiavelli, N. (2006). *The prince.* Urbana, IL: Project Gutenberg. Retrieved March 12, 2017, from https://www.gutenberg.org/files/1232/1232-h/1232-h.htm.

PriceWaterhouseCoopers. (2003). *Global economic crime survey.* London: PwC.

PriceWaterhouseCoopers. (2009). *Global economic crime survey.* London: PwC.

Rubington, R., & Weinberg, M. (Eds.). (1968). *Deviance—The interactionist perspective.* New York: Appleton-Century-Crofts.

Solomon, R. (1992). *Ethics and excellence.* New York: Oxford University Press.

Taylor, C. (1991). *The ethics of authenticity.* Cambridge: Harvard University Press.

Organizational Anti-corruption: De-normalization Through Anxiety, Superego, Courage and Justice

Thomas Taro Lennerfors

Introduction

Corruption is an important problem in the world, and businesses and other organizations are often implicated in it. According to the United Nations campaign United Against Corruption (United Against Corruption 2017), corruption is held to be the single greatest obstacle to economic and social development around the world. It is estimated that 5% of the world's GDP is stolen annually through corruption. Corruption is the side door, the shortcut, the way to have access to places which one should not have access to. In that way, corruption is a key problem that can fuel world evils such as human trafficking, human smuggling, and as Noonan (2004) adds, child labour, child slavery, child prostitution and child pornography.

There are several challenges for fighting corruption, but one major challenge is our predominant conceptions about corruption and the

T. T. Lennerfors (✉)
Uppsala University, Uppsala, Sweden
e-mail: thomas.lennerfors@angstrom.uu.se

S. Arvidsson (ed.), *Challenges in Managing Sustainable Business*,
https://doi.org/10.1007/978-3-319-93266-8_14

lack of alternative, creative theorizations about both corruption and anti-corruption (Breit et al. 2015). Given that corruption is still not fully eradicated, but perhaps even seems to be an increasingly salient sustainability issue, perhaps we are not fighting it in the right way. Our theories of corruption and anti-corruption shape how we fight it and if we rethink corruption and anti-corruption we might develop more effective ways to fight it. In this chapter, I respond to this theoretical challenge by trying to think about organizational perspectives on corruption in a novel and creative way. The paper turns an already existing theoretical framework upside down, and it also draws inspiration from philosophy for thinking about anti-corruption subject positions—how we as subjects relate to anti-corruption.

Let us return to the above-depicted scenario where corruption is an important evil, perhaps the root cause of all evil. With that description, it is likely that all are united against corruption, but what is corruption? One view is very general, the one that implicitly says that corruption is "that which is bad". Few researchers or policy makers dare to define corruption thus, but in practice in research and policy documents, this definition is used. For example, Ashforth and Anand (2003) write about institutionalized sexual harassment as corruption. Measurements of corruption, particularly aggregated ones, most likely also adhere to this definition. Corruption here becomes an umbrella concept for all kinds of deviance, bribery, cultural decay, laziness and perhaps even sexual promiscuity. A well-known description based on this definition is that Socrates was "corrupting the youth", which led to his death sentence.

But, the most well-known definitions of corruption are more narrow. The World Bank defines corruption as the misuse of public office for private gain, and Transparency International means that corruption is the misuse of entrusted power for private gain. Beneath these definitions, I argue, there is an idea about a way the office is supposed to function. For example, a teacher is supposed to grade examinations giving higher grades to those who have provided better answers to their questions. A public official in charge of approving whether a person will be allowed to drive a car or not should do so based on an accurate judgment (most probably supported by a checklist) of the driver's capacities. A police officer dealing with traffic violations should give out tickets in a fair way, only tickets to those who have violated traffic rules. When the function is not fulfilled in the way we expect, one can say that there has been a deviance (compare with Brytting's chapter), and this deviance can happen due to several reasons of which corruption is one. For example, they can be due to error—sometimes things just happen, but not of ill will—it was just a mistake. The traffic police officer could have misread her speed metre and therefore issued a ticket. Sometimes the deviance is because of incompetence or ignorance—that the person does not have the competence to fulfil her role. Perhaps the police officer did not know that she cannot issue a ticket to an ambulance, or perhaps she cannot accurately read the speed metre. The third possibility is corruption—where the agent is swayed by private gain, or perhaps some kind of influence from the outside, for example norms of reciprocity, where someone has favoured you in the past and you are bound by an "obligation to reciprocate" even though you have now entered into a formal position which does not allow for this. Deviance here would, for example, mean to not give a ticket to a person who offers the police officer a token of gratitude (often cash) in exchange for the kind gesture. Or not giving a ticket to a relative, or movie star, who is guilty of speeding. In almost any role, you could do something you are not supposed to do, in order to make money out of your position—money which is above and beyond the salary that you are paid. Therefore, everywhere there are possibilities of being corrupt, but all form of deviance is not corruption.

Moreover, I would like to argue that the issue of corruption is never as easy as that described above. An office can have several functions, several conflicting values. Therefore, I argue that there are several corruptions, and all corruptions are in relation to something that we promote at the same time (Lennerfors 2017). Such values could be fairness, efficiency, meritocracy, demands for reciprocity, the virtue of gratitude, the legitimacy of hierarchy, affirmative action, equal treatment, maximizing benefits for the greatest number, that one should mind one's own business and not interfere with those of the others, and so on (perhaps even in the "moral space" there are conflicting values with no clear hierarchical relation, see Brytting, in this book). In the business setting, a few examples could illustrate this point. A company, as a part of their corporate social responsibility work, promoted the inclusion of marginalized groups in the workforce. One such group were criminals who had served their sentence and were now looking for a way back into society. However, the anti-corruption part of a due diligence process found this inclusion of former convicts, convicted of economic crime, a clear breach of their anti-corruption measures. Here, there are at least two values that stand in conflict: affirmative action to compensate for injustice and discrimination against former convicts on the one hand and anti-corruption as excluding potentially corrupt people—former economic criminals—on the other.

Another, perhaps more trivial example concerns a public agency which controls vehicles and assesses if these are allowed to drive on the roads. In this organization, they have a strict no-gifts policy. At times, the vehicle inspectors are given a home-baked cake, not as a bribe, but as a kind gesture, most often from a "grandma". This issue has become discussed in the compliance organization of the vehicle inspectors, and it was assessed that if the cake is not taken home but consumed on the premises, then it is acceptable to receive it, in order not to hurt the feelings of the grandma, although there is a no-gifts policy. In this case, one can say that a strict no-gifts policy stands in contrast to the value of human decency. The point with these two examples has been to show that there are always corruptions. In other words, when we make trade-offs, there is always some value that is compromised, corrupted. In the first case, the principle of affirmative action was corrupted by anti-corruption measures. In the second case, the no-gifts policy was breached due to the fact that one wanted to promote the value of human decency. One major challenge when fighting corruption is that by fighting corruption, we might also be corrupting other totally legitimate values, just as collateral damage.

As was written in the first paragraph, we are all united against corruption. But on the other hand, it is not given that we should always let anti-corruption corrupt other values. That is, because we promote a plethora of values, it is inevitable that there are corruptions of those values. One of these corruptions can be what we generally call corruption, the misuse of public office for private gain. In other words, we are most probably both for and against various kinds of corruption. So if we should know our enemy—who are we really fighting—the enemy is us (Cf. Sampson's chapter in this book).

Corruption is all about shades of grey. Quite few people are that utterly corrupt (in the sense of misusing public office for private gain) that they would use any situation to enrich themselves. Quite few would never let themselves be influenced. Most are somewhere in between, on a grey scale. Some lean more towards this kind of corruption. And this presents major challenges in the organizational context. In an organizational context, it might very well be the case that a person who starts working is already contemplating ideas and strategies for engaging in corruption. She might know in what places of the organization it is easier to make corrupt deals and would seek to work in those parts. A compliance officer in a multinational corporation told me that they had just discovered that one person, together with a select few in competing organizations, had been running a cartel. From the perspective of the multinational, this was certainly the case of a bad apple, connected to other bad apples in other organizations. It is of course important to problematize this description. Maybe, the organization just described the person as a bad apple in order to compartmentalize the evil, and thus to be able to externalize it by sacking the corrupt employee. However, if we trust the description of the company, there might be bad apples. They could have been corrupt from the beginning, but perhaps, they could have been sliding into corruption due to factors that were present before they entered the organization. Others might be more ambiguous and could either tilt towards corrupt behaviour or not, depending on circumstances. Still others might be leaning more towards formally correct behaviour, but organizational structures and processes might compel or encourage them to become more corrupt (in order to reach performance targets, for example). An example of this was when a reputable airplane manufacturer was going to influence a public procurement process. From the company's perspective, this was illustrated on a chart by the colours of red, yellow and green, where green were the ones who had already been corrupted to serve the briber's ends, the yellow were undecided and needed more influencing, and the red were the absolutists, denying any attempts to be influenced. So potential corruption, as we know, is not only dealt with in the recruitment phase, such that if we just make sure that we recruit honest people, everything will be fine. Even the very honest people might start engaging in corrupt actions, depending on the situation that surrounds them. Some of the social processes are directly related to how the organization is functioning, but one must remember that there are also processes that affect the organization from the outside. Individuals working in the organization are also part of networks and social relations that go beyond the formal boundaries of the organization, affecting them and their way of viewing what is legitimate and what is not. These external relationships can work to the benefit of the culture of the organization—for example when a social campaign such as #metoo spreads into the organization, changing its policies. Conversely, outside events can also work to the detriment of the organization. This is particularly the case with the entry of corrupt practices into the organization. We will now turn to the processes which corrupt individuals working in organizations.

Normalization: Rationalization, Institutionalization and Socialization

The internal organizational processes which normalizes corruption in organizations have been termed rationalization, institutionalization and socialization. Ashforth and Anand (2003; Ashforth et al. 2008), who are the main proponents of this very popular conceptualization, adopt a view of corruption as a very broad concept, including almost all practices that we would otherwise call "deviant" (as mentioned above, one of their examples concerns sexual harassment).

Regarding the process of rationalization, the research on corruption in organizations has benefitted from studies of criminals, and how they rationalize and establish the legitimacy of a criminal act (Sykes and Matza 1957, see also Brytting, in this book). First of all, one might claim that the deviance is indeed *not illegal.* One might claim that it is legal to donate a sum of money to a charity in a country where one wants a business deal. But behind the charity, there might be an illegitimate owner. The criminal can also *deny responsibility*, saying that she had no choice, no power to act, or even no knowledge that what she was doing was illegal or corrupt. For example, in the border control, the officer might solicit a bribe, and then the bribe-payer can easily say that she had no choice but to pay. A third rationalization is *denial of injury*—that no one is really harmed if I steal a few pens from work (misusing my office for private gain), or if I as a public official receive a couple of hundred dollars in exchange for me selling a driver's license. Sure, the driver did a few errors, but will most probably not harm anyone when driving. Also, the driver gladly paid the bribe, since she wouldn't have to retake the exam. And for me, it was a bonus to increase my low salary. There seems to be no loser here. This is denial of injury. From this condensed explanation of rationalization, it is obvious that discourses, ways of speaking, stories and examples are central. If we speak as if corruption were acceptable, then it is more likely that corruption will be acceptable to those who are part of the practices. Similar to our responsibility for spreading stereotypes, telling racist jokes and so on (May 1992), we are also responsible for the discourses regarding corruption (and other issues) that are used within the company. There can be discourses about the acceptance of corruption—that "as a purchasing manager, it is part of the job to get Christmas presents". There can also be discourses about the compliance department or the headquarters: "This is yet another silly and irrelevant anti-corruption policy from the headquarters [who have no clue about how our business works]". Such discourses are not only "talk". They have performative effects—they affect practice. There can, of course, be productive discourses about the honour of people working in a particular company, examples of people being subjected to attempts at being corrupted and which they have resisted. One needs to understand, as well, that the discourses do not fully determine the actions of a person. Each person has some kind of distance to discourses. Hence, they might feel that the way people talk in an organization is not really acceptable to them, but they just play along with the system.

Institutionalization, here meant as the institutionalization of corrupt practices, is a three-stage process. It starts with a corrupt act; someone pays a bribe, takes a bribe, embezzles and steals. These kinds of acts can be motivated in various ways; it can stem from self-interest, as is well-expected from the definitions of corruption. It can also be a form of protest which comes from dissatisfaction with laws and policies in the workplace. One obvious example is when political subjects are tired of the government spending their money in the wrong way, and thus try to divert funds from government through corrupt acts, for example by not paying taxes. Another example could be when an employee is dissatisfied with the salary, lack of fringe benefits, or was unable to have legitimate expenses refunded for some reason, and then takes revenge by an act of corruption, once again misusing her position for private gain. Another reason could be the lack of a specific reason whatsoever—the corrupt act could be performed out of stress, lack of time, or because of a genuine unawareness of laws, guidelines and policies. It is important here to point out that this throws some additional light on the rationalizations that I just described, in that what may appear to be mere rationalizations are more or less legitimate reasons. The difference seems to be that we call them "rationalizations" when something is already deemed to be corrupt, while we call them "reasons" when it is not yet decided whether something was corrupt or not, or when a practice is deemed to be legitimate.

Starting from this corrupt act, institutionalization means that this corruption becomes part of the everyday organizational structure and routine. One theoretical resource to explain this according to Ashforth and Anand (2003) would be path dependency; that one thing leads to the next, some form of light determinism. Indeed, as the argument of the slippery slope says, it is easier to repeat a corrupt act than to perform the first one, and it is easy to understand how such acts can become increasingly severe. Furthermore, such corrupt acts, if they become known, become stored in the collective unconscious, or organizational memory as Ashforth and Anand (2003) put it. It thus becomes an act that others can draw on to justify and legitimize their own behaviour. In the third phase, when the organization has become corrupt, corrupt acts are routine, they seem necessary and even normal, and people are desensitized to it.

Institutionalization is deeply tied to the third dynamic—that of socialization. Socialization explains how new people are introduced, connected and tied to corrupt schemes. One way this happens is cooptation, which in its essence means that newcomers are induced by rewards to skew their attitudes towards certain corrupt behaviour, so that they eventually corrupt themselves. It can also consist of "having to" enter into corrupt schemes. For example, in a governmental agency, an employee took a bribe and then felt obliged to share the bribe with her superiors, thus implicating them in the corrupt practice. Because of the social cohesion in the work team, the corrupt employee was not reported. Conversely superiors can take a share of the corrupt money, as a kind of corruption tax on subordinates. The second socialization strategy is incrementalism, which is the argument of the slippery slope. Being treated to a coffee is acceptable, so why not a lunch, or a business lunch, or a dinner, or a night out, or a free trip? The third avenue is held to be compromise, where the corrupt act is the better of the two alternatives, the lesser of two evils. An interpretation of the socialization perspective is that rather than basing our understanding of corruption on the perspective of individuals, the basic unit of analysis becomes social relationships. Within these, there are always ongoing reciprocal demands and expectations. Whether you call them networks, Chinese *guanxi*, or Swedish *nätverk*, they are part of all societies to varying degrees. In some places, it might seem perfectly fine to act out responsibilities to those in one's social network even though one occupies an entrusted position where all clients must be treated equally; in some other societies or settings, it is seen as morally illegitimate not to give special treatment to one's network.

Anti-corruption as De-normalization: De-rationalization, De-institutionalization and De-socialization

Ashforth and Anand (2003) claim that there is often a need for a strong shock to fight corruption—for example the scandal of media coverage. But since weeding out corruption is complex, the authors suggest five forms of prevention that should be deployed. First, ethical values and awareness should be inculcated. Second, individuals should know that they will be accountable for their acts. Third, individuals should have access to confidential ethics officers for advice. Fourth, organizational practices should be more transparent. Fifth, ethical control should be equitable in order to avoid informer cultures or too extensive control that could make individuals turn against each other or against the organization as such.

Although Ashforth and Anand (2003) highlight the processes of normalizing corruption in organizations, their anti-corruption programme does not entirely cohere with their theory of corruption. The five forms of prevention are certainly important and relevant, but they have no explicit relation to their theory of why corruption is normalized in the first place. In other words, they do not explicitly relate the five anti-corruption measures to the processes of rationalization, institutionalization and socialization.

In this paper, however, I am interested in turning their framework upside down in a thought experiment to try to invert the three processes of rationalization, institutionalization and socialization in order to elaborate an anti-corruption strategy. I will cover already existing elements of anti-corruption programmes in business, but I will also try to go beyond them to suggest new strategies informed by turning the principles of organizational corruption on their head.

De-rationalization

If we first turn to rationalization, we know that individuals and groups rationalize their corrupt behaviour through discourse. A countermeasure would thus be to de-rationalize corruption discourse. An obvious way to de-rationalize corruption is to create an alternative discourse: to educate and constantly talk about ethics and anti-corruption in the organization. In this discursive strategy, by means of principle and example, corrupt acts are described for what they are. For example, in several companies, there is a no-gifts policy, and if organizational members produce discourses about the illegitimacy of giving and receiving gifts, this discourse will act as opposing the euphemistic rationalization discourse that “gifts are OK, because they aren’t bribes”. With additional discourses describing the same practices, the organizational members will have to make a choice as to whether to choose the discourse that coheres with the organization's anti-corruption programme, or not.

There are obstacles to discourses which promote anti-corruption. First of all, like visions and mission statements in organizations, they can be seen as "business bullshit" (Spicer 2017, Cf. Sampson's chapter, particularly the cynical view) and thus completely illegitimate from the perspective of organizational members. The organizational members would thus see the discourse as something necessary solely for external relations, investor relations and so on, but with no bearing on their everyday business routines. One therefore always needs to consider who is the bearer of such kinds of discourses. For example, in the anti-corruption literature, it is well known that we need a "tone at the top"—that the CEO or similar is producing an anti-corruption discourse. However, it is important to engage others in such discourse, not the least the middle management: factory managers, regional managers and so on, something called by a compliance manager *the permafrost of business*, the echelon that is much harder to convince than the CEO. Indeed, part of the CEO position is purely symbolic, and if a message is needed for external stakeholders, she will hardly be difficult to convince. Second, such discourses can be impossible to fulfil. Some scholars, like Gustafsson (1988), have argued that there is a need for double standards in business that there is a need to preach water while drinking wine. This also coheres with an argument I have made in another study that organizations both externalize and thrive on corruption (Lennerfors 2012). Third, these discourses run the risk of being so general and vague that they provide little practical guidance. In any case, one way to derationalize corrupt practices is to produce anti-discourses.

Yet another, more radical strategy is to forbid certain kinds of discourse. Some more ethically permissible, perhaps ethically debatable, or even outright illegal discourses can be prohibited. One can compare this to historical laws against speaking bad about the king. Similarly, one could institutionalize a prohibition against using euphemisms, against saying that "everything is a grey zone", or that "the rules are unclear". In some organizations where the cultural control is high and all members easily buy into the corporate message, such a strategy might work, while in others this could lead to a number of drawbacks; for example, the organization's members might turn against the organization and manifest resistance through corrupt acts. In any case, there are several examples of how certain discourses are silenced in companies.

Another, less familiar, strategy is to go beneath discourse to play on the non-linguistic registers of human experience. Here, one draws on the unspoken that which is beneath discourse. Some would say this is a direct connection with the dimension of the real, since we are not fully determined nor can we express ourselves fully by recourse to discourse. One way is to use humour and multivocality—in other words, a kind of disruption of discourse, to de-rationalize corruption. The disruption can consist of statements which do not explicitly say that corruption is not OK, but definitely doing it with an obvious underlying message. For example, in a Swedish company, the anti-corruption organization constantly spreads humorous, or "ridiculous", challenges to their employees. The employees would be asked if it's OK to treat a buyer to champagne, and give options such as "yes", "no", "maybe", "depends on how tasty it is" and so on. This creates an underlying emotional layer to the anti-corruption discourses, which could make them much more interesting and relevant to discuss among organizational members. In this way, the message can spread by itself, go viral, which typical anti-corruption discourses seldom do. One of course wonders whether it is acceptable to take the seriousness out of the discussion of corruption. Indeed, one might argue the opposite that since everybody knows that corruption is a serious matter, it might not always be desirable that it is always treated seriously.

A similar strategy going beneath discourse is to work with pictures to evoke feelings of anti-corruption. On cigarette packs sold in various countries today, there are pictures of kids smoking cigars, kids with lung cancer, a person with heavy respiratory aids, etc. This is because discourse is sometimes not enough. Although it says on packs of cigarettes that you will definitely die earlier if you smoke, we can easily distance ourselves from this message. But it is somewhat more difficult to do if you see a disgusting image. There are quite a lot of corruption semiotics and pictorial representations. The usual image is of handshakes between the bribe-payer and the bribe-taker. Another representation concerns roads to the same end, one without using bribery, which is represented as a long, narrow, winding road. The other, using bribery, is a wide road straight to the goal. The point, if we draw on the cigarette pack semiotics, is perhaps to show images of the consequences of corruption, that one is sacked, that one's family life is ruined, and that one might lose one's friends—that one becomes a *persona non grata.*

To sum up, anti-corruption strategies that concern de-rationalization are about (1) producing alternative discourses and (2) going beyond, or beneath discourse, to convey the message.

De-institutionalization

As we remember, corruption can become institutionalized by a corrupt act which becomes multiplied by processes of path dependence and the drawing of an organizational memory. If we first turn to organizational memory, it is important to state that an organization can remember things in different ways. Certainly, it is possible that a corrupt act has taken place, but what happened to those who were corrupt? If actions are accompanied by discourse, a kind of sense-making about actions, it would be possible to reprogramme the organizational memory, to create narratives about what happened to the corrupt. For example, an existing management consulting company circulates e-mails with stories about corruption, and how this led to bad consequences. In other words, they collect, or perhaps produce, stories about how not to do, to make people remember the issue of corruption and its vicissitudes. One such true story concerned a consultant who started a meeting with some public officials in the morning. The meeting went on and on, and by the time of lunch, there was no sign of ending the meeting. Good-hearted as the consultant was, she went to buy some sandwiches and drinks for the officials. They of course refused to eat them, and the consultant felt horrible and had to discard the sandwiches. This is something that indeed happened in the past, and the action of the consultant was seen as both right and wrong. Right from the perspective of human decency and hospitality, but wrong from an anti-corruption perspective in that the lunch gift might be construed as some kind of undue influence.

This story has probably led some people, who read this e-mail explaining the story, to recall, and perhaps even rethink their relationship with public officials. In other words, one can use the organizational memory, or the collective unconscious, not only to normalize corruption (as Ashforth and Anand argue) but also to help the organizational member learn about and remember stories of anti-corruption.

Furthermore, path dependence can also be counteracted. It is very common to be a servant to the TINA discourse: *there is no alternative*. And from hindsight, historical events might neatly lead up to the future. But regarding future action, one always has some kind of agency to change the course of events, to decide otherwise. One is not fully determined by the force of path dependence; one is not structurally nor processually determined. Some historians illustrate this point by working with counterfactual history: to argue that the current state of the world was only one of several equally real possibilities. One can go back and ask, for example, what would have happened if the Bolsheviks have not retained power in Russia after the revolution; how would the world have looked? Similarly, this can apply to corrupt acts. One can study examples of corruption that have taken place and turn them into only one possibility among several acts. In that sense, one can make history more malleable and transpose this sentiment towards future action. Faced with a bribery case between a supplier and a public official, we could ask, "What could this supplier have done rather than paying this bribe to the public official – and still make a profit?"

In the fully corrupt organization, corrupt acts become routine and people are desensitized. In this kind of organization, all members are still connected to the outside world, and the few members who have not fully succumbed to corruption may plant a seed from the outside, that is, introduce an "event" from the outside, indicating that things in this organization are not fully OK. They can draw on alternative discourses, allow practices happening outside the organization to penetrate it and counteract more deviant practices already present within the organization. It might be true that in the fully corrupt organization, there is a need for a strong shock from the outside to stop corruption, a Rothsteinian big bang. The goal, however, is to work from the vision of the future that one wants.

To sum up, anti-corruption strategies based on de-institutionalization attempt to (1) tamper with the organizational memory, including those memories related to the detrimental consequences of corruption and to (2) indicate that there is an alternative to corruption, by counteracting a determinate TINA discourse.

De-socialization

What would then de-socialization be? What kind of processes causes organizational members to be somehow excluded from customary social practices? A preliminary remark is that the very idea of organizational members who leave their self at the doorstep when entering the organization, becoming the perfect organizational member, is indeed a form of de-socialization. One could call this de-individualization, but the individual self is to a large extent constituted in and by its social relations, so I choose to call it de-socialization. Uncorrupt organizational members are expected to leave their personal interests and values outside the organization. They are now expected to serve the needs, interests, goals and mission of their organization. They are supposed to be angels in the original meaning of the term: messengers delivering the message of someone, not themselves. This is the view of *corruption of means*, where corruption means the fallen angel, the person who no longer has the ability to leave herself behind (Lennerfors 2008, 2017).

Another thing that is left outside the organization by means of anti-corruption as de-socialization is reciprocal ties. Maybe you owe something to someone outside the organization, and you could reciprocate in your organizational role, but de-socialization processes forbid you to do this. There are also discursive means to remind oneself, for example saying that "the suppliers are not your friends".

Becoming this empty receptacle, the angelic messenger, was for a long time the idea of anti-corruption. However, it is now more common to think of organizational life as very personal, emotional, as that which gives meaning, and that you can also make a better career and better consequences for the organization by bringing in your full self. Then, rather than trying to exclude all of yourself, you now need to exclude only some parts of your private self, but it is not as clear which parts need to be excluded. The organizational and private roles become more intermingled, and it could be even harder to know what practices constitute corruption. The difficulty arises from the fact that there is no longer a clear division between the organizational member/employee and the private self.

Further aspects of de-socialization concern the exclusion of agency. Rather than having to make a personal decision, which can indeed be corrupt, we could possibly outsource decision-making to some external, more objective entity. When it comes to testing of suspension in car inspection, two radically different attitudes exist in two different countries. In one country, it is common knowledge that an inspector, by test driving the car, could determine much more accurately than a machine whether the suspension is acceptable or not. In the other country, the machine is preferred because the machine cannot be bribed to give a positive reply. Outsourcing decision-making to a machine could be a way to avoid corruption. For example, imagine line judges in badminton. They could theoretically be corrupted to favour one of the players. However, since one can now use a technological hawk-eye, the process of judging the lines is potentially less corrupt. But we can never be sure. In the end, one could tamper with machines (as occurred with the VW scandal), so it is not entirely clear that de-socialization by means of machines is the way to go.

Another way of excluding agency is to introduce unpredictability and complexity into the decision-making process so that a single individual or group cannot create a corrupt outcome. This could be done by means of an algorithm. This algorithm will then take the decision, based on input from various individuals—and it is likely that each individual cannot have full control over the outcome. This would be a splitting up of the decision to several people, thus limiting the power of each individual.

A further aspect that would correspond to de-socialization is to remove people from reciprocal ties or corrupt relationships by constantly rotating people in the organization, which leads to de-socialization of their current relationships, but of course also re-socialization into other relationships. There is a risk that this leads to more need to learn, with a potential to corrupt the principle of efficiency. Nevertheless, rotation is certainly a way to disrupt the socialization of corruption (which is why it is often done among diplomatic representatives, the fear being that they will become too close to the local interests in the country in which they are stationed and underprioritize the mission).

Whistleblowing, which is another one of Ashforth and Anand's (2003) anti-corruption strategies, is also a de-socialization strategy, since it allows for reporting on your colleagues and superiors which would be totally unacceptable from the perspective of collective effort and loyalty.

The de-socialization dimension of anti-corruption aims to (1) exclude the personal and (2) to exclude social processes and demands that might lead to corruption. The three processes are depicted in Fig. 1.

I have now introduced a number of anti-corruption strategies in the three dimensions of anti-corruption. Now I would like to turn towards the subject positions of anti-corruption; that is, how we as organizational members could relate to anti-corruption. For this, I have sought inspiration in Alain Badiou, a French contemporary philosopher.

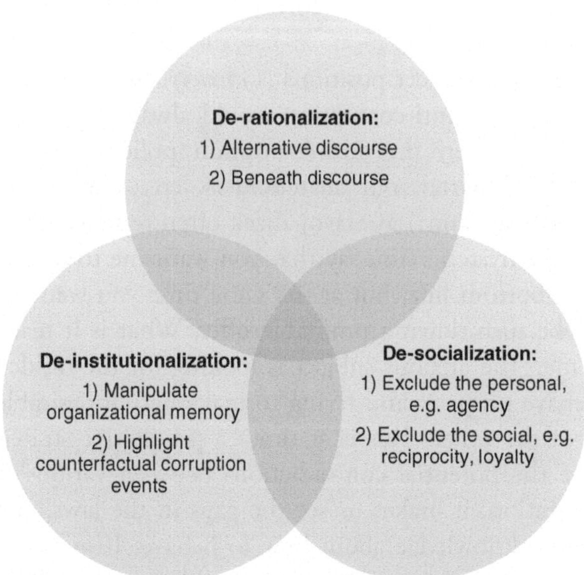

Fig. 1 Anti-corruption as de-rationalization, de-institutionalization and de-socialization

Anti-corruption Subject Positions

We always have a self-conception about how we relate to anti-corruption. I have hinted that some relate to anti-corruption in a cynical way. Although cynicism can be fun and relieving, I am not sure about its productive potential or performative effects. A cynical attitude about corruption (that it's always there and there is nothing we can do about it) could possibly lead to a kind of resentment, a true dissatisfaction with organizational life, but dissatisfaction where one fails to take any sort of remedial action. The best attitude towards anti-corruption policies might also not be the strict policy of following anti-corruption guidelines and enforcing them in every situation, report every person who does something suspicious, and so on. How should we relate to anti-corruption? This is the question I wish to dwell on in this latter part of the paper.

I believe that the four subject positions described by Alain Badiou (2009a, b) are useful for thinking about our engagement in any kind of ethical project (including anti-corruption), in any collective body in which we participate.

The first of these subject positions is *anxiety*. In my reading, an anxious way to relate to anti-corruption would always be to wonder what the codes of conduct, the anti-corruption policies, the compliance officers, the headquarter, our shareholders, etc. want from me. *Che vuoi?* (what do you want?) as Slavoj Zizek often represents the motto of the anxious, the hysteric. You say that you want me to do business and maximize the bottom line, but at the same time you want me to comply and maybe turn down a profitable offer. What is it really that you want from me? The anxious subject is looking for the hidden message, trying to behave properly and trying to make herself desirable from the perspective of the other. This is at times a productive strategy, since it makes us see the potential contradictions between various injunctions in the organization, it makes us see the gaps in the laws, and it makes us question our knowledge about how to behave. It makes us vulnerable, weak, but also open to see the flaws and learn from it. This kind of perspective is sometimes very needed, particularly considering the other subject positions. Anxiety calls upon the strengthening of law, which here can mean codes of conduct, compliance documents and so on. The anxious subject wants a strong law to be installed, something which almost sadistically forces her to do what is right. This would be the call for the superego.

From the *superego* perspective, which is sometimes called "terror" (Badiou 2001), the perspective on anti-corruption is very rigid. Here, we deal with a scenario where everybody is superfluous, and everybody is suspicious. Adopting this stance, every encounter is embedded in a cloud of suspicion, that this, and that, person probably is corrupt. Here, the compliance programme is followed to the maximum, and there are no exceptions and no tolerance, and everything is reported. Here, the compliance management has run amok, potentially even prosecuting itself for being corrupt. The whistle is blown constantly, until the point where everyone is under suspicion of being corrupt, until perhaps everybody is fired, or in jail. This is obviously not a functional subject position, but it can be valuable at times, for example in situations where there is ongoing corruption in an organization, or in situations where one must change to a more rigid scheme. Superego, or terror, jolts the system. There is no space for interpretation, and there is no space for rationalization.

Courage operates by way of deregulation. It is the sister position to anxiety. However, rather than looking to the other to give meaning (*Che vuoi?*), the courageous subject chooses one's own way and sticks to it. In contrast to anxiety, which is very dependent on the law (the codes and the policies) and tries to make sense of what the law says, courage could possibly break the law. But the courageous subject is certain that this way of (organizational) life is correct. In anti-corruption, it could possibly be the excess invested in one's own integrity, the proud feeling of being untouchable, incorruptible. This puts the law to test, since codes, compliance organizations, etc. might not be necessary if people are pursuing their own courageous paths.

Justice, the last subject position, is acceptance that the world is an intricate structure of various intersecting value structures. The courageous way is here deemed insufficient, since we need to integrate and merge various claims on the good. This is the subject position that acknowledges the concept of corruption*s*, and it is distinguished from the superego in its absence of desire to institute the new world in one single blow. The subject position of justice accepts plurality and multiplicity. Justice problematizes both the anxiety seeking subject position, who tries to find the truth behind it all, and the courageous position, going its own way. It sees anti-corruption as constant negotiation between various goals, where there is no obvious right and wrong. The four subject positions and their relation to anti-corruption are shown in Fig. 2.

While one might think that the reasoned, justice attitude might be the best, it is not always productive. Sometimes, as I have stated, there is a need for the superego, particularly when change is needed. There is no room for negotiation, which there is when the subject position of justice dominates. Also, it might also be healthy at times, to adopt the anxious, in some ways hysterical, subject position, who wonders about the ultimate meaning of all these anti-corruption discourses and cannot figure out what these policies really want from her. At times, we need strong, courageous individuals with pride and highly perceived integrity, but at other times, these kinds of individuals are precisely the problem, for these are the ones who lead us into corrupt practices.

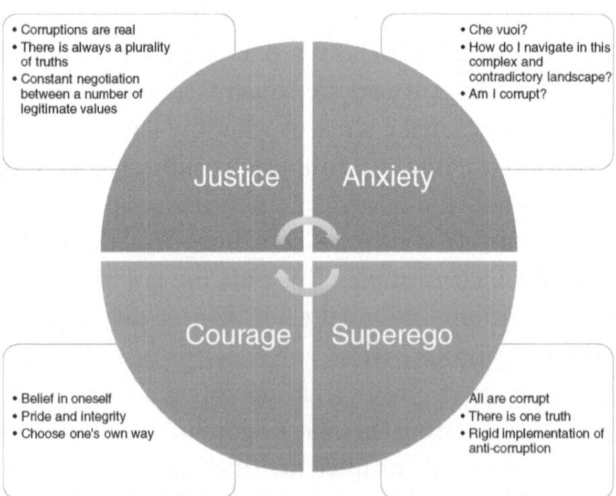

Fig. 2 The four subject positions of anti-corruption

Conclusions

In this chapter, I have first introduced three kinds of definitions of corruption, one definition that views corruption as all that is bad, a second set of definitions based on private gain as a fundamental principle and my own third definition, which replaces the concept of corruption with plural corruptions, thus signifying the degeneration of a legitimate value. I then followed one of the most well-known, and most cited, work on corruption in organizations to explain how corrupt behaviour, in the broad view, is dependent upon processes of rationalization, institutionalization and socialization. Although the authors propose a number of anti-corruption strategies, I took the liberty of devising a de-normalizing anti-corruption programme by inverting their processes as de-rationalization, de-institutionalization and de-socialization. With this inversion, I have therefore developed a conceptual framework with which corruption might be fought. As a final addition, I have also explained in what way one could or should relate to this anti-corruption programme. I have argued that a viable anti-corruption programme can be implemented only if we recognize the need for at least four different subject positions, all with their own strengths and weaknesses.

By doing this theoretical development, I have intended to rethink corruption in an idiosyncratic way, not falling back into standard theorizations of corruption. This addresses one fundamental challenge, namely to understand corruption and anti-corruption in its all different manifestations, and not directly conclude that the fight against corruption is just a practical endeavour. Our theories of corruption and anti-corruption shape how we fight it and given that our anti-corruption measures are still not fully functional, we need to rethink corruption and anti-corruption without throwing out the baby with the bathwater. More work is needed to think thoroughly about the nature of corruption and anti-corruption, drawing on alternative theorizations from various fields as well as conducting empirical investigations using these novel theoretical perspectives. The challenge remains.

References

Ashforth, B. E., & Anand, V. (2003). The normalization of corruption in organizations. *Research in Organizational Behavior, 25,* 1–52.

Ashforth, B. E., Gioia, D. A., Robinson, S. L., & Trevino, L. K. (2008). Re-viewing organizational corruption. *Academy of Management Review, 33*(3), 670–684.

Badiou, A. (2001). *Ethics—An essay on the understanding of evil.* New York: Verso.

Badiou, A. (2009a). *Theory of the subject.* London: Continuum.

Badiou, A. (2009b). *Logics of worlds.* London: Continuum.

Breit, E., Lennerfors, T. T., Olaison, L. (2015). Critiquing corruption—A turn to theory. *Ephemera: Theory and Politics in Organization, 15*(2), 319–336.

Gustafsson, C. (1988). *Om företag, moral och handling.* Lund, Sweden: Studentlitteratur.

Lennerfors, T. T. (2008). *The vicissitudes of corruption—Degeneration, transgression, jouissance.* Stockholm: Arvinius.

Lennerfors, T. T. (2012). Corruption and hosophobia. *Electronic Journal of Business Ethics and Organization Studies, 17*(1), 16–21.

Lennerfors, T. T. (2017). Corruption: Maximising, socialising, balancing, and othering. In M. Assländer & S. Hudson (Eds.), *The handbook of business and corruption: Cross-sectoral experiences* (pp. 25–48). Bingley, UK: Emerald Publishing.

May, L. (1992). *Sharing responsibility.* Chicago: University of Chicago Press.

Noonan, J. T. J. (2004). Struggling against corruption. In W. C. Heffernan & J. Kleinig (Eds.), *Private and public corruption.* Oxford: Rowman & Littlefield.

Spicer, A. (2017). *Business bullshit.* Abingdon, Oxon: Routledge.

Sykes, G. M., & Matza, D. (1957). Techniques of neutralization: A theory of delinquency. *American Sociological Review, 22,* 664–670.

United Against Corruption. (2017). Anti-corruption factsheet. Retrieved December 10, 2017, from http://www.anticorruptionday.org/actagainstcorruption/en/factsheets.html.

Part V

Ethical Taxation and Tax Transparency

Sustainable Tax Governance and Transparency

Hans Gribnau and Ave-Geidi Jallai

Introduction

The relationship between tax and sustainability is not an easy one. Separately, both topics are in general well understood and given considerable attention in most corporations. Nevertheless, tax specialists do not readily combine tax and sustainability with regard to public tax governance, let alone the tax governance of corporations. One troubling aspect of this relationship is transparency, which is also the central topic of this chapter.

Recent tax scandals such as the so-called Paradise Papers, Panama Papers and Lux Leaks have set international tax planning (tax planning with a cross-border dimension) in the spotlight. Many taxpayers appear to pay very low or no (corporate) income taxes in the countries where

H. Gribnau (✉) · A.-G. Jallai
Tilburg University, Tilburg, The Netherlands
e-mail: J.L.M.Gribnau@uvt.nl

A.-G. Jallai
e-mail: A.G.Jallai@uvt.nl

S. Arvidsson (ed.), *Challenges in Managing Sustainable Business*,
https://doi.org/10.1007/978-3-319-93266-8_15

they have economic activities. Tax planning as such is quite normal and every taxpayer does it to a certain degree. However, tax planning is morally not acceptable when it is aimed at minimising one's tax liability—enjoying a tax-free ride at the cost of other members of society. This kind of tax avoidance is often called aggressive tax planning—a global problem with societal, political, economic, legal and moral dimensions. If some taxpayers pay less or no taxes, other members of society have to pay more taxes or they have to face more expensive public goods and services or are deprived thereof. Moreover, a situation where a selected group of members of society can enjoy the benefits of society without paying for it is unjust and increases inequality.

Taxation plays an important role in society, for it supports societal cooperation and provides resources to finance essential public goods and services. Taxation is an essential precondition for the sustainable development of society. Sustainable development "involves meeting the needs of the present without compromising the ability of future generations to meet their own needs" (Ferrell et al. 2017, p. 347). For instance, in terms of sustainability, most of the countries in the world (UN members) have agreed to contribute to Sustainable Development Goals (SDGs) that are aimed at achieving a better future. Taxes are crucial for achieving SDGs. Therefore, it is a responsibility of a state to create a legal system where every taxpayer pays his or her fair share of taxes. Many countries and international organisations adopt general standards of good governance agendas that "focus on reforming the *relationship* between the government, civil society, and the market" and they mostly focus on topics such as "increased public accountability and transparency", strengthening of the rule of law, "increased civil society participation in development", and "respect for human rights and the environment" (Panayi 2017, pp. 2–3). In the same vein, good tax governance is about the relationship between the state, market and civil society, but also transparency and cooperation between states. Moreover, an important objective should be a fair and well-functioning tax system. Good tax legislation is a key element of good public governance.

Legislatures bear the responsibility to establish a fair and well-functioning system of tax laws. Having said that, no legal system is perfect. In a society, there are moral norms and values that regulate the behaviour of the members of society beyond the law, for morality is wider than law. That goes also for corporate members. Corporations (multinationals) nowadays accept their moral responsibilities towards society in the frames of corporate social responsibility (CSR). In general, CSR means that corporations accept responsibility towards society for the effects of their actions. CSR companies aim to go beyond strict compliance with the letter of the law (Carroll 1991; McBarnet 2007, pp. 48–50). Combining this understanding of CSR with the fact that taxes are fundamental contributions to society means that aggressive tax planning conflicts with the concept of CSR.

Corporate scandals and media attention on corporate tax behaviour have shown that society expects them not to engage in aggressive tax planning. Moreover, there is an increased demand for corporate accountability. Without greater transparency, it is, however, impossible to hold corporations accountable for their tax behaviour. Therefore, in this chapter, we argue that a tax strategy that views transparency as a key element of CSR can also be conceptualised as good tax governance. More specifically, good tax governance that is future oriented can be qualified as sustainable tax governance. Both public and private actors should commit themselves to this kind of long-term governance, that is sustainable tax governance.

The structure of this chapter is as follows. First, the relationship between tax and sustainability is explored. Sustainable taxation traditionally refers to environmental taxes. Sustainable tax governance is a broader concept. Sustainable tax governance from a governmental perspective requires the state to establish and implement a fair, well-functioning and stable tax system (section "Sustainable Tax Legislation"). Next, tax governance is connected with sustainable development and SDGs (section "Sustainable Development and Taxation"). As this chapter focuses mainly on the multinational corporation's perspective, it will be further analysed how to connect multinational tax planning practices with sustainability (section "Corporations and Sustainable Tax Governance"). It will be discussed whether paying taxes can be seen as a company's obligation towards society. Here, we will take CSR as a proxy for sustainability. Multinationals are in this respect in a special position, because of their (corporate) power. Their presence in many jurisdictions and their tax expertise offers opportunities with regard to their tax planning. However, society increasingly demands accountability in this respect (section "(Corporate) Power and Accountability"). Corporate accountability is impossible without transparency (section "Transparency"). As a result, tax administrations and investors increasingly focus their attention on corporate reporting and disclosure rules with regard to corporate tax behaviour (section "Tax, Transparency and Disclosure Obligations"). Then, CSR's key feature of going beyond compliance with the law is integrated into good tax governance (section "Good Tax Governance and Transparency"). The last section (section "Conclusion") concludes.

As for methodology, this article first explores legal and philosophical literature and policy documents to show the close connection between taxation and sustainable development. From a business ethics perspective, it is then argued that sustainable corporate tax planning has to take into account the moral dimension of taxation. Business should exercise self-restraint in their tax planning practices. Finally, accountability and transparency as means to enable public evaluation of the way power is exercised are translated to corporate tax planning As a result, accountability and transparency constitute basic elements of sustainable tax governance.

Thus, this chapter aims to make three contributions to academic theory. First, it investigates the connection between governance, good tax governance and sustainable tax governance. Second, it applies the latter concept to public authorities and (private) corporations. Third, transparency, enhancing accountability, as a key element of sustainable tax governance is elaborated upon.

Sustainable Tax Legislation

When asked about the connection between tax and sustainability, most tax experts will probably answer by pointing at environmental taxes—taxes aimed at achieving a positive effect for the environment. These taxes on carbon and energy actually are incentives in order to steer citizens' behaviour to achieve positive effect be achieved for the environment. Such taxes are introduced to reduce negative externalities related to the environmental consequences of production and use—the effects of (carbon) emissions on other people that are not included in the price of the (use) of products such as cars. In a wider sense, environmental levies include charges for public services (such as collection and incineration of waste, and water purification) and environmental taxes aimed at internalising external cost (such as pollution or carbon dioxide emission) in the price of goods and services ('the polluter pays' principle).

Environmental taxes have two objectives: to generate tax revenues for the government (at central and/or lower, for example local, level) and to achieve a change in business behaviour, and eventually consumer behaviour, in favour of the environment (instrumental use of taxation). Public economists even see "green taxes" as an economic instrument with two different goals resulting in a so-called double dividend: they discourage or encourage certain activities and raise revenues which could be used to finance reductions in other kinds of taxes (Mastellone 2014, p. 482). Environmental taxes do not distort behaviour—unlike many other taxes which introduce "inefficiencies in the allocation of resources and hence a decline in social welfare compared to the (undistorted) optimum" (Jaeger 2012, p. 212). On the contrary, these taxes correct behaviour in a way that eliminates the inefficiencies from environmental damage. Thus, they fit well in the economic notion of optimal taxation which is about raising revenues necessary to finance public expenditures in the most efficient, that is not distorting, way. Environmental taxes thus could be set higher than it would be otherwise, not only resulting in a change of (environment-friendly) behaviour but also generating revenues which enable a decrease in other distorting taxes (Jaeger 2012).

There are alternative policy instruments aimed at protecting the environment. These instruments include command and control regulation, permits and subsidies (OECD 1989). These instruments have different distributive and (other) ethical consequences (Posner and Weisbach 2010, pp. 41–58). Environmental taxes are but one example of the use of taxation to implement government policies. The current prevalence of the instrumental or regulatory function often causes shifts in the distribution of the tax burden among taxpayers, which may violate the underlying value of everybody paying a fair share. Furthermore, instrumentalist legislation usually underestimates the importance of legal principles in modern law such as the principle of equality and the principle of legal certainty (Gribnau 2012). Moreover, such incentives in tax law are a means of exerting power and influence over taxpayers. They impact liberty, autonomy and character. Consequently, they may be judged to be paternalist, manipulative or even exploitative if not carefully designed (Grant 2011).

With regard to environmental taxes, it should be noted that there is no internationally harmonised notion of "environmental tax". Several countries consider energy taxes on mineral oils (excises), gas, coal and electricity as "environmental" or "green" taxes, although such energy taxes already existed long before climate change became a main political issue (Kogels 2016). From an international point of view, moreover, national businesses may choose suppliers of goods and services in other countries with lower environmental taxes, and multinationals may decide to replace (part of) their production activities to countries with lower environmental taxes, in order to reduce the internalisation of external (environmental) cost in the prices of their final products.

After all, in a global economy, environmental taxes (as well as taxes on labour and profits) are considered as costs, so from a global sustainability point of view such "environmental tax avoidance" could (in theory) only be attacked by global measures (at least at UN level) restricting the fiscal autonomy of individual countries. Looking at the (60 years old) EU, we learn that the 28 individual Member States want to keep their fiscal autonomy as much as possible, also with respect to environmental taxes (Deak 2017). There is hardly any harmonisation on vehicle and road taxes and no agreement on levying excise on aviation fuel for international flights (for which a fundamental change in the ICAO Chicago Convention (1944) would be required). It is to be seen whether the Paris Climate Agreement (2015) will lead to (global) harmonisation of environmental taxes.

An example may explain the many complexities of environmental taxation. In the Netherlands, car taxes were used to incentivise consumers to buy hybrid cars. Car buyers started to buy hybrid plug-in cars which were a real bargain thanks to the tax incentives with serious budgetary impact for the state. Its success in terms of car sales made it too costly, and therefore, this tax incentive was changed repeatedly. Some car manufacturers reacted on these incentives by gaming the rules. They carefully engineered hybrid cars, which fulfilled just the statutory conditions, and enabled in this way car buyers to exploit the available tax subsidies as much as possible. Some cars could, for example, drive on electricity but only for a (very) limited number of miles (the 1.930 kilo Volvo XC90 T8 Twin Engine, driving only 25 miles on the rechargeable battery, is an well-known example; Kleijwegt 2016, p. 28; Love 2016)—not exactly a good example of a sustainable business policy to counter climate change.

Thus, tax incentives promoted creative compliance. Car manufacturers enabled car buyers (taxpayers) to comply with the letter of the law, while actually undermining the rationale behind the rules. Thus, these car manufacturers indirectly engaged in creative compliance which "may pass the test of legality but fail on the test of social responsibility" (McBarnet 2007, p. 51). In practice, many car owners drove their hybrid cars, often SUVs, hardly on electricity, thus increasing rather than reducing the emission of carbon dioxide. In a 2016 interview, the Dutch State Secretary of Finance concluded that the climate effect of tax incentives amounting to 6 billion euros over the past six years was nil (Kleijwegt 2016, p. 28).

The tax legislator responded to this such calculating behaviour by changing the legislation. For several years, the legal rules were changed quickly and frequently partly due to changes in environmental policy objectives and in response to calculating behaviour of taxpayers and car producers that played with the rules in a very creative way (Kogels 2015). The regulation that tried to incentivise (corporate) citizens to behave in a sustainable way thus was not durable. People who want to plan their activities with foreknowledge of its potential legal implications cannot rely on this kind of ever-changing regulation. As a consequence, the legislature became less reliable, less trustworthy.

Such all too frequent changes of rules point at an important meaning of sustainability with regard to taxation: sustainable, reliable law or regulation. In a state under the rule of law, government should exercise power via general legislation. This requirement of general legislation serves as an important protection against arbitrary interferences with individual rights and liberties by the public authorities. Predictability of law protects those subject to the law from arbitrary state interference with their lives. The value of legal certainty enables people to plan their future. This also goes for taxation for the levying of taxes is a way of exercising power (Gribnau 2010).

As shown above, tax legislation used as a regulatory instrument to change citizens' behaviour is not very stable. It changes (too) frequently due to ever-changing policy preferences and due to the calculating use of the (incentivising) rules by (corporate) citizens. This interplay between tax legislatures and taxpayers results in unstable, not sustainable, tax legislation. Of course, states have the primary responsibility for a fair and stable tax system, setting the rules of the game. Good tax governance (see section "Good Tax Governance and Transparency") requires careful law-making and law-application, and international cooperation in these matters (Végh and Gribnau 2018; Panayi 2017). But there is no denying that rules can often be used in different ways. Citizens enjoy a certain freedom of choice, which entails responsibility.

Responsible behaviour adds to durable legislation, for irresponsible, calculating behaviour leads to quickly changing legislation. Responsible behaviour thus contributes to the stability, and in this sense, sustainability of tax legislation. Corporations may thus show responsibility by not gaming the rules. This does not only apply to the use of domestic tax incentives but also to the use of the international tax system. Corporations choosing for good tax governance should not engage in irresponsible international tax planning practices as will be shown (section "Good Tax Governance and Transparency"). However, before it will be explained what the concept of good tax governance exactly means, it is necessary to understand what kind of responsibility tax paying involves in a larger picture. In other words, how is paying taxes related to sustainability.

Sustainable Development and Taxation

Taxes are means to provide public goods, such as the military to protect the country, education, health care, legal system and infrastructure. Taxation serves also distributive justice, and it is an important means to redistribute wealth between citizens (Gribnau 2017, p. 13). Distributive justice is based on principle where society is responsible for taking care of the less well. Distributive justice and public goods are indispensable for a sustainable society.

Taxes thus enable government to provide a (legal) framework for the functioning of society and economy. Enforcing contracts for instance supports trust in markets without which corporations could not operate. But taxes also contribute to the well-being of corporations in other ways for the state fosters innovation, encourages investment for sustainable growth, boosts worker productivity and stimulates the efficient use of scarce resources. This is done by subsidies paid for by taxes but also by tax (dis)incentives. Taxation is thus an important fundament for well-functioning and sustainable societies and markets.

Also, the UN Sustainable Development Goals are aimed at achieving well-functioning and sustainable societies and markets. In recent years, SDGs have received much attention in the context of state as well as corporate responsibilities. SDGs are 17 goals to fight against poverty, inequality and climate change, adopted in 2015 by UN Member States. SDGs are built on Millennium Development Goals (MDGs) and they "call for action by all countries, poor, rich and middle-income to promote prosperity while protecting the planet". SDGs "recognize that ending poverty must go hand-in-hand with strategies that build economic growth" (UN, The Sustainable Development Agenda). It is governments' responsibility to establish regulatory frameworks in order to achieve SDGs by 2030.

Achieving the ambitious SDGs is dependent on taxes. Most SDGs, such as ending poverty, developing infrastructure or reducing inequality, are (based on) essential public goods that are financed thanks to taxation (Sepúlveda Carmona 2014, p. 1). Therefore, achieving the SDGs is in large part dependent on government's sustainable tax legislation as described in the previous section (section "Sustainable Tax Legislation"). Indeed, "taxation has a key role to play in financing the SDGs" (Platform for Collaboration on Tax 2018, p. 1). Achieving SDGs depends on whether and how governments succeed in improving and enforcing their tax systems (Lustig 2015). In order to achieve and implement effective tax laws to fight against aggressive tax planning practices (as will be explained in section "Corporations and Sustainable

Tax Governance"), states also need to strengthen the cooperation on the international level (e.g. OECD 2013b or EU ATAP). States are, however, not always eager to eliminate all possible tax planning gaps because they want to stay attractive for multinationals and foreign investment which may contribute to goal of sustainable development. In practice, states therefore have to balance these two goals (see section "(Corporate) Power and Accountability"). Creating the fiscal system that allows states to deliver on the SDGs is one of the key challenges of sustainable governance (Christian Aid 2014; Kagan 2016). For achieving SDGs, states need to ensure the "sufficiency of resources, equality in the distribution of burdens and benefits of resourcing, and accountability over all levels of domestic and global policy making" (Christian Aid 2014).

It is often argued that states are responsible for the tax system and its fairness. "Fairness in corporate taxation is not a corporate responsibility; it is the responsibility of the nation states" (De Wilde 2015, p. 22). Corporate taxpayers may thus deftly bend the rules, because states fail to create a perfect tax system. To our minds, not only states but also multinationals bear responsibility when it comes to achieving SDGs. Companies should show positive commitment in this respect. Indeed, as a group of leading companies maintains, "fairer, more transparent tax systems, should be supported and upheld by business" (*The B Team* 2018, p. 1). Multinationals are often capable to play around tax legislation and avoid paying their fair share of taxes. This goes at the expense of public revenue and shifts the tax burden to less expert taxpayers (see section "Corporations and Sustainable Tax Governance"). Tax avoidance has an important influence on achieving SDGs. For instance, corporate tax avoidance can negatively affect human rights of socio-economic nature that are related to poverty, such as right to education or other elementary public goods and services that should be provided by means of tax money (IBA 2013). Such deprivation occurs especially with regard to poor (developing) countries when they are involved in tax planning schemes (Weyzig 2013, pp. 75–80; Pogge and Mehta 2016, pp. 2–5). Taxation is "instrumental to state-building" (Panayi 2017, p. 22); by not contributing his or her fair share to the society, a taxpayer limits the state's possibility to provide essential public goods and services. This, in turn, has a negative effect on achieving SDGs. In other words, "tax abuses deprive governments of the resources required to provide the programmes that give effect to economic, social and cultural rights, and to create and strengthen the institutions that uphold civil and political rights" (IBA 2013, p. 2).

Moreover, it is morally unacceptable that corporations, driven by profit-maximisation, erode living standards of other members of society (Gribnau and Jallai 2017, pp. 71–75). Multinationals have the power (see section "(Corporate) Power and Accountability") to avoid tax regulations that would impose higher costs on companies. Such behaviour is in conflict with corporate sustainability. Defining the concept of sustainability is challenging for it is culture bound but in general it is related to CSR, "maximizing positive and minimizing negative impacts on stakeholders" (Ferrell et al. 2017, pp. 347–348). RobecoSAM, a sustainable investment research organisation, defines corporate sustainability as "a business approach that creates long-term shareholder value by embracing opportunities and managing risks deriving from economic, environmental and social developments" (RobecoSAM). What kinds of corporate tax practices can be considered as in conflict with social norms and sustainability will be discussed next.

Corporations and Sustainable Tax Governance

The upshot of the foregoing is that states bear primary responsibility for good tax governance and sustainable taxation but that taxpayers also bear some responsibility in this respect. This demands some further explication on the nature and function of taxation. Why does taxation entail responsibility for different actors? The answer is that taxation is a moral phenomenon, for the tax system reflects important values such as liberty, reciprocity, solidarity and distributive justice. Taxation embodies fundamental societal values (Gribnau and Jallai 2017, pp. 71–73). Taxes are the main funding for society and for individual liberty to flourish. Moreover, they are an important means to enhance distributive justice, reducing the unequal distribution of income and wealth. Taxation, however, first and foremost aims at raising revenue to pay for public goods such as defence, the legal system, health care, public education, infrastructure for transport and communications, social security, culture, clean energy and sustainable development (Brauner and Stewart 2013; *The B Team* 2018, p. 3).

Thus, paying taxes can be seen as an investment but there is more to it, for it is also a matter of moral responsibility. Paying taxes is an obligation towards society because it is a contribution towards society which enables corporations to thrive. The principle of reciprocity demands members of society who enjoy the benefits of this kind of social cooperation to do their fair share. This principle applies also to corporate members for corporate citizens are part of society, engaging with other citizens (Gribnau 2017). This goes all the more for corporations that endorse CSR because they voluntarily accept ethical obligations beyond (strict) compliance with the law (Carroll 1991, pp. 39–48).

This view must have tax consequences. A company that takes its social responsibility seriously should extend this responsibility so as to include taxation, thus paying its share to sustain societies in which it exists. Of course (corporate) taxpayers may plan and structure their affairs to achieve a favourable tax treatment within the limits set by law. They are under no obligation to pay as much tax as possible. CSR companies, however, should interpret such limits from an ethical perspective. Hardly paying any (corporate) taxes at all by strictly complying with the letter of the law is clearly inconsistent with professing to accept ethical obligations beyond what is required by the law.

Every company has to engage in tax planning. Tax planning is a legal way to take into account the tax effects of various laws and rules, and adapt ones' actions accordingly. This is something that every taxpayer does to a certain extent whether this is intentional or not. Tax planning means that a taxpayer is in control of his/her finances by being aware of the impact of taxation and by adjusting the behaviour accordingly, for instance to avoid double taxation (Gribnau 2015a, p. 226). Also, the European Court of Justice has repeatedly confirmed that "taxpayers may choose to structure their business so as to limit their tax liability" (ECJ Halifax case 2006). A company can also opt for tax avoidance which refers to the behaviour of taxpayers designed to reduce tax liability by legal means, it is not just about adapting one's behaviour but actively looking for possibilities to diminish one's tax liability within the legal framework.[1] Some multinationals, however, go very far when engaging in tax avoidance; they exploit inconsistencies and loopholes of legal systems in such a way that they eventually pay almost no tax in any country in which they operate. The OECD points out that even though such arrangement could be strictly legal, it is considered as in conflict with the intent of the law it purports to follow (OECD Glossary of Tax Terms). Such tax planning is in tax literature and discussions often addressed as aggressive tax planning.

Although there is no commonly agreed upon definition of aggressive tax planning, for the purpose of this paper we need not go in detail. We use the definition that has been given by the European Commission stating that "it exploits the differences in tax systems by taking advantage of the technicalities of a tax system or of mismatches between two or more tax systems for the purpose of reducing tax liability" (European Commission 2012).

Tax planning practices can therefore be more or less responsible. Tax laws leave taxpayers leeway to structure their affairs in a tax-favourable way. Many multinationals expertly exploit the international tax system so as to minimise their tax liability. Shifting the tax burden to other taxpayers may seriously impact distributive justice, solidarity and society's sustainability. Choices made have impact on society and other taxpayers' well-being. This suggests that taxation has a moral nature; it is necessary for sustaining society, liberty and other important human values. Therefore, by definition, CSR companies who accept ethical obligations towards society should integrate tax in their CSR philosophy. Multinationals engaging in aggressive tax planning deprive countries of financial means necessary to sustain society and shift the tax burden to other more compliant taxpayers, impacting their liberty. For these reasons, aggressive tax planning is irresponsible behaviour.

Companies that acknowledge (moral) obligations towards society can opt to implement social responsibility policies (we refer them CSR companies). CSR can have many different definitions depending on the context and subject from which viewpoint the definition comes. According to the European Commission, CSR "refers to companies voluntarily going beyond what the law requires to achieve social and environmental objectives during the course of their daily business activities" (European Commission CSR). The OECD (CSR FAQ) refers to "the mutual dependence of business and society" where corporate responsibility concerns the corporate role in this relationship. Moreover, the OECD expects that businesses comply next to the written laws also with the "societal expectations that are not written down as formal law" (CSR FAQ). These elements of the OECD and EU definitions both signal the significance of (voluntarily) moving beyond pure compliance with the law, which fit with Carroll's pyramidal framework on CSR (Carroll 1991). According to Carroll are corporations expected to pursue their economic missions within the framework of the law, but that also conform to ethical responsibilities that go beyond the law and profit making. The ethical responsibilities—which are seen as the obligation to do what is right, just and fair—should be fulfilled (Carroll 1991, p. 42). Ethical considerations go beyond compliance with the law. Behaving ethically should be fundamental in all business matters, including tax planning practices.

How corporations could promote good tax governance will be discussed in section "Good Tax Governance and Transparency". It is, however, clear that sustainable tax governance entails tax planning practices that follow ethical considerations. Multinationals possess corporate power that places them in a position to steer sustainable development. Such power means, however, also increased accountability; multinationals need to account for their choices and actions.

(Corporate) Power and Accountability

Large corporations can have an immense impact on the societies in which they operate. The fact that multinational is one economic organisation means that multinationals are in position to combine "the most favourable regulations of different countries within a single contract" (Ruggie 2017, p. 12). This has caused, as also Hirst and Thompson (1996, p. 11) point out, that transnational corporations "could no longer be controlled or even constrained by the policies of particular nation states". Instead, such corporations "could escape all but the commonly agreed and enforced international regulatory standards" (Hirst and Thompson 1996, p. 11). This can be called a regulatory vacuum, which means that national regulations cannot tackle international problems and international rulemaking is not sufficiently developed yet (Scherer and Palazzo 2008, p. 423). Such regulatory vacuum of international standards has created for transnational corporations a possibility to use mismatching national tax laws to extremes, as explained in previous section (section "Corporations and Sustainable Tax Governance").

Such phenomenon where corporations can achieve their goals against the will of governments, for instance, can be called corporate power. In political science, power is typically defined as "the ability of A to get B to do something that B otherwise would not do" (Ruggie 2017, p. 5). Multinationals are among the most powerful organisations. This is not an autonomous development for many governments have ceded power to markets. They have, for example, privatised state-owned industries or provided various (tax) incentives which have boomed the success of private corporations. As a result, powerful corporations impact people's lives increasingly and are more visible than ever before and are more likely to attract criticism in case of perceived misbehaviour (Tapscott and Ticoll 2004, p. 184).

In the context of international tax planning, the multinationals' corporate power is multidimensional. It appears, for instance, in a form of knowledge and possibilities to (ab)use mismatching national tax laws to extremes. Multinationals have sufficient possibilities for moving (parts of their operations) to other jurisdictions that would allow them to plan their taxes as they wish. They are often mobile or they can reshape their business operations by setting up a "letterbox company" in certain states for escaping some applicable rules—for instance, by setting up various business entities in different countries for taking advantage of various tax treaty rules and involving therefore in so-called treaty shopping. This creates next to competition distortion a situation that is perceived as unfair. Multinationals have also power to affect the law-making process by engaging in corporate lobbying (Corporate Europe Observatory; Ruggie 2017; Christians 2017). In relation to corporate tax planning, multinationals often lobby very effectively, which according to Christians (2017, p. 152) "results in tax policy as favourable as possible to those who have recourses to shape it". There is evidence that lobbying activities result in significant tax benefits for companies. In addition, multinationals can use their knowledge and strong negotiation position in the law enforcement phase when they have to deal with tax authorities (Muchlinsky 2007, p. 8). For instance, the so-called Lux Leaks scandal revealed that many multinationals (nearly 340) such as Pepsi, IKEA and Deutsche Bank had "secured secret deals from Luxembourg that allowed many of them to slash their global tax bills" (ICIJ Lux Leaks). When negotiating for such favourable deals, multinationals have a strong position for they are very mobile, which means that if they do not get the deal from one state, they can always turn to another state.

The special character of multinationals allows them to operate on a global level where often exists a regulatory vacuum—a situation where multinationals are involved in problems that cannot be eliminated on the nation-state level due to the transnational nature of the problem. However, in such transnational situations, global governance is usually weak (Scherer and Palazzo 2008, pp. 423–425). This is also happening with international tax planning. Moreover, it is clear that societal expectations for multinationals in this arena are changing; the general public nor regulatory authorities are accepting that multinationals do not contribute—in the form of taxes—in the societies in which they operate. Therefore, corporations need to be accountable to the societies in which they operate. Corporate accountability stands for the fact that the excessive corporate power needs to be tamed (Valor 2005).

The business dictionary defines corporate accountability as the obligation "to account for its activities, accept responsibility for them, and to disclose the results in a transparent manner" (Business Dictionary). Valor argues that "accountability should be understood as social corporate control" because "corporations are accountable for the creation of organisational wealth for its multiple constituents" (Valor 2005, pp. 196–197). Accountability requires transparency for "organisations should account for their actions through the *provision of information* to stakeholders and society" (Swift 2001, p. 16). Swift claims that "essentially accountability is about the provision of information between two parties where the one who is accountable, explains or justifies actions to the one to whom the account is owed" (Swift 2001, p. 17). Thus, for keeping multinationals accountable towards the societies in which they operate, transparency is very important; it is a primary requirement of accountability. Without information, it is hardly possible to acquire the knowledge needed to hold those who wield power over others accountable. Accountability enables people to check the exercise of power.

Transparency

In the international law context, transparency "is universally perceived as a positive value", whereas "the opposites of transparency, such as secrecy and confidentiality, have taken on a negative connotation" and "although they remain paradigmatic narratives in some areas, overall they are largely considered as manifestations of power and, often, of its abuse" (Bianchi 2013, p. 2). Thus, transparency is necessary to tame the corporate power (Tapscott and Ticoll 2004, pp. 13, 225). Naturally, "transparency" is a broad and complicated concept (Schnackenberg and Tomlinson 2014). In this contribution, transparency is considered as a principle of being open about one's tax planning practices.

In the fight against certain types of tax planning, transparency is often considered to be a key principle (Peters 2017, pp. 218–231). The European Commission, for instance, states that "transparency is a crucial element in securing fairer taxation", adding that the Commission has "given high priority to improving tax transparency in the Single Market" (European Commission 2015a). One of the reasons why various international regulatory approaches aim to create more transparency in tax planning discussions is to minimise the information gap between corporations and other interested parties such as tax authorities, states or society at large. In economics, such information gap is referred to as information asymmetry, which describes situations in which one party to a transaction or agreement has less information than the other (Stiglitz 2002, pp. 469–470; Hood 2006, p. 18). Multinationals, as described, possess corporate power that gives them a favourable position in relation to information asymmetry. Therefore, transparency is an important door to corporate accountability. Transparency in itself is never a goal but rather a means towards a certain outcome—accountability in this case.

The demand for transparency in tax affairs has become very urgent. This is clearly visible in the 2013 OECD report to the G20: "Leaders, civil society and everyday taxpayers are renewing demands for greater transparency and (…) changes to the international tax rules to restore fairness and integrity of their tax systems and the global financial systems more generally. The message is clear: all taxpayers must pay their fair share" (OECD 2013a, p. 2).

Transparency as one of the principal democratic values should help citizens to gain a clear insight and understanding of the democratic decision-making processes. "It allows citizens to control the activity of their elected representatives, to verify respect for legal procedures, to understand decision-making processes, and to trust politicians" (Innerarity 2016, p. 89). More generally, transparency enables citizens to hold to account those who exercise some kind of power over them, such as politicians or corporations (Florini 1999). "In a transparent world with unprecedented access to information, employees, shareholders, business partners, and even, to a degree, consumers want evidence that firms are trustworthy and behaving according to their values" (Tapscott and Ticoll 2004, p. 19). Stakeholders want information in order to assess corporations' conduct.

But there are also limits to transparency. Transparency refers first of all to public access to information which is relevant for democratic decision-making (Fung et al. 2008, pp. 24–25). But access to public data as such does not guarantee public understanding. Moreover, it should not be taken for granted that people will use the information they obtained to make rational judgements and decisions. Leaks such as Paradise Papers or Lux Leaks do not by definition lead to rational debate among people who are not tax experts. Nonetheless, they create a sense of urgency for multinationals (and states) to reflect on the propriety of their tax behaviour. Individuals, groups and organisations are prone to cognitive distortions (bounded rationality). Consequently, mandatory information disclosure entails incentives for organisations to "game" the release of information to take advantage of common cognitive distortions (Fung et al. 2008, p. 34). It is sometimes hard to tell what information is trustworthy.

Nonetheless, without information, no evaluation of the way power is exercised is possible. Though transparency is not a panacea, it still is a precondition for accountability to the people. Decision-making procedures and their results should be transparent. Such transparency can be either mandatory (disclosure rules section "Tax, Transparency and Disclosure Obligations") or voluntary (part of good tax governance section "Good Tax Governance and Transparency").

Tax, Transparency and Disclosure Obligations

The requirement of transparency is well known in tax matters, for example in the relationship between taxpayer and tax authorities. Information asymmetry is a fundamental feature of this relationship. The tax inspector depends on the taxpayer for his knowledge of the facts and circumstances relevant to determine the taxpayer's tax liability. Information gathering powers, for example, enable the tax authorities to request information needed for the assessment—information which is available to the taxpayer and/or third parties such as employers, banks and insurance companies. The taxpayer (and other parties) has many corresponding statutory obligations to disclose the information needed for assessment, e.g. to file a tax return, to provide data and information on request and to make available books, documents and other data carriers for audit (Gribnau 2015b, pp. 201–202). International exchange of information enhances transparency, diminishing information asymmetry.

Tax authorities exchange data with regard to income and wealth of taxpayers. This exchange can be done upon request but many data are exchanged automatically between the tax authorities in an increasing number of countries. By way of transnational tax information exchange networks, tax administrators can cooperate actively with administrators from other countries and achieve the capacity to enforce national tax laws in respect of multinational and mobile capital and labour. Exchange of tax-relevant information is an important means for tax authorities to combat tax evasion and tax avoidance (Grinberg 2016, pp. 14–30; Zucman 2015, p. 92). Tax administrators must cooperate actively with administrators from other countries and work to build inclusive transnational institutions and networks. The legitimacy of these transnational information networks based on, e.g., accountability to democratic institutions, professional expertise, and procedural fairness and effectiveness, will be crucial for their sustainability and effectiveness in the long term (Stewart 2013; Mosquera Valderrama 2016). Transparency may also be achieved by mandatory disclosure rules for taxpayers who are involved in "aggressive or abusive transactions" (OECD 2015a, p. 9).

The latter measures are part of initiatives launched by G20/OECD and European Commission to coordinate among countries measures against to base erosion and profit shifting, a particular form of aggressive tax planning (Hilling and Ostas 2017, pp. 46–54). Good tax governance requires these kinds of measures. In practice, regulatory attempts to promote sustainable tax governance, such as the OECD BEPS Action Plan (OECD 2013b) and the EU Action Plan (European Commission 2016a). The European Commission, for instance, "promotes the three principles of good tax governance – namely transparency, exchange of information and fair tax competition – in relations between states" (European Commission 2011). Also, enterprises are encouraged, where appropriate, to work towards the implementation of these principles.

The European Union (EU) is fighting against tax avoidance with its action plan for fair corporate taxation in the EU,[2] which focuses among others on transparency between the Member States in order to eliminate information and knowledge gaps (European Commission 2015b). For instance, the EU has introduced the country-by-country reporting by corporations and sharing this information with Member States' tax authorities to enhance transparency (European Commission 2015c, 2016c). The EU's country-by-country reporting is largely based on the OECD country-by-country reporting (CbC reporting) measure as developed under Action 13 of the BEPS Action Plan (OECD 2013b). The aim of CbC reporting is to increase taxpayers' transparency towards tax authorities for tackling aggressive tax planning issues (OECD 2015b). Moreover, as a consequence of Panama Papers scandal (ICIJ) in April 2016, there is a proposal for public country-by-country reporting to enhance public scrutiny of corporate income taxes borne by multinationals which will “further foster corporate responsibility” (European Commission 2016b, p. 9; Panayi 2017, pp. 17, 36).[3]

Next to disclosure rules, corporations often face also disclosure rules from private actors. Private standardisation actions such as VBDO Good Tax Governance (VBDO 2014, 2017) and ISO 26000 focus on transparency. Many investors also put growing attention to corporate sustainability. RobecoSAM that conducts corporate sustainability assessment for investors puts much attention to “media and stakeholder commentaries and other publicly available information from consumer organizations, NGOs, governments or international organizations to identify companies’ involvement and response to environmental, economic and social crisis situations that may have a damaging effect on their reputation and core business” (RobecoSAM 2015, p. 10). With regard to corporate tax planning, this might be important for media as well as NGOs and governments have in recent years put much (negative) attention on corporate tax practices (e.g. Starbucks case in the UK). According to RobecoSAM, which is a part of Dow Jones Sustainability Index, as a result of recent financial crisis that “exposed significant risks associated with short-termism”, there is a growing demand among investors for “long-term oriented strategies that integrate economic, environmental and social criteria within their portfolios” (RobecoSAM 2015, p. 16). Therefore, sustainability considerations have become an important part of investors’ decision-making (Dixon and Sharma 2018). Such (external) stimulus should, nevertheless, not be the only motivation for corporations to switch to good tax governance.

Good Tax Governance and Transparency

The concept of good tax governance does not only regard states but it also regards taxpayers. “Governance” is indeed a broad concept that applies to the purpose, management and functions of nations, governments, communities and organisations such as corporations. With regard to companies, corporate governance is according to Charkham “about the way companies are directed and controlled, and relate their source of finance” (Charkham 2005, p. 1). As for the purpose of the company, he argues "that this is to provide *ethically and profitably* the goods and services people need and want" (Charkham 2005, pp. 2, 21). Corporate governance, which determines in general "a pattern of relationships between a company's management, its board, its shareholders and stakeholders", should include tax—requiring tax governance.

Indeed, tax governance is for businesses an element of corporate governance. According to Williams, tax governance is "the answer, or the totality of the various answers, that the board of directors of a company gives to the questions 'What responsibilities and opportunities are we presented with in relation to the tax affairs of the company?' and 'How can we best respond to those responsibilities and opportunities for the benefit of the shareholders and of others to whom we have an obligation?'" (Williams 2007, p. 4).

Bronzewska and Van der Enden (2014, p. 636) elaborate on the implementation of tax governance. It is a board responsibility. They argue that "[T]he role of the board is to set general guidelines for the company's global tax philosophy and the framework for the governance of tax issues and processes". Such tax philosophy should in their opinion be integrated into "the overall business mission and vision". Multinationals that aspire to be regarded as responsible corporate citizens are expected to have "an internal validation system" (Tax Control Framework) in place in order to "explain their tax strategy, what the tax risks are and how these are managed" (Bronzewska and Van der Enden 2014, pp. 635–636).

Corporations have to deal with moral and societal choices when planning taxes. The society has "certain expectations for appropriate business behavior and outcomes" (Wood 1991, p. 695). According to Ruggie, "social norms exist over and above compliance with laws and regulations" (Ruggie 2013, p. 91). Therefore, businesses are not free to do as they wish to increase their income, market share or alike. Corporations that use the power to minimise their tax liability as much as possible behave irresponsible in the eyes of the public (Jallai 2017; Jallai and Gribnau 2018). The fact that taxation is a moral phenomenon places tax also at the heart of the notion of CSR. Corporate commitment to CSR should be consistently applied to all of the company's dealings and activities. For companies that present themselves as sustainable corporations, there are also ethical considerations in addition to legal and economic ones when defining and implementing a business strategy and making decisions. Multinationals that claim to be CSR companies should not engage in fiscal engineering in order to pay (almost) no corporate income taxes in the societies in which they operate.

Socially responsible, sustainable companies should pay their fair share of tax (or at least not unfair), and they should be willing to discuss their tax planning, which demands certain openness on their part. Thus, one could distinguish a substantive approach and a procedural approach to sustainable tax governance. A substantive approach focuses on the amount of tax that a company pays, and asks whether this is more than is demanded by mere compliance with the letter of the law (stripped to the bone by gaming the rules; section "Corporations and Sustainable Tax Governance"). A procedural approach provides information on a company's tax strategy, for instance on how much corporate income tax it pays in all countries it operates. Here, transparency, going beyond compliance with legal disclosure requirements and reporting obligations, is key (Gutmann 2010, pp. 546–547).

When a corporation is convinced that its tax planning practices are legal and legitimate (responsible), it should be able to report this openly to the public. If a corporation does feel the need to hide something, it should be seen as a red flag. Naturally, companies are economic entities and will not actively search for the possibilities to pay more tax. Full transparency over its payments and tax choices is usually even opposed by companies that have nothing to hide. There can namely be many downsides to this, such as threat to taxpayers' privacy, weakening its competitive position or risking with misinterpretation of information by misinformed receiver. However, it is also not acceptable that multinationals use their corporate power at the considerable cost of society's welfare. Therefore, multinationals have their role to play in taking into account the effects of their tax planning practices. If they fail to do so, they may suffer for instance reputation damage (Gribnau and Jallai 2017, pp. 77–79). Therefore, they need to communicate their tax strategy.

Indeed, it is unclear which tax practices exactly are considered as illegitimate and it is government's responsibility to provide more guidance in this matter. However, transparency from the corporations' side opens a door for discussion in order to establish what are legitimate or acceptable tax planning practices. Transparency and openness, from the perspective of corporations, are a precondition for a focused discussion, for it is necessary to get the facts right and take on board different perspectives. This, in turn, helps corporations to protect (or where necessary to re-establish) or advance their reputation. Furthermore, transparency and the inclusion of tax in CSR reporting would help to minimise the information asymmetry gap that, in current debates, seems to confuse the understanding of the problem. One of the most significant procedural elements of CSR is reporting and openness (see, e.g. McBarnet 2007, pp. 32–37; GRI Sustainability Reporting). Transparency should ideally be driven by an intrinsic motivation to do consistently the right thing. Inconsistent reporting is not sustainable, and business should not engage in opportunistic reporting (cf. Holland et al. 2016, p. 338). Of course, transparency is never an end in itself; it is always a means to some other value, for example accountability. In any case, transparency and openness are first steps towards moral tax behaviour. Moreover, for transparency is a precondition for accountability and open debate, it is crucial in creating a better tax compliance environment. A debate promotes a better understanding of factors business take into account in their tax decisions and the moral acceptability of tax planning practices. A fruitful debate is indispensable for developing standards of substantive good tax governance.

Behaving ethically should be fundamental in all business matters, including tax planning practices. However, in order to foster a debate regarding what exactly is ethical, companies should communicate about their practices in tax matters, as this opens a door to discussion and paves the way towards a better understanding of tax morale. At the end of the day, aggressive tax planning cannot be resolved merely by changing the laws, for all laws can be gamed; it demands also that the mindset and attitude are changed (McBarnet 2007, p. 48).

Conclusion

This chapter focused on the relationship between tax and sustainability. The central issue was that many taxpayers appear to pay very low or no (corporate) income taxes in the countries where they have economic activities. This kind of aggressive tax planning is a global problem with societal, political, economic, legal and moral dimensions. It is unjust and undermines sustainable development of societies for taxation supports societal cooperation and provides resources to finance essential public goods and services.

Both public and private actors should commit themselves to sustainable tax governance, long-term future-oriented (good) tax governance. Sustainable tax legislation and enforcement as well as sustainable tax planning are essential preconditions for achieving SDGs. States should create, implement and enforce a fair, well-functioning and stable system of tax rules. Legislatures bear the responsibility to establish a fair and well-functioning system of tax laws. With regard to international taxation, enhanced cooperation among states is required. Having said that, no legal system is perfect and business therefore has to uphold it.

Consequently, multinationals have to accept their moral responsibilities towards society. Here, corporate social responsibility is used as a proxy for sustainability. Corporate scandals and media attention have shown that society expects corporations not to engage in aggressive tax planning. Moreover, an increased societal demand for corporate accountability requires more transparency with regard to corporate tax behaviour. Corporate taxpayers that want to show moral leadership should balance their right to structure their affairs to achieve a favourable tax treatment within the limits set by law with the obligation not to abuse the inevitable imperfections of the legal system. They should account for their tax behaviour. Companies willing to engage in sustainable tax governance need to be transparent about their tax strategy and discuss it with their stakeholders. These companies have to take up the challenge to develop innovative strategies with regard to tax transparency evidencing sustainable tax planning.

Acknowledgements The authors wish to thank Han Kogels for his valuable suggestions with regard to environmental taxation.

Notes

1. We assume that a responsible company will not engage in tax evasion which refers to illegitimate actions to reduce tax (Filipczyk 2017, pp. 15–66).
2. See European Commission's Agenda for the Fair Corporate Taxation in the EU information chart: http://ec.europa.eu/taxation_customs/sites/taxation/files/resources/documents/taxation/company_tax/anti_tax_avoidance/timeline_without_logo.png. Accessed 2 March 2018.
3. For more detailed discussion of CbC Reporting, see OECD (2015b), European Commission (2016b).

References

Bianchi, A. (2013). On power and illusion: The concept of transparency in international law. In A. Bianchi & A. Peters (Eds.), *Transparency in international law* (pp. 1–20). Cambridge: Cambridge University Press.

Brauner, Y., & Stewart, M. (Eds.). (2013). *Tax, law and development*. Cheltenham: Edward Elgar.

Bronzewska, K., & Van der Enden, E. (2014). Tax control framework—A conceptual approach: The six nuances of good tax governance. *Bulletin For International Taxation, 68*(11), 635–640.

The B Team. (2018). *A new bar for responsible tax: The B Team responsible tax principles*. Retrieved February 22, 2018, from http://bteam.org/announcements/responsibletax-2/.

Business Dictionary (online). Retrieved March 3, 2018, from http://www.businessdictionary.com/definition/accountability.html.

Carroll, A. B. (1991, July–August). The pyramid of corporate social responsibility: Toward the moral management of organizational stakeholders. *Business Horizons*, 39–48.

Charkham, J. (2005). *Keeping better company: Corporate governance ten years on* (2nd ed.). Oxford: Oxford University Press.

Christian Aid. (2014). *Statement: A post-2015 fiscal revolution*. UN Sustainable Development Knowledge Platform. Retrieved March 3, 2018, from https://sustainabledevelopment.un.org/index.php?page=view&type=255&nr=9282&menu=35.

Christians, A. (2017). Trust in the tax system: The problem of lobbying. In B. Peeters, J. L. M. Gribnau, & J. Badisco (Eds.), *Building trust in taxation* (pp. 151–173). Cambridge: Intersentia.

Corporate Europe Observatory webpage. *Exposing the power of corporate lobbying in the EU*. Retrieved March 3, 2018, from http://corporateeurope.org/power-lobbies.

De Wilde, M. F. (2015). *"Sharing the pie": Taxing multinationals in a global market*. Doctoral dissertation, Erasmus University Rotterdam.

Deak, D. (2017). Environmental tax harmonization and competition-centred legal practice of EUCJ. *EC Tax Review, 26*(6), 303–316.

Dixon, C., & Sharma, A. (2018, January 24). *Weil discusses 2018 10-K and proxy season: Spotlight on corporate sustainability*. Columbia Law School's Blue Sky Blog on Corporations and the Capital Markets. Retrieved January 25, 2018, from http://clsbluesky.law.columbia.edu/2018/01/24/weil-discusses-2018-10-k-and-proxy-season-spotlight-on-corporate-sustainability/.

European Court of Justice. (2006, February 21). Case C-255/02, *Halifax plc and others v. commissioners of customs & excise*, [2006] ECR I-1609.

European Commission. (2011). *A renewed EU STRATEGY 2011–14 for corporate social responsibility*. Communication from the commission to the european parliament, the council, the European economic and social committee and the committee of the regions, Brussels, 25 October 2011 COM(2011) 681 final. Retrieved March 3, 2018, from http://eur-lex.europa.eu/legal-content/EN/TXT/PDF/?uri=CELEX:52011DC0681&from=EN.

European Commission. (2012). *Recommendation on aggressive tax planning*. C(2012) 8806 final, 6 December 2012. Retrieved March 3, 2018, from http://ec.europa.eu/taxation_customs/sites/taxation/files/resources/documents/taxation/tax_fraud_evasion/c_2012_8806_en.pdf.

European Commission. (2015a). *A fair and efficient corporate tax system in the European Union: 5 key areas for action*. Communication from the Commission to the European Parliament and the Council, Brussels, 17 June 2015 COM(2015) 302 final.

European Commission. (2015b). *Combatting corporate tax avoidance: Commission presents tax transparency package*. Press release. Brussels, 18 March 2015. Retrieved February 22, 2018, from http://europa.eu/rapid/press-release_IP-15-4610_en.htm.

European Commission. (2015c). *Proposal for a council directive amending directive 2011/16/EU as regards mandatory automatic exchange of information in the field of taxation*. Brussels, 18 March 2015 SWD(2015) 60 final, COM(2015) 135 final, 2015/0068 (CNS).

European Commission. (2016a). *Anti-tax avoidance package: Next steps towards delivering effective taxation and greater tax transparency in the EU.* Communication from the commission to the european parliament and the council, Brussels, 28 January 2016 COM(2016) 23 final. Retrieved March 2, 2018, from http://eur-lex.europa.eu/legal-content/EN/TXT/PDF/?uri=CELEX:52016DC0023&from=EN.

European Commission. (2016b). *Proposal for a directive of the European Parliament and of the council amending directive 2013/34/EU as regards disclosure of income tax information by certain undertakings and branches.* Brussels, 12 April 2016 COM(2016) 198 final. Retrieved February 22, 2018, from http://eur-lex.europa.eu/legal-content/EN/TXT/?uri=CELEX:52016PC0198.

European Commission. (2016c). *Proposal for a council directive amending directive 2011/16/EU as regards mandatory automatic exchange of information in the field of taxation.* Brussels, 28 January 2016 COM/2016/025 final (CNS). Retrieved February 22, 2018, from http://eur-lex.europa.eu/legal-content/EN/TXT/?uri=COM:2016:25:FIN.

European Commission Employment, Affairs & Inclusion. *Corporate Social Responsibility (CSR) in the EU.* Retrieved March 3, 2018, from http://ec.europa.eu/social/main.jsp?catId=331.

Ferrell, O. C., Fraedrich, J., & Ferrell, L. (2017). *Business ethics: Ethical decision making and cases* (11th ed.). Boston: Cengage Learning.

Filipczyk, H. (2017). *Tax avoidance and rationality of law.* Warsaw: Wolters Kluwer.

Florini, A. M. (1999). *Does the invisible hand need a transparent glove? The politics of transparency.* Paper prepared for the Annual World Bank Conference on Development Economics Washington. Retrieved February 22, 2018, from http://siteresources.worldbank.org/INTWBIGOVANTCOR/Resources/florini.pdf.

Fung, A., Graham, M., & Weil, D. (2008). *Full disclosure: The perils and promise of transparency.* Cambridge: Cambridge University Press.

Global Reporting Initiative (GRI). *About sustainability reporting.* Retrieved March 1, 2018, from https://www.globalreporting.org/information/sustainability-reporting/Pages/default.aspx.

Grant, R. W. (2011). *Strings attached: Untangling the ethics of incentives.* Princeton: Princeton University Press.

Gribnau, H. (2010). Legal certainty: A matter of principle. In J. L. M. Gribnau & M. Pauwels (Eds.), *Retroactivity of tax legislation* (pp. 69–93). Amsterdam: EATLP.

Gribnau, H. (2012). Legislative instrumentalism vs. legal principles. *International Tax Law Review, 3*, 9–42. Retrieved March 27, 2018, from http://papers.ssrn.com/sol3/papers.cfm?abstract_id=2445038.

Gribnau, H. (2015a). Corporate social responsibility and tax planning: Not by rules alone. *Social and Legal Studies, 24*(2), 225–250.

Gribnau, H. (2015b). Horizontal monitoring: Some procedural tax law issues. In R. Russo (Ed.), *Tax Assurance* (pp. 183–216). Deventer: Kluwer.

Gribnau, H. (2017). The integrity of the tax system after BEPS: A shared responsibility. *Erasmus Law Review, 1*, 12–28.

Gribnau, H., & Jallai, A.-G. (2017). Good tax governance: A matter of moral responsibility and transparency. *Nordic Tax Journal, 1*, 70–88. Retrieved March 3, 2018, from https://papers.ssrn.com/sol3/papers.cfm?abstract_id=3021914.

Grinberg, I. (2016). Building institutions for a globalized world. Automatic information exchange. In T. Pogge & K. Mehta (Eds.), *Global tax fairness* (pp. 14–30). Oxford: Oxford University Press.

Gutmann, D. (2010). L'évasion fiscale des sociétés. *Revue Internationale de Droit Comparé, 62*(2), 533–551.

Hilling, A., & Ostas, D. T. (2017). *Corporate taxation and social responsibility*. Stockholm: Wolters Kluwer.

Hirst, P., & Thompson, G. (1996). *Globalisation in question*. Oxford: Polity Press.

Holland, K., Lindop, S., & Zainudin, F. (2016). Tax avoidance: A threat to corporate legitimacy? An examination of companies financial and CSR reports. *British Tax Review, 3*, 310–338.

Hood, C. (2006). Transparency in a historical perspective. In C. Hood & D. Heald (Eds.), *Transparency: Key to better governance?* (pp. 3–23). Oxford: Oxford University Press.

International Civil Aviation Organization (ICAO). (1944). *Convention on international civil aviation*. Chicago: International Civil Aviation Organization.

International Consortium of Investigative Journalists (ICIJ Lux Leaks). (2014). *Luxembourg leaks: Global companies' secrets exposed*. Retrieved March 3, 2018, from https://www.icij.org/project/luxembourg-leaks/.

International Consortium of Investigative Journalists (ICIJ Panama Papers). (2016). *Panama papers project*. Retrieved March 3, 2018, from https://panamapapers.icij.org/.

International Consortium of Investigative Journalists (ICIJ Paradise Papers). (2017). *An ICIJ investigation paradise papers: Secrets of the global elite*.

Retrieved January 23, 2018, from https://www.icij.org/investigations/paradise-papers/.
Innerarity, D. (2016). *Governance in the new global disorder: Politics for a post-sovereign society*. New York: Columbia University Press.
International Bar Association (IBA). (2013, October). *Tax abuses, poverty and human rights. A report of the international bar association's human rights institute task force on illicit financial flows, poverty and human rights*. Retrieved March 3, 2018, from https://www.ibanet.org/Article/NewDetail.aspx?ArticleUid=4a0cf930-a0d1-4784-8d09-f588dcddfea4.
International Organization for Standardization (ISO). ISO 26000: Social responsibility. Retrieved March 1, 2018, from http://www.iso.org/iso/home/standards/iso26000.htm.
Jallai, A.-G. (2017). Restoring stakeholders' trust in multinationals' tax planning practices with Corporate Social Responsibility (CSR). In B. Peeters, J. L. M. Gribnau, & J. Badisco (Eds.), *Building trust in taxation* (pp. 173–201). Cambridge: Intersentia.
Jallai, A.-G., & Gribnau, J. L. M. (2018). *Aggressive tax planning and corporate social irresponsibility: Managerial discretion in the light of corporate governance* (TLS Working Paper). Retrieved March 3, 2018, from http://ssrn.com/abstract=3119552.
Jaeger, W. K. (2012). The double dividend debate. In J. E. Milne & M. S. Andersen (Eds.), *Handbook of research on environmental taxation* (pp. 211–229). Cheltenham: Edward Elgar.
Kagan, S. (2016). High-level meeting on SDGs. *Environmental Policy and Law, 46*(3/4), 196–197.
Kleijwegt, R. (2016). Staatssecretaris Kraakt Subsidiebeleid Voorgangers. *Autoweek, 32*, 24–28.
Kogels, H. A. (2015). De jungle van de vergroende autogerelateerde belastingen. *Maandblad Belastingbeschouwingen, 1*, 4–11.
Kogels, H. A. (2016). Ontwikkeling van de belastingvergroening. *Maandblad Belastingbeschouwingen, 9*(10), 335–342.
Love. M. (2016, April 24). Volvo XC90 T8 twin engine momentum car. *The Guardian*.
Lustig, N. (2015). A missing target in the SDGs: Tax systems should not reduce the income of the poor. *International Growth Centre*. Retrieved January 22, 2018, from http://eprints.lse.ac.uk/81887/1/A%20missing%20target%20in%20the%20SDGs_%20Tax%20systems%20should%20

not%20reduce%20the%20income%20of%20the%20poor%20-%20IGC.pdf.

Massing, M. (2005, December 1). The end of news? *New York Review of Books*.

Mastellone, P. (2014). The emergence and enforcement of green taxes in the European Union—Part 1. *European Taxation, 54*(11), 478–490.

McBarnet, D. J. (2007). Corporate social responsibility beyond law, through law, for law: The new corporate accountability. In D. J. McBarnet, A. Voiculescu, & T. Campbell (Eds.), *The new corporate accountability: Corporate social responsibility and the law* (pp. 9–56). Cambridge: Cambridge University Press.

Mosquera Valderrama, I. J. (2016). The rights of multinationals in the global transparency framework: McCarthyism? *Derivatives and Financial Instruments, 18*(1), 92–101.

Muchlinsky, P. T. (2007). *Multinational enterprises & the law* (2nd ed.). New York: Oxford University Press.

OECD. (1989). *Economic instruments for environmental protection.* Paris: OECD.

OECD, *Glossary of tax terms*. Retrieved January 23, 2018, from http://www.oecd.org/ctp/glossaryoftaxterms.htm.

OECD. (2013a). *Secretary-general report to the G20 leaders restoring fairness to the tax system*. Paris: OECD.

OECD. (2013b). *Addressing Base Erosion and Profit Shifting (BEPS).* Paris: OECD Publishing.

OECD. (2015a). *Action 12: Mandatory disclosure rules*. Paris: OECD.

OECD. (2015b). *Action 13: Country-by-country reporting—Implementation package*. Paris: OECD.

OECD. *Corporate social responsibility: Frequently asked questions*. Retrieved March 1, 2018, from http://www.oecd.org/corporate/mne/corporateresponsibilityfrequentlyaskedquestions.htm.

Panayi, C. H. J. I. (2017). The europeanization of good tax governance. *Yearbook of European law* (pp. 1–54). Oxford: Oxford University Press.

Peters, C. (2017). Improving democratic international tax governance: On the power of citizens, transparency and independent watchdogs. In B. Peeters, J. L. M. Gribnau, & J. Badisco (Eds.), *Building trust in taxation* (pp. 205–234). Cambridge: Intersentia.

Platform for Collaboration on Tax. (2018). *Taxation and the Sustainable Development Goals*. Retrieved February 20, 2018, from http://www.oecd.org/tax/platform-for-collaboration-on-tax-conference-statement-2018.pdf.

Pogge, T., & Mehta, K. (2016). Introduction: The moral significance of tax-motivated illicit financial outflows. In T. Pogge & K. Mehta (Eds.), *Global tax fairness* (pp. 1–13). Oxford: Oxford University Press.

Posner, E. A., & Weisbach, D. (2010). *Climate change justice*. Princeton: Princeton University Press.

RobecoSAM. (2015). *Measuring intangibles ROBECOSAM's corporate sustainability assessment methodology*. Retrieved January 23, 2018, from http://www.sustainability-indices.com/images/Measuring_Intangibles_CSA_methodology.pdf.

RobecoSAM. *Corporate sustainability*. Retrieved January 23, 2018, from http://www.sustainability-indices.com/sustainability-assessment/corporate-sustainability.jsp.

Ruggie, J. G. (2013). *Just business: Multinational corporations and human rights*. New York: W. W. Norton.

Ruggie, J. G. (2017). Multinationals as global institution: Power, authority and relative autonomy. *Regulation & Governance* (online). https://onlinelibrary.wiley.com/doi/full/10.1111/rego.12154

Scherer, A. G., & Palazzo, G. (2008). Globalization and corporate social responsibility. In A. Crane, A. McWilliams, D. Matten, J. Moon, & D. Siegel (Eds.), *The Oxford handbook of corporate social responsibility* (pp. 413–431). Oxford: Oxford University Press.

Schnackenberg, A. K., & Tomlinson, E. C. (2014). Organizational transparency: A new perspective on managing trust in organization-stakeholder relationships. *Journal of Management* (pre-publication version). Retrieved March 3, 2018, from http://jom.sagepub.com/content/early/2014/03/06/0149206314525202.

Sepúlveda Carmona, M. (2014). *Report of the special rapporteur on extreme poverty and human rights*. Retrieved January 22, 2018, from https://www.ms.dk/sites/default/files/filarkiv/dokumenter/a_hrc_26_28_eng.pdf.

Stewart, M. (2013). Global tax information exchange networks: Legitimacy in a global administrative state. In Y. Brauner & M. Stewart (Eds.), *Tax, law and development* (pp. 316–344). Cheltenham: Edward Elgar.

Stiglitz, J. E. (2002). Information and the change in the paradigm in economics. *The American Economic Review, 92*(3), 460–501.

Swift, T. (2001). Trust, reputation and corporate accountability to stakeholders. *Business Ethics: A European Review, 10*(1), 16–26.

Tapscott, D., & Ticoll, D. (2004). *The naked corporation: How the age of transparency will revolutionize business*. London: Penguin Canada.

United Nations (UN) Framework Convention on Climate Change (2015). *Paris climate agreement*. Retrieved March 27, 2018, from http://unfccc.int/paris_agreement/items/9485.php.

UN. *The United Nations Millennium Development Goals (MDGs)*. Retrieved January 18, 2018, from http://www.un.org/millenniumgoals/.

UN. *Sustainable Development Goals (SDGs)*. Retrieved January 18, 2018, from https://sustainabledevelopment.un.org/post2015/transformingourworld.

UN. *The sustainable development agenda*. Retrieved January 18, 2018, from http://www.un.org/sustainabledevelopment/development-agenda/.

Valor, C. (2005). Corporate social responsibility and corporate citizenship: Towards corporate accountability. *Business and Society Review, 110*(2), 191–212.

VBDO. (2014). *Good tax governance in transition: Transcending the tax debate to CSR.* Retrieved January 18, 2018, from http://www.vbdo.nl/files/media/VBDO_A5_Good_Tax_Governance_D.pdf.

VBDO. (2017). *Tax transparency benchmark 2017, A comparative study of 76 Dutch listed companies*. Retrieved December 23, 2018, from http://www.vbdo.nl/files/news.

Végh, G., & Gribnau, J. L. M. (2018). Tax administration good governance. *EC Tax Review, 27*(1), 48–60.

Weyzig, F. (2013). *Effects of Dutch tax policy on taxation of multinationals in developing countries*. Ph.D. thesis. Nijmegen.

Williams, D. (2007). *Developing the concept of tax governance*. KPMG.

Wood, D. J. (1991). Corporate social performance revisited. *The Academy Management Review, 16*(4), 691–718.

Zucman, G. (2015). *The hidden wealth of nations: The scourge of tax havens*. Chicago and London: The University of Chicago Press.

Perspectives on Corporate Taxation from a Sustainable Business Perspective

Roger Persson Österman

Introductory Remarks

A well-functioning taxation is extremely important to society. The state, especially the welfare state, cannot exist without taxes. It is also important that the tax system is perceived as legitimate, fair and just on both a collective general level and on an individual level.

The general collective requirements are assumingly different from the individual requirements. The general public must believe in the system as such and the general public must also believe that the single taxpayers actually honestly pay their taxes. The single taxpayer must of course also trust the system and thus in good faith comply with the tax rules. Very important, the single taxpayer must as an individual level find the rules and procedures just and foreseeable.

Therefore, a sustainable corporate business taxation must in order to work well fulfill the expectations from society but also the expectations

R. P. Österman (✉)
Stockholm University, Stockholm, Sweden
e-mail: Roger.Osterman@juridicum.su.se

S. Arvidsson (ed.), *Challenges in Managing Sustainable Business*,
https://doi.org/10.1007/978-3-319-93266-8_16

from the individual taxpaying corporation. The latter will be in focus in this chapter. I will explore some of the challenges such an ideal system must address. The study critically evolves about the important discourse about corporate responsibility/sustainability and corporate taxpaying. The discourse is about how CSR and ethics could work as a pressure on corporations to take on a higher degree of tax responsibility. The idea behind the thinking is that tax avoidance and aggressive tax planning, which is deemed legal by the tax system, thereby would decrease. The effect would come by a strengthening of "tax morale" (that is the social norm to pay taxes in good faith) and also by strengthening the role of ethics.

In my analyze, I will raise critique to the view that taxation should be based on social or ethical norms. I do not, of course, deny the great importance of the interest of society that taxes are paid in good faith by honest taxpayers. The issue is about how that interest is best protected. The rational foundations for a strictly law-based regulation that is properly designed, in order to make sure that the individual taxpaying corporation pays its share of the tax, should be explored.

I will argue for the benefit of "*the rule of law*" basis for taxes. I will also argue for the importance of a high level of "*procedural justice*". The legitimacy and fairness of the system are mainly studied from the taxpayer angle. The hypothesis is that "the rule of law basis" and the "procedural justice" are of utmost importance for maintaining a sustainable corporate taxation. A critical view on the ideas of CSR and ethics as tools for enhancing taxation is thus maintained. The view, then, is necessarily mainly the corporate and business view. Other views are also of importance, nevertheless, they are out of scope of this chapter. In short, I will put forward the argument that a truly sustainable taxation must be firmly based on the rule of law concept, despite obvious shortcomings.

To raise the "rule of law" concept might be seen as somewhat conservative and boring in contemporary discourse. Of course, it must be admitted that the legal order is by nature a conservative concept as it slows down all kind of regulative actions. Nevertheless, in these times, I do think it is appropriate to raise the basic underlying arguments for the rule-based liberal society. An authoritarian leader hates the legal order as it hampers the leaders penchant for quick and drastic changes. The legal order and the concept of rule of law create an obstacle to the power holders of society (MacCormick 2011). As the legal order cannot change very quickly, it also produces stability and foreseeability. Especially the business environment needs regulatory stability and foreseeability. You know the playing field, and furthermore, the playing field is level. That is the whole point with the law.

The chapter should not be seen as a purely scientific enterprise rather it is an essay regarding basic issues in a very complex and also quite a broad area. The method is eclectic and the aim is to put together aspects from legal science, social science, economic science, and ethics in one single text. A difficult aim, however, done in good faith. Deliberately, references in the text are kept to a minimum.

What Is Rule of Law

The legal order could be described as a set of legal rules. Embedded in the legal order is the concept of the rule of law. The concept of rule of law is not a phenomenon which was dropped down to the earth by mystic. Nor did it occur from one day to another. The concept has very slowly developed since at least ancient times. It is said that Plato and Aristotle brought forward essentials of the concept (Cormacain 2017). Conventionally, it is said that the Magna Charta is the first genuine "rule of law" document produced (https://www.bl.uk/magna-carta/articles/magna-carta-an-introduction). The founder of the actual English words "Rule of Law" is said to be Dicey in 1885 (Cormacain 2017).

First, we must bear in mind that rule of law is an Anglo-American term. However, more or less simultaneously did similar notions emerge in other Western cultures. Well known is the German term rechtsstaat, and the French term Etat de droit. The roots are different. Rule of law is historically more about legal protection of the individual and Rechtsstaat is more about governing society. Today the view is that the various terms express more or less the same content (MacCormick 2005; Wennerström 2009).

It is of great importance to observe that there is a duality to the rule of law. At one level, the rule of law is a basic principle that we are all subject to the law. At another level, the rule of law is the ideal of the values that a legal system ought to possess (Cormacain 2017).

Furthermore, rule of law could be seen in a formal, substantive, functional, or sociological way (Wennerström 2009; Ziegert 2009). Formal is about procedures, substantive is about content, functional is with focus on desired outcomes, and lastly sociological is about structural coupling between the family system, the economic system, the political system, and the legal system. The family, the economic and the political systems are per se un-coordinated and conflicting, thus, law is the answer to make the communication and cooperation between the systems possible. Also, the rule of law according to the sociological concept delivers an independent legal review of political operations within the political system and a more effective exercise of state power with higher levels of certainty/legitimacy (Ziegert 2009).

The borders between the various concepts are blurred and overlapping. It must be emphasized that the notion of rule of law is by no means clear. The basis to the concept is according to my view of a functional character. It is a system to govern society and at the same time a system to protect individuals. It is more a cluster of values about achieving desired specific outcomes. Thus, in my analyze, I will maintain a functional concept of rule of law which puts the desired outcomes in focus.

As a starting point to the analyze, we must explore the arguments in favor of a rule-based tax system—*the notion of the tax rule of law.*

Why Is It Important to Stress the Value of the Rule of Law Concept in Tax Matters

Introduction

As an illuminating starting point, I would like to cite a few words by the ECJ Advocate-General Bobek in his opinion in a European VAT-case (C-251/16, delivered 7 September 2017).

The Advocate-General in the ECJ case says:

> 63. (…) The Court has confirmed on several occasions that 'a trader's choice between exempt transactions and taxable transactions may be based on a range of factors, including tax considerations relating to the

> VAT system … *taxpayers may choose to structure their business so as to limit their tax liability*'.
>
> 64. In other words, there is *no legal obligation to pay the maximum tax possible*. (…)

Clearly, the citation implies that a corporation from a legal perspective is entitled to tax planning. It also implies that, as a matter of fact, the corporation as a legal entity is entitled to the rule of law protection for its tax-saving activities. What, then, is tax planning and tax avoidance?

The definition of tax planning is when a taxpayer structures the business in a tax-optimized way. Tax avoidance could be defined as an activity by legal methods to minimize the tax burden in a way which the legislator did not intend (OECD tax glossary). Generally speaking, the root of tax avoidance is a strict letter-based interpretation of tax law. Absent tax text—loopholes—creates possibilities to minimize the tax burden. The taxpayer, the corporation, structures and organizes its business in order to use the loopholes. Often tax planning is perceived as fair and tax avoidance/aggressive tax planning as unfair.

The border between the two concepts tax planning/tax avoidance is nevertheless blurred both in legal and moral terms (Kasper et al. 2018). That is mainly because the path to achieve the two outcomes is the same—the structuring of your enterprise and your business. Outside the field of tax experts, it is quite difficult to understand if a certain way of structuring a business is tax planning or tax avoidance. Even among tax experts, there are different opinions. Furthermore, states do compete with each other by creating favorable tax regimes, and it is quite difficult to state if a corporation who takes advantage of a state's tax law is morally questionable.

Tax evasion is also a term commonly used. It should, however, not be mixed with tax avoidance. Tax evasion is a crime. Tax evasion does normally involve concealing information or lying. The crime is the mis-reporting of the facts. The successful tax avoider has no reason not to be transparent toward the tax agency about his actions.

Why, then, is it the case that the corporate taxpayers, as the general-advocate states, may choose to structure their business so as to limit their tax liability? Why do such a thing as tax avoidance enjoy the protection of the rule of tax law?

Not so few would argue that such a state of the tax law is both non-efficient and non-ethic, and also, that it puts some corporate taxpayers in a better situation than other. Not all corporate taxpayers have the opportunity to optimize their taxpaying. Tax planning will often decrease the fiscal budget of the state. Especially, when it comes to tax avoidance or aggressive tax planning, the Ministers of Finance, of course, cannot foresee the budget effects. Of course paying tax is buying civilization, and why should some throw their invoice in the knees of others? Surely, the *volksgeist* cannot be in favor of corporate tax planning. Thus, a truly sustainable corporate tax system cannot rely on a concept which leads to such bad side effects. The CSR thinking and the business ethical view tell a different normative story—even if you according to the legal world are entitled to the fruits of tax avoidance you must not pick them.

Or is this intuitive reasoning misleading? It is easily and tempting to look upon the rule of tax law as something problematic and a hamper to the well-functioning state. In essence, the issue is why is it important that taxation is strictly based on the rule of law when it has quite bad effects? The issue is explored in the next section.

Arguments in Favor of a Strictly Rule-Based Tax System

Introduction

There are of course a number of very powerful and well-known arguments in favor of taxation being governed only by law (Persson Österman and Svernlöv 2016). These arguments deal with the core of what could describe as the citizens acceptance of taxation and of the fundamental legitimacy of taxation as a part of society. It is impossible to neglect the fact that paying taxes is not voluntarily. It is impossible for the citizen to opt out of society (besides by migration of course). An individual does not freely enter the "social contract". The metaphor buying society is actually misleading. The taxpayer is forced to agree on the terms of the contract. The tax bill is something you cannot protest against. The same goes for the corporate citizen. A truly sustainable corporate tax system must put this fact into the fabric. The next section digs further into this issue.

The Functions and Desired Outcomes of the Rule of Tax Law

First, the need for *democracy and the will of the people*—the publicly elected assembly should be the one and only enacting tax laws. "No tax without representation". Decisions about spreading the tax burden on the citizens and corporations are very complex and involve a lot of balancing of contradictory goals. The balancing should, thus, take place in a transparent democratic order. The desired outcome does also fulfill requirements based on the theory of democratic justice (Weale 2013).

All other public entities (government agencies and courts) must simply respect the enacted law. Traditionally, constitutional legal protection is regarded as encompassing the notion of the hierarchical structure of the law—nobody under a publicly elected assembly has the right, without specific legal grounds, to expand or change the meaning of the law. It would undermine the notion of a "government by the people" if a body whose officials are not politically replaceable were to have the authority to expand the areas of application of laws. Tax law always comes from above.

Secondly, the citizens important demands for not being treated worse than anyone else—consequently there are strong demands for *equal treatment.* It seems obvious that equal tax treatment presupposes a legal standard (a legal provision) that meets some form of clarity—or at least by way of the standard's positioning in the legal system could become clear and thus enable subsequent equal treatment. Without a benchmark (the law), it would of course be impossible to achieve equal treatment.

Thirdly, a desired outcome is *normative clarity.* The benchmark cannot be vague or ambiguous. Thus, within the framework of the concept of rule of law, the surrounding legal system (the internal legal context) is also of vast significance for legal clarity and certainty. The legal text written by the legislator is not the only source of law. The normative tax law phenomena must thus be a system in which the independent courts play a major role in producing legal clarity—for example, the Swedish Supreme Administrative Court's (SAC) solely task is to produce precedents that are to increase the clarity of legal norms and thus ensure the equal treatment of taxpayers. There are scholars who suggest that you should not pay too much attention to case law and precedences (Hilling and Ostas 2017). My view, however, is that the functional rule of law-based system must include the courts of law and their methods of interpretation of the laws.

Fourthly, a desired outcome is *ensuring the absence of arbitrariness and ensuring objective treatment*. Arbitrariness and a lack of objectivity undermine the citizens trust in the administration. Ensuring the impartialness and objectivity requires legal norms that embody a certain level of clarity that enables the decision-maker to make the decision without the decision-maker having to involve their private, subjective perceptions. Of course, very important is that the decision-maker is obliged to stick to the law, and nothing but the law.

Fifthly, a very important outcome is *dispute resolution and independent review of the administration*. The legal system possesses an advanced apparatus in the form of independent courts to allow individuals the ability to be able to appeal decisions that government agencies have made. The court check the governmental decision-maker. The courts have thus been given a mandate of power, to use interpretation doctrines developed within the legal system, to interpret and apply legislation to the individual case. In the interest of trust in the functions of society, it is of the utmost importance that a citizen can have their matter tried by an objective and independent body, a court of law. Often, the term *procedural justice* is used (Tyler 2006, 2013). Procedural justice is about the forms for decision taking. Shortly, it is about involving and listening to the people affected by negative decisions. A high level of procedural justice, according to the scientific studies, leads to a high level of rule compliance.

Furthermore, a problematic weakness regarding reviews of administrative tax decisions inherent in the administrative legal system is that reviews are generally limited to an individual or corporation protesting a negative decision. This means that an individual able to enjoy a benefit that others are not able to enjoy is hardly likely to protest. So-called sweetheart deals could occur and, thus, spawn corruption. The dilemma must be addressed. First, a very important condition in order to make sure that unmotivated advantages do not arise for individuals or corporations is that the rules that are applied are so clear that deviations generally should not occur. Secondly, transparency is presumed to be an important safeguarding factor. Transparency is generally not presumed to be a component of the rule of law, yet it must be presumed to be assigned a high value in a society governed by law.

Accordingly, one can conclude that there are strong and powerful arguments in favor of taxation being based on rule of law. The democratic requirement, the requirement for equal treatment, the requirement for objectivity, and the absence of arbitrariness, as well as the requirement for independent judicial reviews (procedural justice), can hardly be met without the existence of a rule of law-based system. This may seem apparent, yet it is nonetheless worth highlighting. After all, it is not a matter of a meaningless abstraction. In summary, the notion of the rule of law can be described in concrete and functional terms—it serves a key function in safeguarding a number of highly fundamental requirements that must be regarded as deeply rooted in social values.

It must of course be emphasized that the rule of tax law contains a duality—tax law entails an obligation to pay taxes under the pain of sanctions. The rule of tax law is not all about protection of individual rights, it is equally important also a system of governing society (supra).

Finally, we must bear in mind that we are discussing a notion which by no means is clear. My definition is based on a functional approach, and it contains a cluster of values. Ideally, all these values should be upheld. However, as the notion itself is vague, it is difficult to argue that a functional rule of tax law notion must fulfill all the stated desired outcomes. For instance, it cannot be ruled out that a system that lacks in terms of democratic grounding could be defined as based on the rule of law in functional terms. Democracy in itself is not a self-evident notion. It is therefore more a question of fulfilling the outcomes to a larger or lesser extent.

Shortcomings of the Rule of Tax Law

The problematic drawback of the rule of law-based taxation is that it is as well the facilitator of tax planning and also tax avoidance. Tax avoidance is (supra) an activity by legal methods to minimize the tax burden in a way which the legislator did not intend. The key is the legality of the action—the tax avoider is protected by the tax rule of law.

As a matter of fact, there are remedies within the legal system in order to challenge such methods of avoidance. Especially the General Anti Avoidance Rule ("GAAR") tax concept is world widely used in order to combat tax planning grounded on a letter-based interpretation of tax legislation (Krever 2016). The interpretation and application of the tax GAAR should be based on the so-called *spirit of the law*—the underlying principles and purpose of the tax statutes.

Actually, there are several scholars who argue that tax GAARs are in breach of the rule of law (Hultqvist 1995; Krever 2016; Prebble and Prebble 2017). The arguments stem from the fact a GAAR is vague and obscure, thus, it does not meet the formal requirement of the law. Instead, it wrongly gives the judiciary a discretionary power. The critique is mainly based on the formal concept of the rule of law (supra). As shown, the concept of the rule of law is, however, not clear. Based on my functional definition of the rule of law (supra), my firm view is that the GAAR is a genuine part of the intrinsic legal "rule of law" fabric. GAARs are introduced by parliament action and they are construed, applied, and checked by independent courts of law. Freedman, who states that tax law cannot always be clear and precise, requires that tax law should be "ascertainable within an equitable system" (Freedman 2011). The courts in their adjudication, according to the functional definition, clarify the vagueness of the GAAR and thus the required clarity is produced within the legal system. The desired outcome of the function of the rule of law is secured. Furthermore, a powerful argument is that the GAAR contributes to the equality under law. A skilled tax avoider should be treated in the same way as an "honest" non-avoiding taxpayer (Skar 2017). The GAAR would then actually enhance an important functional outcome of the rule of law. MacCormick's argument of defeasible legal certainty does also fit in well (MacCormick 2005).

Of course, you must in the process of applying a GAAR find out the specific spirit or purpose of the relevant tax legislation by using some method. The issue is in my view a legal issue—it does not involve ethics or moral standards, as those normally are out of the context of tax legal phenomena. The spirit of the law must be defined as a certain legal source of law. Tax legislation is also, generally speaking, drafted in very technical terms. To find the specific purpose behind technical text is not an easy task. The legislator cannot due to established constitutional principles present interpretation guidelines nor give evidence about its intentions outside the scope of the formal procedure of enacting the legal texts. To construe the law, you use sources of law, nothing else. Thus, the legal system by itself and only by itself contains the criteria utilized to find out the spirit or the purpose of the tax law (Skar 2017). The "spirit of the law" is an abstract notion discovered by justices applying the law on a specific situation. It is worth to highlight, as it seems that non-lawyers often misunderstand the legal concept. They might believe that the spirit must be found from the outside of the law, instead of from within.

As a matter of fact, it is almost impossible on beforehand to define the notions of tax avoidance or aggressive tax planning in abstract terms. The notions are not clearly defined in tax legislation. It is in the process of adjudication, when a court of law rules that a transaction should be deemed as against the spirit or purpose of the law, you discover the line between black and white. Law has a hermeneutic character. Thus, and important, it is in the end of the day the justices of the court of laws who decide what can be done and what cannot be done in terms of tax avoidance. First when knowledge exists, a legislative action could be taken.

Hilling and Ostas (2017) view the power of the justices as a weakness in the legal system and they argue that the justices should change interpretation style and apply a "pragmatic jurisprudence" or "legal pragmatism". Then would social norms and policy goals, instead of literalism, be the guide. V. Braithwaite has also taken a critical attitude toward the judiciary (2009). Of course, you must be able to criticize the courts and the judiciary, however, conventionally and by good reasons judges feel reluctant to deviate from stable norms of interpretation. It is also of great value for the legislator to be able to feel confident about the norms of interpretation when drafting legislation. Thus, it is not realistic nor for the good that the judiciary would throw out methods of interpretation developed under hundreds, even thousands, years.

It is, however, widely acknowledged that GAARs do not eliminate neither problematic tax planning nor tax avoidance. One reason is the above-mentioned methods of interpretation. Another important reason is the international global setting, whereby a corporation takes advantage of two or more separate sovereign national state's limits of jurisdiction. To put it simply, a GAAR is a national rule and cannot effectively combat cross-border tax avoidance. An exception is the jurisdiction of the European Union, in which a European GAAR is present (supra). The latter of course show that international cooperation on the legislative level is crucial.

To summarize, it is in the light of the obvious shortcomings of the rule of law-based taxation the discourse regarding CSR and ethics in taxation must be seen. If the corporation maintains a good tax morale, and if it acts as a responsible corporate citizen the setback of the rule of tax law would vanish. Is that the magic stick to solve the problems of tax avoidance? Next section deals with the role of CSR and ethics in taxation.

The Role of CSR and Ethics in Order to Minimize Tax Avoidance—Possibilities and Challenges

Introduction

An intense discourse about CSR/ethics and taxation has come to the fore as a tool in order to decrease aggressive tax planning and tax avoidance (Persson Österman and Svernlöv 2016; Hilling and Ostas 2017). It is all but what is labeled tax morale—the social norms governing the behavior of the taxpayer. A corporate citizen should behave "well" and refrain from tax avoidance behavior. The legality of the tax avoidance structuring should be seen as irrelevant and, thus, the shortcomings of the rule of law-based taxation would be fixed. It would secure a more legitimate and therefore a sustainable corporate taxation system.

A lawyer would probably at first adopt a highly skeptical position to the idea of letting the power of society be exercised through the setting of social norms or ethics. Philosophers have also expressed doubts. Kant recognized that individuals would not agree on what is right and wrong. If each person simply did as they thought right, there would still be conflict in society, even violent conflicts (Cormacain 2017). Different ethical views could definitively produce different outcomes in terms of the view on tax avoidance—a utilitarian could very well find arguments in favor of tax avoidance (Baron 2012). There is then a need for individual moral reasoning to submit to an agreed set of societal rules to avoid this conflict. The civilized person must let heteronomous rules take precedence over autonomous moral reasoning (Cormacain 2017).

It must nevertheless be acknowledged that social norms can be just as powerful as legal norms. Assumingly, the individual does not always reflect on why she acts in a certain way. Naturally, working with moral teachings is not foreign to lawyers. On the contrary, lawyers can often perceive formal rules and regulations as giving expression to powerful social and ethic norms (e.g., rules of law concerning human rights). In terms of CSR and taxes, gaining a better understanding of the attitudes that can be presumed to govern the behavior of corporate taxpayers is naturally of considerable interest. It must of course be noted that the issue is all about the collective general interest of society. CSR and ethics put duties on the taxpaying corporation, without providing the corporation any rights. Immediately, the great difference between the rule of tax law system and the CSR/morally just/ethic system becomes clear. The duality of the rule of tax law puts duties on the taxpayer and at the same time gives rights and judicial protection to the taxpayer. The question must be asked if such a one-sided system really is the best system in terms of sustainability.

Next section will deal with the factors explaining the behavior of taxpayers and corporate taxpayers. Is there such a thing as "tax morale", and if so, can it be influenced, and if so, what methods should be most effective? Or, is the arguments in favor of the rule of law taxation so strong that the conclusion should be that CSR and ethics are to be held outside the scope of tax issues?

Money, Punishment, or Morale—What Is the Taxpaying Motif?

A hypothesis that many lawyers probably hold is that the actual paying of taxes, as dictated by tax laws, is predominantly a product of the existence of strict sanctions and the fact that there are tax audits or other systems in place to detect inadequate regulatory compliance. Penalties are the ultimate consequence of improper behavior. In the words of Olivecrona, it is a matter of the taxpayer internalizing a norm due to fear. It is thus a matter of power and coercion (Spaak 2014).

Neoclassical microeconomic research has seemingly affirmed this view. An often cited, by now a classic study by Allingham and Sandmo is *Income Tax Evasion: A Theoretical Analysis* (1972). The so-called *AS model* demonstrates that the paying of taxes is a function of sanctions and the risk of getting caught (or the perception of the likelihood of being caught). Sandmo has seemingly not changed his view (Sandmo 2005).

The degree to which the AS model holds true bears evident consequences for CSR. CSR involves adhering to a setting of norms other than legal ones. It seems intuitive that the relevance of CSR in taxation would be limited if the decision to comply with tax rules predominantly involved assessing the risk of sanctions in the form of tax surcharges or other punitive sanctions being imposed. The pure legal force is exercised strictly on the basis of the legal rules' area of application.

Based on the AS model's prediction on taxpayer behavior, advanced, even aggressive, legal tax planning that significantly reduces a corporations tax burden will therefore probably take place.

On the other hand, other respected social science research has demonstrated and argued that the "AS model" is marred by shortcomings, namely that the model forecasts a substantially higher degree of tax evasion than what actually appears to be occurring (Torgler et al. 2007). The research shows that taxpayers do not act in the pure economically rational way as is predicted by the AS model. Taxpayers simply pay more tax than the model predicts. This phenomenon is called "the puzzle of tax compliance".

The firm conclusion is that there may be other motives governing taxpayers than a strictly economically rational approach: The term "tax morale" has come into use as a collective way of describing the foundation for these motives. Taxpayers may "voluntarily" tend to comply with what is termed a social norm instead of a legal norm. The term social norm could be defined as rules and standards that are understood by members of a group, and that guide and/or constrain social behavior without the force of law (Bobek et al. 2007). Of course, it must be emphasized that a social norm could be sanctioned by *social sanctions* (as damaged reputation). A corporation would assumingly also put a prize on "bad will". I will come back to that later (infra).

Accordingly, the message is that taxpayers to a greater extent pay more tax than predicted by the AS model, and that the taxpayer's social values and attitudes are of considerable significance. The research that argues in favor of it being a matter of social attitudes rather than economic rationality is particularly extensive (Posner 2000; Lederman 2003).

However, what does influence tax morale is a highly complex matter—it involves a vast number of elusive factors. The literature in this field is enormous. A good overview is Lago and Lago-Penas (2010).

Tax morale involves the composition of the population group, in terms of age, gender, education, political views, political culture, and attitudes to what society spends tax money on. The complexity of the tax system is also an influencing factor—complicated rules have a negative effect. Corruption, trust in government agencies, trust in officials at government agencies, and trust in the legal system are also key factors.

Taxpayers are also heavily influenced by how they perceive the actions of others: thus making it a matter of "group mentality". A taxpayer is rarely inclined to pay more taxes than anyone else if the other party is perceived as being in a similar or equal situation. On the other hand, the taxpayer can be inclined to pay taxes as long as "everyone else" so does. If others are perceived as cheating or engaging in tax avoidance and "getting away with it", then the individual's inclination to follow suit increases. If numerous corporations successfully use tax shelters, this most likely significantly increases the likelihood of more corporations opting for such structures. Tax planning and tax avoidance spread.

Furthermore, the significance of social norms leads to the insight that individuals can come to act in unexpected ways. One phenomenon is termed "over-compliance", or "extra-role behavior" (Tyler 2006).

The fact that "over-compliance" can occur is of course not unusual given the research observation that individuals appear to "voluntarily" comply with norms without reflecting on the underlying legal requirement. Deliberately, I use citation marks, as you might comply with a social norm because of the social sanctions. If you are "voluntarily" engaging in an action, you can clearly also "voluntarily" refrain from tax avoidance. The individual who "voluntarily" complies with tax laws has no reason to thoroughly contemplate the strict boundary between what is legally possible and what is not legally possible.

However, the discussion within social science research is by no means over. A rather recent study attempting to address the problem of the AS model's noted shortcomings was conducted by Kleven, Knudsen, Thustrup Kreiner, Soren Pedersen, and Saez is *Unwilling or Unable to Cheat? Evidence from a Tax Audit Experiment in Denmark* (2011). The study seems to confirm the AS model. The conclusion deserves to be cited at length:

> While we do not deny the importance of psychological and cultural aspects in the decision to evade taxes, the evidence presented in this paper points to a more classic information story. In particular, we show that the key distinction in the taxpayer's reporting decision is whether income is subject to third-party reporting or if it is solely self-reported.
>
> For self-reported income, our empirical results fit remarkably well with the basic AS model: tax evasion is substantial and responds negatively to an increase in the perceived probability of detection coming from either a prior audit or a threat-of-audit letter. Interestingly, evidence from bunching at kink points shows that the elasticity of tax evasion with respect to the marginal tax rate is very low, which suggests that rigorous tax enforcement is a much more effective tool to combat evasion than cutting marginal tax rates.
>
> For third-party reported income, tax evasion is extremely modest and does not respond to the perceived probability of detection, because this probability is already very high. This shows that third-party reporting is a very effective enforcement device. Given that audits are very costly and eliminate only a part of tax evasion, enforcement resources may be better spent on expanding third party reporting than on audits of self-reported income.

Finally, a very interesting observation has been made by Kasper et al. (2018). They observe that tax avoidance appears to be more socially accepted than tax evasion. Furthermore, their results indicate that cheating on taxes is not necessarily perceived as a crime, but rather as a game played by smart people. They therefore suggest that tax policies that aim at increasing compliance should thus not only diminish the opportunities to evade or evade taxes, but also highlight the negative social effects of tax avoidance.

The important conclusion, nevertheless, is that there is no absolute clear social norm regarding tax avoidance.

Corporate Tax Morale and Corporate Tax Behavior

The previous heading had the individual human taxpayer in focus. What could be said about the findings relevance in terms of the behavior of corporations? Alm and McClellan state that a main lesson of their scientific work is that tax morale considerations apply to both individuals and firms (Alm and McClellan 2012). Social pressures and social norms can thus be presumed to affect influential corporate owners, corporate executives, and key employees when reaching the decisions that are taken in the name of the corporation.

However, the corporate context raises an important extra level of complexity. The reason is that corporate executives and key employees are bound by specific restrictions. When making decisions they cannot follow their private moral convictions. They are bound by various legal instruments as corporate law, labor law and legally valid loyalty clauses to the owners. They are also bound by social norms developed in their social professional group of business people.

One important restriction is that the management must focus on the economic benefit of the corporation. Knuutinen states that it is clear that a corporation needs economic success in order to take any kind of responsibilities (2014). Gribnau and Jallai (2018), however, argue that corporate managers in different corporate governance regimes have sufficient room for aligning their tax planning strategies with societal expectations and thus avoiding aggressive tax planning.

What do we know, then, about the corporate view and behavior in terms of tax planning and tax avoidance? The European Commission has summarized that there is almost no economic behavior literature on firms tax avoidance activities (EU Taxation paper no 41, 2014). An exception to that is a number of highly interesting surveys conducted at the Oxford University Centre for Business Taxation (OUCBT) in the UK focus on topics including the attitudes held by tax officers in major British companies (Freedman et al. 2009, 2014). The first study is slightly old (2009) but has nevertheless kept its general value. In brief and simplified terms, the following was concluded in the study:

Most executives believed that openness and transparency concerning the corporate tax policy could be motivated. The boards of most major corporations also maintained a stated tax policy. However, these policies were most often of a general and vague nature (infra more about tax policies). The executives emphasized that tax planning must be regarded as constituting a right and that decisions concerning tax planning must be taken pursuant to a strict "cost/benefit" analysis. None of the executives believed that the corporation should pay more tax than was legally required. However, they were very well aware of the fact that there are circumstances in which achieving the greatest possible shareholder value over time may require taking into account the perceptions of stakeholders rather than the owners. The executives believed that tax matters in general were of limited value to shareholders (of publicly listed companies) or analysts. However, "reputational risk" was outlined as being a reality that should be taken into consideration when it comes to tax planning as well. However, the determining factor was whether a bad reputation in terms of tax planning could lead to lower sales or otherwise yield a lower profit. Most felt that any such correlation was missing. However, companies in certain markets and companies with public contracts could clearly see such a correlation.

The OUCBT study thus indicates that tax matters in the corporate sector are primarily determined on the basis of an economic perspective, and that social norms play a minor role. It could of course definitively be argued that the reputational risk today regarding tax planning is considerably higher than ten years ago. However, it is assumingly still a matter of cost/benefit analyze. The reputation risk is to be seen as the sanction of breaking the social norm. Of course, important in that respect is the strongness of the social norm and there is no absolute clear social norm about tax avoidance (supra).

A rather recently published study by Davis et al. (2016) provides empirical evidence that high-CSR firms actually avoid more taxes, which suggests that CSR and taxes act as substitutes rather than complements. The results provide evidence that the relation between corporate tax payments and social welfare is complex. Furthermore, the results of the study suggest that, at least for US public corporations, the payment of taxes is not viewed as an important socially responsible activity by an influential subset of firms' stakeholders. They acknowledge, however, that it may be the case that stakeholders' views on corporate taxes as a socially responsible activity will change or are changing.

Elbra and Mikler (2016) suggest that a concern for shareholder value and financial drivers are likely to be more globally generalizable than more socially relational forms of capitalism. They state that if corporations do not primarily judge their standing and brand value on the basis of social responsibility, being less concerned with an obligation to society than shareholders, then they are unlikely to be voluntary payers of tax. Their conclusion is that governments must take the lead in developing effective taxation regulations, rather than relying on self-regulation or working with multinational corporations (MNCs) to address their tax minimization strategies. Because global corporate tax avoidance is not caused by market forces, but regulatory competition between states, the states must agree on international regulatory approaches to prevent this.

Social norms is one thing, ethical norms is of course something else. An issue is if the application of an ethical norm would be helpful in terms of combatting tax avoidance. Hilling and Ostas (2017) state that tax avoidance given the documented negative impact of it on essential societal values and functions is unethical, taken from a teleological, deontological, and virtue ethics. Baron (2012), however, argues that a utilitarian, on the other hand, would not necessarily view tax avoidance as bad. On the contrary, it could be seen as positive. Baron also argues that a deontologist might not condemn tax avoidance, as the tax avoider "in his special way", obeys the tax law.

One undisputable fact is, furthermore, that ethics does not define what tax avoidance is. Hilling and Ostas (2017) seem to define tax avoidance as an activity which avoids paying the "fair" share of tax, but that is not very helpful as "fair" is also a very ambiguous notion. Gribnau and Jallai (2018) state that there is no international consensus on ethical principles that solidifies the ideal of paying a fair share of taxes.

To summarize, the corporation is a creature affected not only by legal rules but also by social norms. An added complexity compared to the individual is that the decision-makers of the corporation are bound by specific corporate norms—the most important is the norm of profit-making. Empirical studies seemingly show that the corporation is governed by a cost-benefit thinking in terms of tax compliance and tax planning behavior. However, it cannot be ruled out that a corporation would be willing to adhere to social norms and ethical norms. The great dilemma is the vagueness of those norms. The norms are, to put it simply, not produced in the same way as the legal norms. The norms are not founded in democracy; the norms cannot be construed by independent bodies as courts of law, and so on. Social norms and also ethical norms contain no procedural justice whatsoever which is highly undesirable.

Some of the problematic issues surrounding the social and ethic norms in terms of taxation could presumably be solved by creating and applying *soft law*. One source of soft law is self-regulation, and examples of self-regulation by tax policies and tax strategies have started to emerge. In the next section, a few examples of such soft law will be presented.

Tax Policies and Tax Strategies—A Few Examples

The OUCBT study (Freedman et al. 2009) showed that most major UK corporations maintained a more or less stated tax policy (supra). Such a tax policy could be described as a kind of soft law. The corporation creates and sets up a guideline "a soft law norm" and then in its business makes sure to follow it. The purpose of the internal self-regulation could be to provide the management guidance for decisions in the daily business. A tax policy could also be transparent to the public. Interested parties and stakeholders would then have the opportunity to learn about the view of the corporation soft law. The interested parties and stakeholders would also be able to check if the corporation complies with its norms.

Great Britain has since the OUCBT study come further and introduced binding legal rules regarding tax policies. According to paragraph 16(2) Schedule 19, UK Finance (No. 2) Bill 2016, corporations must under certain conditions publish a tax strategy. In the context of this study, it is of considerable interest to take a closer look on some of these tax strategies.

I have chosen to briefly highlight some of the content of the published tax strategies/policies from the following corporations; *Apple, Astra Zeneca, Atlas Copco, Electrolux and Starbucks*. The excerpts should only be regarded as a sketchy illustration of the contents of published tax policies.

Apple states: “Taxes play a necessary and important role in our society and Apple believes every corporation has a responsibility to pay all the taxes they owe”. “Apple’s tax positions and reporting reflect the business activities undertaken in the UK. Apple does not enter into artificial or abusive arrangements in order to reduce its liability to UK taxes”.

Astra Zeneca states: “Our approach is to manage tax risks and tax costs in a manner consistent with applicable regulatory requirements and with shareholders’ best long term interests, taking into account operational, economic and reputational factors.” “Substantive business transactions, for example, acquisitions and divestments, intragroup trade and expansion in global markets, determine our approach to tax planning and consequent tax liabilities. We access government sponsored tax incentives where appropriate and in line with substantive business activities (e.g., UK patent box and R&D tax credits).”

Atlas Copco states: “To pay the right amount of tax required of it under the laws and regulations of the countries in which we operate” “The UK Group’s tax planning aims to support the commercial needs of the business by ensuring that the companies affairs are carried out in the most tax efficient manner whilst remaining compliant with all relevant laws.”

Electrolux states: “Tax costs should be managed as any other cost within the Group”. “Considering shareholder value involves taking due account of long-term considerations and risks, including the maintenance of corporate reputation and relationships with governments. Short term gains through aggressive planning in the area of tax may, and likely will, have long term negative consequences for Electrolux Group's brand, reputation and customer relationships, and should therefore be avoided."

Starbucks states: "Our approach to tax aims to align with the needs and long-term interests of our various stakeholders - including governments, shareholders, partners (i.e., employees) and the communities where we operate and source products." "We always consider the company's corporate and social responsibilities, brand and reputation when considering tax affairs." "The tax department assesses the appropriate tax treatment of the operating models which are determined by the business. This may include the identification of tax efficiencies, such as use of or application for local tax incentives, reliefs, or exemptions, where legally available and permissible. However, it is not the role of the Starbucks tax team to determine how the business is operated."

While indeed interesting to observe the tax policies, the content of the tax policies cannot be described as very clear and precise. It should thus be quite difficult to use the tax policies as benchmarks. One obvious and important conclusion is that tax generally is regarded as a cost. Some (but not all) of the corporations acknowledge the issue of reputational risk. Most of the corporations stress the rule of law aspect. One corporation, Electrolux, dismisses aggressive tax planning, however without defining the notion. Also, there are expressions which easily should be labeled as marketing.

To conclude, there is definitively a great potential to enhance the wordings and normative value of the tax policies.

Conclusion

A legal rule-based taxation which contains the rule of tax law concept is highly desirable. The obvious failure is that in such a system the tax avoider receives protection by the tax rule of law.

The pro of using CSR and social/ethics as a pressure in tax compliance is self-evident. Should corporate executives be subjected to requirements greater than those dictated by formal tax legislation, let it be by "ethics" or by reputational risks, would tax planning and most important aggressive tax planning decrease (Kasper et al. 2018). On a collective level, that would lead to a more sustainable business taxation.

There are also a few but nevertheless very important cons.

First, a clear and indisputable weakness is that what can be regarded as constituting ethic behavior or taking good social responsibility is not established in a formalized manner within the framework of a democratic system. It leaves room for different views held by non-elected intellectuals and also a lot of power to media and various organizations outside the scope of the democratic system. It would also open the door to populism. In a global world, you must also pay attention to the fact that moral and social values differ from one world region to another. A global corporation does business not only in the Western world and it cannot maintain one single view of ethics. Thus, such an ambiguous and complex setting of norms would not create a stable and foreseeable fabric to follow. It is difficult to argue against the view that a sound, effective, and sustainable business environment should be stable and foreseeable.

Secondly, there are no generally accepted formalized systems for construing and applying norms for good social and ethic behavior. Obscureness and vagueness are companions. It may thus be difficult to establish what can be perceived as being socially responsible for a corporation in terms of taxpaying. As a matter of fact, there can be many different and probably contradictory perceptions about that. A norm requiring a corporation paying a "fair" amount of tax is not so clear it can be satisfactorily used. The term "tax avoidance" is also very obscure and the precise content of the notion can only be discovered by a court of law in adjudication.

Thirdly, it must be stressed that a level playing field is of great importance for the general tax morale (supra). There are apparently great risks that a corporation could suffer from non-equal treatment and even arbitrariness when facing ethic and moral critique by various and independent agents in society. Some corporations would suffer more than others. For instance, corporations who mainly deal with the states (public contracts) must assumingly maintain a much higher degree of perceived "ethics" than others. "Bad corporations" who already carry a lot of bad will without economic suffering could keep on tax avoidance. "Good" corporations would thus be penalized in economic terms which does not seem just, apparently.

Thirdly, there is of course not a generally established system that offers independent dispute resolution or review. A corporation who believes it has been wrongly accused of bad ethic behavior in terms of tax avoidance has difficulties in seeking redress. The important concept of procedural justice is more or less completely missing.

The apparent problematic issue is that we cannot identify the key elements of the rule of tax law in other normative structures than the legal order. In order to secure the willingness of corporations to behave well and pay the tax, the elements of the rule of tax law and procedural justice must be present. No other system but the legal system can provide the very important desired outcomes. The shortcomings of the system of the rule of tax law must therefore be fixed within the very system, by designing effective remedies against tax avoidance, such as GAARs and international cooperation. The belief that other norm-systems could save the legitimacy of the legal system is not well founded.

The most important lesson the social science research provides should be that the willingness to pay taxes is a function of complicated processes and that there is no single explanation as to why an individual or a corporation choose to pay their taxes or to engage or not engage in tax planning or tax avoidance. Research also indicates that the social norm is not very clear in terms of the view on tax avoidance. Ethical norms cannot be described as very clear, either. A very problematic issue is that neither "tax avoidance" nor "fair share" is defined in a way that enables a benchmarking. The corporations published tax strategies tell us that they behave well—but how do we know that? Marketing instead of regulatory compliance.

A key insight is also that research findings concerning taxpayer behavior can be difficult to transfer directly to the corporate sector. The reason for this is that, while corporate executives can be governed by values and by attitudes, their ability to make decisions can be limited by a substantial number of restrictions. There is a reason to assume that economic considerations play a major role in the corporate sector. The coercive content of the legal rules is of considerable significance, as the sanctions against non-compliance directly decrease the profit.

Sanctions in economic terms are thus the most effective driving forces. Nevertheless, the reputational risk could depending on the corporate circumstances be an important factor, if less profit is attributed to the realization of the reputational risk. As a matter of fact, that could lead to an economic sanction against the "good corporation".

References

Litterature

Allingham, M. G., & Sandmo, A. (1972). Income tax evasion: A theoretical analysis. *Journal of Public Economics, 1,* 328–338.

Alm, J., & MacClellan, C. (2012). Tax morale and tax compliance from the firm's perspective. *Kyklos, 65,* 1–17.

Baron, R. (2012). The ethics of taxation. *Philosophy Now* (Vol. 90), pp. 26–28.

Bobek, D. D., Roberts, R. W., & Sweeney, J. T. (2007). The social norms of tax compliance: Evidence from Australia, Singapore, and the United States. *Journal of Business Ethics, 74,* 49–64.

Braithwaite, V. (2009). *Defiance in taxation and governance—Resisting and dismissing authority in a democracy.* Cheltenham: Edward Elgar.

Cormacain, R. (2017). Legislation, legislative drafting and the rule of law. *The Theory and Practice of Legislation, 5,* 115–135.

Davis, A. K., Guenther, D. A., Krull, L. K., & Williams, B. M. (2016). Do socially responsible firms pay more taxes? *The Accounting Review, 91,* 47–68.

Elbra, A., & Mikler, J. (2016). Paying a 'fair share': Multinational corporations' perspectives on taxation. *Global Policy, 8,* 181–190.

Freedman, J. (2011). Responsive regulation, risk, and rules: Applying the theory to tax practice. *UBC Law Review, 44,* 625–662.

Freedman, J., Loomer, G. T., & Vella, J. (2009). Corporate tax risk and tax avoidance: New approaches. *British Tax Review, 1,* 74–116.

Freedman, J., Ng, F., & Vella, J. (2014). *HMRC's relationship with business* (Draft report Oxford University Centre for Business Taxation no. 19).

Hilling, A., & Ostas, D. T. (2017). *Corporate taxation and social responsibility.* Stockholm: Kluwer.

Hultqvist, A. (1995). *Legalitetsprincipen vid inkomstbeskattningen.* Stockholm: Juristförlaget.

Jallai, A.-G., & Gribnau, H. (2018). *Aggressive tax planning and corporate social irresponsibility: Managerial discretion in the light of corporate governance* (Tilburg Law School Research Paper No. 5).
Kasper, M., Olsen, J., Kogler, C., Stark, J., & Kirchler, E. (2018). Individual attitudes and social representations of taxation, tax avoidance and tax evasion. In N. Hashimzade & Y. Epifantseva (Eds.), *The Routledge companion to tax avoidance research* (pp. 289–303). Abingdon: Routledge.
Kleven, H. J., Knudsen, M. B., Kreiner, C. T., Pedersen, S., & Saez, E. (2011). Unwilling or unable to cheat? Evidence from a tax audit experiment in Denmark. *Econometrica, 79,* 651–692.
Knuutinen, R. (2014). Corporate social responsibility, taxation and aggressive tax planning. *Nordic Tax Journal, 2014,* 36–75.
Krever, R. (2016). General report: GAARs. In *GAARs—A key element of tax systems in the post-BEPS world,* IBFD.
Lago, I., & Lago-Penas, S. (2010). The determinants of tax morale in comparative perspective: Evidence from European Countries. *European Journal of Political Economy, 26,* 441–453.
Lederman, L. (2003). The interplay between norms and enforcement in tax compliance. *Ohio State Law Journal, 64,* 1453–1514.
MacCormick, N. (2005). *Rethoric and the rule of law: A theory of legal reasoning.* Oxford: Oxford University Press.
MacCormick, N. (2011). Civil liberties and the law. In *Legal right and the social democracy—Essays in legal and political philosophy* (Reprinted). Oxford: Clarendon Press.
Olaf Weber, T., Fooken, J., & Herrmann, B. (2014). *Behavioural economics and taxation* (European Commission Taxation Papers no. 41).
Posner, E. A. (2000). Law and social norms: The case of tax compliance. *Virginia Law Review, 86,* 1781–1820.
Prebble, R., & Prebble, J. (2017). General anti-avoidance rules and the rule of law. In N. Hashimzade & Y. Epifantseva (Eds.), *The Routledge companion to tax avoidance research* (pp. 61–78). Abingdon: Routledge.
Sandmo, A. (2005). The theory of tax evasion: A retrospective view. *National Tax Journal, 58,* 643–663.
Skar, H. (2017). *Den ulovfestede omgåelsesnormen i skatteretten. En analyse av rettsanvendelsesprosessen i omgåelsessaker.* Norway: University of Bergen.
Spaak, T. (2014). *A critical appraisal of Karl Olivecrona's legal philosophy.* Berlin: Springer.

Svernlöv, C., & Person Österman, R. (2016). *Corporate social responsibility and corporate taxation*. Stockholm: The Confederation of Swedish Enterprise.

Torgler, B., Schaffner, M., & Macintyre, A. (2007). *Tax compliance, tax morale and governance quality* (No. 225 School of Economics and Finance Discussion Papers and Working Papers School of Economics and Finance Queensland University of Technology).

Tyler, T. R. (2006). *Why people obey the law*. New Haven: Yale University Press.

Tyler, T. R. (2013). *Why people cooperate—The role of social motivations*. Princeton: Princeton University Press.

Weale, A. (2013). *Democratic justice and the social contract*. Oxford: Oxford University Press.

Wennerströmm, E. O. (2009). Measuring the rule of law. In *Rule of law promotion: Global perspectives, local applications*, Skrifter från juridiska institutionen vid Umeå universitet nr 21.

Ziegert, K. A. (2009). Is the rule of law portable? A socio-legal journey from the Nordic Mediterranean Sea via the Silk Road to China. In *Rule of law promotion: Global perspectives, local applications*, Skrifter från juridiska institutionen vid Umeå universitet nr 21.

Others

OECD Glossary of Tax Terms. http://www.oecd.org/ctp/glossaryoftaxterms.htm (2018-04-12).

Opinion of the Advocate-General Bobek, European Court of Justice Case C-251/16, delivered 7 September 2017.

apple.com/legal/more-resources/docs/uk-tax-policy.pdf.

astrazeneca.com/content/dam/az/PDF/AstraZeneca%20Tax%20Policy%20Dec%202017%20FINAL.pdf.

atlascopco.com/content/dam/atlas-copco/local-countries/united-kingdom/documents/Atlas-Copco-UK-Group-Tax-Strategy.pdf.

electroluxgroup.com/en/tax-policy-22164/.

globalassets.starbucks.com/assets/77CB10D4E6DD403A92D568DE90148166.pdf.

Index

S. Arvidsson (ed.), *Challenges in Managing Sustainable Business*, https://doi.org/10.1007/978-3-319-93266-8

The manufacturer's authorised representative in the EU is Springer Nature Customer Service Centre GmbH, Europaplatz 3, 69115 Heidelberg, Germany. If you have any concerns regarding our products, please contact ProductSafety@springernature.com

Printed and bound by CPI Group (UK) Ltd, Croydon, CR0 4YY
25/09/2026
02222848-0004